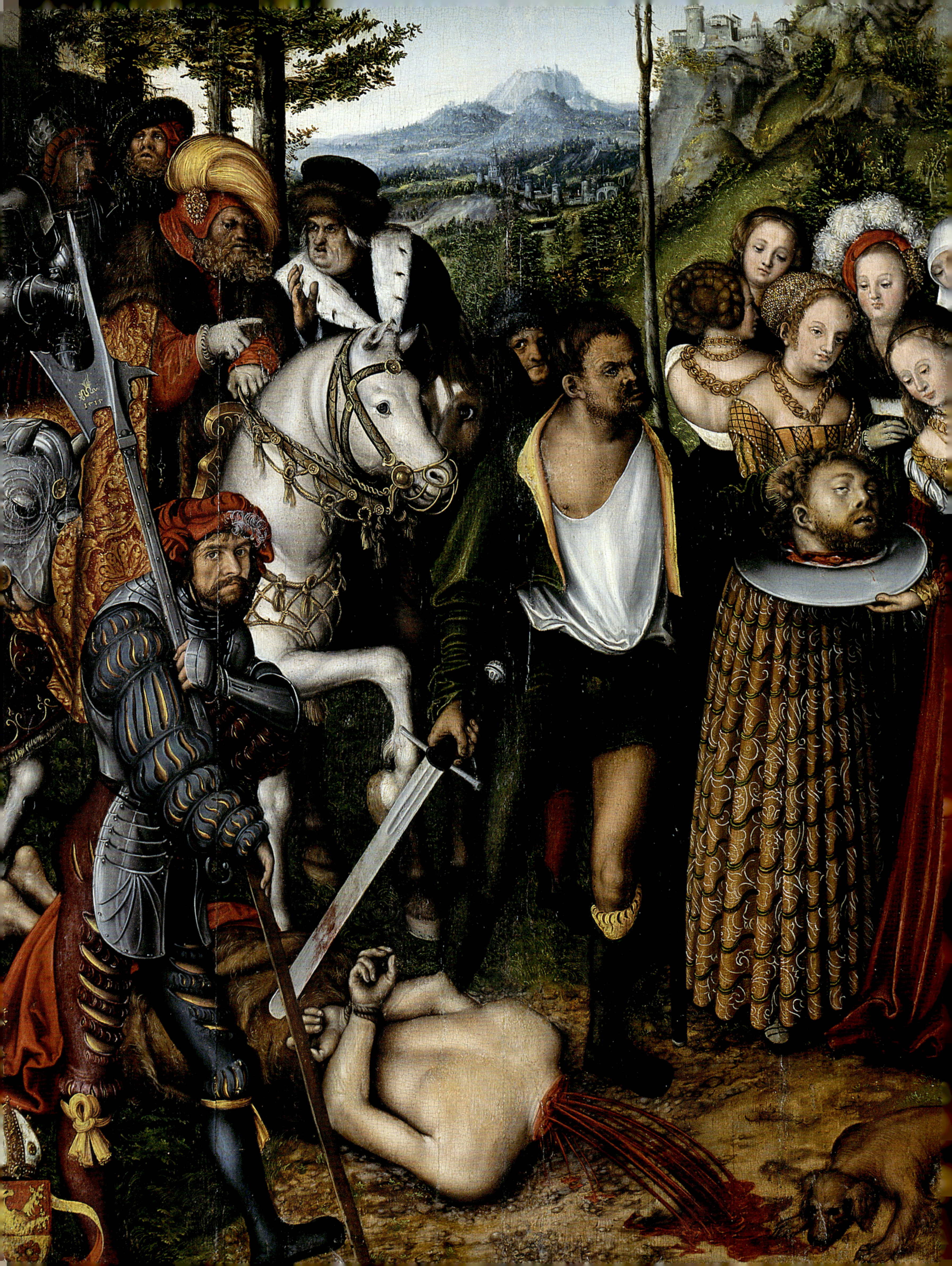

CRANACH

Edited by Bodo Brinkmann

Royal Academy of Arts

This edition first published on the occasion
of the exhibition 'Cranach'

Städel Museum, Frankfurt am Main
23 November 2007 – 17 February 2008

Royal Academy of Arts, London
8 March – 8 June 2008

2008 Season supported by

Sotheby's

The Royal Academy of Arts is grateful to Her Majesty's Government for its help in agreeing to indemnify the exhibition under the National Heritage Act 1980 and to the Museums, Libraries and Archives Council, for its help in arranging this indemnity.

EXHIBITION CURATORS
Städel Museum, Frankfurt am Main
Bodo Brinkmann
Gabriel Dette

Royal Academy of Arts, London
Sir Norman Rosenthal
Cecilia Treves

EXHIBITION ORGANISATION
Royal Academy of Arts, London
Idoya Beitia
Cayetana Castillo
Caroline McCarthy
Hillary Taylor

PHOTOGRAPHIC AND COPYRIGHT CO-ORDINATION
Royal Academy of Arts, London
Miranda Bennion

CATALOGUE: ENGLISH-LANGUAGE EDITION
Royal Academy Publications
David Breuer
Harry Burden
Carola Krueger
Peter Sawbridge
Nick Tite

Translation from the German, copy-editing, typesetting and proofreading: Translate-A-Book, Oxford
Book design: Heine / Lenz / Zizka, Frankfurt / Berlin
Colour origination: Dr Cantz'sche Druckerei, Ostfildern
Printed in Germany

British Library Cataloguing-in-Publication Data
A catalogue record for this book is available from the British Library

ISBN 978-1-905711-14-7 (paperback)
ISBN 978-1-905711-13-0 (hardback)

Distributed outside the United States and Canada
by Thames & Hudson Ltd, London

Distributed in the United States and Canada
by Harry N. Abrams, Inc., New York

EDITORIAL NOTE
Measurements are given in centimetres, height before width.

The majority of catalogue entries are the work of Bodo Brinkmann; those by Gabriel Dette are signed with his initials.

ILLUSTRATIONS

Contents

Patron's Foreword

I am delighted that the Royal Academy of Arts is holding this wonderful exhibition of the art of Lucas Cranach, the great German Renaissance master. It was with much pleasure that I accepted the invitation to become Patron.

Lucas Cranach was one of the finest and also most versatile painters of his era. My congratulations go to the Royal Academy, which has succeeded in assembling outstanding masterpieces from all phases of his career, thus providing the perfect window on his exquisite world.

This exhibition is yet another example of the excellent cooperation between our two countries in the arts. At its heart is the remarkable collection of works by Lucas Cranach held by the Royal Academy's partner institution in Germany, the Städel Museum in Frankfurt, where the show first opened. Further significant contributions have been made by many German museums and private collections.

I would like to thank all the generous individuals who have helped to make this beautiful and fascinating exhibition possible. I am sure these marvellous paintings will inspire further interest in the United Kingdom in one of the most renowned German painters of the sixteenth century. May they give joy to a great many people.

Wolfgang Ischinger
German Ambassador to the Court of St James's

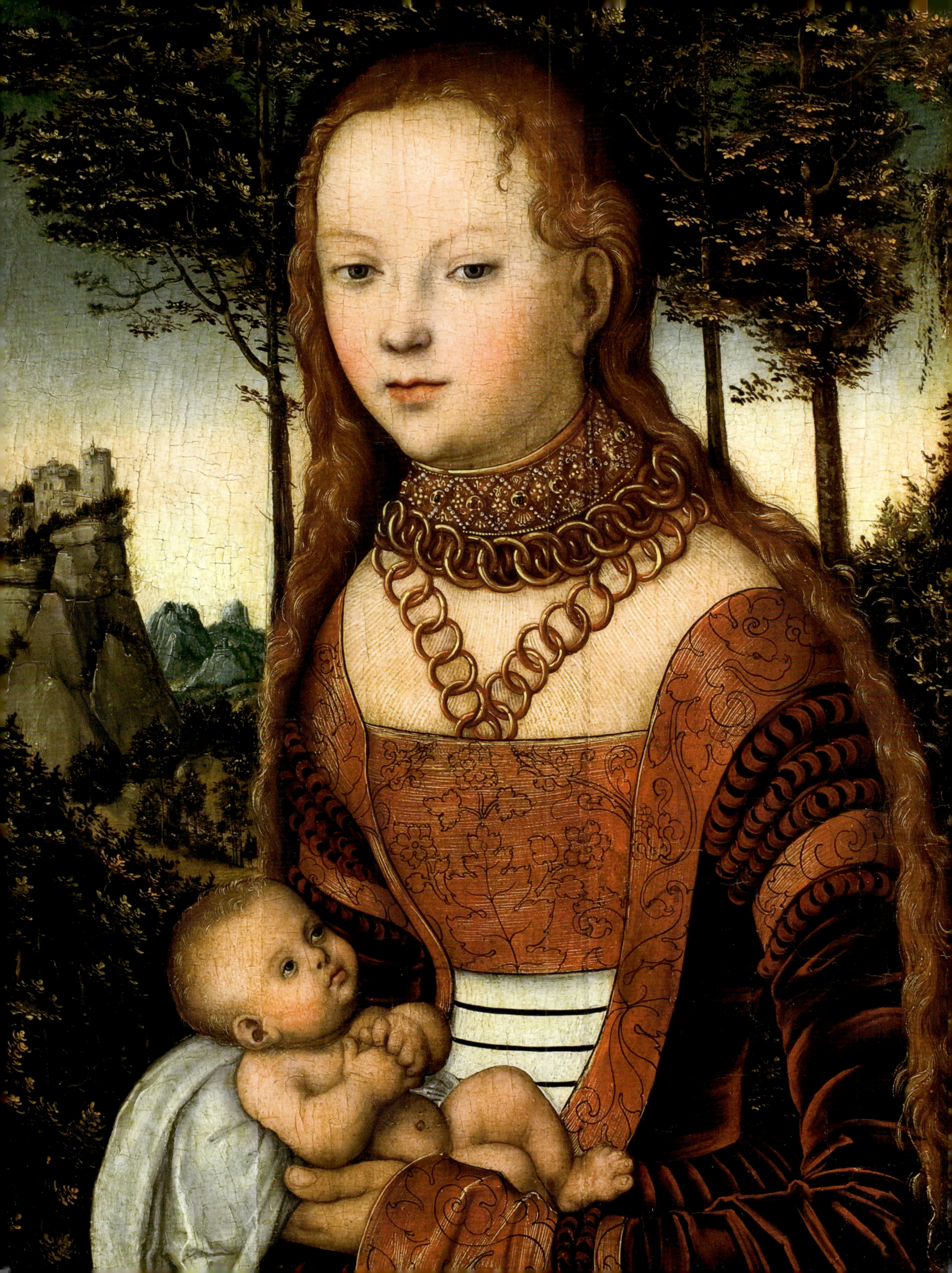

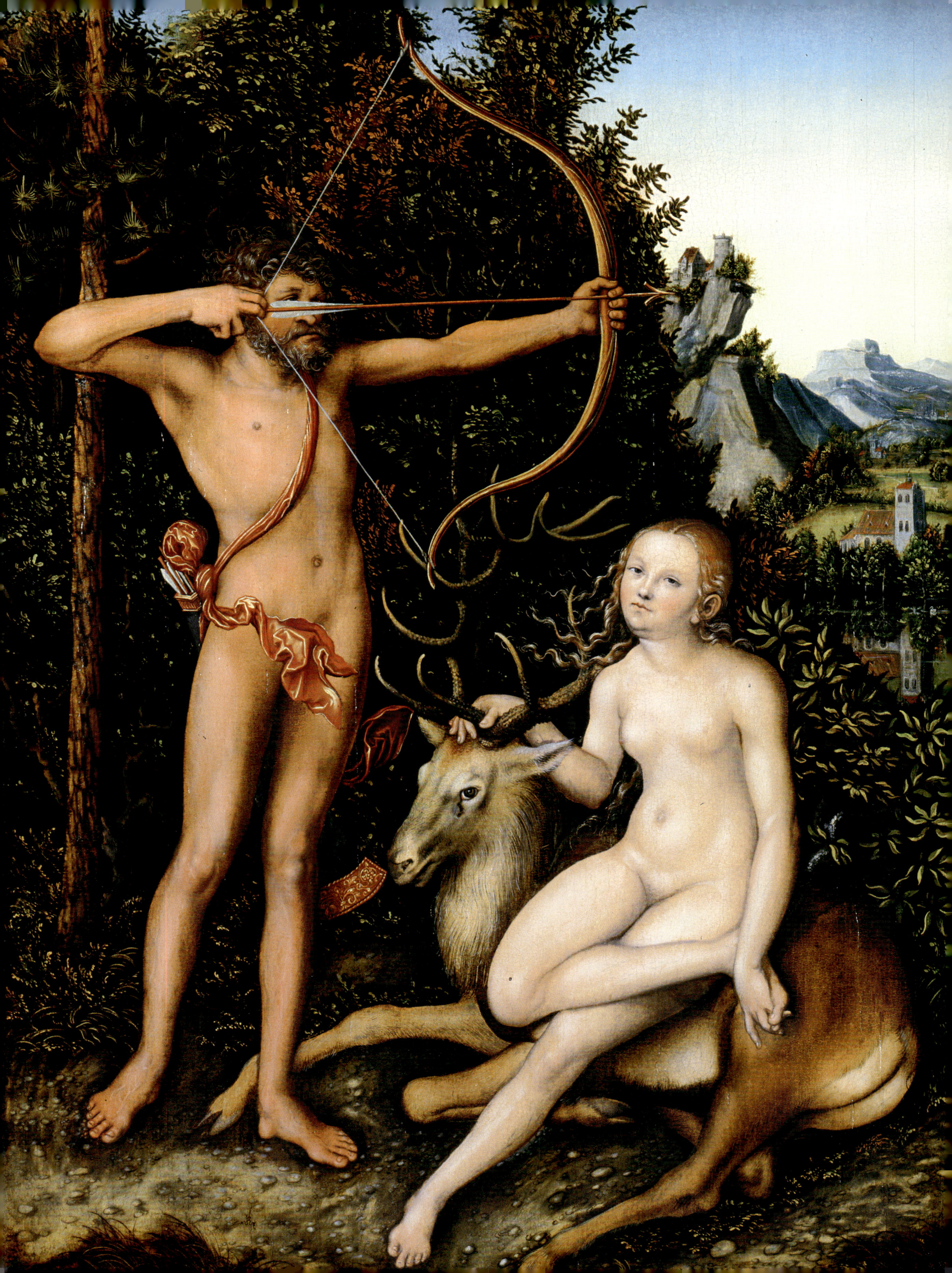

President's Foreword

Lucas Cranach the Elder, one of sixteenth-century Europe's greatest artists, is the archetypal painter of the Reformation. Until the Courtauld Institute of Art's recent exhibition and catalogue *Temptation in Eden: Lucas Cranach's Adam and Eve*, there had never been in Britain an exhibition devoted to him, a reflection of the underestimation of the artist outside Germany.

The exhibition at the Royal Academy of Arts, organised in collaboration with the Städel Museum, Frankfurt am Main, is the first major survey in this country of the artist's career. It seeks to build on the Courtauld's significant contribution, further stimulating our appreciation of the artist by bringing together works of many different themes, both sacred and profane, notable for their originality. Cranach's outstanding gifts are evident not only in his portrayal of landscape, animals and the female nude, but also in devotional paintings and portraiture, in his later work as chief propagandist of the Protestant cause, and in his inventive treatments of biblical and mythological subjects.

In mounting an exhibition devoted to Cranach, the Royal Academy found a willing partner in the Städel Museum, the exhibition's first venue. Our colleagues in Frankfurt were thinking along similar lines so it seemed natural for us to collaborate on such a project. The exhibition would not have been possible without the support of the Städel and other institutions and individuals who have so kindly agreed to lend their works. The core of loans from the Städel has been supplemented not only with works of the highest quality that reside, in large part, in German collections but also with important loans from elsewhere in Europe and the United States that travel but rarely.

The Städel's remarkable collection of paintings, drawings and prints by Cranach, ranging from all periods of the artist's career, was made available to the Academy with the greatest generosity; foremost among its works is the *Altarpiece of the Holy Kinship* dated 1509, specially conserved for the exhibition. To its Director Max Hollein and all his colleagues we owe a special debt of gratitude. In particular, Bodo Brinkmann, the principal curator, has played an instrumental role in bringing about the exhibition and its catalogue. We are deeply appreciative of his scholarship and commitment to our project.

It is with pleasure and appreciation that we extend our thanks to the many people who have contributed to the exhibition and its catalogue. At the Royal Academy Sir Norman Rosenthal initiated the project, working with Cecilia Treves on its realisation. We wish to thank the catalogue's authors and all those at Hatje Cantz and RA Publications who have been involved in its production and design.

We are most grateful for the valuable support of our 2008 Season Supporter, Sotheby's, Konrad Bernheimer and Katrin Bellinger for Colnaghi, Andreas and Catherine Heeschen, and George W. von Mallinckrodt KBE. We would also like to thank the German Ambassador, His Excellency Wolfgang Ischinger, for agreeing to be Patron of the exhibition. It is our sincere hope that this major presentation of the artist's achievements will make a lasting contribution to the re-evaluation of Cranach.

Sir Nicholas Grimshaw CBE
President, Royal Academy of Arts

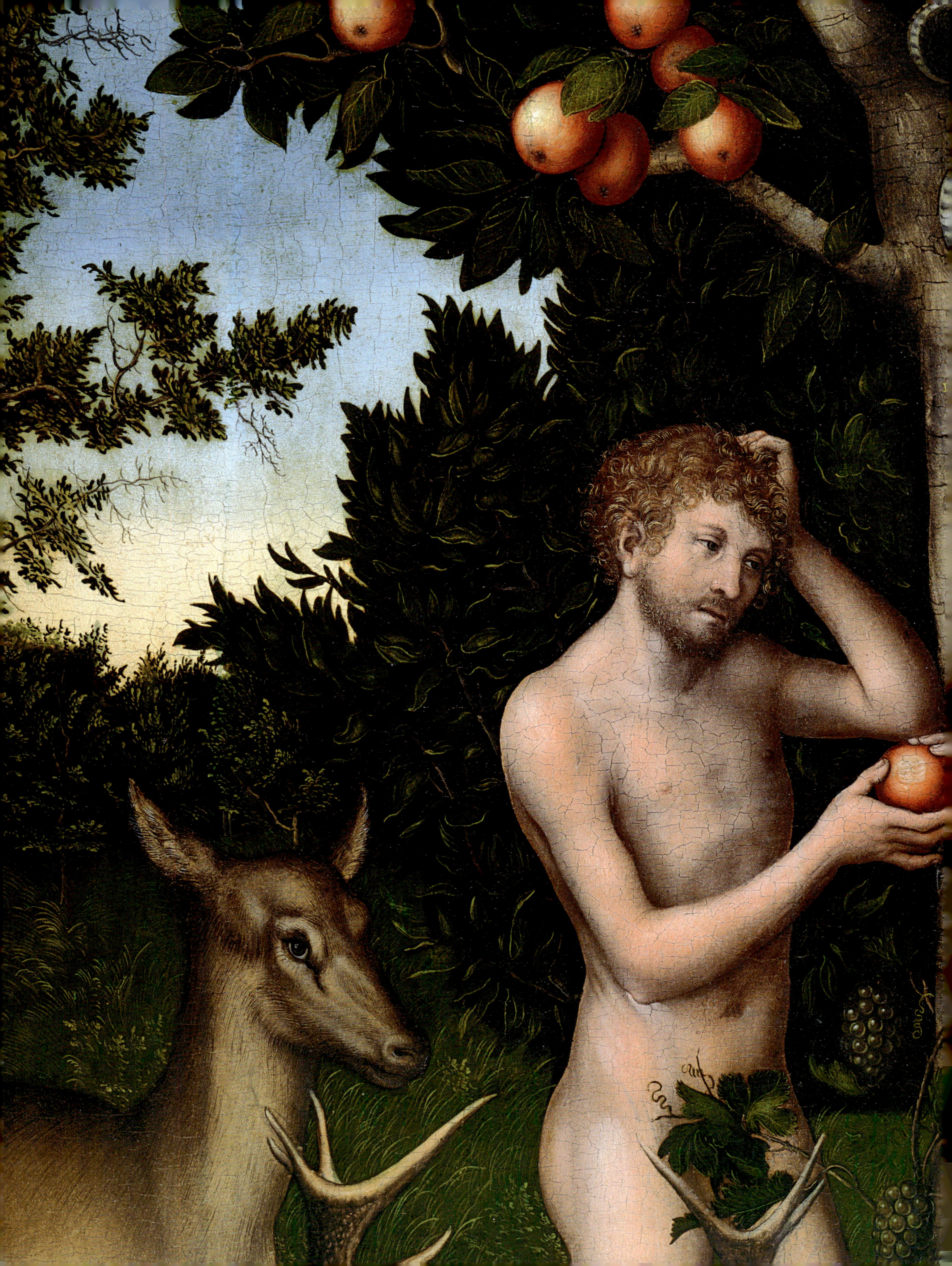

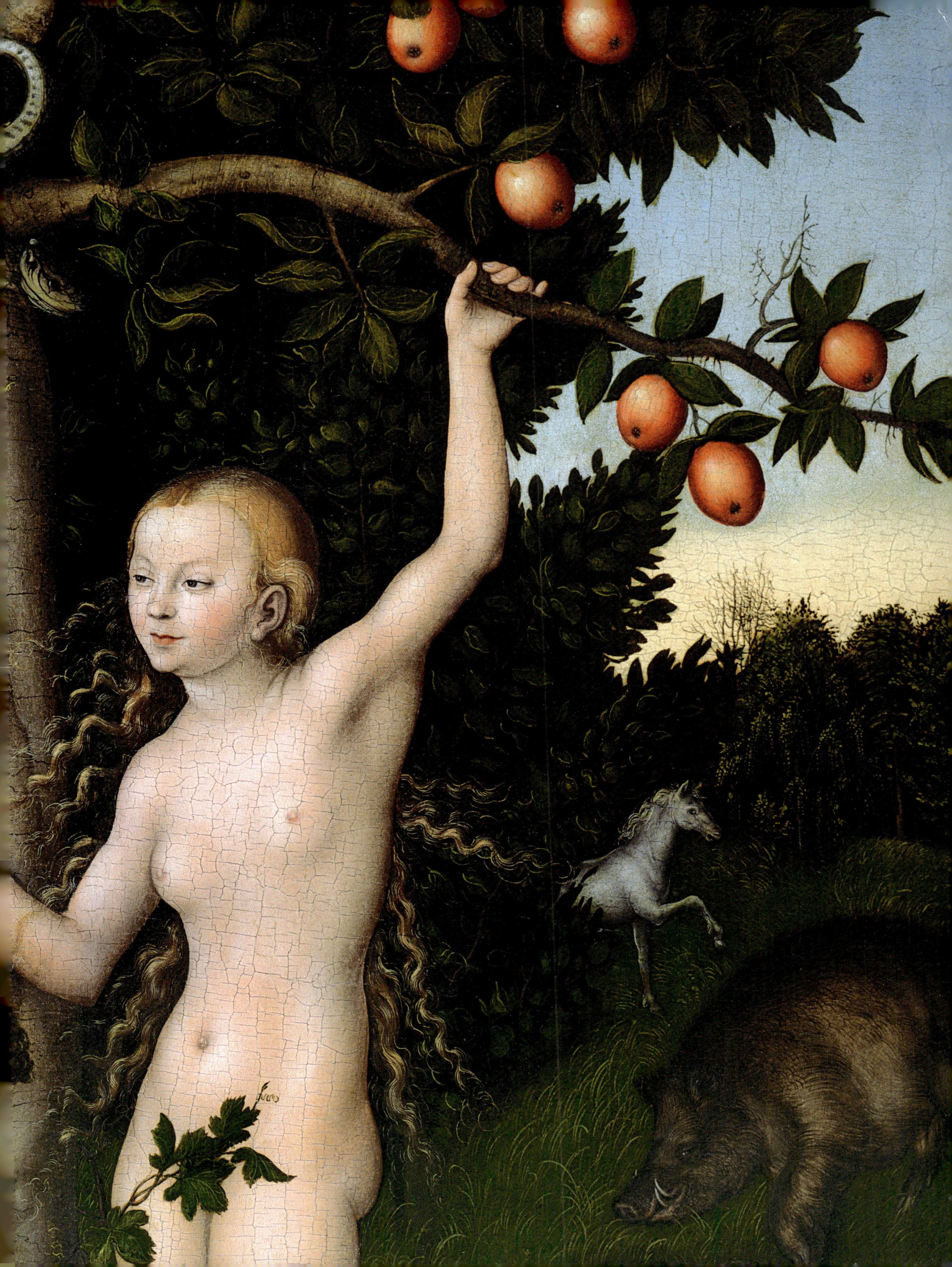

Lenders to the Exhibition

Austria
Tiroler Landesmuseum Ferdinandeum, Innsbruck
Gemäldegalerie der Akademie der bildenden Künste, Vienna
Kunsthistorisches Museum, Vienna

Belgium
Musées royaux des Beaux-Arts de Belgique, Brussels

Czech Republic
Moravská Galerie, Brno
Archiepiscopal Palace, Kroměříž
Klášter premonstrátů, Nová Říše

France
Musée des Beaux-Arts et d'Archéologie, Besançon
Musée d'Unterlinden, Colmar

Germany
Stadtmuseum, Bautzen
Gemäldegalerie, Staatliche Museen zu Berlin
Kupferstichkabinett, Staatliche Museen zu Berlin
Jagdschloss Grunewald, Stiftung Preußische Schlösser und Gärten Berlin-Brandenburg
Museum im Roselius-Haus, Kunstsammlungen Böttcherstraße, Bremen
Galerie Neuse Kunsthandel GmbH, Bremen
Kunstsammlungen Veste Coburg
Wallraf-Richartz-Museum and Fondation Corboud, Cologne
Hessisches Landesmuseum, Darmstadt
Anhaltische Gemäldegalerie, Dessau
Gemäldegalerie Alte Meister, Staatliche Kunstsammlungen Dresden
Stiftung Museum Kunst Palast, Düsseldorf
Wartburg-Stiftung, Eisenach
Dr Karl Graf von und zu Eltz-Kempenich, Burg Eltz
Städel Museum, Frankfurt am Main
Sammlungen der Herzog von Sachsen-Coburg und Gotha'schen Stiftung für Kunst und Wissenschaft, Stiftung Schloss Friedenstein, Schlossmuseum, Gotha
Niedersächsisches Landesmuseum, Hanover
Staatliche Kunsthalle, Karlsruhe
Gemäldegalerie Alte Meister, Museumslandschaft Hessen, Kassel
Hessische Hausstiftung, Kronberg
Museum der bildenden Künste, Leipzig
Alte Pinakothek, Bayerische Staatsgemäldesammlungen, Munich
Germanisches Nationalmuseum, Nuremberg

Hungary
Ráday Library of the Hungarian Reformed Church, Budapest
Szépmüvészeti Múzeum, Budapest

Italy
Galleria degli Uffizi, Polo Museale Fiorentino, Florence
Museo e Galleria Borghese, Rome

Mexico
JAPS Collection, Mexico City

Poland
Muzeum Narodowe w Warszawie

Portugal
Museu Nacional de Arte Antiga, Lisbon

Spain
Museo Nacional del Prado, Madrid
Museo Thyssen-Bornemisza, Madrid

Switzerland
Kupferstichkabinett, Kunstmuseum Basel
Museum zu Allerheiligen, Schaffhausen
Kunsthaus, Zürich

United Kingdom
City Museum and Art Gallery, Bristol
The British Library, London
Courtauld Institute of Art Gallery, London
National Gallery, London
Her Majesty The Queen, Royal Collection, London
Private collection on loan to the National Gallery of Scotland, Edinburgh
Salamander Fine Arts, London
Royal Cornwall Museum, Truro

United States of America
Cincinnati Art Museum
Kimbell Art Museum, Fort Worth
The Nelson-Atkins Museum of Art, Kansas City
J. Paul Getty Museum, Los Angeles
The Metropolitan Museum of Art, New York
The John and Mable Ringling Museum of Art, State Art Museum of Florida, Sarasota
National Gallery of Art, Washington DC

and others who wish to remain anonymous

Acknowledgements

The Royal Academy of Arts would like to thank all contributors to this exhibition catalogue. In addition to those mentioned in the President's Foreword we acknowledge the assistance of the following individuals:

Hein-Th. Schulze Altcappenberg
Karen Ashworth
László Baán
Giulia Bartrum
Ágnes Berecz
Hilary Bird
Stephanie Buck
Véronique Bücken
Lena Bühl
Caroline Campbell
His Excellency the Ambassador of the Czech Republic
The Bishop of the Danubian District of the Hungarian Reformed Church
Gabriel Dette
Inka Drögemüller
Susan Foister
Edward Glover
Emilie Gordenker
Christiane Haeseler
Anita Haldemann
Lada Hlavackova
Heike Höcherl
Isabel Horovitz
Clio Jones
Stephan Knobloch
Joseph Koerner
Marek Pokorný
Hanne Kolind Poulsen
Armin Kunz
Lola Landa
Michael Leitch
Ewa Manikowska
Harald Marx
Lucinda Middleton
Christian Müller
The Premonstratensian Abbey of Nová Říše
Barbara O'Connor
The Archbishop of Olomouc
David Organ
Doris Prade
Yasmin Qureshi
Sophie Richard
Catherine Rickman
Helmut H. and Petra Rumbler
José Alberto Seabra Carvalho
Desmond Shawe-Taylor
Anne-Marie Schleich
Julia V. Shea
Martin Sonnabend
Sheena Stoddard
Lajos Szelestey
Eelin Thomas
Ernst Vegelin van Claerbergen
Malcolm Warner
Lucy Whitaker
Jon Whiteley
Linda Whiteley
Martin Wyld
Adam Zamoyski
Antoni Ziemba

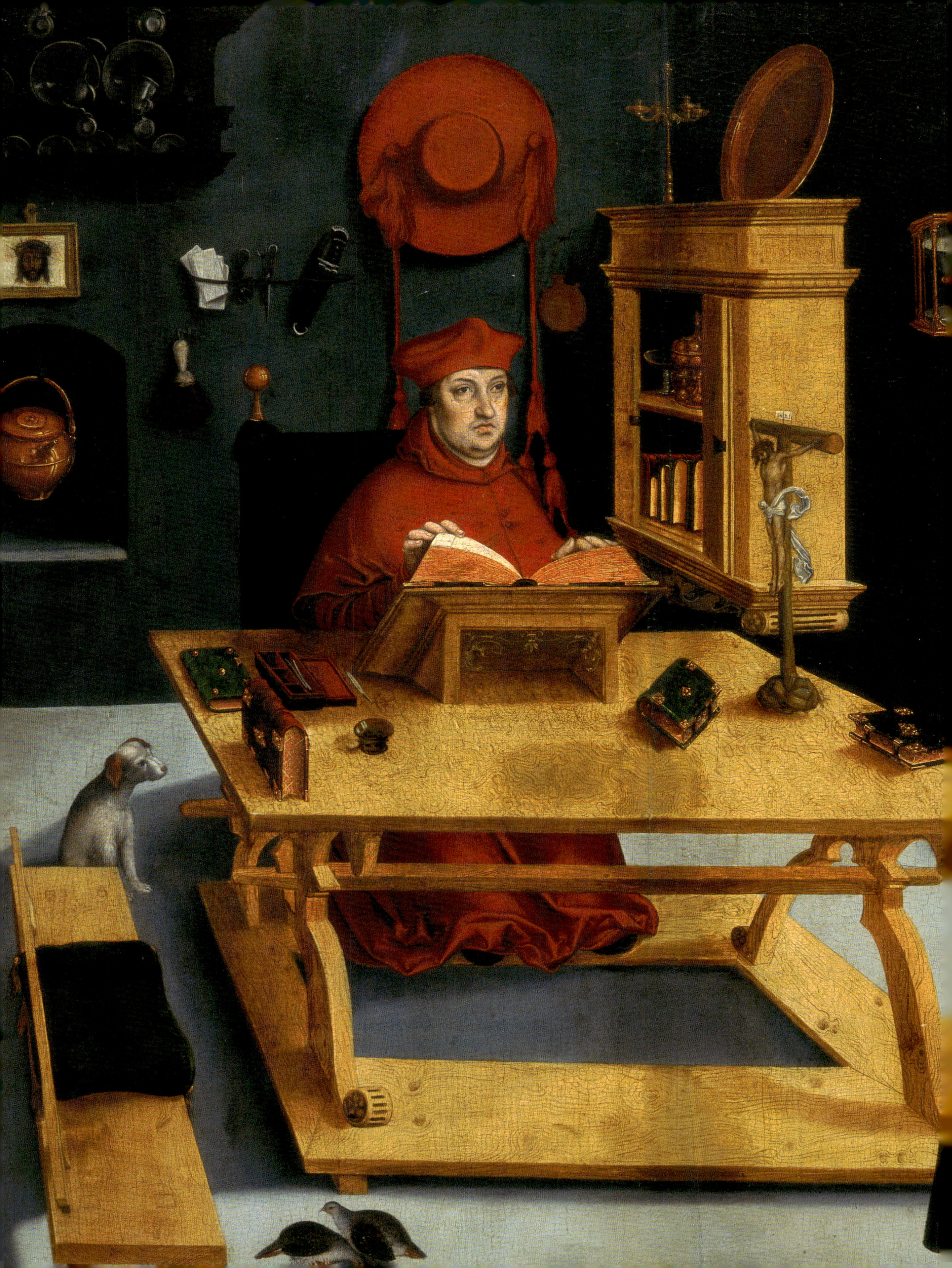

Essays

Bodo Brinkmann
Gunnar Heydenreich
Mark Evans
Dieter Koepplin
Andreas Tacke
Werner Schade
Elke Anna Werner

All captions and catalogue numbers that do not name the artist refer to works that we consider to be by Lucas Cranach the Elder – in the specific sense that he made them independently. Only those works revealing traces of another distinct artistic character are described as workshop creations.

The abbreviations relating to key reference works (FR, R, JB, SMS, Hind, Hollstein, IIIB) are explained at the beginning of the Bibliography on p. 388.

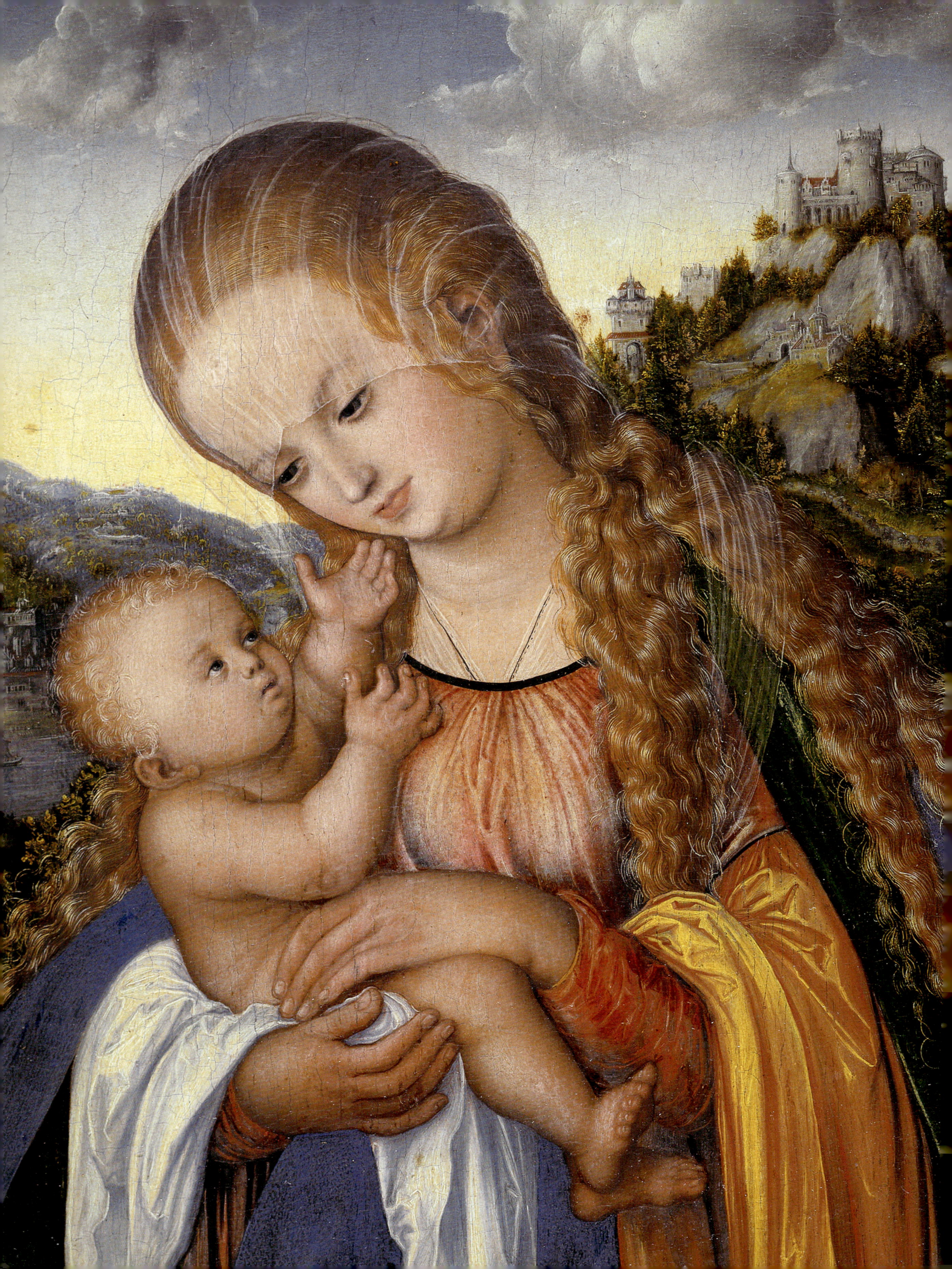

The Smile of the Madonna. Lucas Cranach, a Serial Painter

Bodo Brinkmann

I

'A Cranach has been stolen from the art museum in Konstanz. The restorer who worked on the painting lies dead near the empty frame. Stabbed in the heart with a thrust from a scalpel.' So began ARD's official description of the episode of the famous crime series *Tatort* (Scene of the Crime) which was first transmitted on Boxing Day 2005.[1] Its title was *The Smile of the Madonna* and at first glance it did not look very promising. In a plot involving, among others, a corrupt and diabetic restorer, an adulterous female museum director, her unscrupulous assistant and a very sharp and likeable art thief with a father complex, the object of the crime was one of the most magical small panels of the Virgin Mary by the early German master (cat. 62) – even though the picture does not usually live in Konstanz but a good 200 kilometres further down the Rhine.

Cranach's Karlsruhe *Virgin Mary*, which in 2005 was to appear before a million paying TV viewers, has nevertheless been outstripped in media terms by another work by the master from Franconia. According to the TV channel, an average of 119 million viewers watch the American cult series *Desperate Housewives* and there – provided they do not switch on after the credits – they are greeted by a picture of the Fall of Man which again is by Cranach.[2]

But why Cranach? Why not the more famous Albrecht Dürer or even the legendary Leonardo? Even if an element of chance plays a part when famous Old Masters turn up in the media today, I believe there are reasons in both cases for choosing a work by Lucas Cranach the Elder. With *Tatort* it may have been relevant that Cranach is not known to the general public as the creator of one famous masterpiece or a handful of such works, but as the creator of a whole range of fine and very varied paintings. The popular memory of him is not limited to a particular work; Lucas Cranach never created a *Mona Lisa* but he did produce a range of excellent portraits and attractive images of the Virgin Mary. If, therefore, someone wanted to ascribe a famous Old Master painting to a fictional medium-sized Museum X for the purposes of a television script, a Cranach *Virgin Mary* would be a good choice because it would immediately seem plausible to the viewer that a museum of that kind might own such a work. At the same time, the viewer would associate the name of Cranach with exceptional quality and high value. Although there are so many pictures of the Virgin Mary by Lucas Cranach that Museum X might indeed manage to own one of them, each one is nevertheless distinctive: 'The picture is like our shop sign,' says the art historian Siegfried Wagner (Rainer Will) as he eagerly assists Inspector Blum (Eva Mattes): 'It's everywhere. Posters, postcards, shopping bags – no-one could miss it, not even a philistine like me.'

Despite the large number of pictures of the same subject, true replicas, workshop repetitions such as were customary in Cranach's day, in Netherlandish painting for example, were seldom produced by the Wittenberg master. His workshop, under the master's supervision, generated a constant supply of new variants, even of subjects of which whole series have survived. They showed great inventiveness in the way they regrouped figures, changed motifs, and exchanged and adapted gestures and poses. By using samples and models and assembling them in new combinations they created a method of working which is close to the technique of making collages. The American makers of *Desperate Housewives* made use of this collage-like feature of Cranach's art for their credits sequence.[3] The Cranach picture opens a short cartoon in the course of which Eve takes the apple from the serpent and more apples tumble down from the tree, until finally an enormous one buries Adam beneath it. The fluency of the animation is surprising, but because Cranach's figures are rather like puppets,

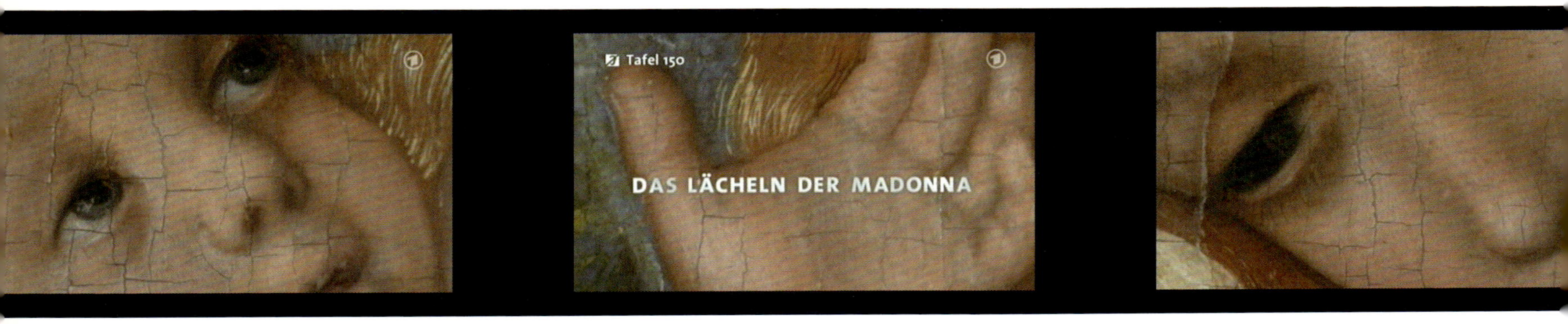

1 Film stills from the *Tatort* episode 'The Smile of the Madonna'

constructed so that individual parts can be interchanged, they withstand the manipulation relatively unscathed. A few seconds after the animated Fall of Man one can actually put to the test the idea that this is indeed a feature of Cranach's art. Next comes a second slapstick sequence involving the two protagonists in Jan van Eyck's *Arnolfini and His Wife* (National Gallery, London) – the husband drops a banana skin which his wife sweeps up. However, in marked contrast to the first scene the animation here is faltering, looks forced and less successful. Jan van Eyck's figures resist being made to move; it is as though they were nailed down – when discussing the Netherlandish painter's art someone once referred to a 'freezing of the look'.

The American creators of the credit sequence thus intuitively captured Cranach's method of composition for their own aims. The designers of the German crime film counted on their audience having similarly intuitive powers of memory. The two television programmes offer two aspects of the way in which Cranach is durably and subliminally fixed in the collective consciousness. In 1932 Max J. Friedländer, co-author of the first *catalogue raisonné*, described the public's attitude as follows: 'His well-known paintings, found in galleries all over the world, gave an impression of sound craftsmanship [...]; they were immediately recognisable, and invariably elicited a fleeting, superior smile.'[4]

Our memory of Lucas Cranach was and still remains thoroughly alive, but it seldom goes very deep. Thus we know a great deal about the life and work of the master, but beneath the surface there are some quite astonishing facts which are most unusual for a painter of his time.[5]

II

Lucas Cranach was born in 1472 in Kronach, the son of a 'Hans Maler' (in documents the name is also spelt 'Moller' or 'Müller'). This was a time when the use of surnames was gradually beginning to be established; they were taken from careers, origins, colours of clothing and other features and could vary even for one and the same person according to their situation. The name at any rate suggests that Lucas's father practised the craft of painting. The son may thus have learned his trade in his father's workshop; a note from 1556 confirms this. Later in Wittenberg he was only rarely called by his father's surname, and always signed his name 'Cranach', which clearly meant that he came from Kronach.

The use of a name based on origins naturally makes it possible to identify someone convincingly when they leave their home town. Where Cranach's *Wanderjahre* took him we do not know, but it is likely he had some contact with Nuremberg. By the time we can confirm that he was working as an artist, that is to say, in about 1500, he was almost 30 years old, and living in Vienna where among his clients he counted important humanists from university circles. He painted Johannes Cuspinian and his wife (Winterthur, Sammlung Oskar Reinhart 'Am Römerholz'; FR 6, 7) and another scholar (cat. 9). His rapid access to such patrons and later statements about Cranach's knowledge of Latin suggest that before his Vienna period the artist studied at a university. In the Vienna years his style was astonishingly innovative, expressive and lively, as in the *Crucifixion* of 1503 in the Alte Pinakothek in Munich (fig. 3), with its slanting perspective, then lyrical and full of atmosphere as in the *Rest on the Flight into Egypt* of 1504 (fig. 4), in the Gemäldegalerie, Berlin, his earliest signed panel picture. The sparkling colour range he used at the time reveals unmistakable parallels with the Danube School, but it is not clear whether he came into contact with Albrecht Altdorfer, Wolf Huber and others.

While these artists were starting out, Cranach was already moving on. In the year he painted the Berlin panel he was appointed court painter to the Elector of Saxony, Frederick the Wise, in succession to Jacopo de' Barbari (*c.* 1440–1515/16). In 1505 Cranach promptly settled in Wittenberg. His tasks included not just painting pictures of sacred and profane subjects but also the decoration of castles and palaces, designing arms, medals, costumes, festive settings, advising on building schemes, building furniture, sledges and carriages and also painting houses and fences. A fixed salary of a hundred guilders a year mainly covered his attendance at court and readiness to make himself constantly available; the pieces he produced were separately accounted for. His work and official clothes and means of transport were also paid for, including court robes for summer and winter and fodder for a horse. This was not particularly unusual for a court painter in the late Middle Ages, but with Cranach things developed a great deal further. By the end of his life he had served three Electors of Saxony, and this at a time of stormy political upheaval. The artist and his masters clearly shared an extraordinarily trusting relationship and this greatly helped the way Cranach reshaped the institution of court painter to suit a man who wanted to be more than an interior designer and picture producer, in other words to be an advisor and friend to princes. At the same time the Cranach workshop never thought it beneath its dignity to take on routine tasks such as painting houses, sledges and fences.

The earliest monumental work that Cranach completed in his new office was the Dresden *St Catherine* Altarpiece of 1506 (fig. 5 here; FR 12–15). The triptych is the first in a series of magnificent altar retables in which the two brothers Frederick the Wise and John the Steadfast appear either in role portraits or closely associated with the saintly figures in the composition, mostly as half-length donors. Examples of this scheme are the Dessau Princes' Altarpiece (Anhaltische Gemäldegalerie; FR 20) and a former triptych from which only the middle panel and the left wing with Frederick the Wise have survived, today in Copenhagen (Statens Museum for Kunst; FR 36). Cranach's pictorial inventions went down well with his master: in 1508 the Elector awarded the painter a coat of arms in recognition of his achievements; this showed a crowned serpent with batwings and a ruby ring in its mouth. Cranach immediately adopted this mark as his workshop signature. Probably in that same year his master commissioned him to travel to the Netherlands where he painted a portrait of the future Emperor Charles V as an eight-year-old boy, and took advantage of the opportunity of seeing the latest Dutch paintings, especially the works of Quentin Massys.

The year 1509 was one of the most important in Cranach's creative life. He continued the series of retables begun with the *St Catherine* Altarpiece in Dresden, producing the Frankfurt *Holy Kinship* Altarpiece (cat. 19), earlier thought to have been destined for St Mary's Church in Torgau, though this is now doubted. Here he revealed a fresh attitude to composition and colour and a clear debt to his journey to the Netherlands. Since 1506 he had become increasingly involved in the art of the woodcut, and this resulted in a Passion cycle. But his principal work was the 123 woodcuts illustrating the Wittenberg *Heiltumsbuch*, a printed catalogue of the relics brought back by Frederick the Wise and his ancestors.

Cranach was also apparently interested in the new printing processes. In 1507 he made his first attempt at producing coloured woodcuts. That year Frederick the Wise sent Konrad Peutinger, the Augsburg humanist and advisor to Emperor Maximilian, a copy of Cranach's woodcut of St George (fig. 6), printed from two blocks in black and gold on blue paper which had been previously coloured by hand (there are surviving copies in the Dresden Kupferstichkabinett and the British Museum, London). In Augsburg Hans Burgkmair seems to have taken the next step, producing the ground colour of the sheet by pressing down with a so-called tinting block which left white lights in the thinly covered depressions. This was how the coloured woodcut, also known as the light-dark or chiaroscuro woodcut, came into being. A few years later Cranach also made prints using this technique, backdating some of his sheets to 1506; one example is his *Venus and Cupid* which could hardly have been made before 1509. Clearly he wanted to feign authorship of the invention. Cranach was also responsible for designing a medal with which Frederick the Wise wanted to celebrate the temporary office of Imperial Governor that the Emperor had conferred on him. In Northern Europe this was a new challenge and evidently seems to have caused the artist some difficulties.

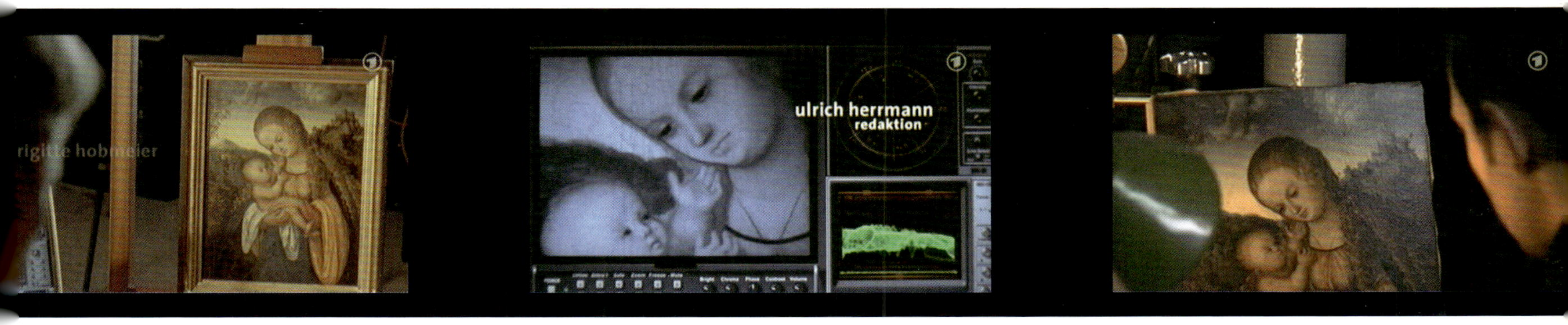

2 Film stills from the *Tatort* episode 'The Smile of the Madonna'

Cranach's wide-ranging activities and the support he received from the court, which outside clients were bound to see as a seal of quality, guaranteed an economic upturn. At first Cranach had lived in accommodation at the palace, and then probably as early as 1507 moved down into the town, clearly because his business was expanding rapidly. In about 1512 he successfully won the hand of Barbara Brengbier (died 1541), the daughter of a city councillor in Gotha, and in about 1513 and then 1515 she gave birth to their sons Hans and Lucas, followed by three daughters, Barbara, Ursula and Anna. Both sons later joined the workshop to satisfy the constantly growing demand for branded products bearing the mark of the serpent. Cranach was clearly making a good profit from all this. In 1528 he was the richest citizen in Wittenberg. By then he owned several houses and gardens, some of them in the best location in the marketplace, which he rented out, and bought and sold others. From 1520 he was running the only pharmacy in Wittenberg, which also sold herbs and spices and served sweet wines for which he took on a manager with the appropriate experience. Together with his increasing wealth his social standing was also in the ascendant. From 1519 until 1549 Cranach was always on the city council; he was elected city treasurer three times (1519, 1531 and 1534) and mayor three times (1537, 1540 and 1543).

In the first two decades of the sixteenth century the workshop's range of products showed a continuous increase. Together with the secular commissions for decorating Electoral palaces and castles and providing the churches of Saxony with altarpieces, Cranach pursued other areas. He established himself as a busy portrait painter. At court he proved his ability in this field with the life-sized double portrait he created in 1514 of Duke Henry the Devout of Saxony and his wife Catherine of Mecklenburg (Staatliche Kunstsammlungen, Dresden, Gemäldegalerie; FR 60/61). Also among his clients were mayors, councillors and, not least, professors at Wittenberg University such as Christof Scheurl (Scheurlsche Familienstiftung, Nuremberg; FR 23). There was also an increase in his mythological and allegorical scenes drawn from pagan Antiquity, which were distributed in print form, and panel paintings which initially were all individual pieces. These include such grandiose works as the life-sized *Venus with the Child Cupid* of 1509 in the Hermitage Museum, St Petersburg (FR 22). In 1508 he produced his woodcut of the *Judgement of Paris*, and a year later came a print with *Venus and Cupid* of similar proportions to the St Petersburg painting.

Antique subjects had long been accepted at court, as Berthold Hinz has shown. The *Description of the Bridal Bed*, which Cranach decorated on the occasion of John the Steadfast's second marriage in 1513, reads like a catalogue of the panels that Cranach was to complete decades later; the amorous pictorial programme included the *Judgement of Paris*, *Venus and Cupid*, *Hercules with Omphale* and *Lucretia* (!).[6] Perhaps the surprisingly early woodcuts of the same subjects had something of the character of court chronicles, like the majority of Cranach prints bearing the Saxony coat of arms. With them citizens of Saxony had an affordable medium with which to decorate their houses, choosing motifs that their rulers clearly found entertaining, leaving the artist free to explore this new market at no great financial risk.

The course of history soon provided Cranach with a new subject area as the situation quickly came to a head after Luther had nailed up his theses in Wittenberg in 1517. Cranach evidently did not hesitate to offer himself as a pictorial propagandist for the new cause. In 1519 he created the first Protestant flyer using the so-called wagon of Andreas Bodenstein of Karlstadt (*c.* 1482–1541), the doctoral supervisor and early campaigner for Luther. In 1520 Cranach provided Luther's polemic *Passional Christi et Antichristi* with allusive woodcut illustrations contrasting papal ceremonies with the Passion of Christ. The text and pictures are co-ordinated in such a way as could not have been achieved without close co-operation and analysis of the content. In the same year he engraved the first, touchingly plain portrait of the runaway Augustinian monk, whose image from then on – and even today – was shaped and reshaped by Cranach's creations.[7] The 'sensitive rebel' of the 1520 engraving was followed in 1521 by the *Scholar in a Doctor's Hat in Profile* in the same medium, and a year later by the energetic *Junker Jörg*, who had completely renounced the church, the title referring to Luther's incognito while he was staying in the Wartburg. Painted portraits soon followed, which to judge from the number that have survived, must, in the course of the sixteenth century, have served to decorate the homes of every well-off Protestant family. Contemporaries certainly found the flood of Luther portraits remarkable. In his eulogy for Cranach's son Hans, following his early death, Johann Stigel maintained that Hans alone had painted nearly a thousand. The fact that from 1525 Luther's portrait was mainly produced in the form of a pair with a pendant (cat. 41), depicting either his wife Katharina von Bora or Philipp Melanchthon, shows that the demand for pictures of the Reformer was not at all motivated by simple worship since

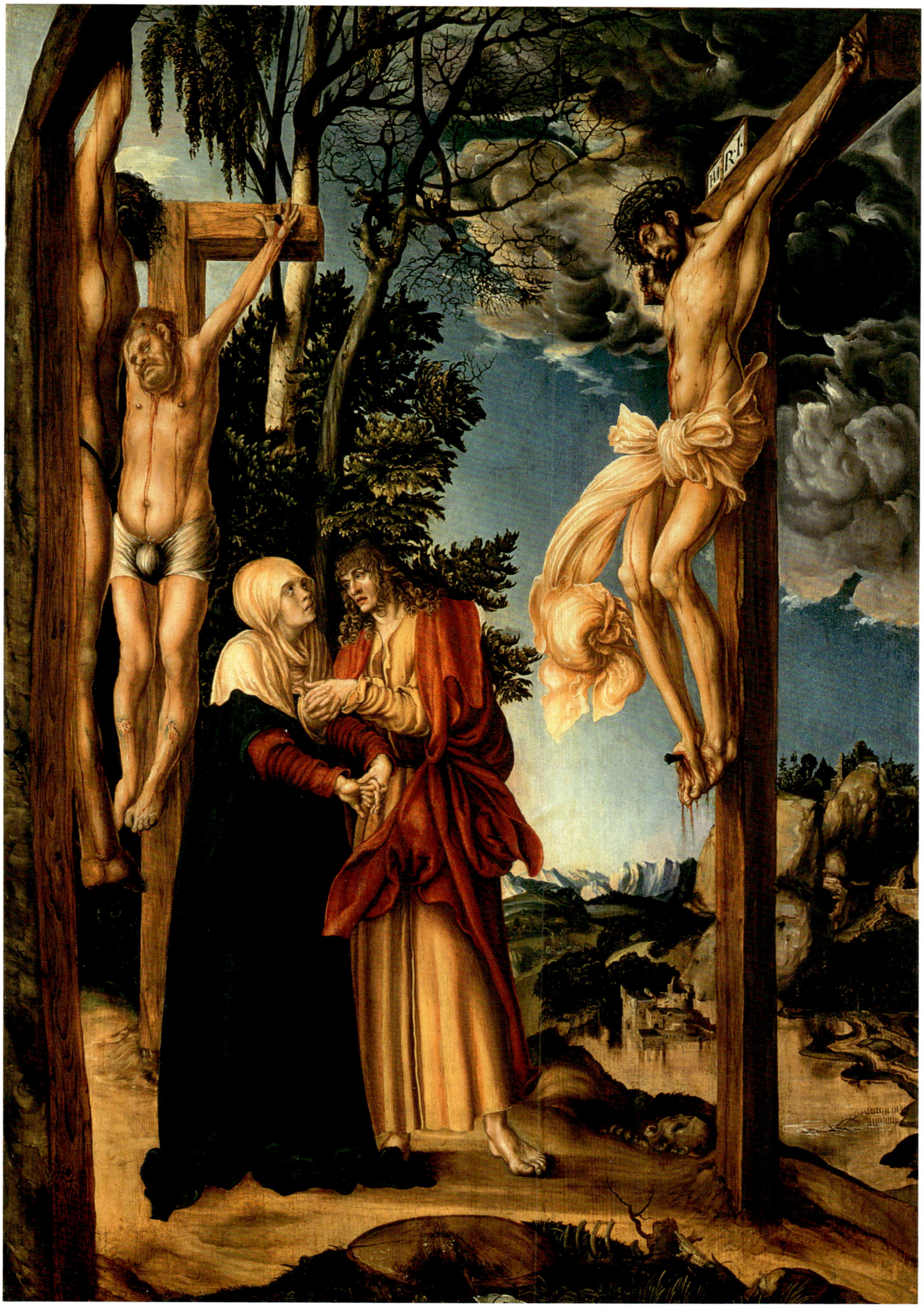

3 The so-called Schleissheimer Crucifixion, 1503,
Bayerische Staatsgemäldesammlungen, Munich, Alte Pinakothek

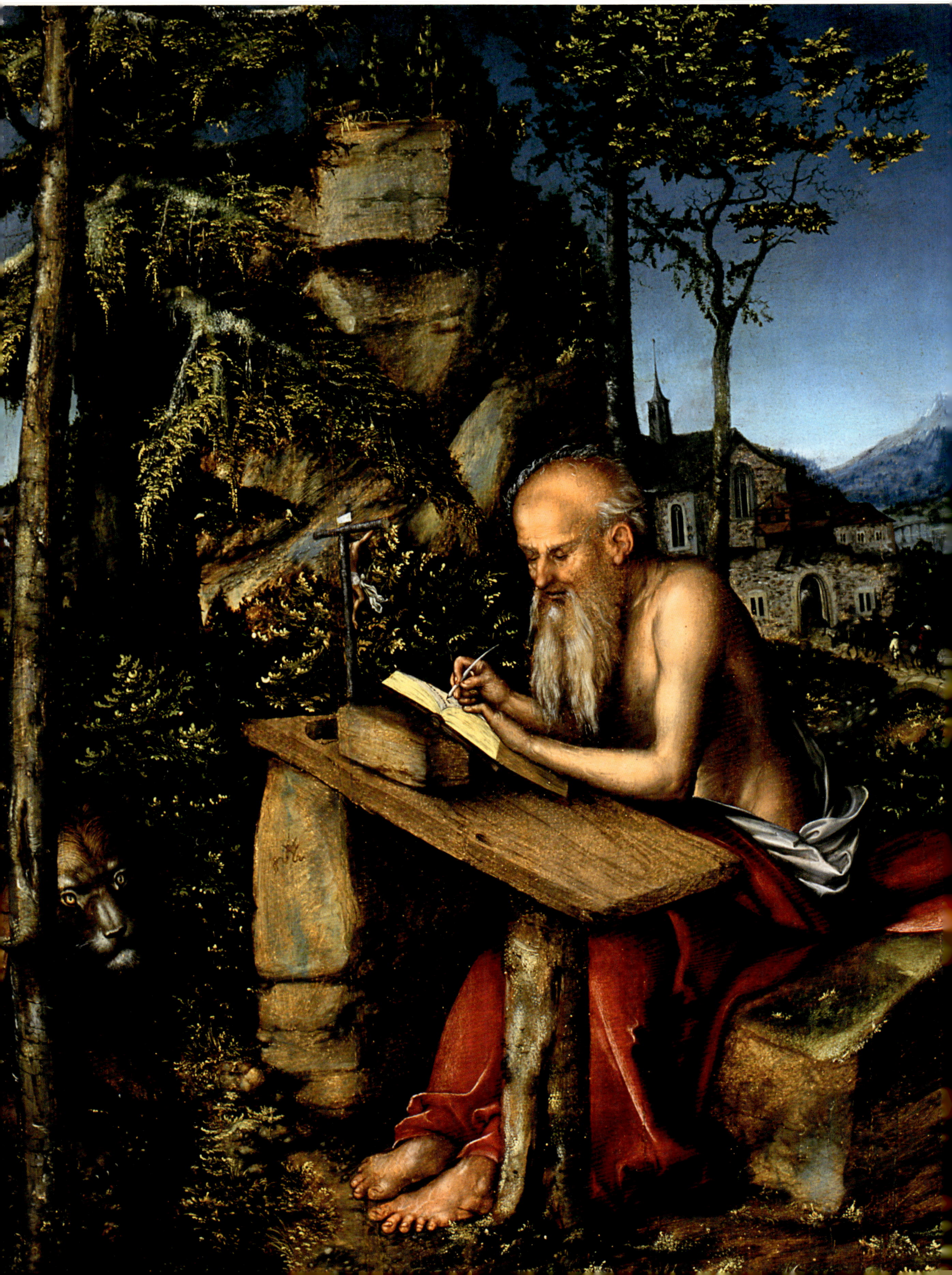

'... that you paint with wonderful speed'[1] Virtuosity and Efficiency in the Artistic Practice of Lucas Cranach the Elder

Gunnar Heydenreich

In his eulogy to Lucas Cranach the Elder, written in 1508, the Wittenberg University Professor Christoph Scheurl praised the realistic painting of the Electorate of Saxony's court painter.[2] Scheurl particularly lauded the 'wonderful speed' with which Cranach completed his paintings, and in which he surpassed all his contemporaries. The learned professor used this reference to Pliny the Elder[3] to introduce speed as a criterion for valuing artistic quality. The mastery of time and efficiency acquired fresh meaning in the Renaissance.[4] It is not quite clear, though, whether Scheurl's praise meant that Cranach actually painted faster than his contemporaries or whether it was primarily a reflection on his skills as an organiser. Cranach took on a large number of commissions in Wittenberg; the decoration of the Saxony castles was a particularly demanding job for the workshop. They produced an extraordinary number of prints and paintings on canvas and panel. Designs by Cranach served as models for, among others, glaziers, tapestry makers, tailors, goldsmiths and bronze foundries. This enormous artistic productivity required both efficient organisation of the workshop and careful allocation of work. This raises a number of questions. Did Cranach use painterly techniques that enabled him to produce pictures more quickly? Were there differences between the painting methods of the *Pictor Celerrimus*[5] and those of his assistants and contemporaries? Was the choice of materials and speed of execution varied according to the commission and what influence had print technology on the painter? The aim of this essay is to find answers to these questions using technical examinations; to explore the rich spectrum of Cranach's design methods, and the changing relationship between material and technical factors and artistic forms of expression in the work of the celebrated 'fast painter'.

Panel Paintings and Book Covers

The dimensions and proportions of a painting support may be determined by assessing the artistic idea as well as the properties of the materials and the commission, including their function and cost. In the period before he was appointed court painter in Wittenberg, Lucas Cranach the Elder developed his compositions on panels of varying size in an almost constant ratio of 4:3.[6] In his early years at the Wittenberg court the formats and ratios varied more widely. The average measurements reveal that the artist at first adopted Renaissance proportions with a more balanced relationship between height and width, while later he seems to have preferred the more Gothic proportion of the tall and narrow format. His interest in proportion was increasingly limited to maintaining a formal canon which he had himself determined, and stands in contrast to Hans Holbein's and Albrecht Dürer's more refined variability.[7]

In its second decade, picture production at the Cranach workshop was submitted to a far-reaching standardisation of formats. Between 1520 and 1535 more than seventy per cent of the surviving single panels conformed to one of six standard formats.[8] The panels for small portraits and large winged retables followed the same pattern. Even the proportions of designs for altarpieces were adjusted to the finished retables in standard formats in a scale of 1:10.[9] In this way, the painter forced himself and his assistants to make their compositions harmonise with the predetermined borders of the picture area. Compositions that were originally developed in individual formats were now increasingly carried out by Cranach and his apprentices on standardised panels. For example, the *St Jerome in a Landscape* (*c.* 1515, cat. 54, fig. 1) was clearly

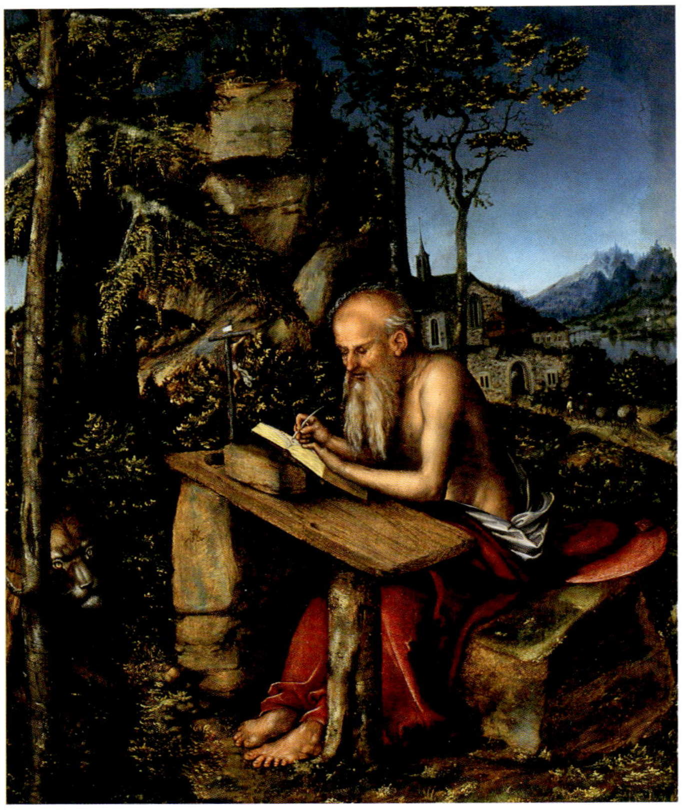

1 Lucas Cranach the Elder, *St Jerome in a Landscape*, *c.* 1515, panel, 67 x 57.5 cm, JAPS Collection, Mexico City

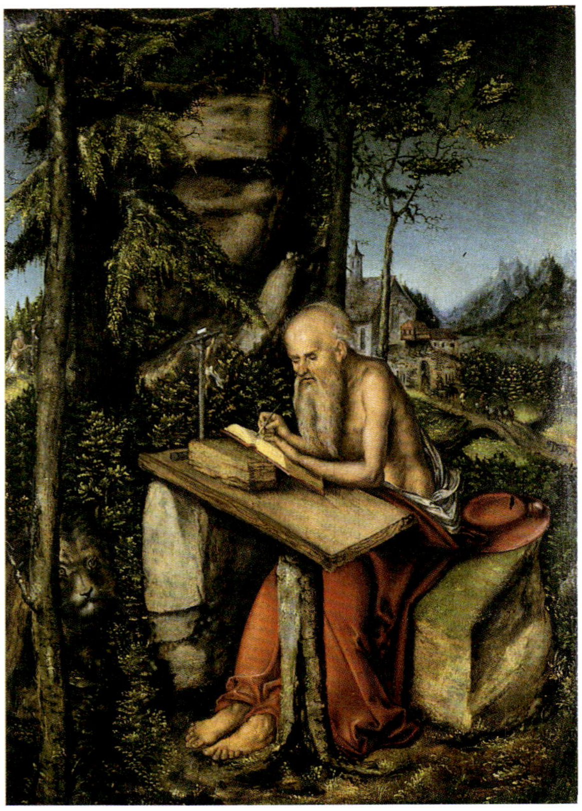

2 Lucas Cranach the Elder and workshop, *St Jerome in a Landscape*, *c.* 1515–1520, limewood panel, 51.3 x 37.7 cm, Staatliche Museen zu Berlin, Preußischer Kulturbesitz, Gemäldegalerie

stretched upwards when it was transferred to the comparatively narrower standard format (*c.* 1515–1520, FR 107, fig. 2).

The standardised panels were mainly of beechwood (*Fagus* sp.), and from 1521–22 to the mid-1530s beech was the preferred type of wood in the workshop of the Wittenberg court painter. The various methods used to prepare the panels suggest that Cranach had at least two carpenters working for him. While one of them produced limewood panels in irregular formats, another made beechwood panels in mainly standard formats.[10] Peter Klein has used dendrochronological analysis to prove that the boards used for various beechwood panels came from the same tree trunk.[11] Evidently, boards taken from one tree were used over a number of years. The storage time varied between one and seven years.[12] Cranach may have bought beechwood trunks, possibly precut, from which 'his' carpenter produced the panels in standard formats. Cranach's extensive use of beechwood appears to have been exceptional for Renaissance panel painting.

In the sixteenth century, wood was generally carried by raft along the Elbe to Wittenberg, and in 1524–25 the Wittenberg shipping accounts recorded the delivery of a larger quantity of *buchbretter* (beech or book boards).[13] By about 1528 at the latest, Cranach had his own timber and carpentry business. Wittenberg city council paid him for 'a quantity of wood and workpieces, to be used to build the city hall, and part of the merchants' shops'.[14] It is not impossible that the artist bought forest land in addition to the other land and property he owned[15] – as Titian is known to have done[16] – to increase the profits of his business.

The extensive use of beechwood in standard formats between 1522 and 1535 also suggests another link: at that time Cranach was involved in Wittenberg's large book-printing business. He and the goldsmith Christian Döring were sponsors of the first edition of Luther's translation of the New Testament, and in May 1522 Melchior Lotter the Younger printed the so-called *September Testament* in Cranach's workshop. Cranach himself contributed a series of woodcuts. The first edition of some 3,000 to 5,000 copies was sold out in a short time and a second edition followed in December (the *December Testament*). In 1523 Cranach and Döring installed their own press, employed Joseph Krug as printer and in the next few years published a number of titles by Luther.[17] In 1525 Cranach may also have owned a book and paper shop. An entry in an account reads:

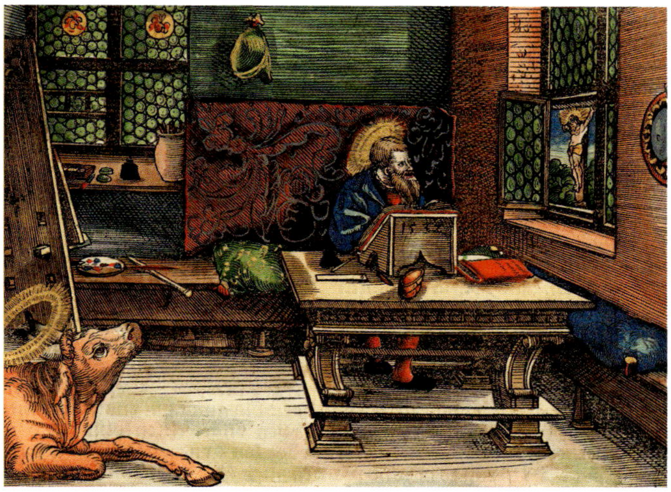

3 Lucas Cranach the Elder and workshop, *St Luke*, woodcut from the Luther Bible, 1534, Herzogin Anna Amalia Bibliothek, Weimar

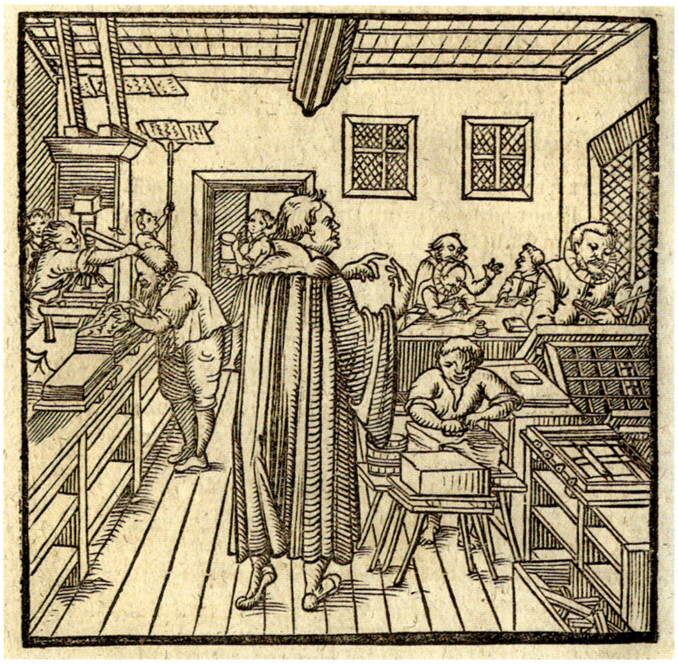

4 Officinae typographicae Delinatio, Woodcut from Hieronymus Hornschuch, Orthotypographia, Leipzig, 1608, Niedersächsische Landesbibliothek, Hanover

'26 Groschen Christoph Schramm in Lucas Cranach's bookshop for 2 reams of paper.'[18] At the beginning of 1526 Cranach and Döring set up their press again, and in 1532 withdrew from the publishing business. Around 1535 the number of beechwood panels used for Cranach's paintings decreased sharply.

With the development of printing businesses in Wittenberg and the thriving book trade, bookbinders also moved to the city; at the time most books were sold in uncut sheets which the buyer had bound later. Wittenberg developed as a centre of the art of bookbinding. Here the Saxon book cover was developed with its characteristic blind stamps of rolls and plates on white pigskin and brown calfskin.[19] Numerous clients, including princes, professors and students had the works of the Reformers bound and decorated.[20] The printed sheets were placed together and fixed inside two wooden covers, for which beechwood was preferred in Germany from the Middle Ages onwards.[21] It seems there was a connection between the extensive use of beechwood in Cranach's paintings between 1521–22 and 1535 and his activity as a publisher between 1522 and 1532. This assumption is further supported by the fact that there are remarkable similarities between the sizes of his paintings and the paper and book formats used in Wittenberg at that time (figs 3, 4).

Book formats depend on the number of leaves or pages a printer can obtain from one sheet of paper, and were traditionally based on the size of a vellum sheet. If a sheet of vellum or paper is folded once, this produces the folio format, then come quarto (4 leaves with 8 pages), octavo and sexto-decimo. The size of the book varied in accordance with the size of the sheets of paper available and was further influenced by various printing, binding and cutting techniques. If the majority of prints and books produced in Wittenberg in the 1520s are compared, the following sizes are most prevalent: octavo: *c.* 15–16.5 x 8.5–10.5 cm; quarto: *c.* 20–23 x 14–16 cm (fig. 5); folio: *c.* 35–37 x 21–24 cm.[22] These book formats correspond with the measurements of numerous smaller panel paintings from the Cranach workshop.[23] In the 1520s Cranach's works included portrait series of Martin Luther and Katharina von Bora on quarto-sized panels (*c.* 19.2–22.5 x 13.3–15.5 cm, fig. 6).[24] This also applies to the portrait pairs of the two electors Frederick III the Wise and John the Steadfast, for which a payment of 109 gulden and 14 groschen was made on 10 May 1533 for '60 panels of the two electors painted in praise

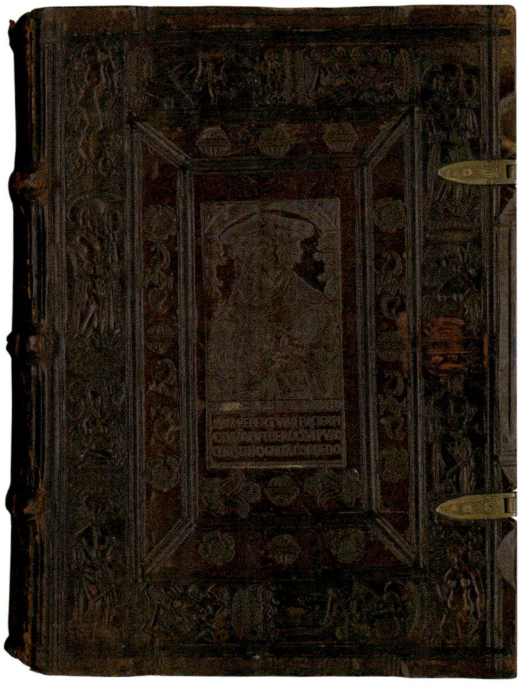

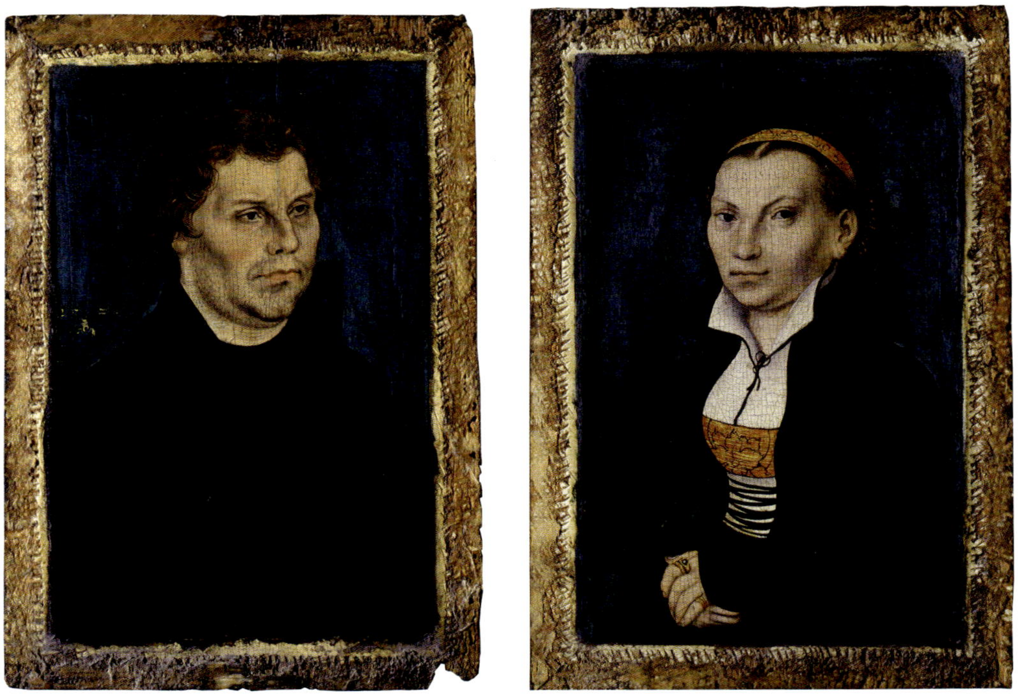

5 Joachim Linck, book cover with portrait of Luther, *c.* 1530, octavo, 22.5 x 16 cm; Contents of the anthology: Martin Luther, *Explanation of the Gospels ...*, Augsburg: Heinrich Steiner 1529; Martin Luther, *The Prophet Jesaia Deutsch*, Wittenberg: Johannes Lufft 1528, Anhaltische Landesbücherei, Dessau (Georg 1557)

6 Lucas Cranach the Elder and workshop, *Martin Luther and Katharina von Bora*, 1526, panels, each 22.5 x 15.9 cm, Wartburg-Stiftung, Eisenach

of their memory ...'; these too were in quarto format (*c.* 20.5 x 14.5 cm).[25] For portraits, Cranach seems to have preferred the historic folio format. As well as the series portraits of Martin Luther and Katharina von Bora from the years 1528–29 (cat. 41)[26] he also used it for numerous single compositions, including, among other works, Venus, Lucretia, Judith and the *Ill-Matched Couple* (cat. nos 91–95).[27] The next largest standard format size used by Cranach (C: 51–59 x 34–40 cm) may well be related to the format of an unfolded sheet of paper.[28]

Presumably Cranach adopted the usual paper and book formats as standard sizes for his paintings. His activities as a publisher and the requirements of book production may thus have influenced the compositions of his paintings, for he used the principle of standardisation to force himself and his assistants to harmonise the preliminary designs within predetermined vertical and horizontal limits. This may account for pictorial solutions that were not always well balanced. However, this way of working made it possible to produce larger quantities of supports in advance and more economically. At the same time it brought with it the advantage of being able to make regular use of preliminary material produced to the same scale. Cranach probably obtained his beechwood panels for painting from a carpenter who also made book covers. However, the rough surfaces on the backs of the painted panels[29] rule out the possibility that he actually painted on finished book covers. The larger formats are also far larger than paper sizes.

One of the earliest works painted on beechwood, possibly towards the end of 1521, is the *Portrait of Martin Luther as Junker Jörg* (FR 149).[30] The panel consists of a particularly wide board (52.8 x 37.3 cm, standard format C), the reverse of which shows carved blossoms and leaf and chain-like decorations.[31] Perhaps the wood was being tested here for other uses such as carving. Possibly, too, Cranach produced designs for book covers[32] and even employed a bookbinder in his bookshop.

The extensive standardisation of formats supported not only a factory-style output of paintings but also the notion that certain subjects could be produced without a commission and delivered immediately to order. Standardised works could be produced more quickly and therefore more cheaply. These paintings could be bought by a broader section level of society, particularly those with smaller financial means. In the process Cranach introduced characteristic features of both woodcuts and book illustration into his painted work, although he preferred to avoid direct copies. Diptychs were traditionally joined with hinges and could be closed like a book. With pictures in book formats and printed texts in pictures the court painter merged his fields of activity. The painting as

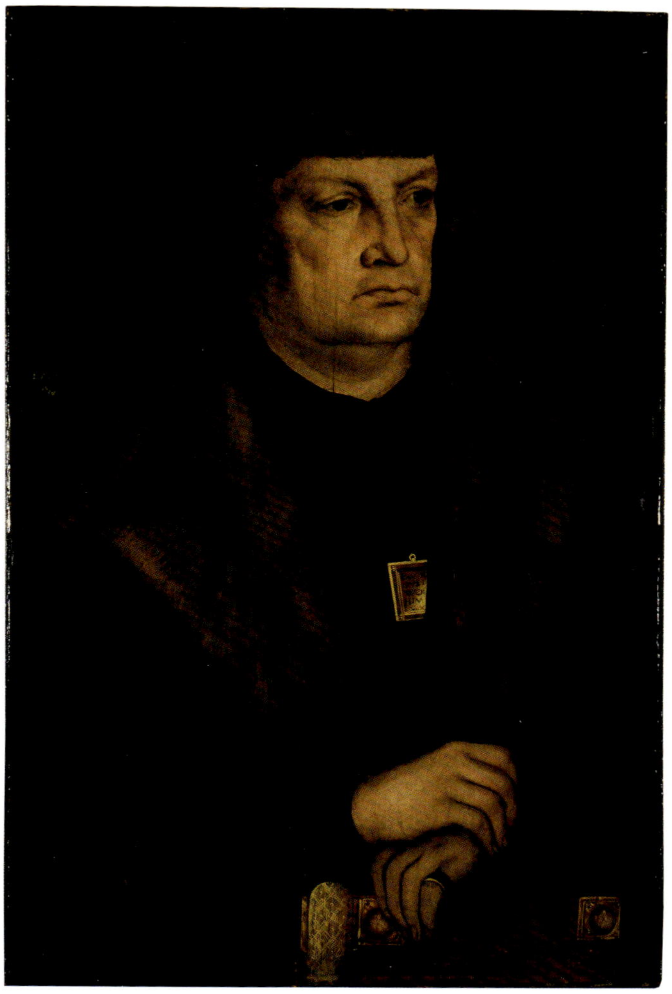

7 Lucas Cranach the Elder and workshop, *Portrait of a Man, possibly a Mayor of Weissenfels*, 1515, parchment on wood, 42.2 x 28.3 cm, Staatliche Museen zu Berlin, Preußischer Kulturbesitz, Gemäldegalerie

book reflected Luther's ideas of explanatory and didactic pictures and was put to work for the New Belief. These and other efficient practices were almost without equal in sixteenth-century German panel painting.

Wood, Canvas, Parchment and Paper

Cranach painted mainly on wooden panels. In addition we know of numerous paintings on canvas in various techniques and with various functions.[33] He also made varying use of parchment and paper, the traditional supports of the graphic arts, in his panel paintings.

In about 1515 he made a sketch in quill pen and black ink on parchment of the *Assumption of St Mary Magdalen*.[34] Over this sketch, and without any further drawing, he painted the portrait of a bare-headed man, perhaps a mayor of Weissenfels (1515, FR 63, fig. 7). The face was captured with rapid, painterly brushstrokes. It seems as though Cranach, driven by a relentless creative urge, gave little thought to the type and preparation of the support and no time at all to erasing the pen drawing before he fixed his sitter's facial features in paint. As a result of the increasing transparency of the flesh paint with ageing, the drawing of *St Mary Magdalen* is today visible in normal light. There is a striking discrepancy between the lively and confident brushstrokes in the face and the schematic execution of the clothing, hands and book. Perhaps this portrait was created in two stages: while the face is mainly rendered wet on wet – the eyelids were put onto the flesh colour while it was still fresh – decorating the book clasps in a sgraffito technique required the first layer of paint to dry. These observations support the theory that Cranach had fluently mastered the transition between the portrait study and the finished painting.

From the twelfth to the early fifteenth century there are many instances in European painting of wooden panels being completely covered with parchment.[35] It is generally assumed that this would have disguised faults in the panel and reinforced the joins.[36] It may also have been done to reduce later cracking of ground and paint layers. Accordingly, there are many panels with strips of parchment covering the joins before the ground was applied.[37]

The parchments used for the *Portrait of a Man, perhaps a Mayor of Weissenfels*, the *Portrait of Martin Luther as an Augustinian Monk* (*c.* 1523–24) and the heads of Christ and the Virgin Mary (*c.* 1516–20, cat. 61) bear no sign of a ground layer.[38] This suggests that Cranach, like Dürer and other contemporaries, regarded the parchment less as an independent support or a protective device for the joins of the wooden panel but rather as a preparatory surface equivalent to a ground for painting. Over successive generations painters were aware of and had appreciated its qualities as a material for their drawings as well as their watercolours and paintings in body colours.[39] The semi-transparent hue of the animal skin and its compact smooth surface may have been particularly useful for refining flesh tones and may have been a reason for its increased use as a support for portraits.

In the *Portrait of a Man* of 1514 (FR 62) and the Elector Johann Friedrich I of Saxony and his Wife Sibyl of Cleves (1532), the coats of arms were painted on sheets of parchment and glued to the reverse of the wooden panels.[40] While in his early years in Vienna Cranach painted coats of arms directly onto the thinly primed backs of the panels, in Wittenberg he laid down illuminated prints on them. The use of parchment could also be linked to his efforts to be more efficient. It may be that preliminary designs and patterns were copied by overlaying a semi-transparent sheet of parchment and tracing them.

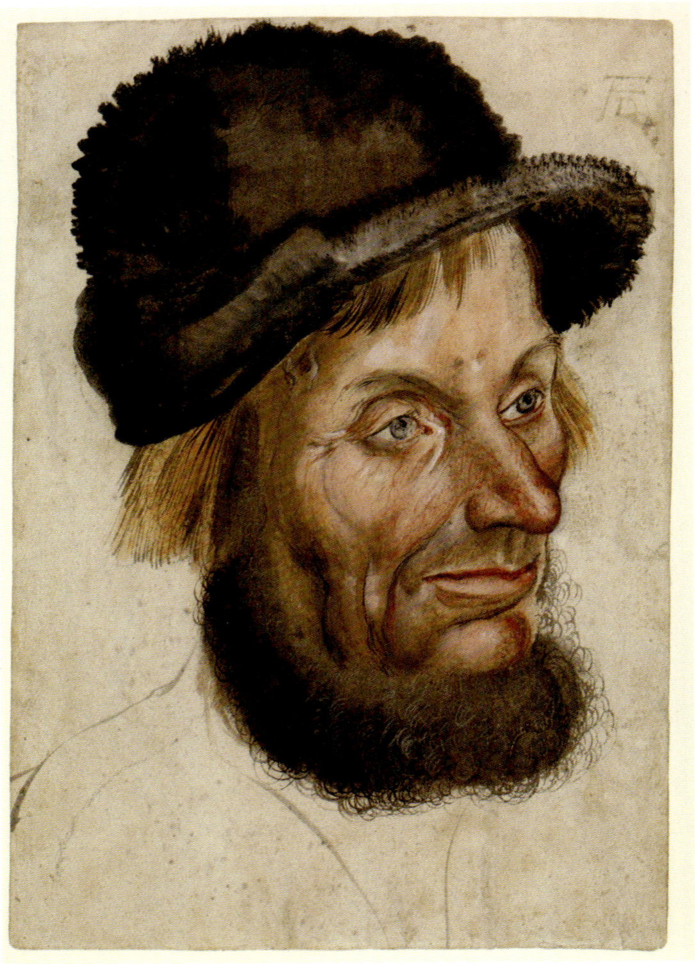

8 Lucas Cranach the Elder, *Portrait Study of a Peasant*, *c.* 1510–20, paper, 23.8 x 16.8 cm, The British Museum, London

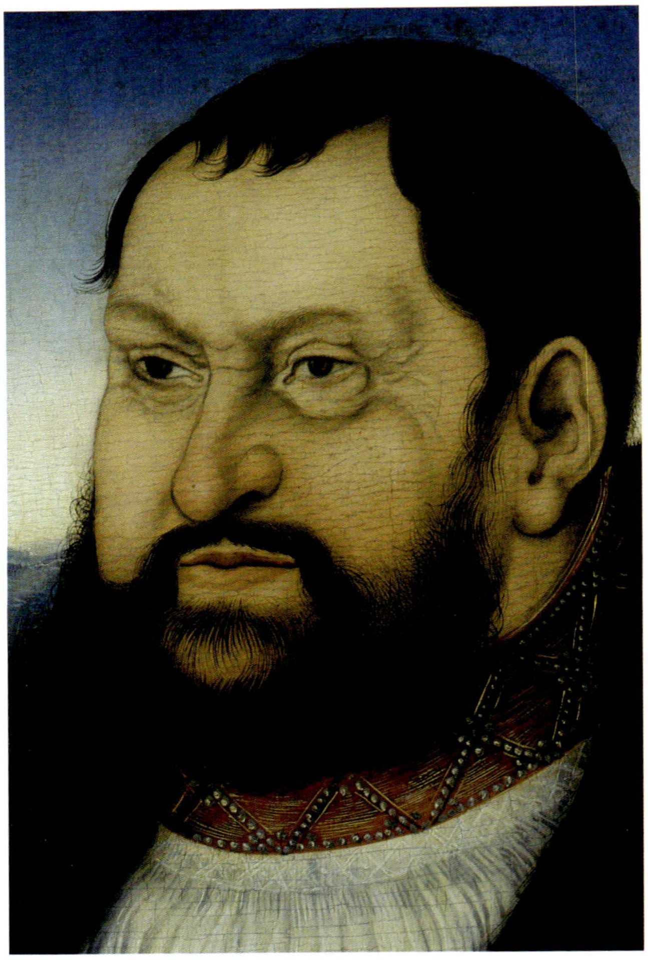

9 Lucas Cranach the Elder and workshop, *Portrait of Elector John the Steadfast* (detail), *c.* 1526, beechwood, Kunstsammlungen Weimar

Paper was often used in Cranach's workshop as a support for studies and models, but was also laid down on wooden panels. The preliminary head study on paper was executed in front of the sitter, recording important physiognomical features in colour (fig. 8). These studies were often produced with a wonderful freedom and at great speed, leaving the clothing only briefly sketched. A number of surviving portrait studies on paper, as well as the finished paintings made from them, document the customary practice in the Cranach workshop.[41] Portrait studies on paper allowed for division of labour in panel painting, and frequent reuse. Other works on paper, such as the *Heads of Three Women* (*c.* 1530–32, cat. 85),[42] could be copies of important elements of paintings also intended for multiple reuse. In contrast to parchment, no finished oil paintings on paper have yet been associated with the Cranach workshop.

A head study of Elector Frederick the Wise wearing a wire cap was clearly used for several years. We find the same likeness in at least eight surviving paintings.[43] Here the workshop model was obviously adjusted to the scale of the paintings by freehand transfer. Other head studies were transferred by tracing. Two that completely match are the portrait study sketched in body colour on paper[44] and the completed portrait painting on wood of Hans Luther of 1527 (cat. 72). Also, in some portraits made in series or variants on them, the mechanical transfer of the same head study is evident (fig. 9). The use of panels in standard formats would have facilitated the repeated reuse of prototypes.

Occasionally, fine and notably long lines of underdrawing are characteristic of tracing using a stylus to transfer black pigment from the reverse of a study to the prepared panel (fig. 9). However, surviving portrait studies bear no evidence of their being used for tracings; there are no impressed lines or pinpricks. This means that the transfer was very probably carried out with the help of a transfer drawing taken from the painted study and then blackened on the verso to serve as a tracing. Foil prepared from animal glue or paper which was oiled to make it semi-transparent, were suitable ways of preparing such a transfer drawing.

The most likely reason for applying paper to panel paintings would be to link text and image and to improve serial production. Traditionally, inscriptions were carried out using brush and paint on completion of the painting process.

However, in some paintings from the 1530s and 1540s that were produced in larger quantities, texts printed on paper were glued on before painting began. Examples include the paired portraits of the two electors, Frederick the Wise and John the Steadfast, dating from 1532 and 1533.[45] The poems extol the activities of the electors. Occasionally they were enhanced with printed nameplates. On the reverse of some of these panels, woodcuts have been preserved of coats of arms from the *Heiltumsbuch* (catalogue of relics).[46] The combination of portrait and text follows the model of Dürer's engraved portrait of Elector Frederick the Wise with inscribed panel, dating from 1524, and can be compared to the propaganda purposes of, for instance, Roman monuments.[47] The use of printed inscriptions spread from portraits to other pictorial productions. In the *Allegory of Redemption* (fig. p. 67), Cranach clarified the powerful pictorial motifs with detailed quotations from the Bible, and in the process succeeded in faithfully illustrating the central ideas of Luther's theology of Redemption, producing the most significant work among Protestant explanatory and didactic pictures.[48]

Chalk Grounds and Frames

Substantial preparatory layers were applied to all panels used in the Cranach workshop. These were usually white grounds bound with an animal glue and contained calcium carbonate as a filler. A few panels from the period before Cranach's appointment in Wittenberg form an exception: *The Penance of St Jerome* of 1502 (FR 4, cat. 3) has a red preparatory layer consisting of red lead, lead white and some calcium carbonate. *The Holy Family* of 1504 (FR 10) seems to be primed in two layers, white on red lead. X-radiographs show that Cranach, driven by his creative urge, did not always pay great attention to his grounds; the pictures show blisters and cracks that occurred before painting began.

The Cranach workshop abandoned the use of the medieval unit of panel and frame. While many panels were still given an engaged frame, others were fitted in rebated mouldings. Applied frames (laminated to the edges of the panel when the work was completed) are well known from smaller portraits (fig. 6). The frame could be made according to the client's wishes; either at the same time or after painting was completed. Here Cranach introduced into painting a principle which was already current practice in book production in the sixteenth century, that is, that frames for completed paintings were made, exactly like book covers, according to the taste and demands of the client.

If the panel was inserted in a frame, in accordance with the medieval practice, before the ground had been applied, there is a so-called 'priming barb' close to the edges of the panel. In some of Cranach's panels there are traces of gilding and paint on the bare wood outside the barb. These suggest that in Cranach's workshop the panel and frame or interim frame were occasionally separated again after priming. This assumption is supported by incisions in the ground along the edges and black painted borders. The function of the incised lines could simply have been to provide an additional indication of the outer borders of the surface to be painted. It is also possible that they helped to prevent the ground from being damaged when the interim frame was removed. The black edges can generally be seen as providing a visual border during the painting process, comparable to the black painted edges in contemporary paintings on textile supports.

Cranach modified the surface quality of the smoothed ground with thin intermediate layers. What appears to be an unpigmented isolation layer over the ground was probably applied to reduce absorption. The pigmented intermediate layer or *imprimatura* served to adjust the surface properties of the ground with a semi-transparent tint. An *imprimatura* that is white strengthened the light reflected by the chalk ground. It was a typical feature of German and Dutch painting at the beginning of the sixteenth century and was part of the repertoire of, among others, Dürer,[49] Hans Memling,[50] Michelangelo[51] and Titian.[52] Early works by Cranach the Elder such as *The Crucifixion* of *c.* 1500 (cat. 2) and the retable wings with SS Valentine and Francis of *c.* 1502–03 (cat nos 4, 5) have an *imprimatura* of lead white in oil. For many decades this technique formed part of the practice of the Wittenberg workshop. The earliest example of a light reddish *imprimatura* in Cranach's work is the *Crucifixion* of 1503. Generally this was a mixture of lead white and red lead. The reddish grounds and *imprimature* on wooden panels can be compared with the reddish tone of the drawing papers that Cranach used for the *Bad Thief on the Cross* (*c.* 1501–02, fig. 10). They suggest a fluent transition between studies and paintings, which may have reinforced Cranach's reputation as a rapid painter.

There is evidence of reddish *imprimature* in North German panel paintings of the fourteenth century and in Dutch and Italian paintings of the fifteenth century.[53] Examples from Nuremberg are the Perkmeister Portrait (1496) from the Wolgemut workshop[54] and the portrait of Barbara and Albrecht Dürer the Elder (*c.* 1490)[55] attributed to Albrecht Dürer. A light reddish *imprimatura* was also discovered on Dürer's panel *Jesus among the Scribes* (1506).[56] For this work,

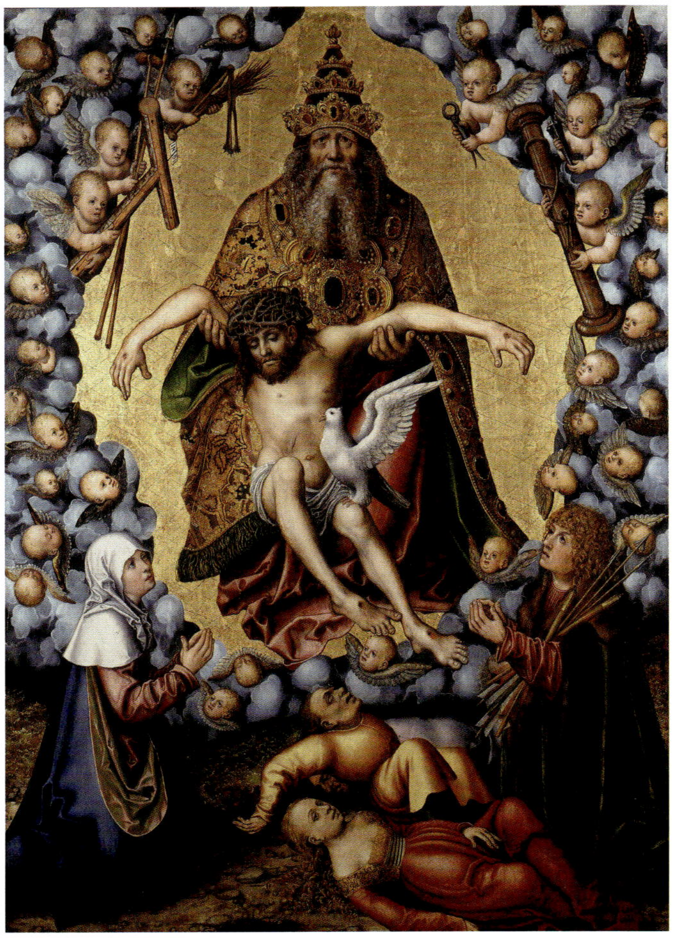

14 Lucas Cranach the Elder and workshop, *The Holy Trinity*, *c.* 1515, panel (transferred), painted area 137.8 x 99 cm, Museum der bildenden Künste, Leipzig

following decades the Wittenberg workshop limited the application of gold leaf mainly to frames and to the polychromy of architecture. When Melanchthon[63] deemed the works of Cranach to be 'pure in their simplicity' in comparison with those of Dürer and Grünewald, he was describing not just a difference in meaning and quality but also the use of materials. Cranach heightened the intensity of his pictorial statements in favour of Reformist ideas and also increased the efficiency of his picture production by incorporating texts printed on paper into his pictures at the expense of material value and painterly virtuosity (fig. 10).

Painting Materials and Technique

Cranach had more than twenty-five different pigments at his disposal, a much larger range than what is known to have been available to his contemporaries Dürer and Grünewald.[64] The pigments and binding media varied just as much within single works as between different commissions. The choice was influenced not only by tradition, the wishes of the client and his financial reserves but also by local availability, artistic exchange and trade. So, for example, the use of expensive natural ultramarine was limited to a short period after his journey to the Netherlands, where Cranach could possibly obtain it more easily (fig.16). With his varied use of a rich palette Cranach pursued a broad spectrum of pictorial activities. In addition, he painted with pigments of different particle sizes and binding media. In, for example, the Neustadt Altarpiece (1511–13, FR 47A) and the panel pictures *The Saviour* (*c.* 1515–16, FR 78) and *Virgin and Child with St Anne* (*c.* 1515–16, FR 79), a finer-grained azurite, which was bound in oil and applied to the blue draperies, forms a contrast with a coarser grade bound in glue and used as a background colour (cf. figs 19, 20). In this manner Cranach also transferred traditional techniques of mural painting and polychrome sculpture to his panel paintings. The diversity of his materials grew smaller with the adoption of serial picture production in the 1520s, when pigments with a smaller particle size began to dominate. The paint layers from that period are often surprisingly thin.

The painting process began with underpainting. This can be divided broadly into three groups: underpainting with coloured pigments, another using grey tones and a third using black. In the panel with St Jerome of 1502 and the Cuspinian portraits (*c.* 1502–03, FR 6, 7), we find an opaque, pale violet underpainting for the blue sky made from a mixture of lead white and fluorite. Then, in the *Portraits of a Jurist and his Wife* completed only a few months later, Cranach replaced the fluorite with black pigment (fig. 17). Later the grey underpainting was extended to robes in various colours. *The Virgin and Child with St John* (*c.* 1512, cat. 17) and the *Virgin and Child* in the Thyssen-Bornemisza Collection (*c.* 1512–14, FR 30) are among the earliest examples of blue drapery underpainted in grey. This grisaille-like modelling allowed an economical and subtle grading of light and shade and resulted in a particular intensity of colour when finally a thin layer of almost pure azurite was applied.

For almost forty years it was normal practice in the Wittenberg workshop to underpaint each part of a picture as a separate entity. It was only in the 1540s that a larger number of Cranach paintings appeared with complete grisaille undermodelling, including the flesh tones, which corresponds to the increasing incidence of this practice both north and south of the Alps. These underpaintings may have been similar to the grisaille paintings that have survived on the backs of some earlier panels. In order to rationalise production efficiently, a comprehensive tonal underpainting of the entire composition replaces the additive technique relying on varying local underpainting, which perhaps evolved from purely practical considerations related to workshop organisation.

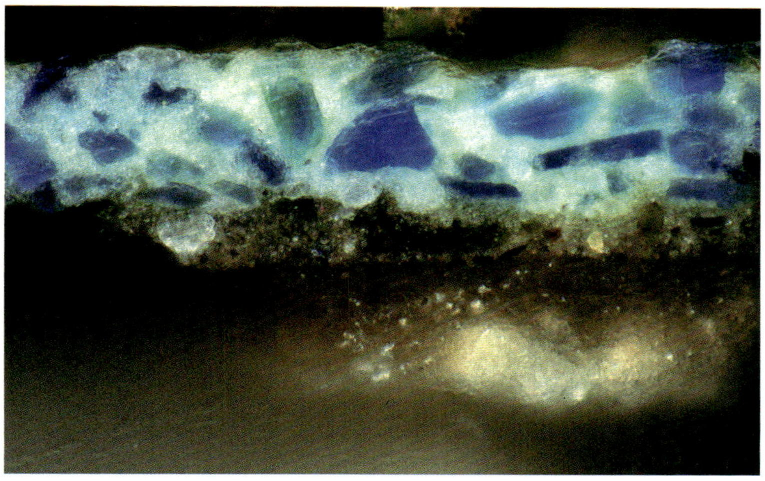

15 Lucas Cranach the Elder, *Portrait of a Jurist*, 1503, Germanisches Nationalmuseum, Nuremberg; cross-section of blue sky (azurite and lead white) on grey underpainting and chalk ground

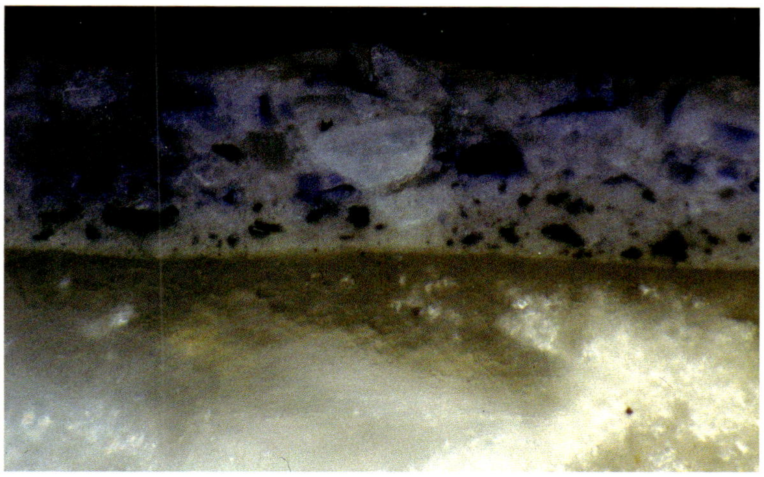

16 Lucas Cranach the Elder, *The Holy Kinship*, 1509, Städel Museum, Frankfurt; cross-section of blue sky (natural ultramarine and lead white) on grey underpainting (lead white, carbon black) and chalk ground

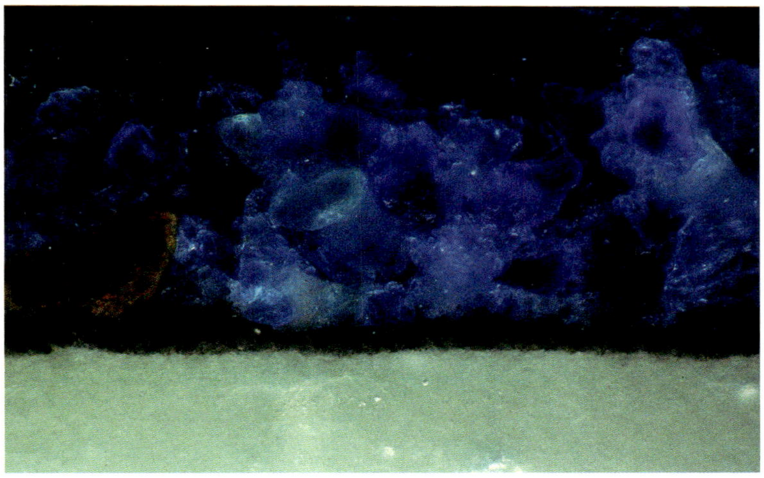

17 Lucas Cranach the Elder and workshop, Neustadt Altarpiece, 1511–13, Evangelische Stadtkirche St. Johannis, Neustadt/Orla; cross-section of the blue decorative painting of the predella with coarse-grained azurite (*c.* 30–60 μm) on dark-grey underpainting (carbon black, calcium carbonate) and chalk ground

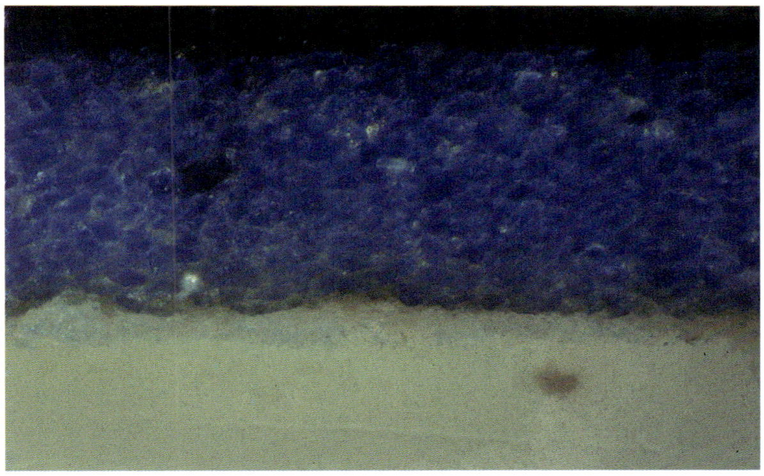

18 Lucas Cranach the Elder, *Cardinal Albrecht of Brandenburg as St Jerome*, 1527, Staatliche Museen zu Berlin, Preußischer Kulturbesitz, Gemäldegalerie; cross-section of blue sky (small-grained azurite, *c.* 3–6 m) on white *imprimatura* and chalk ground

With such a system Cranach could easily supervise and, if necessary, intervene to correct formal and tonal elements of the painting before elaborating them in colour.

Black underpainting was one of the characteristic techniques of the Cranach workshop. In 1555, Johann Neudorffer from Nuremberg noted that Lucas Cranach was praised for his particular virtuosity in painting velvet.[65] These words of tribute are probably closely related to the technique of underpainting this material in black. For more than four decades, numerous red, deep purple and green robes were modelled over extensive black underpainting (fig. 19). The folds are applied with bright opaque colours on the dark ground and then completed with translucent glazes. The disadvantage was that the black paint had to be allowed to dry before the next layer of colour could be applied, and this could have delayed the completion of the whole painting. However, in serial picture production this practice was highly efficient and easy for the workshop assistants to copy.

Some of Cranach's pupils who later opened their own workshops, for example the so-called Master of the Mass of St Gregory, practised this technique so often and so mechanically that it became more characteristic of them than of Cranach himself. For larger works, such as the Altarpiece of the Virgin of 1529 in Halle an der Saale (FR Sup 6A), the underdrawing of the robes is even incised into the ground to keep it visible after the black paint was applied. Lucas Cranach the Younger was clearly drawn to this technique. After the death of his father, if not before, he avoided it.

Cranach experimented with numerous methods of applying paint. Apart from the flesh tones, no other passages

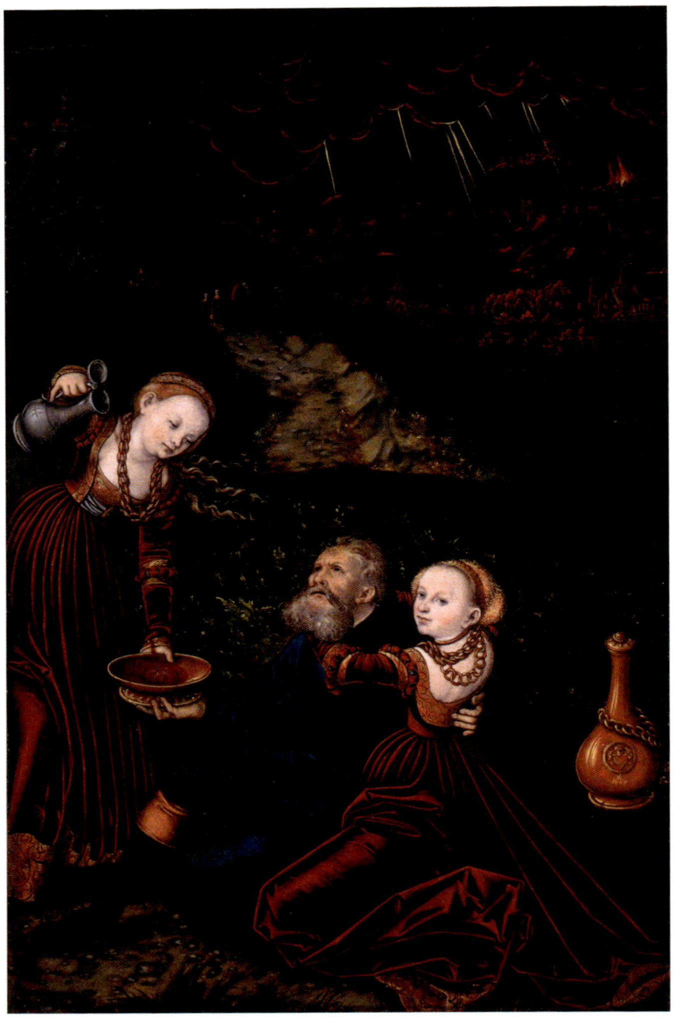

19 Lucas Cranach the Elder, *Lot and His Daughters*, Premonstratensian monastery of Nová Říše, on loan to the Moravian Gallery, Brno

reveal a greater range of materials and techniques than his red robes. He used vermilion, red lead, red iron oxide, and at least two red lake pigments, as well as vegetable-derived carbon black, soot black, lead white and lead-tin yellow to depict fabrics made of wool, plant fibres and precious silky materials including velvet, moiré and satin. Cranach and his assistants used the pigments on several works at the same time and, in the paintings that have been examined, in more than thirty different combinations and sequences. Mostly the colours were built up in layers: one or two layers of opaque colour covered by red glazes.

The inner tension of Lucas Cranach the Elder's paintings is the result of his capacity for poignant composition and the interplay of colour and tonal values. Equally important are the translucency and gloss of the paint, as well as the method of application. In the panel paintings there are contrasts between gently dispersed passages of paint and clearly visible brushwork; stippling is juxtaposed to a stroking or hatching technique, slightly 'pastose' touches of paint accentuate enamel-like smoothness and barely differentiated passages contrast with those rendered in distinct graphic detail (figs 20–25). There is a great variety of combined effects, as when the clear outlines of characteristic pebble-covered surfaces are dispersed with a soft hair brush (fig. 21).

From the earliest works the colour of the sky was stippled on with a broad bristle brush and then probably worked over with the soft brush. Stippling of the paint helped here to apply the crystalline blue pigment more evenly as well as easing the modelling of colour and tonal values. In the *Portrait of a Jurist* (1503, FR 8) the stippled brush differentiates the material of the red hood from the similarly coloured coat with the pomegranate pattern (cat. 9 and fig. 20). Cranach used the brush quite specifically to emphasise the qualities of the fabrics.

Stippling lent softness to textiles, smoothness to flesh tones, airiness to the sky and the roughness of stone. Furthermore, in landscape painting stippling gave the rendering of moss and tree bark an appropriate structure. The alternation of conventional brushstrokes and stippling was one of the characteristic techniques of the Wittenberg workshop for many decades and, as such, contributed greatly to the high regard in which the workshop's paintings were held. This was not, however, Cranach's invention: Stephan Lochner and Robert Campin were already capturing the soft surfaces of fabrics using a similar stippling technique.[66]

In the Frankfurt altarpiece of the *Holy Kinship* of 1509, the hatching application of ultramarine in the Virgin's robe probably reflects impressions which Cranach picked up during his journey to the Netherlands (cat. 19). Soon after this, in his panel with the *Holy Kinship* of *c.* 1509–10 (FR 34), he returned to 'his' technique of brushing and stippling when he modelled the blue areas.

Taking advantage of his technical experience and his love of experimentation, Cranach occasionally also used streaky brushstrokes to capture the structure of fabrics. An almost non-absorbent ground colour is a prerequisite for this effect. A darker colour is then applied unevenly to this surface with a hard bristle brush, in fact 'scratched on' so that the underpainting remains partly visible (fig. 25).

In painting, the sgraffito technique was borrowed from the long tradition of gold and silver sgraffito. The artist uses a pointed wooden stick, the handle of a brush or another suitable object to scratch lines and shapes into paint before it is dry, thereby partly revealing an underlying layer of paint or ground, the varying tone of which forms a contrast with the

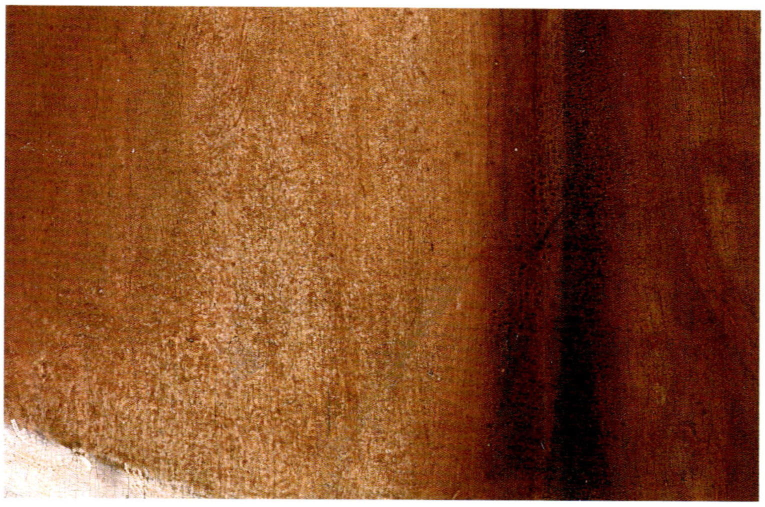

20 Lucas Cranach the Elder, *Portrait of a Jurist* (detail), 1503, sprucewood, Germanisches Nationalmuseum, Nuremberg

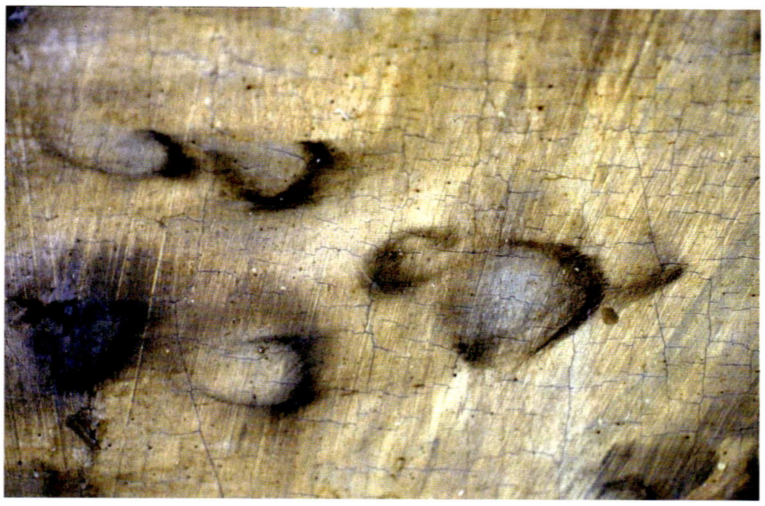

21 Lucas Cranach the Elder and workshop, *Venus* (detail), c. 1518, limewood, National Gallery of Canada, Ottawa

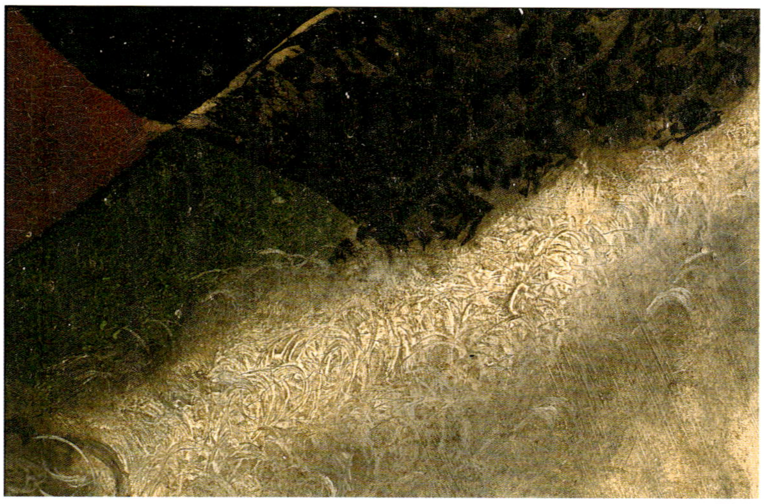

22 Lucas Cranach the Elder, *Christ as the Man of Sorrows* (detail), *c.* 1505–07, limewood, Marienkirche, Torgau

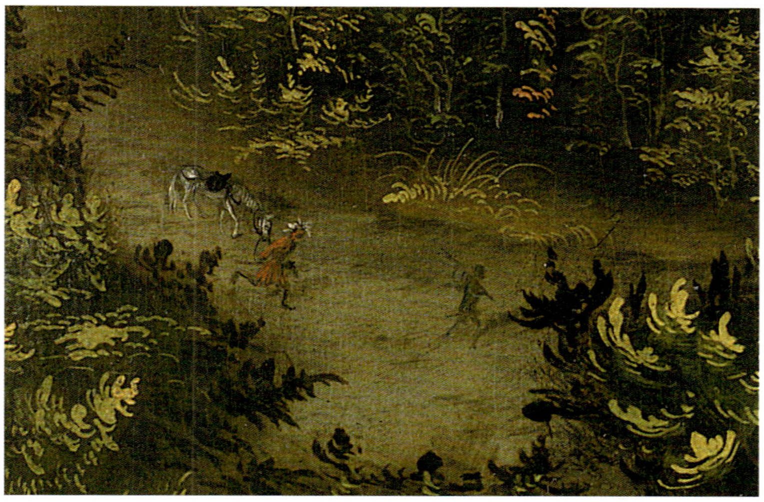

23 Lucas Cranach the Elder and workshop, *Christ Taking Leave of his Mother* (detail), *c.* 1516–20, limewood, Kunsthistorisches Museum, Vienna

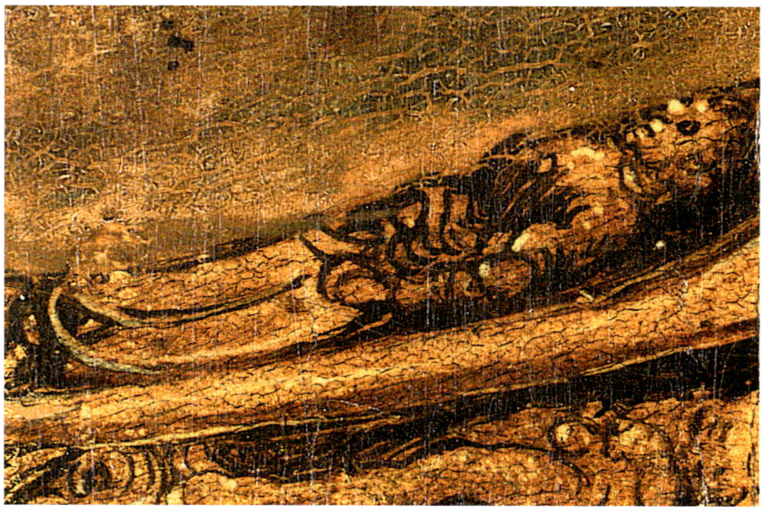

24 Lucas Cranach the Elder, Princes' Altarpiece (detail), *c.* 1510, limewood, Anhaltische Gemäldegalerie, Dessau

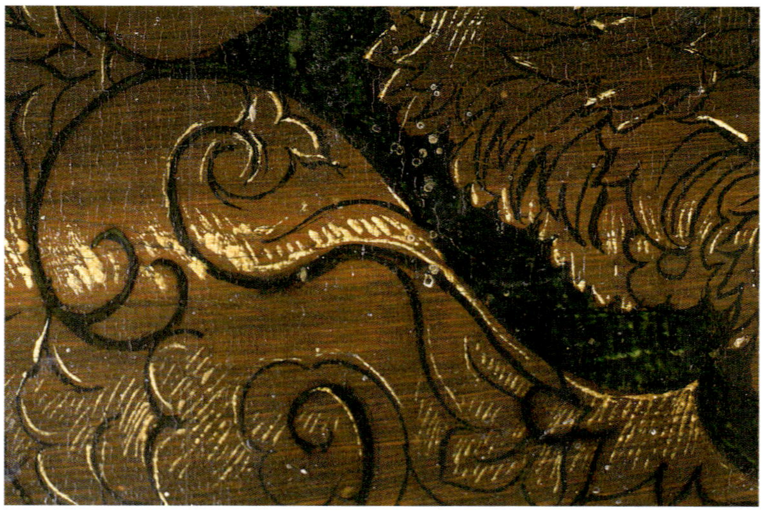

25 Lucas Cranach the Elder, Altarpiece of the *Holy Kinship* (detail), 1509, limewood, Städel Museum, Frankfurt

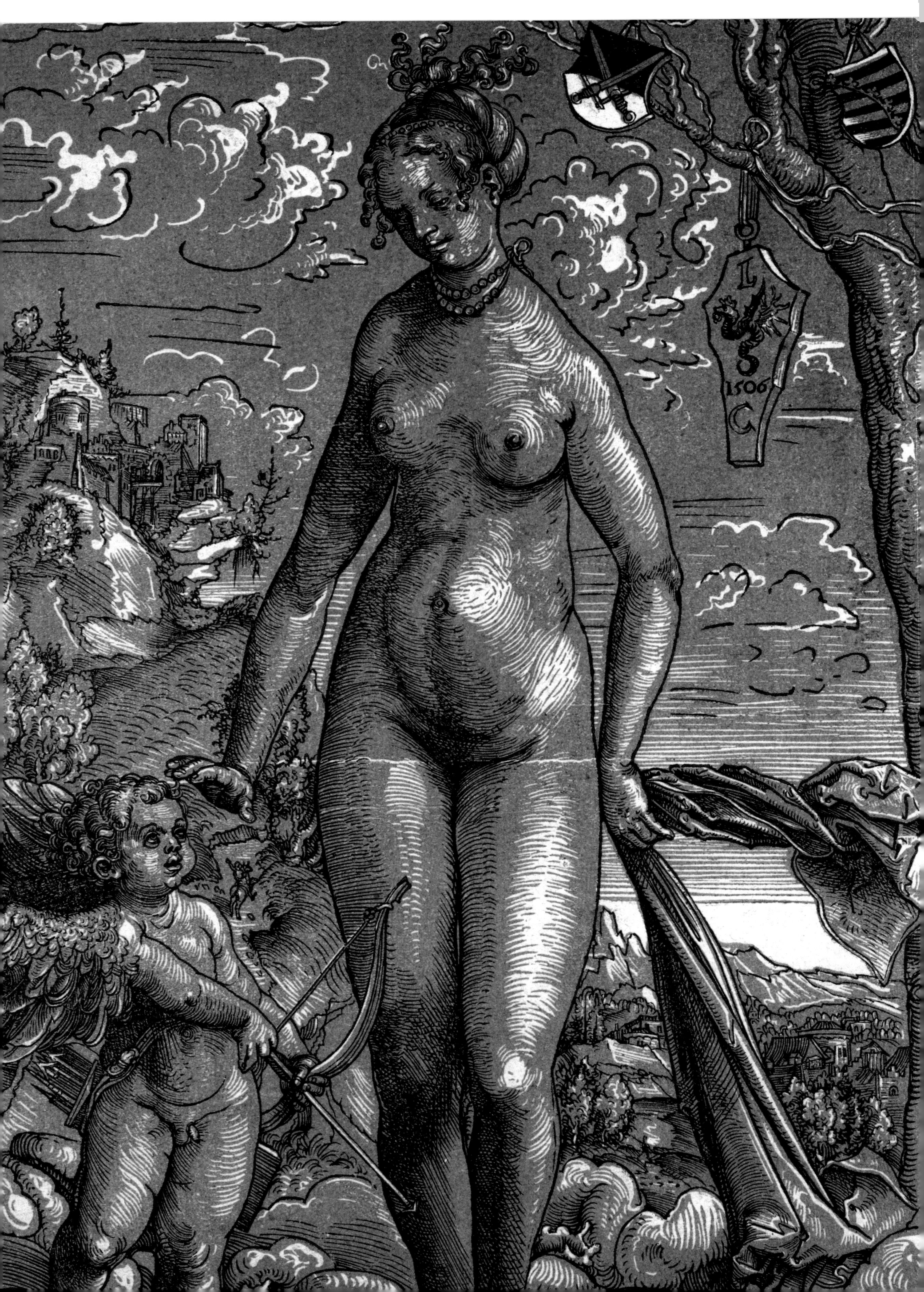
L
1506
C

'The Italians, who usually pursue fame, proffer their hand to you.' Lucas Cranach and the Art of Humanism

Mark Evans

In 1931, in his 'comparative psychological study' *Italien und das Deutsche Formgefühl*, Heinrich Wölfflin emphasised the 'uninterrupted formal development' of Cranach's figurative style from earlier German artists, and argued that its 'fluid movement of form, whose essential trait is the interweaving of serpentine curves' exemplified 'the truly national style'.[1] A generation later, in *The Nude: A Study of Ideal Art*, Kenneth Clark considered that Cranach's 'skill in combining sinuous line with shallow internal modelling is unprecedented in the North', and instead drew comparisons with Botticelli, the art of India and that of ancient Egypt. He regarded Cranach's nudes as 'most artful productions in which elements of Mannerism and revived Gothicism are mingled and concealed' foreshadowing those of the later Mannerist Bartholomeus Spranger. More light-heartedly, Clark found Cranach's 'naked charmers ... as much to our taste today as they were to John Frederick the Magnanimous' and praised his 'sense of *chic* which should make him the patron saint of all fashion designers'.[2] The latter remark recalls the androgynous mannequins of the 1930s, but Clark's emphasis upon Cranach's apparent modernity – which also fascinated Picasso[3] – retains its currency for a generation habituated to images of the model Twiggy or the actress Nicole Kidman. As both the elderly Swiss professor and the former Director of the National Gallery assessed Cranach relative to an essentially classicising canon of form, their appraisals of his style – by turns Germanic or exotic, archaic or avant-garde – may also frame his elusive relationship with the Italian Renaissance.

The foundations of the humanist court milieu which was to nourish Cranach's style were laid in Germany in 1442, when Aeneas Sylvius Piccolomini was crowned poet laureate by Emperor Frederick III, and began a career of imperial service which continued until his election as Pope Pius II in 1458.[4] A milestone in the emergence of German humanism was the rediscovery of Tacitus's *Germania*, which inspired Piccolomini's own treatise on Germany, and was first published at Bologna in 1472.[5] From the 1450s Italian-educated 'wandering poets' and scholars such as Peter Luder and George Peuerbach promoted the humanist curriculum in Germany.[6] Many members of the patrician elite of Augsburg and Nuremberg were educated at Bologna, Padua and Pavia, or had major commercial interests in Venice, where the printing trade was initially dominated by Germans.[7] In 1487 Frederick III crowned the 'arch-humanist' Konrad Celtis poet laureate; Celtis contended that Germany's neglect of the liberal arts had made it a home of 'drunkenness, barbarism, cruelty and whatever is bestial and foolish', and founded the *Sodalitas Litteraria Danubiana* to promote humanism.[8] The marriage of Maximilian I to Bianca Maria Sforza in 1494 strengthened contact with the Milanese court, and in 1497 the Emperor summoned Celtis to Vienna, and funded his ambitious but short-lived College of Poets and Mathematicians which sought 'to restore the lost eloquence of the previous age'.[9]

Intellectual links between north and south had provided a conduit for the visual arts a century earlier, as is apparent from the votive fresco in the style of Altichiero from St Stephen's Cathedral in Vienna, commissioned by Galeazzo di Santa Sofia, an eminent Paduan doctor who was court physician to the Habsburgs and dean of the Viennese faculty of medicine.[10] In 1459 the Augsburg alderman Sigismund Gossembrot (1417–1493) received portrait medals of leading Italian humanists by Matteo de' Pasti, Filarete and Pisanello from his son Ulrich, then a student at Padua.[11] Sigismund's friend, the Nuremberg physician Hermann Schedel, also studied in Padua, as did the latter's nephew Hartmann in 1463–66, where he acquired an impression of the early Florentine engraving *The Fight*

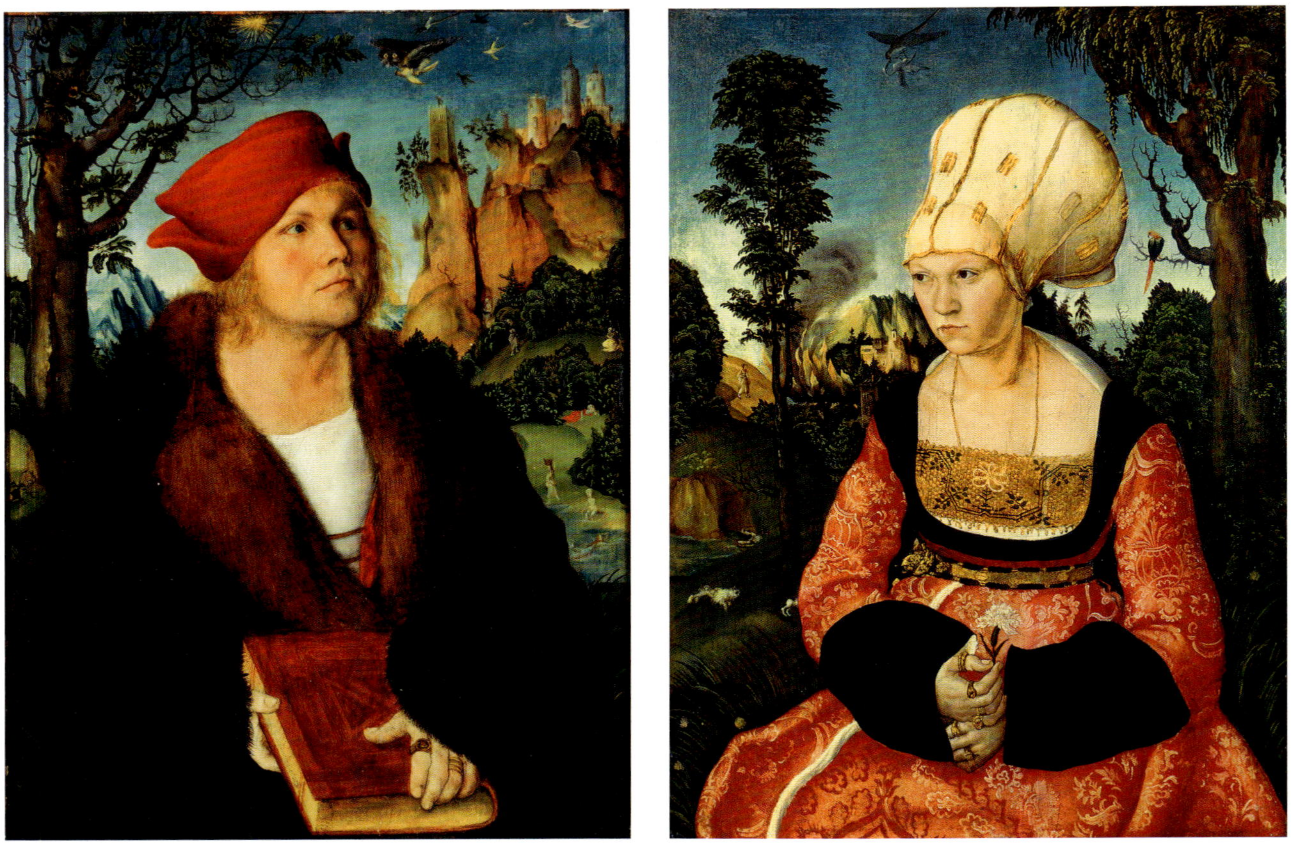

1/2 Lucas Cranach the Elder, *Dr. Johannes Cuspinian* and his wife née *Anna Putsch*, 1502–03, oil on panel, 59 x 45 cm, Oskar Reinhart Collection, Winterthur

for the Hose.[12] Significant commissions from South Germans in North Italy include Giovanni Bellini's forceful oil portrait of the Augsburg merchant Jörg Fugger (1474), as well as the exquisite volume of poems decorated by Giovan Pietro Birago acquired by the Nuremberg humanist Willibald Pirckheimer while a student at Pavia in the 1490s. These provided models for woodcuts in Celtis' *Quattro Libri Amorum* (1502) by Albrecht Dürer, whose recondite engravings made after his first visit to Venice reflect his association with Pirckheimer and Celtis.[13] The Emperor Maximilian employed the Milanese Giovanni Ambrogio de Predis to paint portraits and design coins at Innsbruck in 1493–94, and the Venetian Jacopo de' Barbari as 'portrait painter and illuminator' in 1500–03 at Nuremberg, where he tantalised Dürer with measured drawings of a man and woman, and supplied Hartmann Schedel with more engravings.[14] Cranach probably received intimations of this Italianate visual culture through Dürer's prints during his early years at Kronach, 90 kilometres north of Nuremberg.

Cranach's documented activity begins in 1501–02 at Vienna, where he was employed by prominent humanists from Celtis's circle. The lawyer and imperial counsellor Dr. Johannes Fuchsmagen, a co-founder of the *Sodalitas Litteraria Danubiana* and a collector of ancient coins and inscriptions, engaged him to copy the miniatures of the *Months* in a manuscript chronology by the third-century calligrapher Furius Dionysius Filocalus.[15] These later passed to Fuchsmagen's friend and fellow-member of the *Sodalitas Litteraria*, Dr. Johannes Cuspinian (1473–1529) who, like Cranach, was originally from Franconia.[16] Crowned in 1493 as poet laureate by Maximilian, whom he also served as a counsellor, he was rector and professor of poetry and rhetoric at the University of Vienna, and as Dean of its faculty of medicine held the same post as Galeazzo di Santa Sofia, a century earlier.

Cuspinian commissioned Cranach's three-quarter length double portrait of himself and his wife Anna Putsch (fig. 1/2), customarily dated to their marriage in 1502–03, and now in Winterthur.[17] This spectacular work was described by John Pope-Hennessy as 'the greatest northern emblematic portrait'.[18] By this date, portrait diptychs were common in Germany, but the characterisation of Cuspinian with book in hand derives from representations of Italian scholars such as those painted by Justus of Ghent and Pedro Berruguete for the Studiolo of Federigo da Montefeltro at Urbino.[19] The location of Cuspinian and his wife against a continuous landscape background, repeated in Cranach's

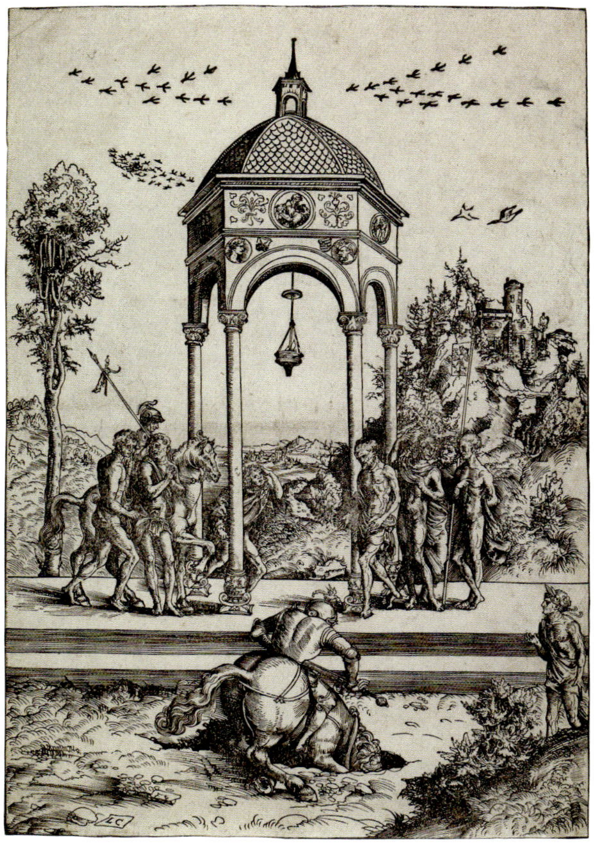

3 Lucas Cranach the Elder, *The Sacrifice of Marcus Curtius*, *c.* 1507, woodcut on paper, 33.5 x 23.5 cm, British Museum, London

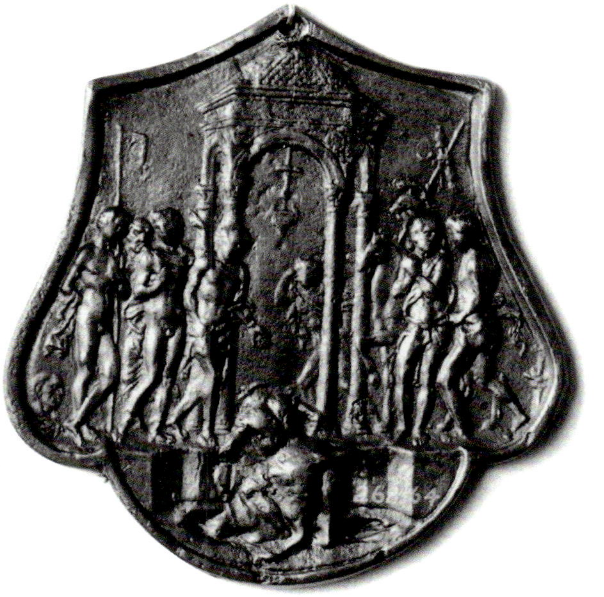

4 Master IO.F.F, *The Sacrifice of Marcus Curtius*, bronze relief, 6.18 x 5.97 cm, National Gallery of Art, Washington, Samuel H. Kress Collection

now-divided double portrait of another scholar and his wife (1503; cat. 9), was previously unknown in Germany.[20] This genre originated in the Netherlands, and was communicated to Italy through pictures of expatriate Italian merchants by Hans Memling. As an example of this Koepplin cited Francesco Francia's portrait of the humanist Bartolomeo Binachini, who knew German students at Bologna.[21] However, it lacks the imagery of mottos, emblems or subsidiary scenes typical of early Italian examples of the genre, such as Leonardo da Vinci's *Ginevra de' Benci*, Luca Signorelli's *Portrait of a Humanist*, and Jacometto Veneziano's double-portrait of Alvise Contarini and his wife.[22] The erudite symbols of cosmology which fill the landscape in Cuspinian's double portrait may emulate lost works by de Predis or Barbari.[23] This order of priority reverses that suggested by Pope-Hennessy, who considered that Lorenzo Lotto's later 'use of emblems to illustrate a psychological condition' reflected the Cuspinian double-portrait.[24] Its mountainous background contrasts with the gentler scenery usual in Italian portraiture, and evokes Tacitus's mordant remark about Germany: 'With its wild scenery and harsh climate it is pleasant neither to live in nor look upon unless it be one's fatherland'.[25] Such Germanic landscapes, similar to that in Cranach's *Rest on the Flight into Egypt* (1504), became a defining characteristic of the so-called Danube School.

In 1505 Cranach entered the service of the Elector Frederick the Wise, who was utilising the wealth from the silver mines of Saxony to transform the modest town of Wittenberg into a capital. The dedicatee of Celtis's *Ars versificandi*, Frederick had engineered the humanist's coronation as poet laureate. In 1492 he procured de Predis's portrait of the future Empress Bianca Maria.[26] He spent some weeks in Venice en route to Jerusalem in 1493, and later sat for his portrait to Dürer, from whom he also acquired the painting of *Hercules Slaying the Stymphalian Birds*; a subject perhaps suggested by Tacitus's claim that the ancient Germans hymned 'Hercules, the first of brave men' before battle.[27] In 1498 the Elector commissioned a bust portrait cast in brass from the Italian sculptor Adriano Fiorentino, whose other clients included Bianca Maria's chamberlain Nikolaus von Firmian, and in 1503 he enticed from Maximilian's service Jacopo de' Barbari, who remained in Saxony for two years.[28] Frederick had founded the University of Wittenberg in 1502, and from 1507 a humanist curriculum was energetically promoted there by its new Rector Dr. Christoph Scheurl (1481–1542), a jurist from Nuremberg who had studied at Bologna

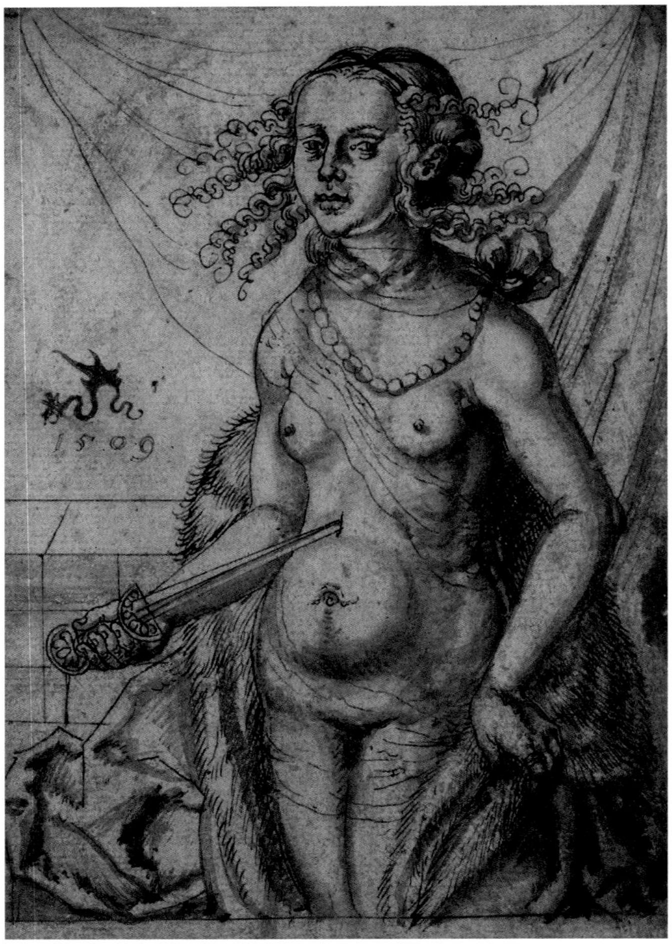

5 Lucas Cranach the Elder, *The Suicide of Lucretia*, 1509, ink and wash on paper, 13.1 x 9.5 cm, Staatliche Museen zu Berlin,Kupferstichkabinett

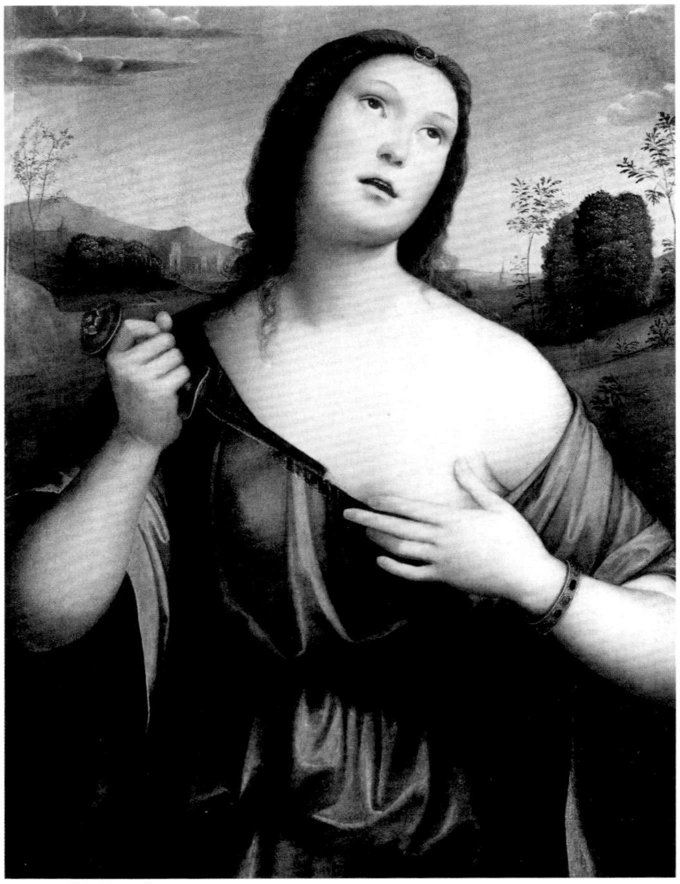

6 Francesco Francia, *The Suicide of Lucretia*, *c.* 1505–06, oil on panel, 64 x 48 cm, Staatliche Kunstsammlungen, Dresden, Gemäldegalerie

where he served as Dürer's interpreter in 1506.[29] Andreas Meinhard's utopian dialogue extolling the beauties of Wittenberg, which was published in 1508, indicates that its castle was decorated with numerous scenes from mythology and ancient history, including a cycle of the *Labours of Hercules*, stories of fortitude such as Horatius and his single-handed defence of the bridge over the Tiber in Rome, and the *Sacrifice of Mucius Scaevola*, who burned off his right hand to save Rome, and edifying examples of female modesty and fidelity.[30] A distinctly neoclassical gloss is apparent in a poem by Georg Sibutus celebrating a tournament in 1508, which likens Frederick to Apollo, his brother John the Steadfast to Mars and Wittenberg itself to Ancient Rome.[31]

An early appraisal of Cranach's activity occurs in Scheurl's Latin oration, given on 16 December 1508. This claimed that, with the sole exception of Dürer, only 'the gifted, quick, consummate painter of the Saxon dukes' is 'worth the first place in painting ... The other Germans are in retreat, the Italians who usually pursue fame, proffer their hand to you, the French greet you as their master'.[32] Scheurl likened Cranach to ancient masters from Apelles to Zeuxis, but mentioned only one other living artist, the Bolognese Francesco Francia, who had been praised by the German scholar's teacher Filippo Beroaldo in his commentary on the *Metamorphoses* of Apuleius, published in 1500.[33] Scheurl extolled Cranach's still-life paintings with a series of elaborations on the theme of Zeuxis's picture of grapes, which deceived birds into attacking it. For all its customary hyperbole, his praise shows first-hand knowledge of the painter's accomplished watercolours of game birds and other wild animals (cat. 86).[34] The benchmark for such illusionism had been provided by Barbari's startling *Still-life with a dead partridge* (1504), now in Munich, which continues a tradition begun by Pisanello.[35] The oration closes with the hope that it will please its recipient 'as much as your panel pleases me, on which you have so carefully represented me and on which I have, not without reason, allowed to be written: "If you, passer-by, know Scheurl, which is more Scheurl, this or the other?"' Cranach's portrait and that of the Wittenberg court tutor Georg Spalatin, both of 1509, depict their sitters against the plain background thereafter usual in his portraits.[36]

Scheurl did not mention the scenes from mythology and ancient history now regarded as Cranach's most characteristic inventions. The earliest of these, the woodcut of *The Sacrifice of Marcus Curtius* (fig. 3) was probably made before January 1508 when Frederick the Wise awarded him the coat of arms depicting a winged serpent, which became his distinctive monogram. His woodcut of this previously seldom-represented story from Livy superimposes a scene copied from a small late fifteenth-century North Italian bronze relief (fig. 4) on a 'Danube' landscape of his invention.[37] This bronze is one of a trio of sword decorations all signed 'IO.F.F' which exist in numerous casts. The others, depicting *Horatius at the Bridge* and *The Sacrifice of Mucius Scaevola*, may have provided models for the pictures of those stories mentioned by Meinhard in 1507 as part of the décor of Wittenberg Castle.[38] Cranach's choice of this motif is especially significant because the bronzes are from the circle of Francia, the very artist with whom Scheurl had compared him, and whom Filippo Beroaldo had praised as 'the greatest goldsmith among painters, and the most perfect painter among goldsmiths'.[39]

Included in various medieval compilations, the Judgement of Paris was a better known story, which became popular in Saxony because of Piccolomini's claim that the duchy had been founded by Trojan refugees, and was interpreted by Celtis, following Marsilio Ficino, as an allegory of the choice between wisdom, power or pleasure.[40] The subject had been illustrated in a Late Gothic idiom in an edition of Darius Phrygius's *Bellum Troianum* published in Wittenberg in 1502. Cranach modernised the theme in his woodcut of 1508 by referring to Barbari's engraving of *Victory and Fame* and Dürer's *Hercules at the Crossroads* and *The Large Horse*.[41]

In 1509, Cranach made a pair of ink and wash drawings of *The Suicide of Lucretia*, now in Berlin (fig. 5), a subject recalling the female paragons reported two years earlier by Meinhard in the bedroom of Sophie of Mecklenburg at Wittenberg Castle.[42] Although this theme from Livy had been treated the previous year by Dürer as a full-length drawing, Cranach adopted the three-quarter length format in Francia's depictions of the subject (fig. 6), the earliest of which date from around 1505–6.[43] Framing

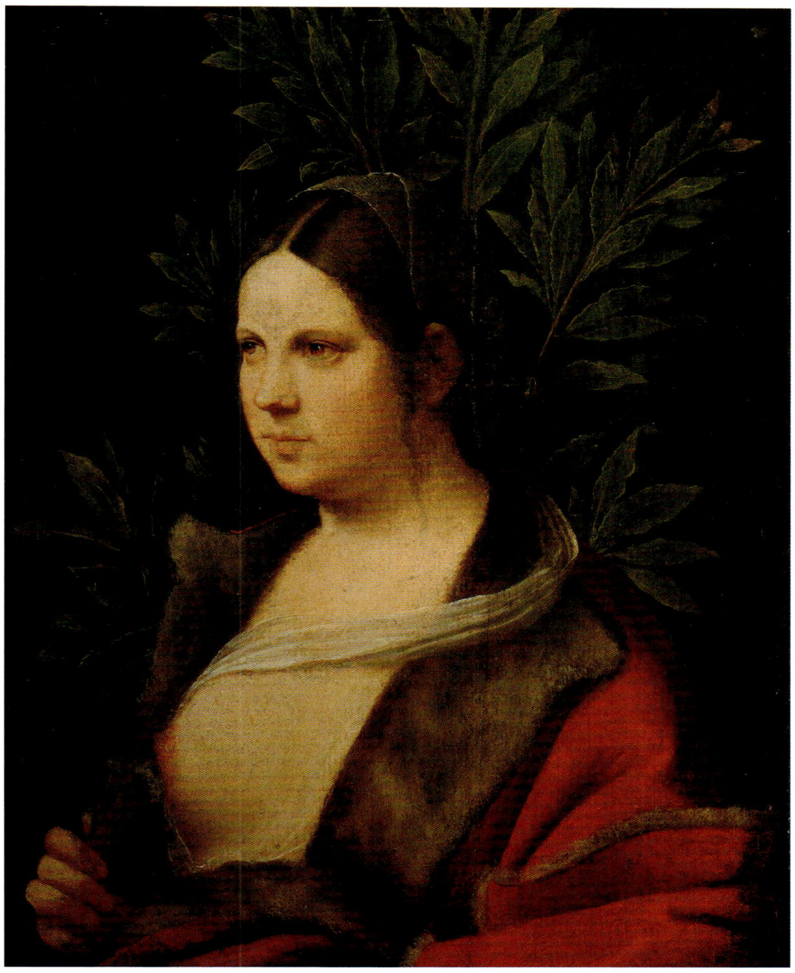

7 Giorgione, *Portrait of a Woman* (Laura), 1506, oil on canvas laid down on panel, 41 x 33.6 cm, Kunsthistorisches Museum, Vienna, Gemäldegalerie

the naked torso of the heroine with vibrant strands of her hair and the fur lining of the mantle falling from her shoulders and hips, Cranach's studies have an erotic charge whose only precedent is Giorgione's *Laura* of 1506 (fig. 7), a work Dürer also seems to have known.[44] The drawings were doubtless utilised in *The Suicide of Lucretia* of 1513 which provided the climax to Cranach's decorations of the bridal bed of John the Steadfast and Margaret of Anhalt, and was described in a nuptial song by Philipp Engelbrecht: 'In the final place is the dishonoured Roman lady. The sword is sprayed with blood, the once starry eyes are half dimmed, Lucretia's raiment glides from her swelling bosom.'[45]

Cranach's most impressive early mythological work is the life-size painting of *Venus and Cupid* now in St Petersburg (fig. 8), whose black background bears his arms, the date 1509, and a stately Latin inscription: 'Resist with all your might the lascivious Cupid, so that Venus does not take possession of your darkened heart.'[46] Such sentiments echo

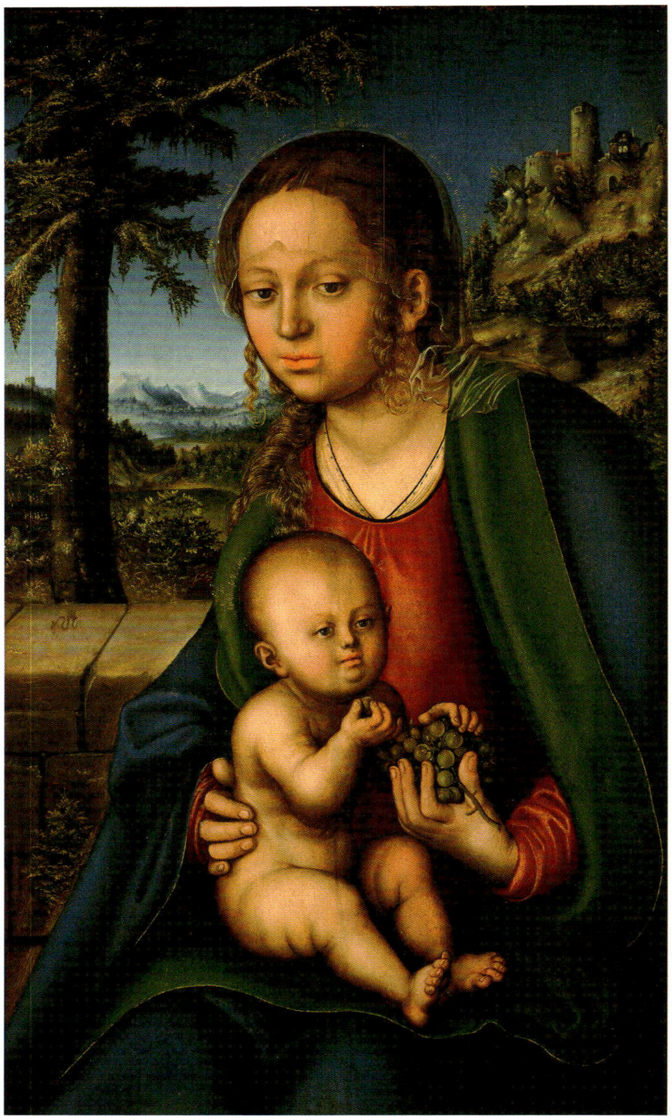

10 Lucas Cranach the Elder, *Virgin and Child Eating Grapes*, *c.* 1509–10, oil on beech panel, 71.5 x 44.2 cm, Museo Thyssen-Bornemisza, Madrid

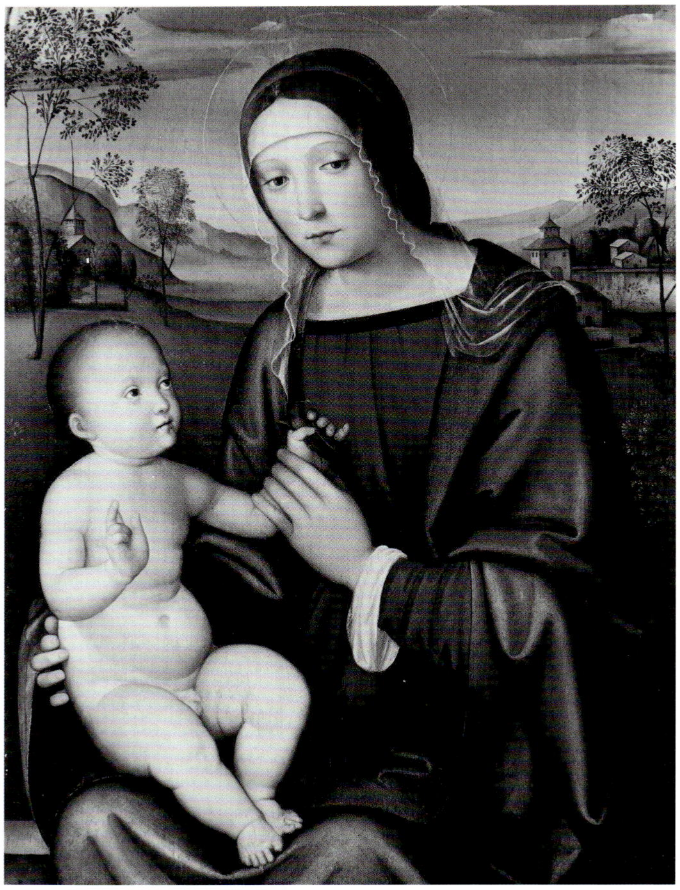

11 Francesco Francia, *Virgin and Child*, *c.* 1502–05, oil on panel, 79.5 x 52 cm, National Trust, Wallington Hall, Northumberland

visible with water pouring into a pond. A drawing made around 1525, formerly in Dresden, adds a herd of deer in the background and a bow and quiver of arrows at the feet of the nymph.[68] These references to hunting, appropriate to the chaste Diana, are accompanied by a pair of partridges, suggestive of Venus.[69] Bow, quiver and partridges reappear in the later versions. These attributes may have been intended to introduce an air of ambiguity, but there can be no mistaking the irony in the nymph's languid half-closed eyes, which seem to countermand the peremptory instruction and positively to invite interruption.

The resemblance of Cranach's versions of the *Nymph of the Fountain* to the Dresden *Sleeping Venus*, begun by Giorgione in 1507–08 and completed by Titian (fig. 12), has been interpreted to show that the former reflects a lost version of the latter, mentioned at Cologne in 1667, which depicted Venus as a resting huntress, with scenes from the chase in the background.[70] According to another theory, Cranach's source was a woodcut of a fountain with 'an elegant carving of a nymph … sleeping comfortably on an outspread drapery' being approached by an aroused satyr and two fauns, in Francesco Colonna's *Hypnerotomachia Poliphili*, published by Aldus Manutius in 1499.[71] Dürer owned a copy of this illustrated book, and as Spalatin wrote to Manutius in 1512 about acquisitions for the Wittenberg University library, its identification as Cranach's source was endorsed by Koepplin and Falk.[72] Recently, the case that Cranach knew the lost version of Giorgione's *Sleeping Venus* has been forcibly re-stated.[73] Campani's epigram could well have been known to Colonna, whose book was probably familiar to Giorgione. However, it is implausible that the resemblance of the *Nymph of the Fountain* to the *Sleeping Venus* is explicable by Cranach's extraction of the schematic figure in the *Hypnerotomachia* and his re-use of it in an independent composition which coincidentally combined the principal elements of the Dresden painting. The bow and quiver in the later versions of the *Nymph of the Fountain* and the herd of deer in the drawing formerly at Dresden suggest that Cranach knew the lost version of Giorgione's picture of Venus as a resting huntress. This link is reinforced by the similarity of Cranach's early drawings of *The Suicide of Lucretia* to Giorgione's Laura.

Cranach's work between 1509 and 1518 suggests a knowledge of paintings by Francia, Giorgione and perhaps Costa, made at Bologna and Venice between 1505 and 1508. There is no evidence that such pictures were then available in Wittenberg or the Netherlands, which he visited in 1508.[74] It is unlikely that Barbari, who had left Italy for Germany in 1500, provided a conduit for such up-to-date notions; especially as Dürer mentioned in a letter from Venice how the local artists 'make fun of Barbari, saying that if he were good he would stay there'.[75] Dürer's drawings of *The Suicide of Lucretia* and the *Nymph of the Fountain* are as distinct from Cranach's interpretations of these subjects as his probable Italian models. Scheurl may have provided the small bronze from Francia's circle on which Cranach's woodcut *Sacrifice of Marcus Curtius* is based. Had Frederick the Wise concluded from the humanist's oration in December 1508 that his court painter should emulate Dürer and Francia, Scheurl could also have facilitated his visit, via Nuremberg, to Bologna and Venice.

On account of the presence of Italianate motifs in his prints, Hans Burgkmair is assumed to have visited North Italy between April and October 1507.[76] Cranach's documented chronology has space for a similar journey between his visits to the Leipzig New Year Fair around 1 January 1509 and the Easter Fair there on about 8 April.[77] The 80 florins he received in Leipzig in January 1509 from the Saxon treasurer Degenhart von Pfeffinger would have sufficed for such a journey.[78] Dürer's return from Venice in February 1507 indicates that the Alpine passes were negotiable in winter.[79] The travel diary that Antonio de Beatis wrote in 1517–18, and other travel reports, suggest that a large party could travel from Leipzig to Bologna or Venice at an easy pace in about 24 days.[80] Communications were facilitated by the truce between Maximilian and Venice from June 1508 until the outbreak of the War of the League of Cambrai in May 1509.[81] Cranach could have spent two months in Bologna and Venice early in 1509. This may explain his apparent knowledge of recent works by Francia and Giorgione. Cranach's elder son Hans may have followed his father's example. In 1537 he died in Bologna, where Francia's workshop was continued by his sons Giacomo and Giulio.[82]

Cranach's early paintings of classical nudes of 1509–18 represent a remarkable new departure. Although Pirckheimer employed Dürer to illuminate his printed copies of ancient texts,[83] few patrons commissioned paintings of such subjects. In this respect, the prescient taste of Frederick the Wise and his brother John the Steadfast required Cranach to satisfy a demand formed by Barbari and Dürer. The latter had a similar influence on the first Flemish painter of mythologies comparable with those of Cranach: Jan Gossaert. In 1508–09 he accompanied Philip of Burgundy (1465–1524), later Bishop of Utrecht, on a diplomatic mission to Rome where he made some of the earliest studies of antiquities by a Northern artist.[84] Philip had studied at the University of Leuven and, like his humanist secretary Gerard Geldenhauer, was fascinated by ancient literature, art and architecture.[85] However, Gossaert failed to capitalise on his experiences in Rome until after Barbari's arrival in 1510 at the court of Margaret of Austria at Mechelen, where he was joined from Wittenberg by the sculptor Conrad Meit.[86] Gossaert and Barbari were hailed by Geldenhauer as 'the Zeuxis and Apelles of our day', and in 1516 the former painted his monumental *Neptune and Amphitrite* now in Berlin: a reconstruction of a classical cult image which relies heavily on two engravings, Dürer's *Fall of Man* and Barbari's *Mars and Venus*.[87] Gossaert's later mythological pictures of 1517–27 make continued reference to prints by Barbari, and to those of Marcantonio Raimondi after Raphael.[88]

After 1518, Cranach painted no scenes from mythology or ancient history for nearly a decade. In 1525 John the Steadfast succeeded his brother as Elector and introduced Protestantism to Saxony. The emergence of a younger and humanist-educated generation, led by Spalatin's pupil John Frederick the Magnanimous (1503–1554), stimulated the demand for such subjects from Cranach's workshop. With the aid of his sons Hans and Lucas the Younger, this became a corporate enterprise, whose later dated classical subjects of 1527–37 include many versions of Lucas's earlier compositions (cats 103, 111).[89] Hans had matriculated at the University of Wittenberg, and Johann Stigel's claim that his power of invention exceeded that of his father may suggest a deeper knowledge of ancient mythology and history.[90] His sketch of the unusual theme of The Mouth of Truth (*Bocca di Verità*) mentioned in an account of the Marvels of Rome, became the basis of a painting (cat. 96) in 1534.[91] One of his two independently signed works, a version

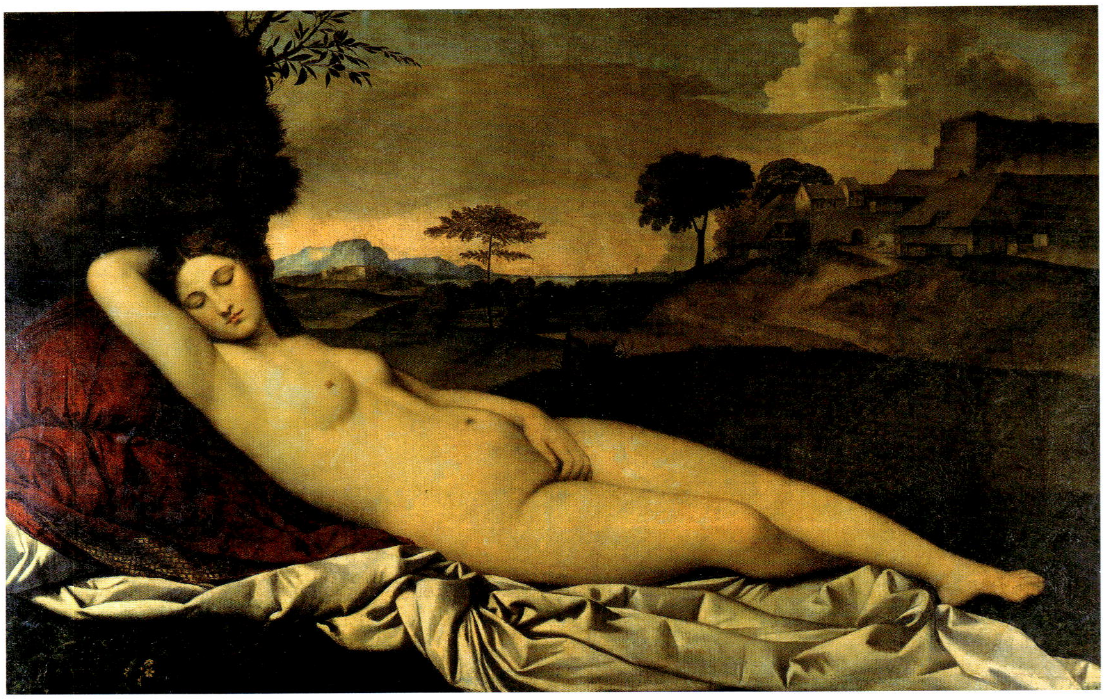

12 Giorgione and Titian, *Sleeping Venus*, *c.* 1507–10, oil on canvas, 108 x 174 cm, Staatliche Kunstsammlungen, Dresden, Gemäldegalerie

of the composition of *Hercules with Omphala*, dates from the year of his death in Bologna.[92] Its half-length format and contemporary costume resemble other moralising genre scenes from the Cranach workshop, while its trophy of dead fowl on the wall provides an ironic allusion to the hero's impotence.

Most of Cranach's later mythological works paraphrase earlier prints by other artists. The compositions of battling nudes (dated examples of 1527 and 1529; cat. 105) depicting the Age of Silver mentioned by Hesiod and other authorities derive from Pollaiuolo's engravings of nude warriors, which had been imitated in northern Europe since the 1490s.[93] As representations of the male and female nude from a multiplicity of viewpoints these were exceeded by more peaceful scenes of *The Age of Gold* (cat. 104).[94] *Bacchus and the Wine Tub* (1530) and *Hercules and Antaeus* (cat. 109) recall prints after Mantegna by Giovanni Antonio da Brescia.[95] The paintings of *Apollo and Diana* (1530; cats 107, 108) and the *Faun and his Family* (1531; cat. 106) revisit engravings by Dürer and Barbari of 1503–05, while the body of the faun in the latter refers to Giovanni Antonio's print of the *Belvedere Torso* of around 1515.[96]

The most successful of Cranach's late mythological scenes – judging by the quantity of its surviving versions – was *Venus with Cupid the Honey Thief* (dated examples of 1530, 1529; cats 111, 112).[97] In 1514, probably following the advice of Pirckheimer, who was a leading Greek scholar, Dürer had treated this theme from the *Idylls* of Theocritus in a watercolour which is quite unlike Cranach's versions.[98] The Latin translation of the *Idylls* by the Paduan Ercole Strozzi, published in 1513, and that of Philipp Melanchthon made in Wittenberg in 1528 probably informed Cranach's paintings, whose accompanying Latin epigram recalls the admonition in his earlier *Venus and Cupid*. It may be translated thus:

> While little Cupid stole from a beehive a honeycomb,
> a bee stung the thief's finger.
> Such is the short-lived pleasure we strive for:
> Harmful and mixed with sad sorrow.[99]

The position of Venus's legs, with the leading left foot at right-angles to the trailing right, derives from Dürer's engraving of *The Oriental Family*, where it suggests the rolling gait of a laden traveller.[100] It strikes an elegant balletic attitude in *Venus with Cupid the Honey Thief*, and other full-length Cranach female nudes.[101]

Venus's head reappears combined with a body from another early Dürer engraving, *The Dream of the Doctor*, in what is arguably the definitive late Cranach nude: the *Venus* of 1532 in Frankfurt (cat. 114). Its relationship to the full-length *Lucretia* in Vienna (cat. 113), which is of similar format, size and date, is suggested by a Han Sachs poem citing the Roman heroine as proof that love is stronger than death.[102] Where the figure in Dürer's print has the developed musculature and rhetorical pose of an antique marble, those in Cranach's cabinet paintings suggest the melting contours and brittle linearity of an ivory relief. In Clark's view, the latter demonstrate 'how necessary it is for the naked body to be clothed by a consistent style.'[103]

Cranach left few, if any drawings from life. The proportions of his earlier nudes are broadly comparable with those in fifteenth-century paintings, both Northern and Italian, but his later figures have a distinctive tendency towards slenderness and elongation, especially of the lower limbs.[104] In his *Four Books of Human Proportions* (published in 1528), Dürer presented five different types of male and female figure, from the 'coarse rural' Type A (short and stocky) to the 'tall and thin' Types D and E.[105] The proportions of his 'median' Types B and C correspond quite closely to Cranach's *Venus and Cupid* of 1509, but the leg-length of Dürer's Types D and E were exceeded by the later productions of the Cranach workshop.[106] This tendency to elongation, also found in contemporary Mannerist works from Italy and France, more probably reflects the growing role of Cranach's sons rather than a recrudescence of 'Late Gothic' sensibility on his behalf.[107]

Despite Dürer's best endeavours, the general lack of German critical commentary at that time makes it difficult to analyse the aesthetic values of Cranach and his contemporaries. Melanchthon's apt comment in 1532 that 'The paintings of Lucas are simple, and if they are also charming a comparison shows how much they differ from Dürer's works.'[108] In search of 'the period eye' of Renaissance Germany, Michael Baxandall explored other sources of stylistic criteria, from the terminology of calligraphy to the metrical-musical patterns of the Mastersingers.[109] The language of dance seems pertinent to Cranach's figures; especially the word 'schleifen' meaning to glide, which Gottfried von Strassburg (d. 1210) had used centuries earlier in *Tristan* to describe Isolde: 'The girl glided gently forward, silently and evenly against the morning sky, upright, lovely to behold, exquisitely formed and slender.'[110] Cranach's *Venus with Cupid the Honey Thief* seems to move in just such a way, which also evokes the Italian term 'leggiadrìa' utilised by sixteenth-century writers such as Castiglione and Matteo Bandello, and later defined by Filippo Baldinucci (1681) as follows:

> '*Leggiadrìa*: a certain way of carrying the body, so light and agile that the figure appears to move but to have no weight, bearing itself with the greatest possible lightness; it is appropriate for youth, and especially for nymphs and figures of a similar kind'.[111]

Hanne Kolind Poulsen interpreted the 'anti-realist' flatness typical of Cranach's later works, such as *Venus with Cupid the Honey Thief*, as a response to Martin Luther's insistence on simplicity and narrative clarity in visual imagery, which the reformer regarded as a tool for dissemination of the Word.[112] Harmonious linearity and flatness are qualities which the late works of Cranach share with those of Botticelli, which Hemsoll has associated with the Neoplatonism of Marsilio Ficino. Founding his position on Plato's belief that art should not represent the superficial appearance of an object, but rather its essential truth or 'image',[113] the Florentine philosopher's *Letters* and sections from his translation of Plato were published in Leipzig and Nuremberg in the 1490s, and he had an influence on Celtis, Cuspinian and Dürer, as well as the leading Wittenberg humanist Otto Beckman (1476–1540/56), whose friends included Cranach, Scheurl, Melanchthon and Luther.[114] The taste for Plato among Augustinians, including Luther,[115] supports the inference that the 'anti-realist' qualities of Cranach's later work may express a preference for higher 'forms' or 'ideas' perceivable by the soul.

More than 60 years after Sigismund and Ulrich Gossembrot had justified reading Terence and other classical poetry with the analogy of bees who sucked honey from flowers while avoiding their poison,[116] Cranach's *Venus with Cupid the Honey Thief* bore a written 'disclaimer' proclaiming its essentially ethical message. However, it seems naive to attribute the evident popularity of this, and similar hedonistic subjects which Cranach painted for his clients, to their efficacy as moral examples, or their pertinence to the self-imaging of the Saxony Electors. Observing that the large-scale mythologies painted by Titian between his completion of Giorgione's *Sleeping Venus* and the mid-sixteenth century had little impact in republican Venice, Charles Hope characterised this genre as 'an essentially aristocratic and courtly taste'.[117] Much the same may be said of Cranach's subjects from mythology and ancient history, whose origins may also be sought in North Italian art of the early sixteenth century, as well as in the works of Dürer.

After painting Charles V's portrait in 1532–33, Titian became the Emperor's favourite artist, although his now-lost reclining *Venus* produced as a personal initiative in 1545 seems not to have been to the ruler's taste.[118] John Frederick the Magnanimous earned Charles's dislike at the Diet of Augsburg in 1530, and after he became Elector of Saxony their antagonism would have been compounded by Cranach's modelling of the Elector's personal iconography on images of Martin Luther.[119] As leaders of the Catholic Imperial and Protestant parties in Germany, the two princes were equals and opposites both in a religious and a political sense. Their principal painters occupied a similar polarity in the artistic

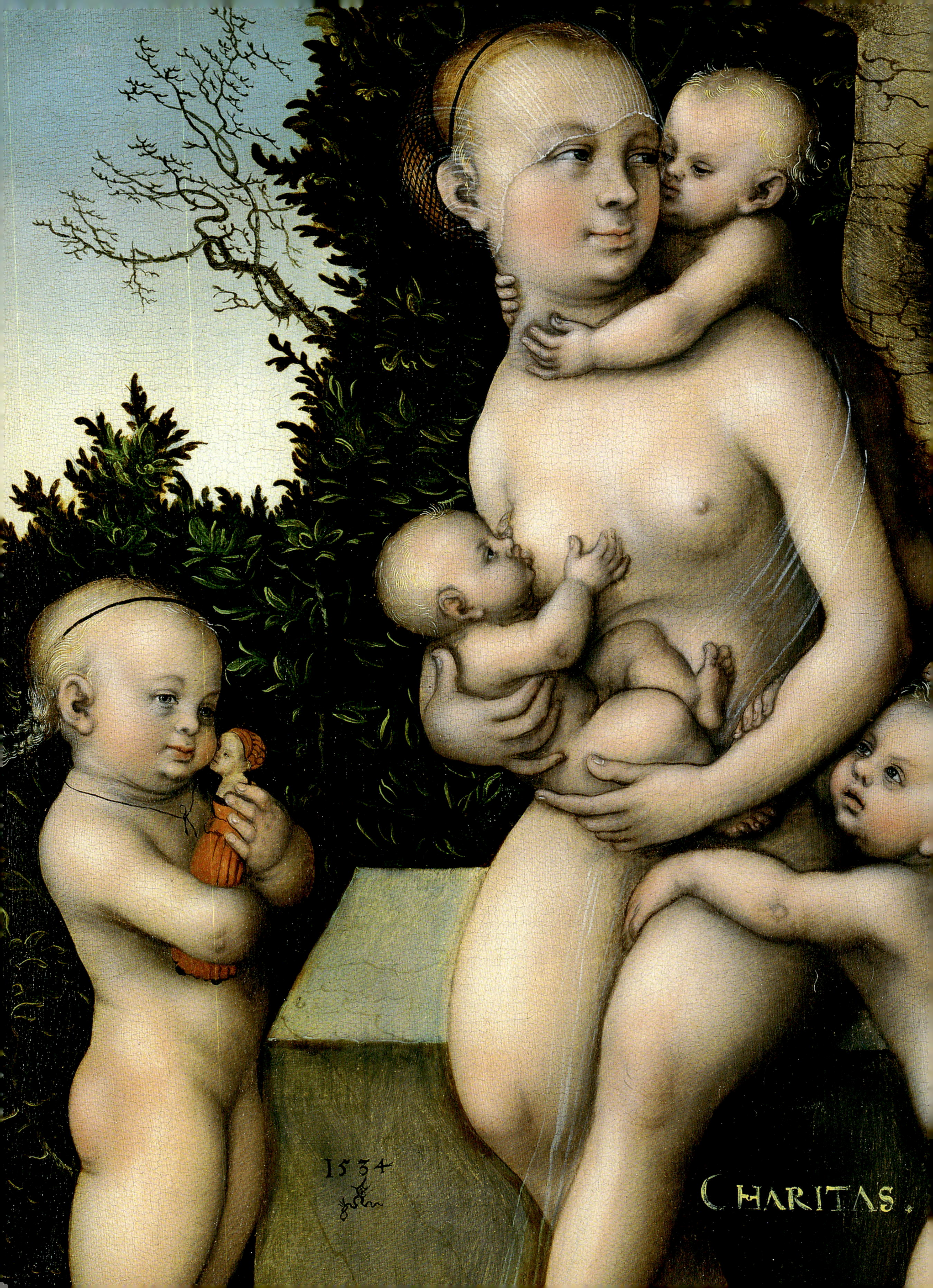
1534
CHARITAS.

Cranach's Paintings of Charity in the Theological and Humanist Spirit of Luther and Melanchthon

Dieter Koepplin

Questions

Why was it that, from 1529 at the latest, Lucas Cranach the Elder and his son Lucas the Younger chose to depict the Christian virtue of Love (of God and of one's neighbour), *Caritas*[1] or *Charitas*,[2] in some dozen different versions (figs 1, 2, 9, 10, 14)? Why did this happen, as far as we can tell, only in individual pictures, where *Caritas* (Charity) does not appear in the company of the seven (or more) virtues and vices? Why is it *Caritas* who appears almost exclusively in the depictions of Virtue by Lucas Cranach the Elder and his son, with the exception of two pictures of Justice in the form of a lightly veiled female nude carrying scales and a sword, and not blindfold,[3] and a picture of a naked *Patientia* of 1535, of which only a very unreliable copy has survived? In contrast to the isolated pictures of Justice of 1537 (fig. 2)[4] and later[5] and the *Patience* of 1535 (fig. 16)[6] there is a long series of depictions of *Caritas*, beginning in 1529. As late as 1552 Lucas Cranach the Elder issued an account for two *Caritas* pictures in Augsburg which he clearly painted himself on linen; these have not survived.[7] The virtuously veiled nakedness of Cranach's *Caritas* and his other personifications is conspicuous and relatively, if not very unusual. Personifications as female figures used either to be winged (like Dürer's and Cranach's figures of Melancholy) or naked, or both, but clothing is much more usual in pictures at that time, for example in Hans Burgkmair's woodcuts of the Seven Virtues of around 1510[8] or in the second picture in the woodcut of the Virtues by Erhard Schön (fig. 6).

Most of the versions of *Caritas* produced in the workshop of Lucas Cranach the Elder and his son Lucas the Younger, i.e. eleven upright or rectangular pictures, are in the *catalogue raisonné* of Max J. Friedländer and Jakob Rosenberg and three of them are illustrated.[9] To them can be added the important earliest version of 1529 (fig. 1)[10] and a later small and pretty panel by Lucas Cranach the Younger with a seated *Caritas* clasping three children against a black background (fig. 3);[11] the girl is holding an apple. Another small picture of *Caritas* painted by Cranach or initiated by him has only survived in an illustration; in the early nineteenth century it was in the collection of Valentin Prehn in Frankfurt.[12] In addition, a few works from Cranach's circle are worth considering, including a painting by the 'Master HB of the Griffin's Head' who was probably taught by Cranach and was possibly active in Magdeburg (fig. 4);[13] he also treated the ancient subject of the *Caritas Romana*[14] and, with a clearly intentional lack of decorum, painted a seated Venus and Cupid with Venus holding an apple in a pose that is very close to the seated *Caritas*.[15] There is also a strange *Caritas* picture in a wide format, bearing the signature of August Cordus, a pupil of Cranach born in about 1520 (fig. 5).[16]

None of these pictures shows a maternal figure in a paradisiacal state of innocence, even though we can read in Luther's words that it is through his righteous faith and not through virtuous works that man 'is admitted to paradise and created anew' and then is ready to do 'free works' of neighbourly love 'for no reward'.[17] The figures shown by Cranach do not represent 'innocent' mankind, rather they personify the concept of *Caritas* to whom traditionally children are given as attributes embodying the ideal love of one's neighbour. These pictures are not connected with representations of the seven Virtues as they were depicted, often in series. in contemporary prints, In Cranach *Caritas* appears alone, in striking poses and relatively often. How can this be explained?

Should we consider these attractive pictures of Love, by a master whose *nacket weyb* or naked women enjoyed great popularity,[18] as religious art? Is it conceivable that such pictures

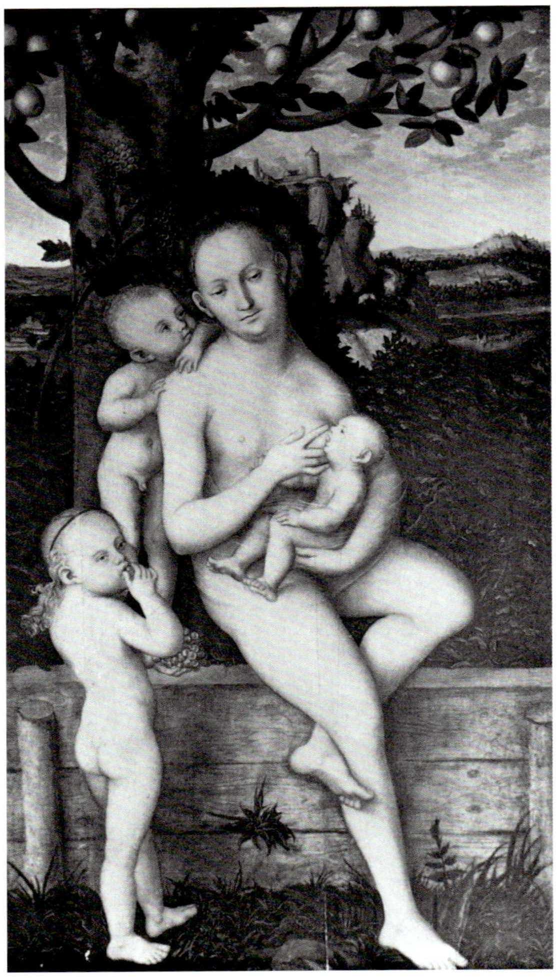

1 *Caritas*, 1529, wood panel

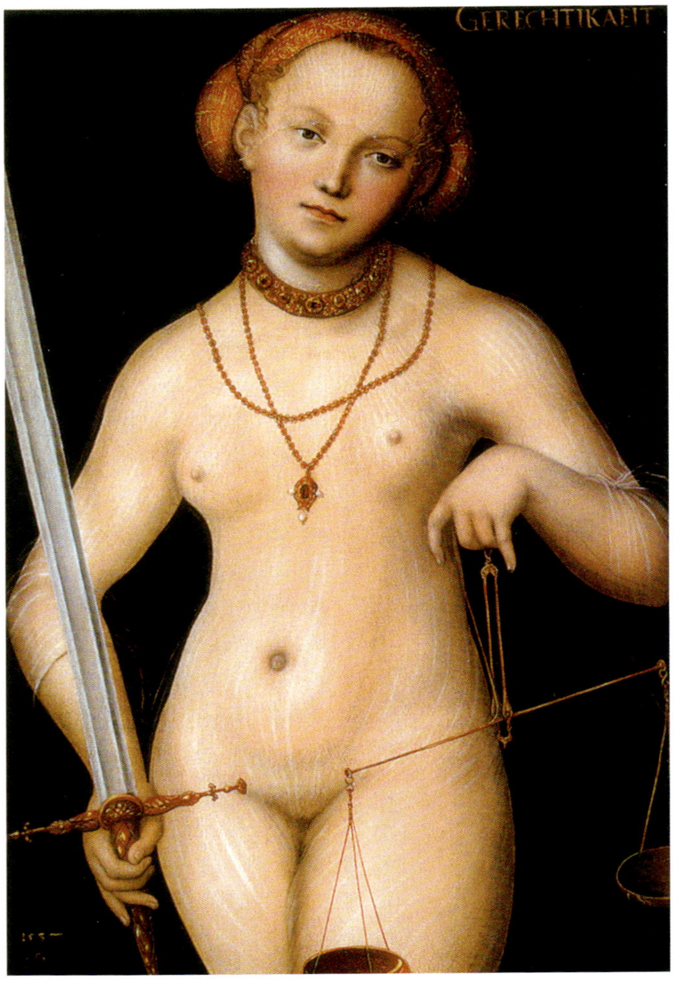

2 Lucas Cranach the Younger, *Justitia*, 1537, wood panel, Fridart Stichting, Amsterdam

of *Caritas* decorated if not churches then perhaps certain priests' houses or even schoolrooms? Were there some devout art lovers available to explain that they showed the love of one's neighbour required by Mosaic Law (3 Moses 19, 18), as Jesus then newly embodied and taught it, the love of God (Matthew 22, 37–40) and the 'fulfilling of the law' according to Paul (Romans 13, 10; Galatians 5, 14; 1 Timothy, 1, 5; 1 John 4, 20–21; James 2, 8)? Was the repeated emphasis on *Caritas* to be linked with the famous words of Paul in the First Epistle to the Corinthians ('and have not charity ...' 13, 3) followed by 'And now abideth faith, hope, charity, these three; but the greatest of these is charity' (13, 13)? Or with the First Epistle of John, chapter 4, verses 8 and 16?

The Three Theological Virtues – Charity in Its Relationship to Faith

Pictures entitled *Law and Faith* and *Law and Gospel* were introduced into the circle of Wittenberg Reformers in about 1525–28, refined in 1529 and often varied after that. If we interpret these as illustrations of Pauline-Lutheran faith,[19] may we see love as a fulfilment of faith in Cranach's pictures of *Caritas*? Could *Caritas*, which Cranach possibly depicted for the first time in 1529 in a large painting (fig. 1), stand beside his more weighty *Fides* (Faith) of 1529 – *Law and Gospel* (fig. 7)? If this is so, then in what relationship to each other do they stand? *Spes* (Hope), the third theological virtue, is concerned with the 'hope of the Gospel' and in the biblical and Pauline sense is part of faith (Colossians 1, 23). Through justifying and peace-bringing faith in the redemption of Christ, sinful mankind, wrote Paul (Romans 5, 1–2), may 'rejoice in hope of the glory of God'. Philipp Melanchthon wrote in his much-read *Loci communes rerum theologicarum* of 1521 that not only love – the love of God and one's neighbour – but 'also hope is a work of faith. [...] There is no reason to separate one from the other.'[20] (This summary of Luther's theology was later rewritten and expanded many times by Melanchthon; this passage is based on a German translation of the original version.) Hope, like love, is also a 'fruit of faith'. The entire group of seven or eight Pauline and Aristotelian virtues (*virtutes*), which were placed in aggressive opposition to

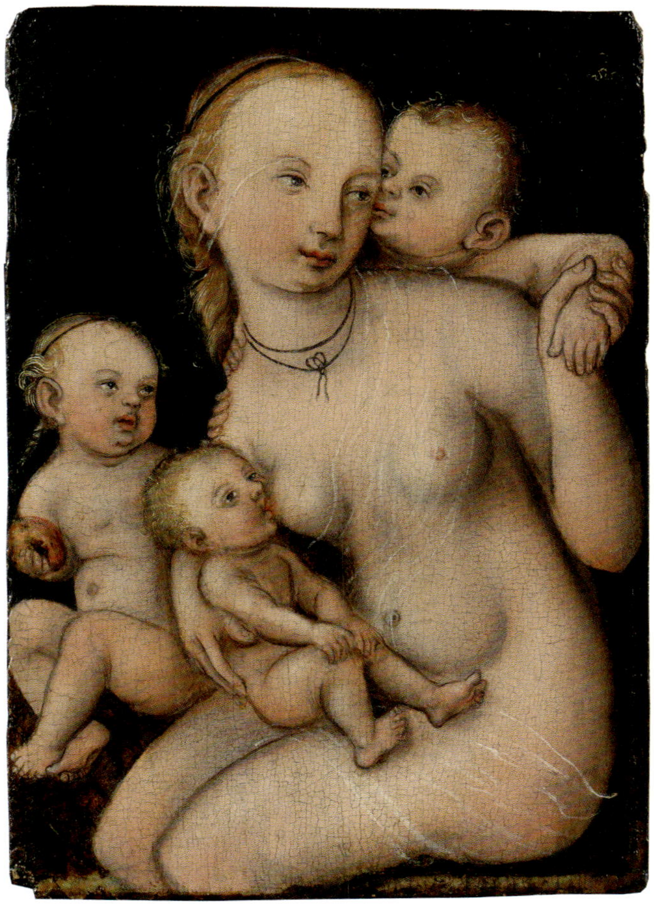

3 Lucas Cranach the Younger, *Caritas*, *c.* 1540–45, wood panel

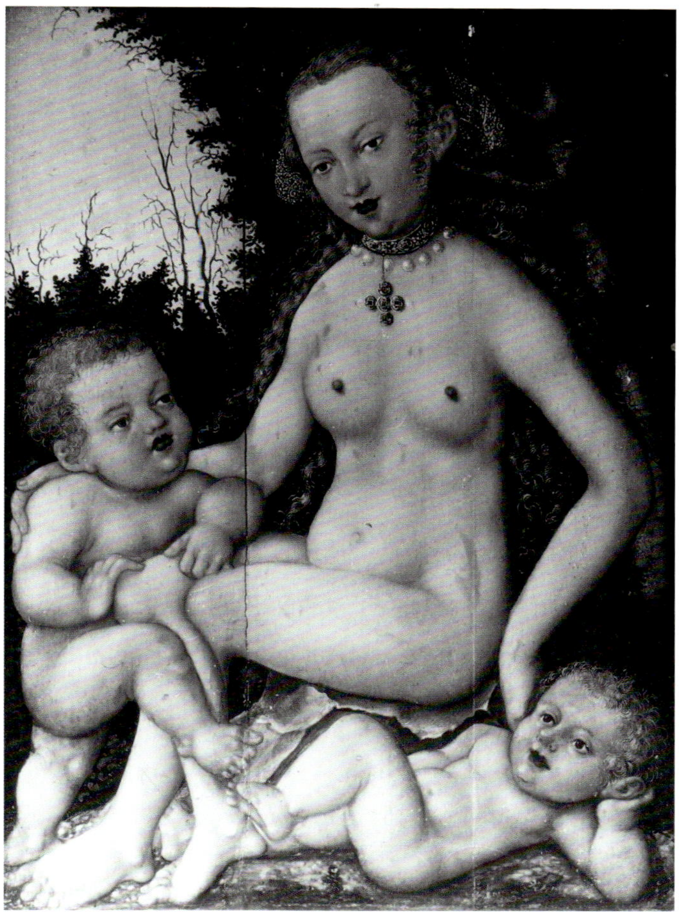

4 Master HB with the Griffin's Head, *Caritas*, *c.* 1530–40, wood panel

the same number of vices (*vitia*) by Prudentius and other authors, appeared later at Cluny in the late eleventh century and in Romanesque and Gothic statues in church portals.[21] These ideas supported man's 'acquired virtues' resulting from commendable works of virtue that allegedly bring happiness, and completely contradicted the theology of Luther. To Luther's way of thinking human virtues were only effective for the here-and-now and not for the future eternal life of sinful mankind in need of salvation.[22] The alleged virtue of *Caritas* had to be understood as a gift of God. As such it arises from faith in the grace of God who sacrificed his son for the salvation of mankind, a God of love who is love itself (1 John 4, 7–21: *Deus Caritas* est).[23] In 1535, in his verses to Erhard Schön's woodcut, Hans Sachs wrote of the 'Six excellent spiritual gifts, from one of which came faith' (fig. 6), or in Lutheran terms: 'Love flows from faith.' Spiritual gifts, gifts from the Holy Ghost, arise from virtues. They require Faith, which opens the picture sequence in the woodcut. Sachs described it as the 'absolute fundamental'.[24]

Faith Overflowing in the Love of One's Neighbour – Love which as the 'Fruit of Faith' 'fills us with joy' and 'is free'

For Martin Luther, Philipp Melanchthon and Hans Sachs, *Caritas* chiefly meant love of one's neighbour, leading us to 'love and praise God'. They did not see love of one's neighbour as a virtue in the sense of a human ability and duty to do good works that would bring salvation for our self-sacrifice. Faith was much more bound up in the Holy Ghost. In his Preface to the Epistle of Paul to the Romans of 1522, Luther wrote: 'Without compulsion man becomes willing and eager to do everyone good, to serve everyone, to suffer a great deal, to be full of love and praise of God, who has granted him such grace [the redeeming love of merciful God] that it is impossible to separate works from faith, as impossible as separating burning and glowing from fire.'[25] 'Without compulsion willing and eager', that is: without fear of punishment and expecting no reward.

While Luther insisted that there was no 'acquired love' for mankind, as scholars maintained, and that only faith, a

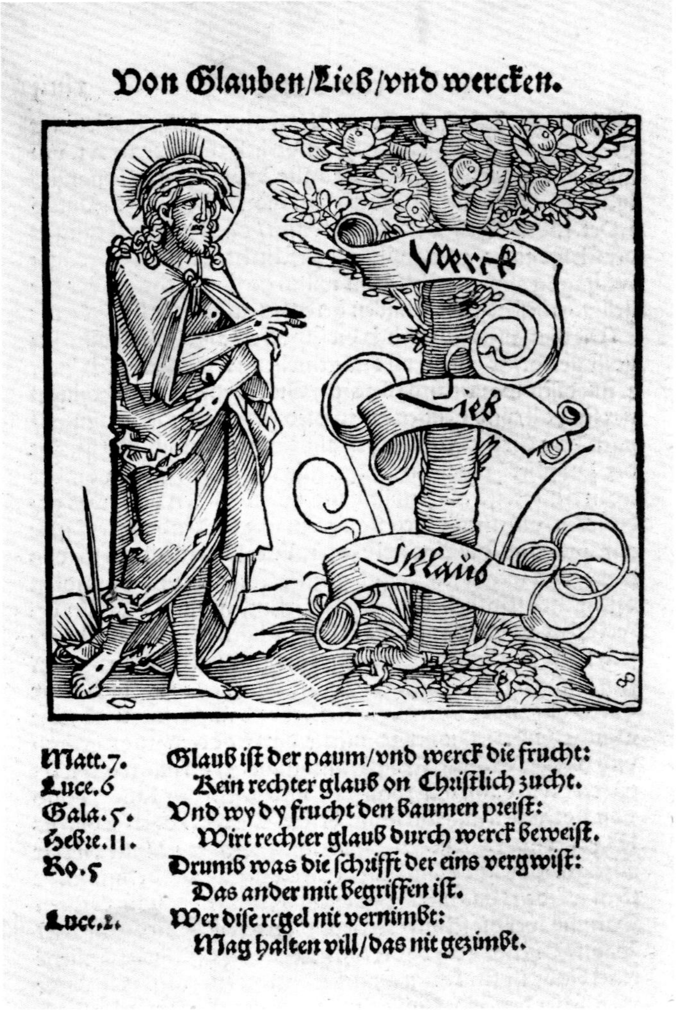

8 Hans Sebald Beham (attrib), *The Tree of Faith, Love and Good Works*, woodcut in: Johann von Schwartzenberg, *Weighing down the devilish serpent with the word of God*, Nuremberg 1525, Staatliche Museen zu Berlin, Kunstbibliothek

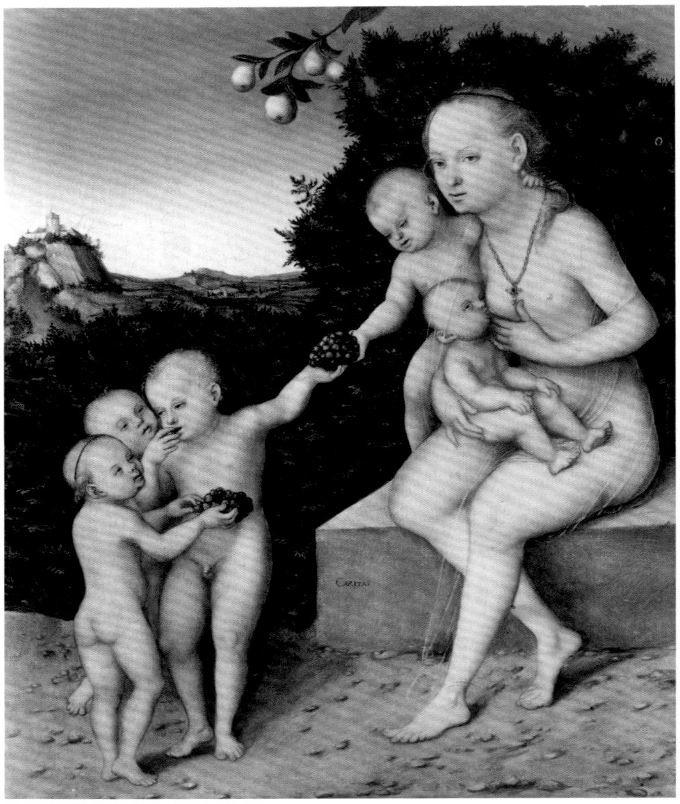

9 Lucas Cranach the Younger, *Caritas*, *c.* 1540, wood panel, Musées royaux des Beaux-Arts de Belgique, Brussels

and bears grapes – a motif we encounter in the earliest *Caritas* picture of 1529 (fig. 1) and also in his painting the Fall of Man (*Adam and Eve*) from 1526 (fig. 11)[39] – we are inevitably reminded of the Fall and Redemption and of the Eucharist.

However, this piece of iconography, which has almost no theological basis, makes no further appearance in Cranach's later *Caritas* pictures. Even if Luther's concept of *Caritas* had an influence on Cranach's pictures, their varying artistic appearance was surely not inhibited by the need to translate Lutheran thoughts and biblical texts literally into paintings. (For reasons of space, Cranach's *art* can be only touched on in this iconographic study.)

In about 1543 Hans Holbein the Younger drew an inscribed *CHARITAS* sign for the Netherlandish Protestant book printer Reynold Wolf, who worked in London. This took the form of an apple tree whose fruits, if one may interpret it so, could be harvested by the 'children of God' (fig. 12).[40] An accompanying text quotes 1 Corinthians 13, 5, which Luther translated as: 'Love does not seek its own.' (Love as in the Greek *agape*, the Latin *caritas*.) Even if there is no connection with this sign for a book printer, it is worth quoting a remark by Luther which suggests a more general meaning for 'fruits'. In 1533 Luther said at one of his Table Conversations: 'I have been reading the whole of the Bible twice a year for a number of years, and if the Bible were a large and mighty tree and all its words were twigs, then I have tapped on all the twigs because I wanted to know what they were and what they were doing. And in all that time I have knocked down only a few apples or pears.'[41] Luther thus saw the Holy Scriptures in pictorial terms as a fruit tree, which offered faith to the devout and also the fruits of faith (apples and pears) as gifts of God ready to be harvested.

Faith does not sleep, it is 'made active by love'

In his *Fastenpostille* of 1525, commenting on Romans 13, 8, Luther described *caritas* not as a human virtue but as a gift of God: 'Faith eradicates sin and makes a person pleasant

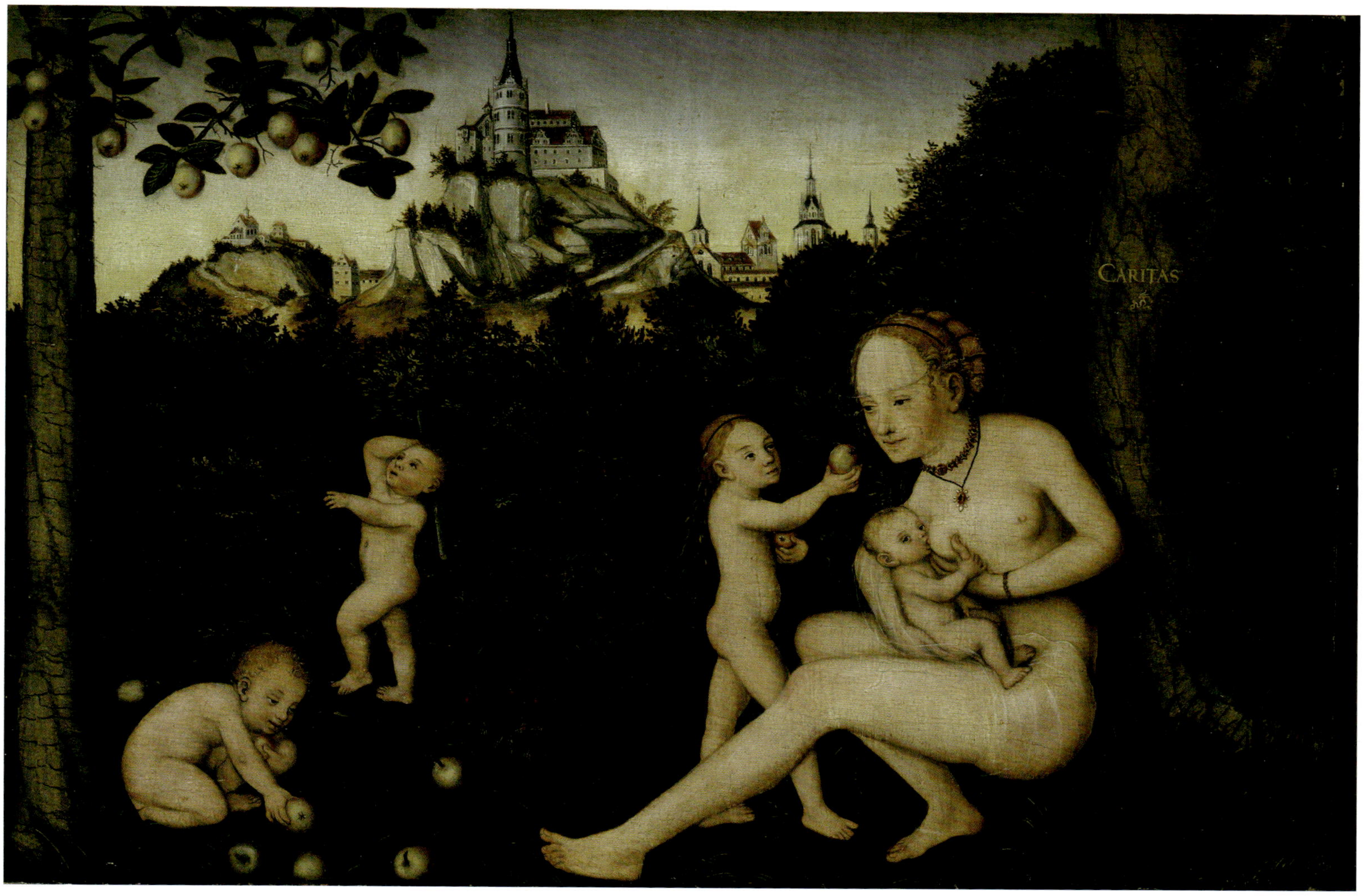

10 Lucas Cranach the Younger, *Caritas*, *c.* 1550, wood panel, Kunsthalle, Hamburg

and righteous [before God]. But when the person has become pleasant and righteous, he will receive the Holy Ghost and love so that he does good with joy.'[42] It is not love (the love of God and one's neighbour) that 'eradicates sin' but faith, and indeed, as it says in Galatians, 'faith which worketh by love'. Luther clarified the reference to doing works in these words from Paul and wanted to exclude being misunderstood when he stated (translated from the Latin): 'It is true that faith alone without works makes a person righteous, but I am speaking of true faith which, after it has made a person righteous, does not fall asleep and do nothing but does works through love.'[43] He also pointed out that 'Faith, if it hath not works, is dead, being alone', as it says in the Epistle of James 2, 17, and similarly in 1 Corinthians 13, 1.

When Melanchthon referred to Galatians 5, 6, he was speaking of a faith 'which overflows with love in our dealings with our neighbours'.[44] To fulfill the law the love of God and our neighbour is, strictly speaking, 'impossible' for mankind; but faith makes us 'love God for his great good deed for the forgiveness of sin for Christ's sake. Thus love for God is a fruit of faith.'[45] As Luther says, the love of one's neighbour flows as a gift from the redemption of faith, causing a love 'that does good with joy'.

A Comparison with *Christ Blessing the Children*

Looking at the mother bringing up her children lovingly and selflessly (Luther might say 'freely'), we can assume – though this is not in Luther or Melanchthon – that she fulfils all her duties and overcomes her difficulties 'with joy'. Such a work of love 'for her neighbours' (or nearest ones) depicted symbolically and at the same time with sincerity by Cranach is fundamentally different both from the non-altruistic earning of indulgences and from being anxiously pursued by others to perform allegedly necessary duties, within the complicated world picture of a late medieval church, which did not wish to address the absolute primacy of faith. If one may risk leaping from allegorical representation to pictures

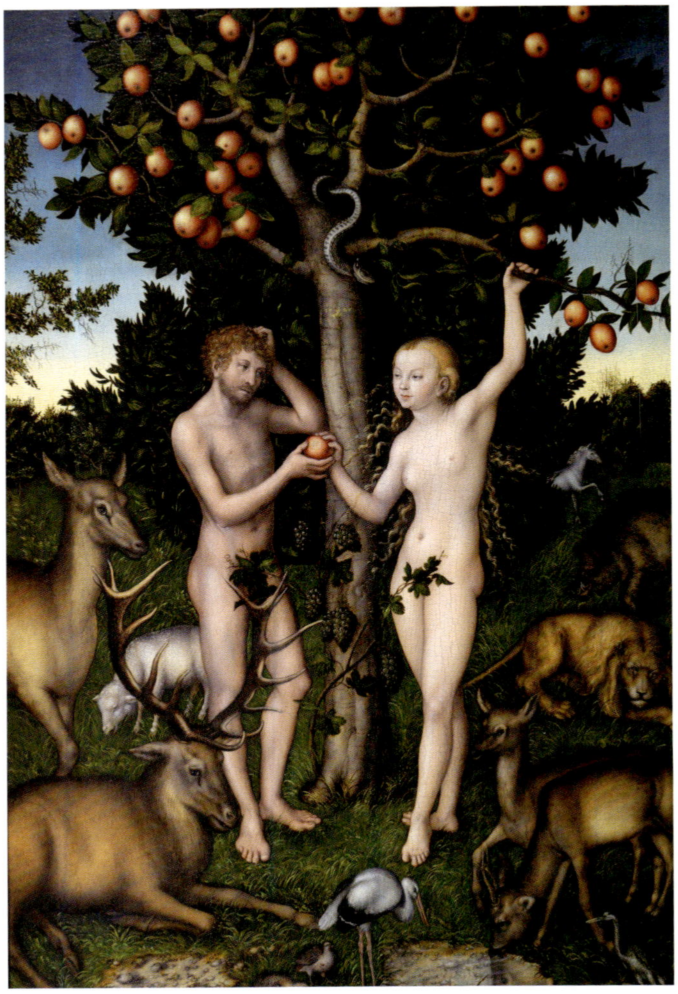

11 Lucas Cranach the Elder, *Adam and Eve*, 1526, wood panel, Courtauld Institute Galleries, London

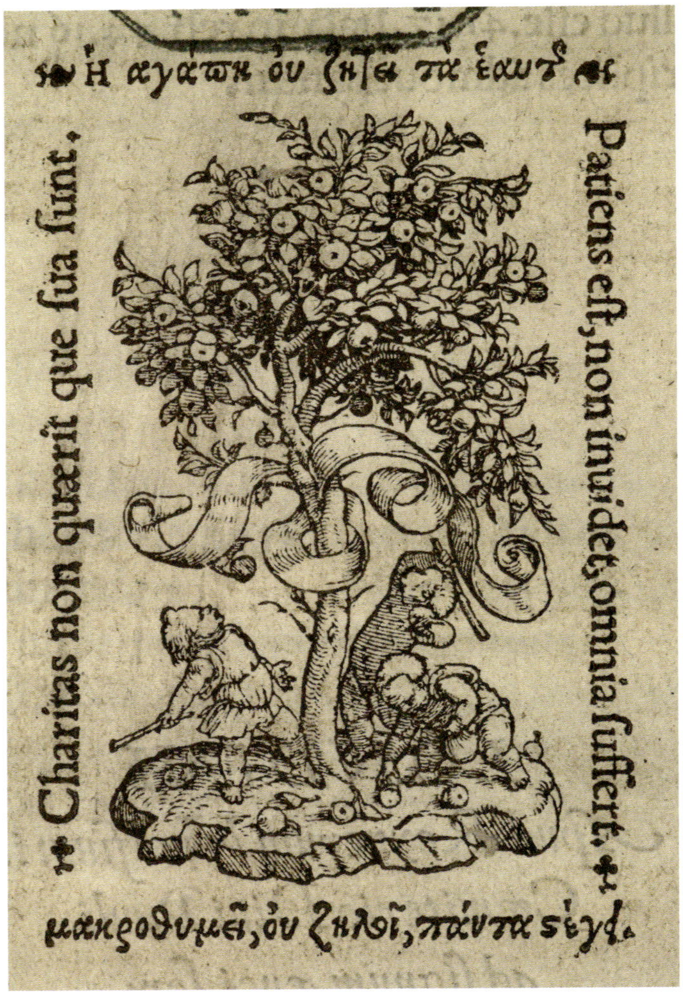

12 Hans Holbein the Younger, *Charitas*, book printer's sign of the Netherlandish Reynold Wolf, 1543, woodcut, British Library, London

of biblical history,– realising that there is a considerable difference between allegorical and historical figures – then one is reminded of the Reformist pictorial subject, often supplemented by written quotations, which in the old inventories was entered as: *How the Lord Jesus called the little children to come to him* (cat. 50). Luther understood the words of the Gospel, especially Mark 10, 13–16, in relation to a simple just faith which should not be complicated but more of a 'childish' faith. 'And they [mothers are not mentioned] brought young children to him, that he should touch them: and his disciples rebuked those that brought them. But when Jesus saw it, he was much displeased, and said unto them, "Suffer the little children to come unto me, and forbid them not: for of such is the kingdom of God. Verily I say unto you, whosoever shall not receive the kingdom of God as a little child, he shall not enter therein." And he took them up in his arms, put his hands upon them, and blessed them.'

Cranach's picture of *Christ Blessing the Children*, of which he produced many variants, was intended to strengthen the devout viewer's belief in a merciful God who loved mankind and revealed himself in Christ. Gottfried Seebass wrote of this picture type: 'As a child receives his life only from the love and care of his parents, so man receives his from God.'[46] Christian love of one's neighbour is linked to the love of God (1 John 4, 11): '[...] if God so loved us, we ought also to love one another'; verse 16: 'God is love; and he that dwelleth in love dwelleth in God, and God in him.' 'Preaching pictures' of this kind were not, like the *Caritas*, an allegory of Christian love; the biblical story picture was about the merging of a love of God with a childish trust in God, and also addresses the baptism of children in the trusting reception of the Kingdom of God.[47]

Reformation of a Ladder of Virtues

Before the Reformation, Cranach drew, for a woodcut, a Ladder of Virtues showing devout mankind ascending to God, the top rung of which is called 'the humble love of

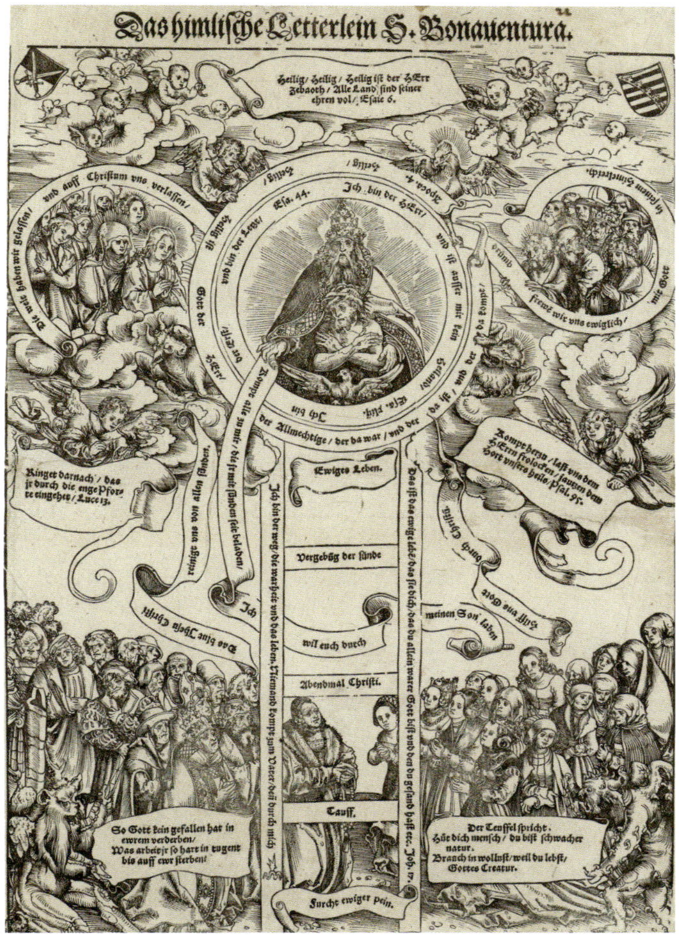

13 *Emperor Frederick of Saxony under the 'Heavenly Ladder of St Bonaventura'* (upper part, without the depiction of Hell which originally appeared beneath). With texts altered to suit Reformist ideas which turned a 'Ladder to God' into a 'Ladder of God to Mankind'. Woodcut *c.* 1510–15, inscription changed at least ten to twenty years later. Kupferstichkabinett, Staatliche Kunstsammlungen, Dresden

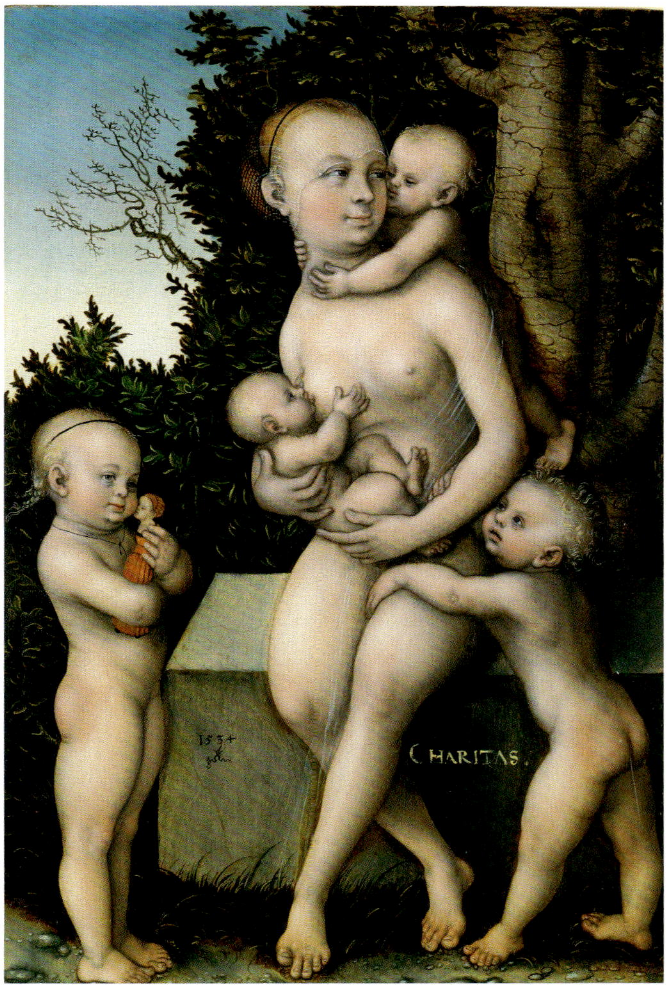

14 *Charitas*, 1534, wood panel, Museum zu Allerheiligen Schaffhausen, Sturzenegger-Stiftung

God'. This stands in opposition to Luther's concept of God's merciful descent to man, who is undeservingly blessed (fig. 13). According to the Reformist view, the ladder is no longer the means of ascent for the virtuous man who is finally 'rewarded', it belongs to Christ and faith in Christ the Redeemer who came down to mankind. Cranach's Catholic picture of the ladder was 'adjusted' as far as possible to the Lutheran mode by extensive changes to the inscription.[48] The active ascent,[49] which was formerly emphasised, is now seen to be a welcoming of faith in Christ, which means welcoming the chief sacraments, baptism and communion.

Cranach's Pictures of Pauline-Lutheran Faith and Love of One's Neighbour

In view of the numerous variants of Cranach's *Caritas* pictures, the earliest of which are dated 1529[50] and 1534[51] (figs 1 and 14), both of them signed and of high quality, we assume there was a close connection between the existence and the form of these works and Luther's reinterpretation of the *Caritas* concept, that is, the way he promoted love of one's neighbour to become the primary power of faith, and which Cranach illustrated in supremely artistic fashion in his 1529 picture *Law and Gospel* in the Gotha Museum (fig. 7).[52]

The reason why no-one until now has examined the Lutheran content of Cranach's *Caritas* pictures more closely[53] must clearly be that it is as difficult to make a connection between Luther's theology and iconography as it is in the case of Cranach's many pictures of the Fall of Man[54] or the Crucifixion of Christ or, for example, with the book cover woodcut of 1526 and the conversion of Paul.[55] This difficulty also applies to the clearly Luther-inspired pictorial themes, *Christ Blessing the Children* (cat. 50) or *Christ and the Adulteress* because, as was rightly said, 'almost every traditional Christian theme treated by Cranach and the artists in his circle at the time of the Reformation received a new meaning under the influence of Luther's teaching.'[56] Perhaps Cranach's *Caritas* pictures seemed too worldly to art historians and theologians, and the art historians, who could point to a long pictorial tradition, did not feel that any iconographic features obliged them to make a connection with Luther's idea of *Caritas*, i.e. his linking faith and love of one's neighbour with Paul's interpretation. The question now is: how did Cranach come to the unusual solution of depicting the theological Virtue, or rather the allegorical figure of *Caritas*, without clothing?

The Nudity both of Cranach's *Caritas* and a *Sophrosyne* of 1523 commissioned from Cranach by Melanchthon

Lightly veiled nudity is a feature not only of all Cranach's depictions of *Caritas* but also of the personifications of *Justitia* depicted nude by Cranach or wearing a transparent veil (fig. 2), and a *Patientia* (fig. 16) of which only a bad copy has survived. As early as 1523, at the request of Philipp Melanchthon, Cranach had produced painted and graphic versions of an almost nude *Sophrosyne* with veiled breasts (fig. 15).[57] Melanchthon, a Greek scholar and theologian, did not call this non-theological figure of Virtue from ancient philosophy *Temperantia*, Moderation, Prudence or Sobriety ('Discipline' in Luther's translation of 1 Timothy 2, 9 and 15). She does not belong in the pictorial tradition of a *Temperantia* who usually mixes wine with water in a moderate way or has a bridle and reins or occasionally a protractor, as she appears on the sign of the publisher Wendelin Rihel, active in Strasburg from 1535–38.[58] Her appearance here is completely original. Melanchthon used the Greek name which she bears in Plato's *Republic* (Book 4) and in Aristotle's *Nicomachean Ethics* (Book 4, Chapter 3) as one of the four cardinal virtues.[59] Aristotle defined *Sophrosyne* as a figure of moderation and sobriety with a reasonable desire for pleasant and joyful things who tries to be basically generous at the right time and in the right manner, i.e. in harmony with reason. Aristotle also discussed the 'discipline' of children and their youthful desire to learn, which seems to be significant with regard to Melanchthon's school and Cranach's small picture. All desires should be 'moderate and limited in number and in no way opposed to correct planning'. This may be what Melanchthon the teacher impressed on his students, who were also encouraged to appreciate the 'joyful' side of learning.

In 1521 Melanchthon wrote about *Temperantia* in his *Loci communes*, which he understood as nothing less than self-control and tolerance (*malorum tolerantia*), which may give rise to devoutness and brotherly love, many phrases which, here given a theological thrust, fit the *Sophrosyne* which Cranach designed and for which Melanchthon provided accompanying verses. In the early years Melanchthon was quite capable of supplementing Lutheran ideas in a general way: 'Now you have the sum of all Christian life: faith and its fruits. It is no use dividing the types [*genera*] and forms of the virtues in the manner of the philosophers and scholars into the [four] moral and [three] theological types, into gifts and fruits, as Aquinas inappropriately does with his. Faith alone is the organ of perception of the mercifulness of God who is the source and the life and the navigator of all good works.'[60]

Melanchthon here denied both the 'redemptive value' of moral and philosophical (Aristotelian) virtues and the false ideas about the justness of works and 'free will', the subject of violent debates between Erasmus, Luther and Melanchthon.[61] Later, however – in the Preface to Cicero's book *On Moral Duty (De officiis)* published in 1534 and in his definitions of concepts, which he added after 1553 to his *Loci* (and there replaced the word *caritas* by *dilectio*, as Erasmus also did from time to time) – he developed a more humanist doctrine of virtue despite his Lutheran inclinations (this was not for him a contradiction) which was partly based outside theology and more on human life on earth.[62] It is characteristic of him that the *Sophrosyne* woodcut which he first used in 1523 was used again in 1532 in the commentary on Aristotle's ethics which he wrote in 1532.[63]

Art was not untouched by the new philosophy as represented by Melanchthon.[64] The ever more sumptuous decoration of Mannerist altarpieces, epitaphs, chancelleries and other works of the late sixteenth and the seventeenth centuries funded by the Reformist movement sought to gain substance in terms of content by commissioning many figures depicting the Virtues.[65] In Augsburg in 1551 Lucas Cranach the Elder had to 'copy' a picture of the Seven Virtues from an unfamiliar model requested by John Frederick the Magnanimous, and Melanchthon's pupil Johann Stigel, whom Emperor Charles V had crowned poet laureate in 1541, had to compose verses for it.[66] Cycles of the Virtues had become fashionable everywhere. But let us return to the early Reformist milieu in the 1520s.

The *Sophrosyne* or *Temperantia* of 1523 conceived of by Melanchthon and executed by Cranach, which teaches moderation, is seated like Cranach's *Caritas* which illustrates the more pleasant, almost paradisiacal condition of the state of being in love, sitting in the open on a block of stone, with gracefully crossed legs.[67] This way of sitting, on a natural seat set at an angle and seen from above, perhaps meant to be a

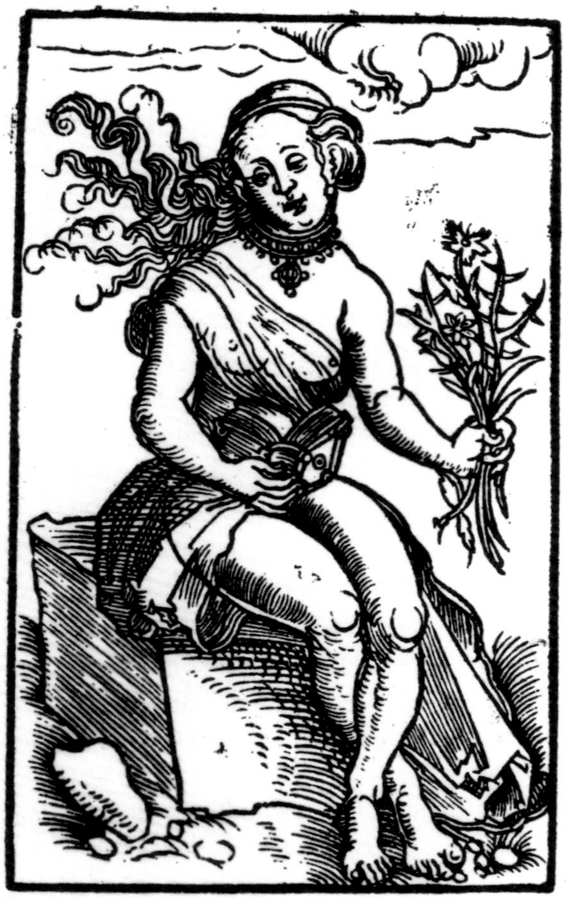

15 *Sophrosyne*, woodcut in: Philipp Melanchthon, *Enchiridion elementorum puerilium*, Wittenberg 1523, Frhrl. von Scheurl'sche Familienstiftung (Freiherr von Scheurl's Family Trust), Nuremberg

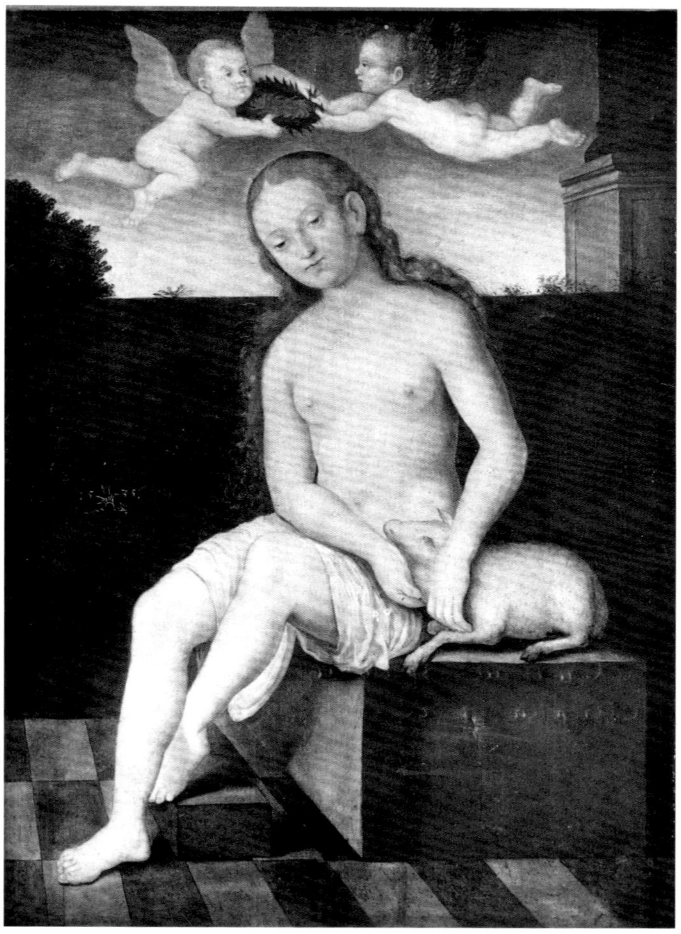

16 Possible copy of a Cranach picture of *Patientia*, 1535, wood panel

sedes quadrata,[68] was used again by Cranach in his image *Joshua in armour* (a woodcut for the cover of the second part of the Old Testament in Luther's German translation, printed in 1524)[69] and the naked *Faun and His Family*, the valiant-looking man armed with a club and the mother who is lovingly occupied with her small children, as in Cranach's *Caritas* pictures.[70] The woodcut of *Sophrosyne* has no landscape background, but there is a small cloud above the head of the virtuous maiden who is reading and holding a symbolic bunch of flowers. Her hair streams in the wind as we have seen it do in contemporary pictures of Venus[71] and other female figures, whether Lucretia, Eve, Mary Magdalen or the Virgin Mary.

The small *Sophrosyne* woodcut was printed first of all in 1523 in Melanchthon's *Enchiridion Elementorum Puerilium* by Joseph Klug in Wittenberg.[72] The accompanying Greek verses expressly name the author of the charming picture of Moderation, Lucas Cranach. They explain that the woodcut reflects one of Cranach's small paintings which hung in Melanchthon's private school near the podium and for which Melanchthon. had devised the iconography. The painting has not survived. The graceful *Sophrosyne* was supposed to encourage the students to work hard at their studies, guided by ancient culture. The accompanying verses by Melanchthon, who when in the school was ideally placed to see an illustration of the happy state of things, as in the Golden Age ('if there had been a Golden Age, if human nature had remained untainted by the Fall of Man and death'),[73] explain the significance of the book of wisdom in the right hand of the young woman (not a Bible!), and in addition the sense of the necklace with its 'moderately sparkling stones', as they were called – Cranach's women in the *Caritas* pictures also seldom do without necklaces – and finally the significance of the bouquet held up by Moderation. Here the beautiful but prickly roses are surrounded by thistles since, as Melanchthon's students must

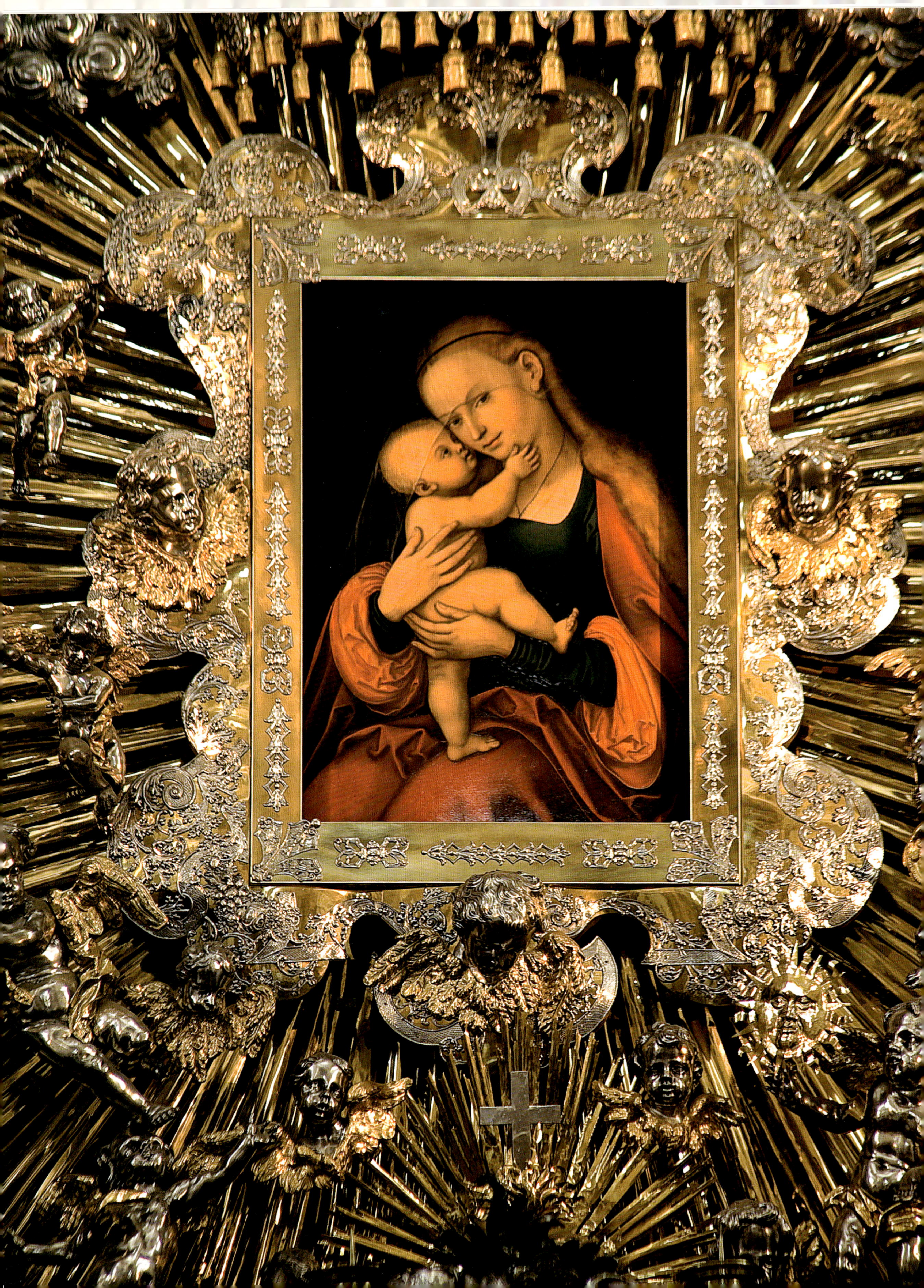

With Cranach's Help: Counter-Reformation Art before the Council of Trent

Andreas Tacke

The sound of the blows of Luther's hammer as he nailed up his theses on the Eve of All Saints' Day 1517 rose to such a thunder pitch in the nineteenth and twentieth centuries that it muffled any kind of objective argument, based on sources, about religious beliefs in the sixteenth century. Objectivity was replaced by a profession of faith. Current research into religious beliefs is still not completely free of this approach; indeed the objective study of Reformation history (or church history reflecting its own religious point of view) is in retreat compared with what the so-called 'grey literature' of the nineteenth and twentieth centuries had to offer. When the 500th anniversary of the epoch-making event comes round in 2017, we may certainly expect a number of further lapses.[1]

In the meantime, while the biased tendencies of nineteenth- and twentieth-century research have themselves become subjects of research and of great interest for the study of a general history of knowledge, it is not sufficiently realised how arguments in related fields developed or how separate disciplines reflected aspects in the game for social and political power.

Despite the occurrence of occasional irritations and lapses into Bismarckian cultural methods, for half a century historians of religion have described the period of the Reformation in a markedly different way. Aesthetics entered the debate only belatedly, and since then has produced considerable results; one may even say that it has developed into a separate research area within art history.[2] Works of art produced for Old Believers during the years of division in order to give visual form to the old religious ideas have also become a subject for research, alongside the new pictorial programmes of the Wittenberg reformers, which have themselves long been the subject of investigation (fig. 1). This research involves other artists in addition to Lucas Cranach the Elder and his workshop;[3] for example in the first period Master HL,[4] Sebald Beham[5] and Hans Baldung Grien.[6] For this reason the publication with the provocative title *Der katholische Cranach* enjoyed huge success, drawing attention to the need for research into the commissions which for example Cranach the Elder and his workshop received from Old Believers after 1517.[7] Then as now, Renaissance artists like their successors in general held firm to the idea that they could as a rule work for one side or the other, irrespective of the religious beliefs they themselves had adopted. The success of *Der katholische Cranach* and the exhibition catalogue *Cranach im Exil*[8] justify the use of provocative titles to encourage those with specialised knowledge as well as the public at large to reflect on the various scholarly approaches possible, and on widely held narratives of history reaching back over generations.

Until then, religious blinkers had almost prevented two major commissions from the workshop of Cranach the Elder, including some 300 paintings (!), from entering the field of Cranach research.[9] The Cranach workshop produced a comprehensive Saints and Passion cycle for the collegiate churches in both Halle an der Saale and Berlin. In Halle the 142 paintings were divided among the 16 altars of the collegiate church, in Berlin 117 paintings were divided among 18 altars; as well as these, other paintings were hung in both churches. The altars were similarly constructed: the weekday sides of the folding altars showed full-length saints, generally four at a time. When the weekday sides were folded over, the feast day page revealed a scene from the Passion, flanked to left and right by the figures of saints. The predella showed a scene from the Old Testament related to the Passion, demonstrating the connection between the Old and New Testaments.

The Saints and Passion cycle completed between 1519–20 and 1523–25 for Cardinal Albrecht of Brandenburg in Halle an der Saale and that painted in Berlin in 1537–38 for Prince Joachim of Brandenburg were seen by the Wittenberg Reformers as extremely dangerous because

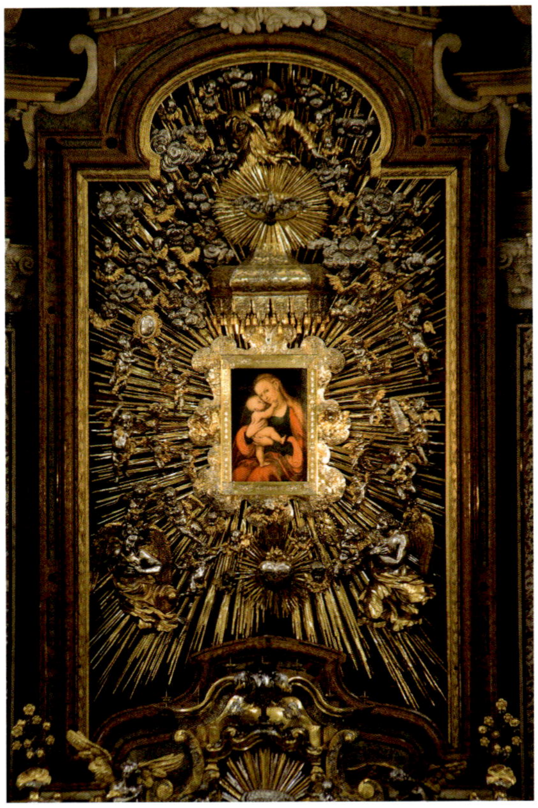

1 Virgin and Child (the Innsbruck 'Maria Hilfbild'), in the Baroque high altar, weekday view, Cathedral of St James, Innsbruck

the pictures they contained were 'improper', connected as they were with the old rites of prayer, liturgy and the cult of relics. These two major commissions from the 1520s and 1530s more than adequately demonstrate both in terms of quality and quantity that works by Cranach the Elder and his workshop depicting the Old Beliefs were by no means created in isolation. It can also be seen from other commissions, for example those which served to enhance princely prestige, that Cranach continued to work for Old Believers after the theses appeared in Wittenberg in 1517. Clients included the Albertine branch of the Wettiners, above all Duke George the Bearded (the 'Luther hater'), for whom, among other works, the Cranach workshop painted the altarpiece in Meissen Cathedral (FR, 1979, no. 219) in 1534. In this painting for the burial chapel, Cranach depicts the views of the Roman Church in an almost dogmatic way.[10]

In other dioceses, too, for instance in Naumberg, other works are to be seen which Cranach and his workshop painted for Old Believers after the historic year of 1517. Two large altar wings painted on both sides (each about 239 x 100 cm) hang today in Naumberg Cathedral deprived of context (figs 3, 4). They are neither signed nor dated but Werner Schade has proposed an estimated date of 1537.[11] They include two bishops of Naumberg. On the left wing we see Philipp of the Palatinate and on the right Johann III von Schönberg (both with their coat of arms, surmounted by mitre and crozier); in front of each man two saints on a gold ground. Since the left-hand side, from the viewer's point of view (which in heraldry is the right-hand side), is the more important, we can assume that Philipp of the Palatinate commissioned this altar, which is no longer complete. In my view, the style of the works suggests a date between *c.* 1520 and the mid-1520s. The history of the diocese lends weight to this dating. From 1512 to 1517 Philipp of the Palatinate was the *Koadjutor* or co-administrator of Bishop Johann III of Schönberg, after whose death in 1517 he became administrator. In 1518 he donated an annual memorial in Naumberg Cathedral to his predecessor in office. The two panels may be connected with this event, particularly since Philipp, who was also Bishop of Freising, was only occasionally in Naumberg from 1517–18 until 1526. This was also when his fine portrait was painted, dated *c.* 1520–22 (FR, 1979, no. 141) and now in the Gemäldegalerie, Berlin (601). In later years, Philipp limited himself to directing the fate of Naumberg Cathedral from distant Bavaria.

Philipp was supported at first by Frederick the Wise, but their religious views drove them apart. Philipp was, and remained, a strict Catholic and withdrew from the Ernestine branch of the Wettiners, forming an alliance with the Albertine branch. With the help of Duke Georg of Saxony and Cardinal Albrecht of Brandenburg he tried as best he could to minimise the influence of the Reformation on the diocese of Naumberg, but was only partially successful. Finally the cathedral was left standing alone, an island of Old Believers in a city that had become Lutheran. A similar situation occurred in Meissen. These were more or less the last bastions of Rome, but they were soon to collapse like a house of cards.

From the dynamic early stages of the Reformation process, Luther and his followers emerged as the victors. It was hardly relevant at the time that the roles of winner and loser might be reversed over and over again in the course of history (fig. 2). Thus, for example, Lucas Cranach's last patron, Frederick the Magnanimous, had to leave Wittenberg and go to Weimar, taking his aged court painter with him into exile. The representatives of the Old Church had already had to withdraw and leave the way clear for the introduction of the Reformation in central Germany. The sheer pace of this development caused people to forget that the 'losers' – Cardinal Albrecht of Brandenburg, for example – had in no way given ground to the supporters of the new doctrine without a struggle; the same could be said of Duke Georg of Saxony and Albrecht's brother, Elector Joachim I of Brandenburg. The historical aspect of these events has been

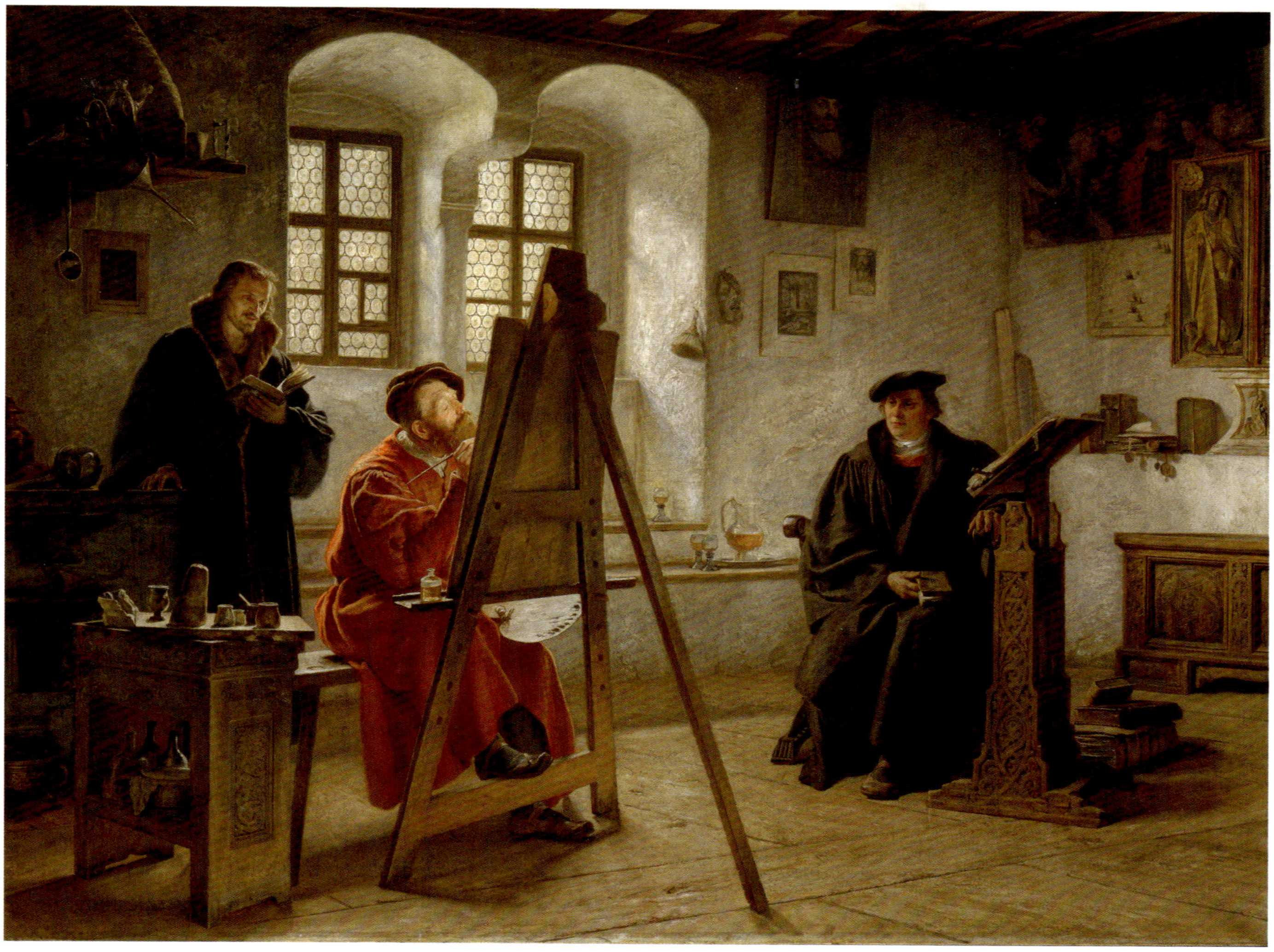

2 Heinrich Stelzner, *Cranach painting Luther at the Wartburg*, c. 1890, Bayerische Staatsgemäldesammlungen, Munich, Alte Pinakothek

widely examined; this research should now be supplemented by studies from an art–historical perspective. The areas to be investigated are those where the Reformation was able to gain a foothold without the help of the regional rulers, in dioceses where the inhabitants gradually turned towards the new doctrine while their rulers stayed with the Old Church and introduced appropriate Counter-Reformation measures. Unlike the systematic implementation that later proved successful, here we are dealing with the uncoordinated, spontaneous actions and reactions of individuals in those areas affected or threatened by the Reformation. Cardinal Albrecht of Brandenburg is the prime example of a figure involving art in the defensive struggle against Luther before the Council of Trent.[12]

The Council of Trent itself forms an important marker because it was here that the resolutions of the council agreed on a united procedure – whatever it looked like in detail. When measured against their effects on the history of art, the pronouncements of the Council of Trent on the subject of the fine arts, resolved on 3 December 1563, surprisingly came to nothing within a short time.[13] And yet the decree is the culminating point at which the foundations for a Counter-Reformation art must be seen. We have to ask how the situation looked prior to this, and whether the representatives of the Old Church, who for centuries had been using the fine arts to give visual form to their religious convictions, had completely renounced this medium in the face of Luther. Had the Roman Church no artistic response to Luther's religious ideas before the middle of the sixteenth century? This is difficult to imagine; the example of Lucas Cranach the Elder and Cardinal Albrecht of Brandenburg shows that the Papal Church still resorted to the fine arts to perform their age-old function of giving visual form to its religious ideas.[14]

Let us remain with Cardinal Albrecht, for whom we still have no biography acknowledging his historical significance.[15] Until now research into the history of art has, like other historical research, been no more than patchy, although we may draw on it to clarify one or two questions that remain unresolved.

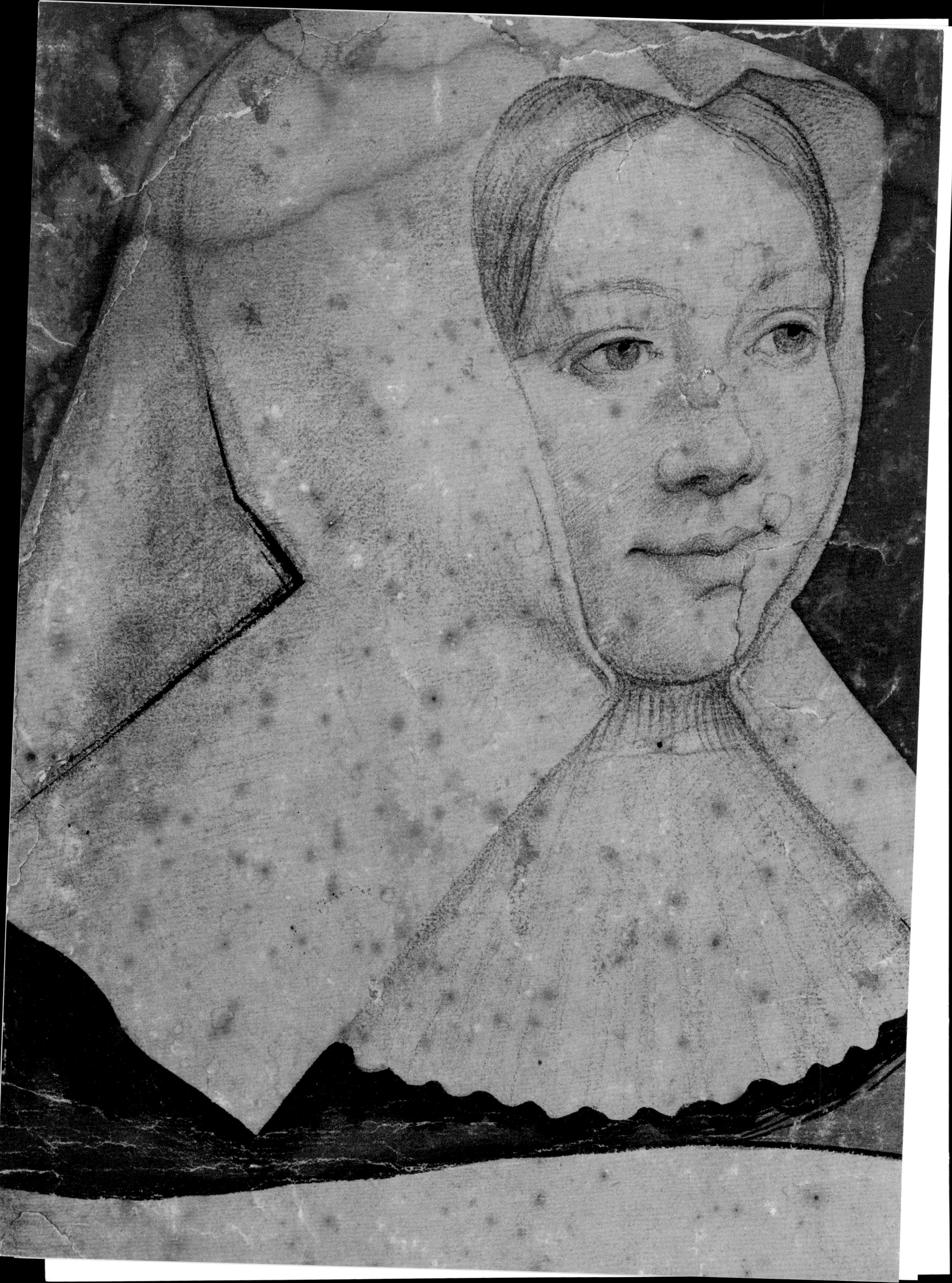

The Veil of Venus: A Metaphor of Seeing in Lucas Cranach the Elder

Elke Anna Werner

I

Lucas Cranach the Elder's small picture of Venus in the Städel Museum, Frankfurt has captivated many viewers (fig.1; cat. 114). While art historians have called this painting 'the most exquisite of Cranach's little pictures of Venus' because of its artistic quality, particularly the graceful pose and the fine execution, and ranked it first among the many variants of its type, many artists have been directly inspired by it.[1] From Ernst Ludwig Kirchner via Otto Müller to Alberto Giacometti there is a whole range of modern artists who studied, copied and paraphrased Cranach's painting. Comparing the modern adaptations with Cranach's original reveals an essential difference, however, demonstrating all the more clearly the specific quality of Cranach's pictorial invention and granting an insight into his artistic view of himself.

It is the veil: the veil which is missing in Kirchner's and Heckel's nude pictures. But, as we shall see, it is precisely this accessory which is essential for an understanding of the Frankfurt painting in particular, and also for Cranach's mythological nude subjects in general. More recent art historians and writers on art have shown what a great impression the debate over the veil has made on art history in Europe.[2] With its sacred and erotic connotations, the veil both masks and unmasks, draws the viewer's attention and at the same time shows itself to be the medium that mediates between the levels of reality (that of the picture) and the imagination (that of the beholder). There have long been theories about the material nature of pictures, for example when Leon Battista Alberti recommended the painter to stretch a thin piece of *velum* over a frame and to use this net or veil to capture the surrounding world.[3] The veil, which for Alberti was a kind of support, assumes an important function in the production of pictures because it can be used as a medium to transfer three-dimensional reality on to a two-dimensional picture. It is from these many connections with processes of production and reception that the veil ultimately derives its quality as a metaphor. On the level of an actual picture, and in accordance with the metaphors of covering and exposing, the veil can be understood as a visual metaphor which, as part of a complex system of mental perception and intellectual understanding, provides access to the various layers of meaning in a picture.

The motif of the veil appears not only remarkably often in Cranach's oeuvre, it also seems that the nature of the materials serving as a veil, the way the figures behave with the veil and the way it is depicted were so precisely and consciously chosen as to make us question the meaning of this motif for the artist. This question might be applied just as well to both his numerous versions of nude pictures of mythological subjects as to his depictions of the Virgin Mary, but here we shall begin our approach by examining some of Cranach's Venus pictures and the changes he made in his artistic interpretations of the subject, especially in the way he painted the figures and the veils, and also look at the shifts in meaning that these produced.[4]

II

From 1509 at the latest Cranach took up the subject of the Antique goddess of love and then continued to return to it, with particular frequency from the late 1520s – in paintings in various formats, both with and without Cupid. It is hard to decide whether a classical model

1 *Venus*, 1532, Städel Museum, Frankfurt

and self-referential references are predominant. This is expressed not least through the veil, which becomes the central element of the picture, leaving its mark both as an object and as a piece of fine painting.[40]

V

The *Kunstkammer*, or private collection for small intimate works, may have been the ultimate destination for Baldung Grien's enigmatic female nudes, and this could well be true of Cranach's unusually elaborate Venus pictures with all their many implications.[41] Certainly the small nude statuettes of Conrad Meit, who worked for a few years in Cranach's workshop, are regarded as early collectors' pieces, their aesthetic qualities particularly well suited to the conditions pertaining to a *Kunstkammer*.[42] Today we know that there must have been examples of the *Kunstkammer* in Northern Europe in the first half of the sixteenth century but we have little evidence of their conception, the collections involved and how they were laid out.[43] The earliest known inventories (1587 and 1598) come from the two princely collections founded in the 1560s in Dresden and Munich.[44] Samuel Quiccheberg, who wrote about the Munich collection in his museological foundation address of 1565, *Inscriptiones vel titulo theatri amplissimi*, described the organisation of a Kunstkammer as a hierarchical and chronological sequence of five divisions whose centre was formed by the natural history and art history collections.[45] These proceeded from natural objects (*naturalia*) and their conversion into works of art (*artificialia*) to technical instruments (*scientifica*), from mineralogical materials as the original form of materials via ancient and historical artistic products to contemporary works of art and mechanical instruments, which were regarded as the height of man's conquest of nature through science. These collections, which had an encyclopedic claim to be the microcosm of the macrocosm, represented not only the material wealth of their owners and their claims to political, economic and cultural power in a territory, but were above all considered to be places of knowledge and understanding, as their libraries made clear.

According to the inventory of the Dresden *Kunstkammer* of 1587, the collection included an *Adam and Eve* – 'made by the old painter Lucas'.[46] In an inventory drawn up for 1595, there were a whole series of other Cranach pictures such as *Adam and Eve, Lucretia*, various pictures of Ill-matched Couples and mention of a reclining Venus 'on a red velvet cushion' by the hand of Cranach.[47] An inventory of acquisitions of 1633 explains the reason for relocating Cranach paintings to the *Kunstkammer*, because works of high artistic quality could be viewed better there (than in the various palaces and castles).[48] Even though these *Kunstkammer* inventories are documents from the late sixteenth and early seventeenth centuries, they do prove that nude pictures by Cranach could be found in a *Kunstkammer*, that they were highly valued because of their special artistic quality, and that for that reason collectors wanted to make them more accessible. In this context artistic quality relates to the technical skill involved in their execution, which linked the paintings to other *artificialia* in a *Kunstkammer* which were admired for their masterly or amazing handling of a particular material. This wonderment in the face of objects from nature, art and technology was – as Horst Bredekamp has comprehensively shown[49] – the preliminary stage, the emotional trigger for a more thorough consideration of the exhibits in order to develop a scientific understanding of the world and its hidden implications. The institution of the *Kunstkammer* represented, therefore, a specific type of understanding: understanding through visual perception.

If one places Cranach's Venus pictures in the conceptual context of the *Kunstkammer* system, then the classical quotations and comparisons, the artistic models of excellence, the play with different materials and levels of reality, the guiding of the beholder's gaze and the refinement of the act of seeing, and finally the ambiguity between the Christian moral interpretation of myths and the direct recourse to Antiquity are given a concrete point of reference. The artistic potential of painting, which Cranach demonstrated at the highest level, and its specific means of conveying understanding could be seen to stand in a direct relationship with nature, other arts and scientific instruments. Whether Cranach's paintings were actually designed for the *Kunstkammer* or whether they sought to stimulate a comparable form of contemplating pictures and intellectual reflection in other functional connections is something for further research to uncover.

1 For a summary: Brinkmann/Kemperdick 2005, pp. 188–195; esp. on the history of research and results, pp. 191–193
2 Krüger 2001; Wolf 2002; for more on art and cultural studies: Endres/Wittmann/Wolf 2005.
3 On Alberti's view of painting as the art of the superficial, see Mary Pardo, 'Veiling the Venus of Urbino' in: Endres/Wittmann/Wolf 2005, pp. 9–33.
4 First considerations of the function of the veil in Cranach's nude pictures with reference to the immanence of the picture in Robert 2003, esp. pp. 109–112.
5 Koepplin/Falk 1974–76, vol. 2, p. 648; on the *Venus Felix* see Hinz 1998, pp. 185–188.
6 On the central meaning of nude and naked figures in the work of Dürer and in German art in general around 1500, see Bonnet 2001; on Cranach's involvement with Dürer's nude figure, Schoen 2001.
7 Lucas Cranach the Elder, *Venus Restraining Cupid*, woodcut, 28.2 x 18.9 cm; on the different conditions, see Koepplin/Falk 1974–76, vol. 2, p. 644.
8 Lucas Cranach the Elder, *Venus and Cupid*, 1509, painted on wood, later transferred to canvas and added to on the sides, 213 x 102 cm (preserved from the old format: 170 x 84 cm), FR 22, Hermitage Museum, St Petersburg.
9 Koepplin/Falk 1974–76, vol. 2, no. 555; Steigerwald assumes that the dating of 1506 is correct for the monochrome woodcut but not for the later coloured one; Köhler/Steigerwald 1973, pp. 6 ff., 59 ff.
10 Koepplin has pointed out in Koepplin/Falk 1974–76, vol. 2, pp. 645–647 that in this picture Cranach merged two pictorial traditions into one: the iconography of the ancient goddess and the late-medieval tradition of Venus as an astrological planetary goddess, who determined events in the world from the heavens. In Cranach she indeed stands on a ruffled ribbon of cloud but is clearly much closer to events on Earth.
11 On the early woodcuts, see Schade 1974, p. 24.
12 Hinz 1998, esp. pp. 38–40.
13 Schnitzler 1996; Scribner 1990; for a summary see also Bushart 2004, pp. 15–19.
14 On the moralising interpretation of ancient mythology see Robert 2003, esp. pp. 103 ff.; on the moralising pictorial tradition of ancient subjects since the late Middle Ages: Koepplin/Falk 1974–76, vol. 2, pp. 645 ff.
15 Koepplin/Falk 1974–76, vol. 2, p. 649.
16 For the translation of the inscription see the versions in Koepplin/Falk 1974/76, p. 649; Schade 2003, p. 178, no. 61; Robert 2003, p. 109.
17 Koepplin/Falk 1974–76, p. 649; Bonnet 1994, esp. p. 142; Koepplin, in: Schade 2003, esp. pp. 157 ff.
18 Robert 2003, p. 104.
19 See note 13.
20 For a summary see Krüger 2001, pp. 11–26; Bushart 2004, pp. 16 ff.
21 Weimer 1999, pp. 30 ff.
22 Weimer 1999, p. 32.
23 Krüger 2001, p. 283.
24 For a more thorough comparison of Cranach and Apelles see also the contribution of Mark Evans in this catalogue, pp. 49–61.
25 000 Gemäldegalerie, Berlin 1996, p. 236.
26 Varese 1967, no. 59 a, b; cf. fig. 9 in the contribution of Mark Evans in this catalogue, pp. 49–61.
27 Heiser 2002, pp. 56 ff.; on Cranach's relationship with Wittenberg University and the court see also the contribution of Mark Evans in this catalogue, pp. 49–61 and other literature.
28 FR 116; Koepplin and Schade doubt that it was painted by Cranach alone despite the signature, Koepplin/Falk 1974–76, p. 655; even if it was a copy, the presentation piece was certainly by Cranach.
29 On the spelling mistakes in this inscription and a variant of the picture (FR 112 B) with the correct inscription in the Niedersächsisches Landesmuseum, Hanover see Koepplin/Falk 1974–76, p. 655.
30 Pliny the Elder, *Naturalis Historia*. Book XXXV, 79.
31 Hesiod, *Theogony*, 156–210.
32 Erwin Panofsky, 'Blind Love', in: Panofsky 1980, pp. 153–202 (first pub. in English. 1939).
33 Erwin Panofsky, 'Blind Love', in: Panofsky 1980, p. 171; FR 246 S.
34 Erwin Panofsky, 'Blind Love', in: Panofsky 1980, p. 178.
35 Vienna, Kunsthistorisches Museum, Inv. 2636; von der Osten 1983, pp. 20 ff., 58–62, no. 10; for a new view of Baldung's nude and witch pictures see Brinkmann 2007.
36 For the iconography of Visus see Kauffmann 1943; Sluijter 1991–92.
37 Brinkmann writes in connection with the structural complexity of Baldung Grien's female nude pictures of the works' discursive structure (Brinkmann 2007, p. 36).
38 Schade also emphasises the artistic quality and the tension between representational and non-representational painting, see Schade 2003, p. 179, cat. 64.
39 On the history of the title see Brinkmann/Kemperdick 2005, p. 191; if the panel was originally to have formed a pendant to a *Lucretia* in Vienna, as Brinkmann suggests, then both figures would 'personify two different forms of love, the fickle wayward passion of Venus and Lucretia's self-sacrificial loyalty to marriage', p. 194.
40 The independent behaviour of the veil also appears at this time in other female nude pictures by Cranach, and also in paintings of Lucretia, the *Judgement of Paris*, etc., e.g. FR 243, 249, 251.
41 Brinkmann 2007, pp. 36 ff.
42 Burk 2006, esp. pp. 35–40.
43 Theuerkauff, 1981, p. 13; Impey/MacGregor 1985; Pomian 1987; Grote 1994; Herklotz 1994 provides an overview of the scholarly literature.
44 On the Dresden inventory see Kolb 2005, esp. pp. 118 ff. and other literature; on the Munich inventory see Diemer 2004.
45 Bredekamp 2002, esp. pp. 33–35.
46 Kolb 2005, p. 118.
47 Chemnitz 2005, p. 561.
48 Kolb 2005, p. 126.
49 Bredekamp 2002.

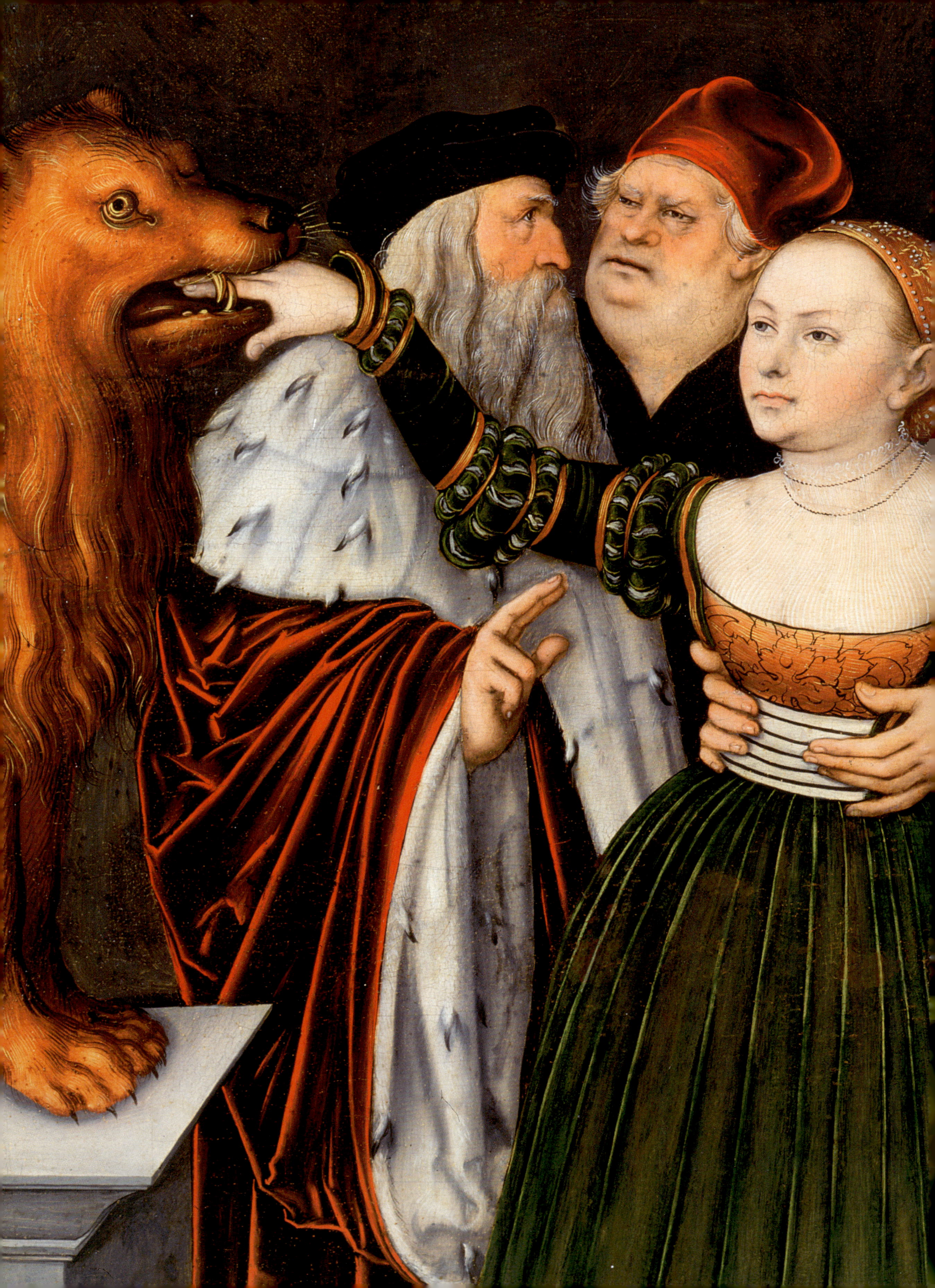

Catalogue

Bodo Brinkmann
Gabriel Dette (GD)

The catalogue numbers 19, 64, 68/69, 89 and 116 were restored for the Exhibition. However, for technical reasons the illustrations show them in their previous condition.

I Landscape (fragment)

Wittenberg, *c.* 1525–30

Oil and tempera on wood
43.2 x 27.6 cm

Private Collection

Provenance:
the Jenny Klever collection, Leverkusen; acquired in 1990

(Frankfurt only)

Selected references:
not in FR; Lempertz, 10. 12. 1990, p. 26, lot 22

This small panel is a fragment, and probably served to enliven a very large interior scene with a landscape view seen through an unglazed window opening, of a kind that Lucas Cranach often employed. The painting has survived being sawn out of its original panel remarkably well: it is in an excellent state of preservation, its reduced scale offering the viewer a complete guide to the finesse of Cranach's landscape art. Its chief motif is the tall young deciduous tree on the left, standing in front of a stretch of water in which are reflected the bushes on the bank and the single swan. Behind it is part of a fortified town. The right half of the picture includes a massive rocky cliff with an extensive fortress and a four-sided corner tower on the fortified walls. In front of it a path winds round the rock formation beside the base and climbs steeply to the right. A tiny rider with a dog can be seen on the path. Bluish thunderclouds gather above the fortress. The cliff shimmers with a reddish glow from the late afternoon sun which bathes the horizon in tones of yellow and pink. Fortress, town and water are, like a distant echo, rhythmically repeated in the background to the left. Cranach successfully combines dramatically opposed objects to form a harmonious exchange in a tight space. Light and dark, close up and far away, steeply rising elements and flat surfaces, barricades and wide-open spaces form a mysterious symbiosis.

This extremely fine work embodies several of the aims of the present exhibition: to draw attention to Cranach's qualities as a painter – up to now somewhat underestimated – to uncover details and from the selection of available works – which is far from complete – to suggest wider connections and relationships.

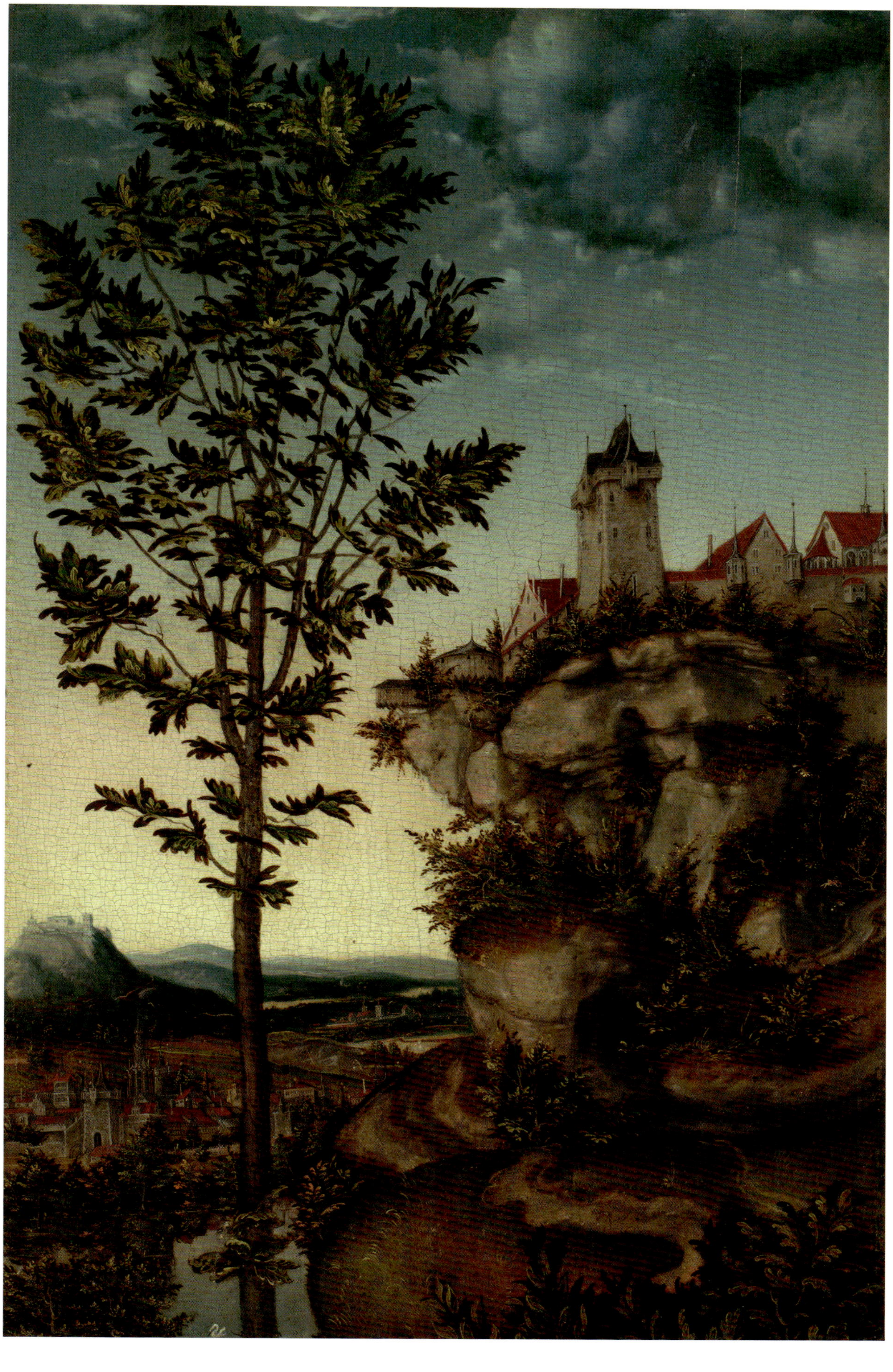

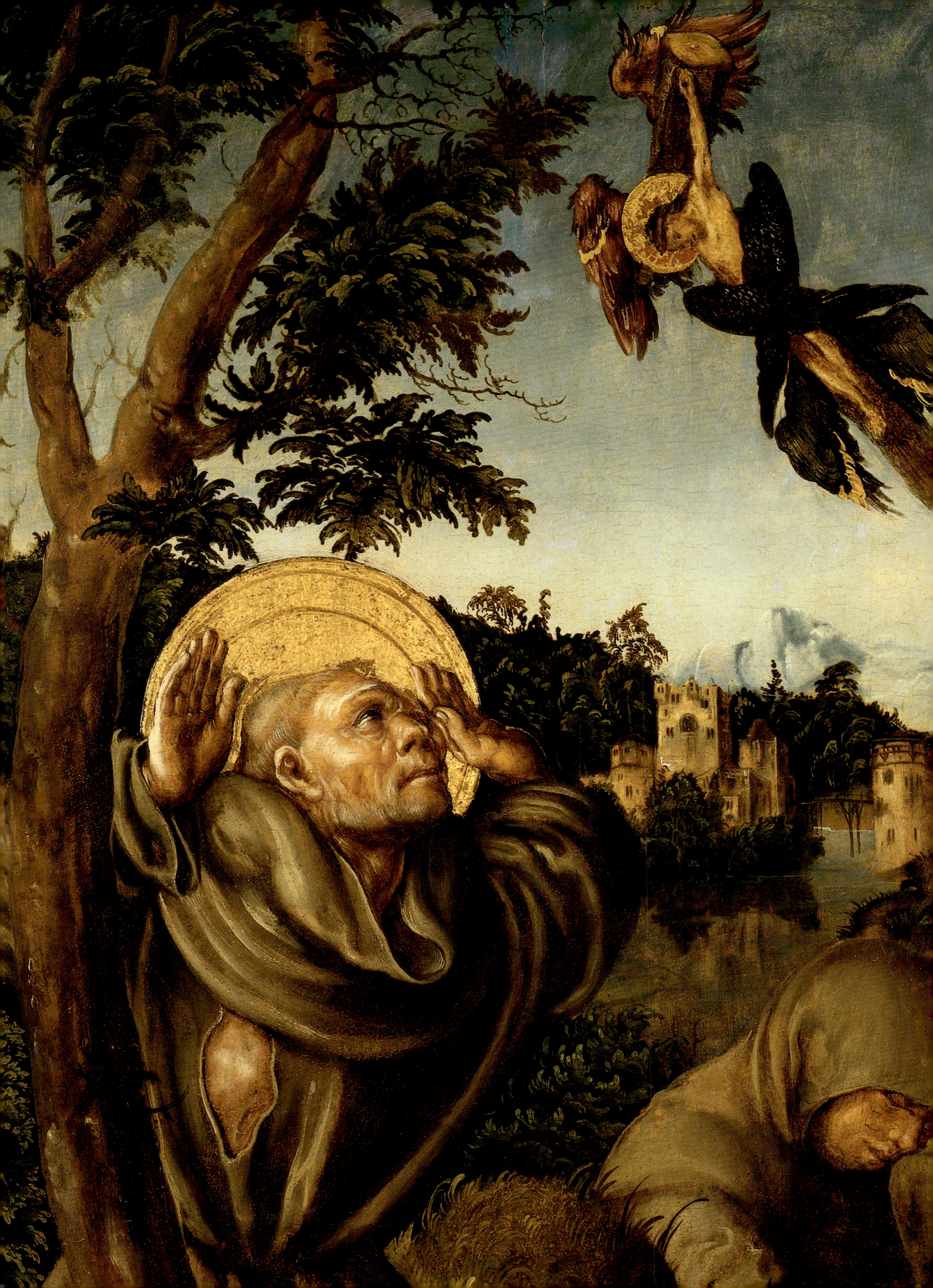

Sturm und Drang in Vienna

We can only make assumptions about the artistic training of Lucas Cranach the Elder. He was almost thirty by the time we find him in Vienna in about 1500, where he quickly found his feet in university circles and in the company of leading humanists. His early works are already no longer youthful pieces but the style is still stormy and expressive, incorporating ideas he may have acquired in Hungary and Poland. With these works Cranach paved the way for the Danube School.

2 The Crucifixion

Vienna, *c.* 1500

Oil and tempera on limewood
58.5 x 45 cm

Kunsthistorisches Museum,
Vienna, GG 6905

Provenance:
acquired in 1934 from the collection of the Abbey of Schotten, Vienna

Selected references:
FR 1; Grimm/Erichsen/Brockhoff 1994, p. 294 , no. 110; Sandner 1998, pp. 96–9, no. 11.1; Anzelewsky 1999, pp. 125–134; Bierende 2002, pp. 55–108; Heiser 2002, passim; Stadlober 2006, pp. 155–164

This panel, known by reason of its provenance as the *Schotten Crucifixion*, is on a small scale for a representation of the Crucifixion, and was probably intended for private use. Its highly distinctive manner is characteristic of Cranach's style at the age of about 30, and is thought to be the earliest surviving painting from his hand. Together with his *St Jerome* (cat. 3), dated 1502, which is also in the Kunsthistorisches Museum, the *Schotten Crucifixion* is associated with the altar wings with Saints in the Vienna Academy (cat. 4, 5), the *Schleissheim Crucifixion* (p. 21) from the Alte Pinakothek in Munich, dated 1503, and the *Rest on the Flight into Egypt* (FR 10) dated 1504 in the Gemäldegalerie Berlin, signed and dated 1504. While these works are in a softer and rather more painterly manner, the outstanding feature of the *Schotten Crucifixion* is its remarkable graphic hardness. Using the tip of his brush, the artist has outlined light areas, drawn in wrinkles and furrows, individual hairs and the edges of leaves within the foliage, and accentuated the contours of limbs with the result that a disquieting ornamental network of lines overlays both the figures and the landscape background. The figure types seem oddly overdrawn to the point of caricature, though their gestures are always expressive. Even the clouds moving across from the right seem to add an eloquent commentary to the scene. This stylistically heightened treatment has led to the assumption that the painting was begun some two to three years before the earliest dated work, in other words in about 1500. This raises the question of the sources and models to be seen most clearly in the painting, if it is indeed the earliest of Cranach's works to survive. On the one hand there are motifs such as the limply drooping arms of Mary and the dog sniffing at the bone, which point towards earlier Franconian panel paintings; on the other hand the costumes of the men on horseback show some exotic traits. The moustachioed man wearing a yellow tunic with conspicuous lacings and the gnomelike bearded figure in the foreground, in his wide-brimmed hat with its jutting crown, are the most striking figures. According to Anzelewsky, these are elements of Slavic dress which Cranach may first have observed in Poland. It seems quite likely that the artist stayed for a time in the royal university city of Cracow before he went to Vienna. At the time of the Jagiellon dynasty, Cracow attracted a number of German artists including Veit Stoss, Hans von Kulmbach and Hans Dürer.

Cranach heightens the drama of his *Crucifixion* by referring back to motifs more common at an earlier date: the body of his crucified figure does not hang symmetrically and is not tautly stretched on the cross but is covered in wounds and sags with bended knees to one side. Both features recall the plague crucifixes of the fourteenth century. Since the Gothic period the feet of the victim were usually fastened with a single nail. Cranach, however, goes back not only with the figure of the Redeemer to the older four-nail type, but inflicts a similar fate on the two Thieves, although traditionally, both were shown simply bound to the cross with cords.

This effective staging, featuring a well-calculated blend of ornament and expressiveness, and depicting figures and landscape on equal terms, became a stylistic hallmark – though not, surprisingly, in Cranach's own work, which inclined towards a formal calmness, but rather, in that of artists such as Albrecht Altdorfer, Jörg Breu and Wolf Huber, who adopted the manner of Cranach's Viennese period and developed it into a characteristic stylistic idiom, which as the so-called Danube School was to dominate painting, the graphic arts and sculpture in Bavaria and northern Austria in the first half of the sixteenth century.

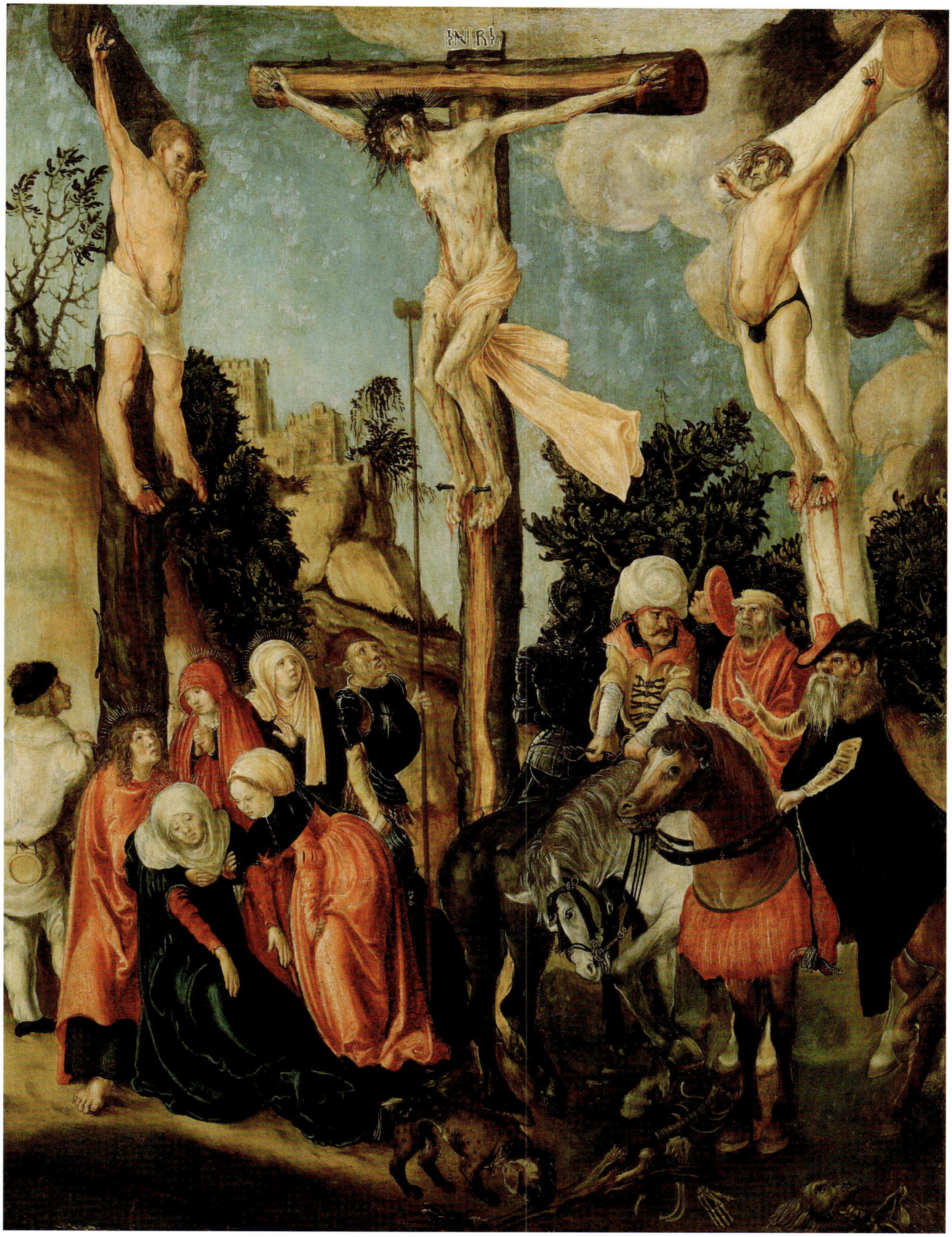

3 The Penance of St Jerome

Vienna 1502

Dated below centre 1502

Oil and tempera on limewood
55.5 x 41.5 cm

Kunsthistorisches Museum,
Vienna, GG 6739

Provenance:
acquired in 1927 from the Refectory of the Bishop's Palace at Linz; previously in the Mondsee Monastery

(Frankfurt only)

Selected references:
FR 4; Schade 1974, p. 17; Sandner 1998, pp. 85 f, 150–2, no. 17.1; Heiser 2002, pp. 73–7; Stadlober 2006, pp. 164–75

The Church Father Jerome (*c.* 347–419/20) rose in the late Middle Ages to become one of the most honoured of saints. He was revered not only as the Pope's confidant and secretary, and thought of as having the rank of a cardinal, though Jerome was never granted this honour, but also as an eloquent philologist and translator of the Bible, highly regarded by worldly minded humanists (see cat. 54, 66, 67). Above all, however, the four years he spent as a hermit in the desert of Chalcis in Syria were seen as exemplary – a time when he undertook eager penance for the sinful years of his youth in Rome and through self-chastisement sought to kill off all desires of the flesh.

For this reason, the saint is generally shown as a penitent in the desert, which for want of knowledge of its true nature is represented as a kind of richly wooded wasteland. Jerome has put aside his cardinal's robe and hat, and wears a simple white cloth about his hips, leaving the upper body uncovered. A lion rests at his feet; according to legend, Jerome extracted a thorn from the animal's paw, after which the lion became his devoted companion. The building with a chapel in the background on the right may indicate the monastery which Jerome later founded in Bethlehem. The central theme of the painting is the saint at his devotions, beating his breast with a stone – a form of self-flagellation about which he wrote, in letters that survive. Cranach portrays the saint's torso in a remarkably correct anatomical manner, even by comparison with his later versions of the subject (cat. 55). He also prepared his scene with great care. The saint draws his arm back as far as possible, while grasping his beard with his other hand so that it might not diminish the force of the blow. This athletic and convincing pose offers a strange parallel with an early work on the same subject by Leonardo da Vinci in the Vatican Museums – strange because in appearance it departs somewhat from the more usual pictorial tradition.

A contemporary viewer was not meant to attend particularly to the notion of flagellation, but rather to the devotion displayed. This is why Jerome, despite his straining physical exertion, retains a fixed gaze upon the crucified figure, rendered as a polychrome sculpture, and standing to the right above a rocky outcrop. The devout owner of the painting was intended to see the Church Father as an example and to honour the crucified figure with a similar ardour – or might at least use the work to claim he was doing precisely that. It is probable that we can even identify the owner. The strange pair of birds – an owl and a parrot – in the tree on the left edge of the picture, was used on another occasion by Cranach, in his double portrait of Johannes Cuspinian and his first wife Anna Kupsch (FR 6, 7; Collection Oskar Reinhart, Am Römerholz, Winterthur) to symbolise the melancholic and sanguine temperaments. Cuspinian (1473–1529) was at the time a historian at the University of Vienna, and later entered the Emperor's service. Cranach's expressive style in his Viennese period was well suited to this new interpretation of what was often treated as a more elegiac subject. He borrowed the lion from Dürer's engraving of only a few years before (SMS 6), and this perhaps also inspired him to depict the saint's torso unclothed; the tautly stretched figure is his own work, however, as is the oblique positioning of the crucified figure. The vegetation going to seed and the ample folds in the garments heighten the dramatic nature of the events shown. Certain exaggerations seem acceptable, such as the enormously long tail of the winding sheet on the crucified figure and the gigantic knot tied at the saint's waist. They were perhaps consciously inserted to guide the viewer's attention to these parts of the painting; the knots in both white cloths are tied in the same way and are placed over the same part of the wearer's body. Perhaps the artist meant to emphasise the point that Jerome, in his 'imitation of Christ', is struggling to achieve true emulation of the Lord, and that the viewer in turn should join him in his efforts.

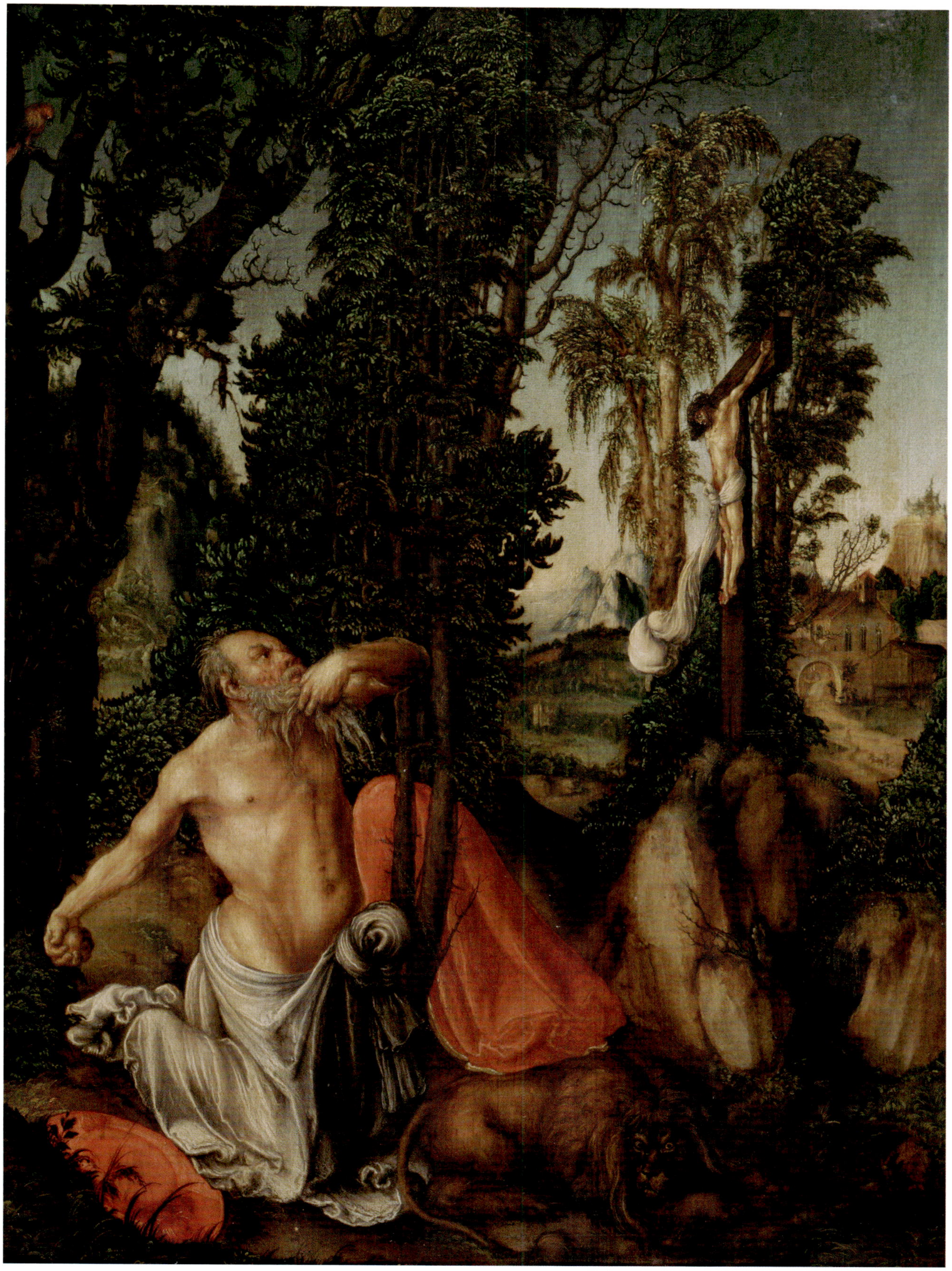

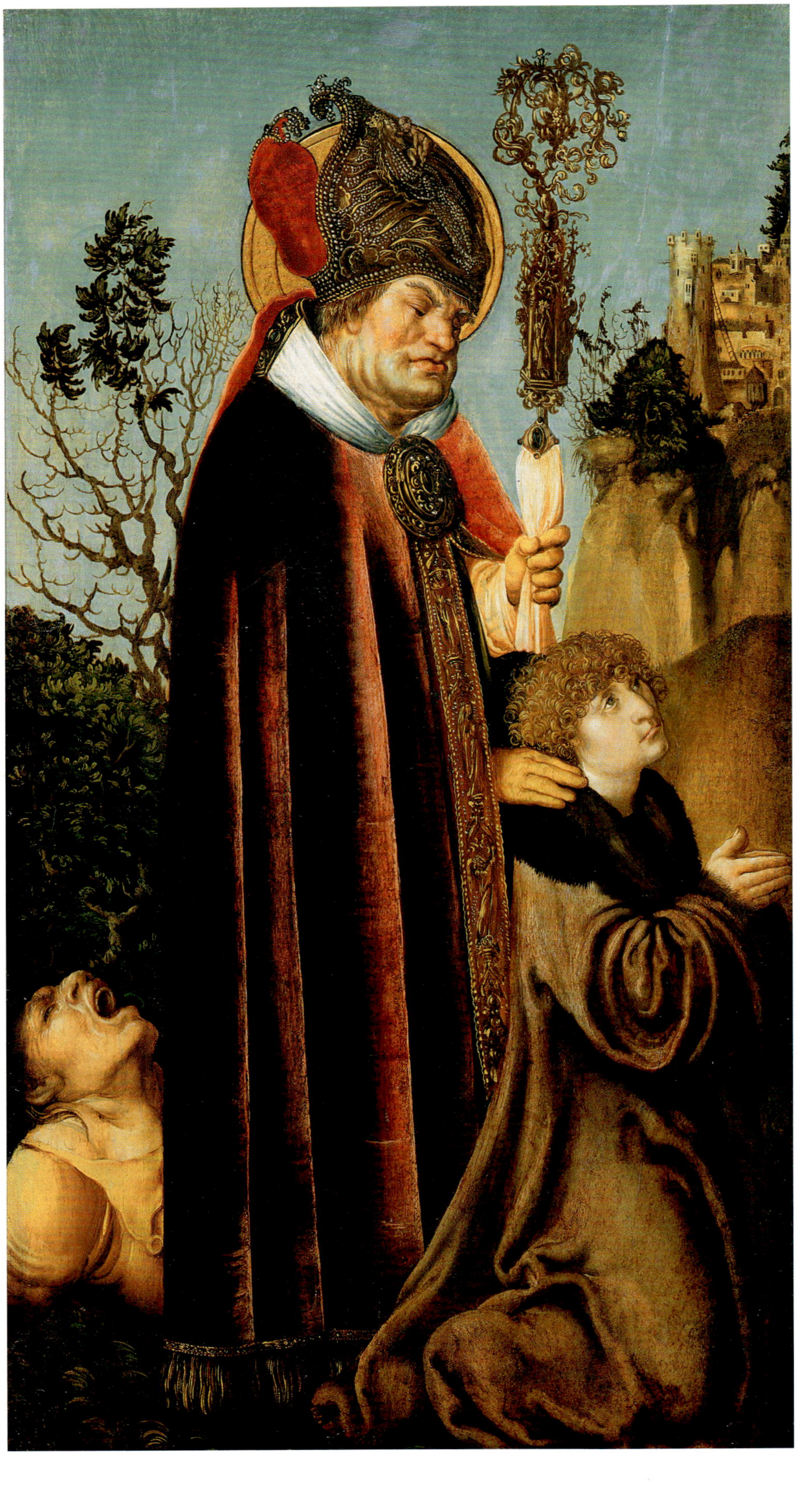

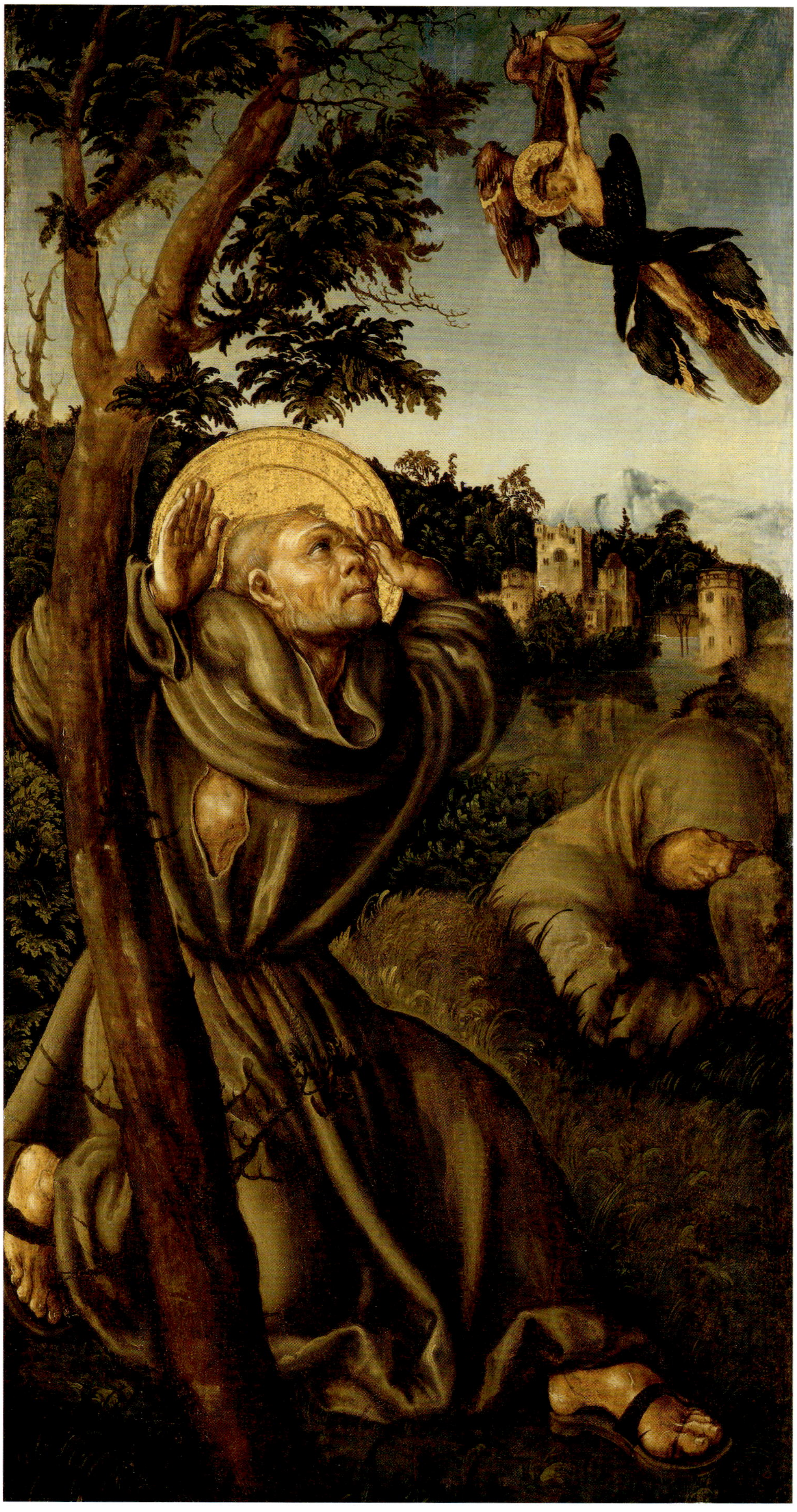

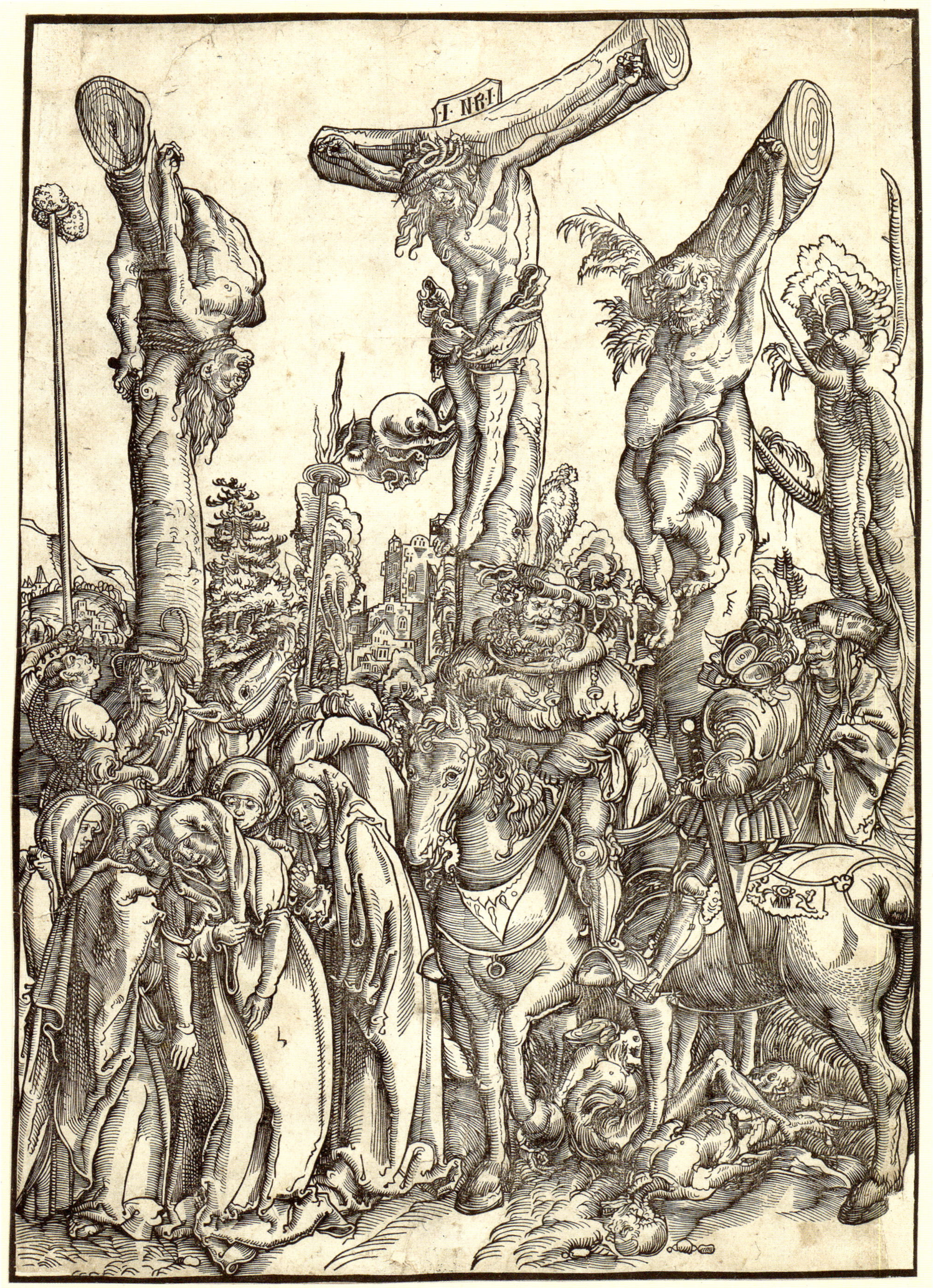
I · NRI ·

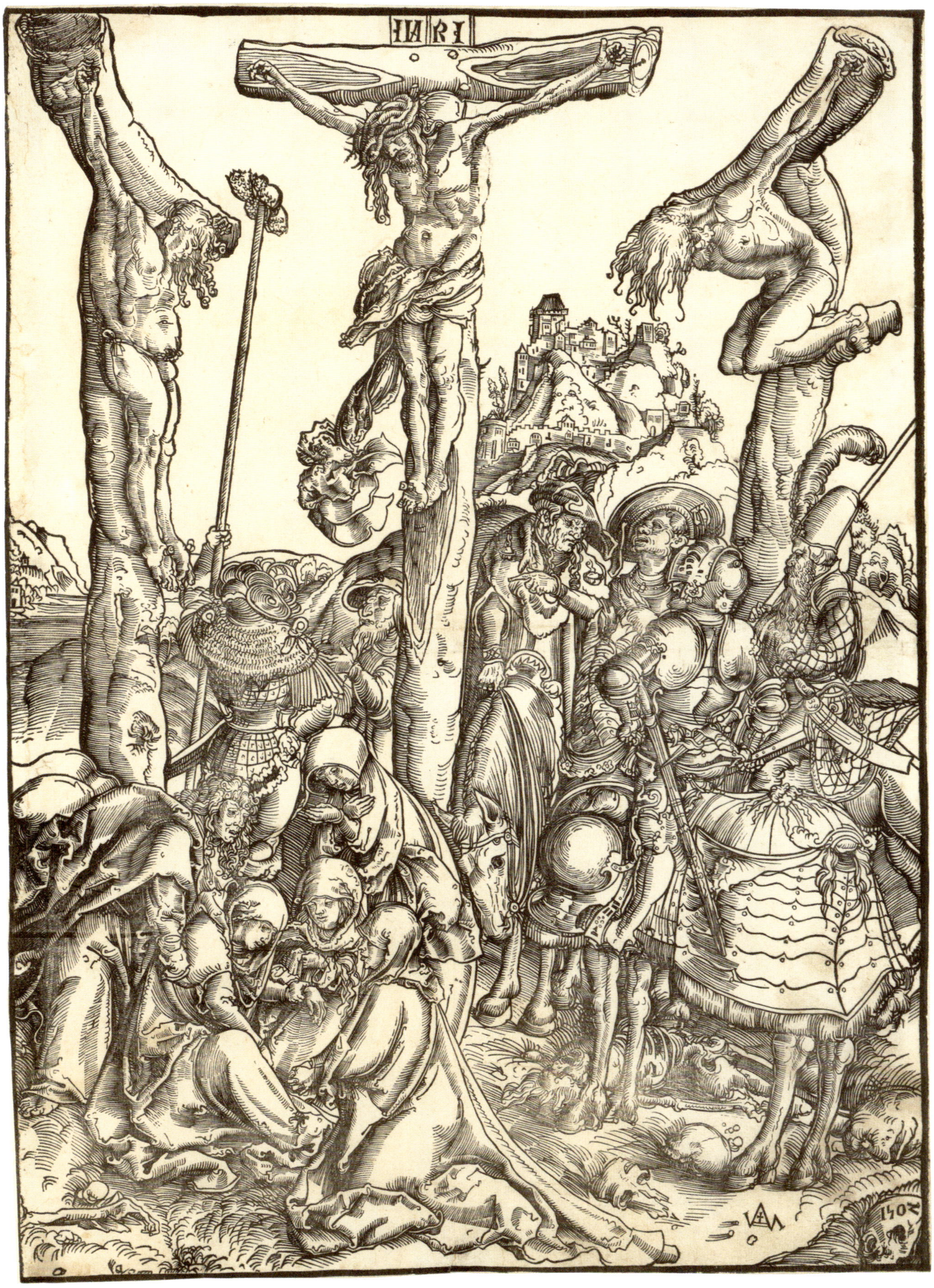

The Crucifixion, 1502 | 125

The Good Thief on the Cross | 127

The Good Thief on the Cross

Vienna, *c.* 1501–02

Black and white chalk on paper

'Verily, I say unto thee, today shalt thou be with me in paradise' (Luke 23, 43). This was Christ's promise to one of the two Thieves crucified with him. In an apocryphal legend, this Good Thief was named

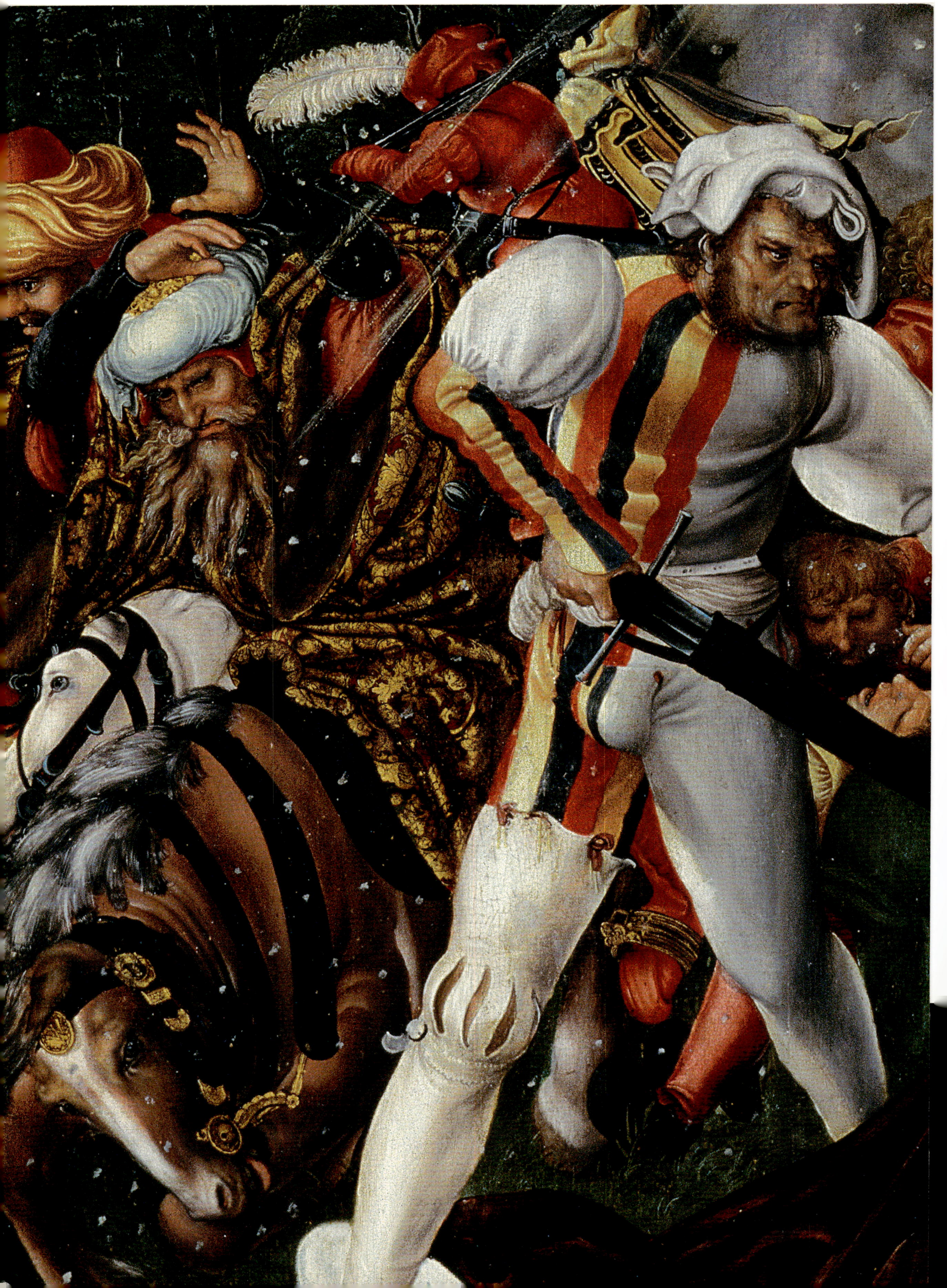

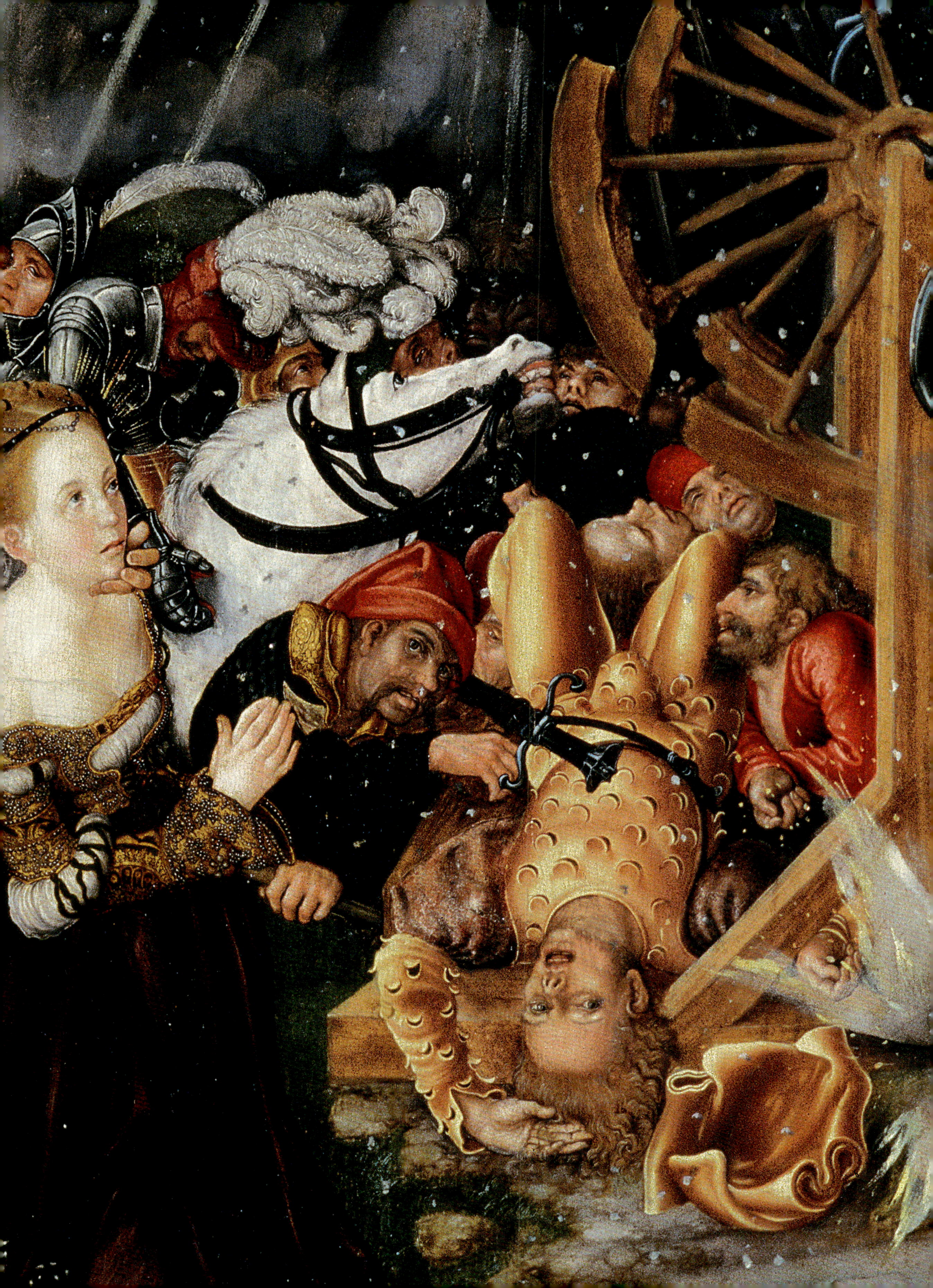

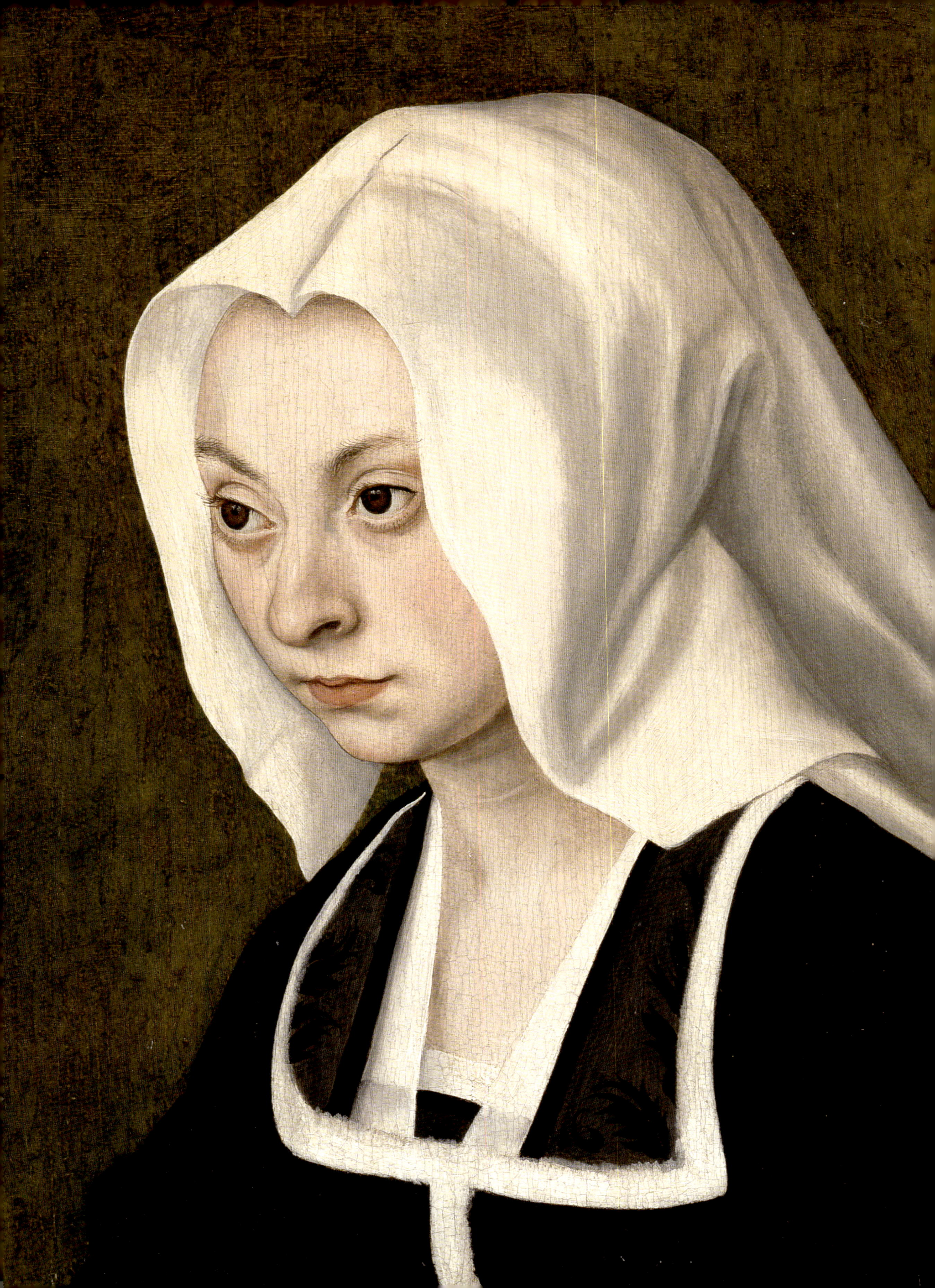

Influences: The Netherlands and Italy

In 1508 Lucas Cranach travelled in the Netherlands, and there is clear evidence of his time there. He began designing costumes in the latest Western fashion, intensified the expressiveness of his portraits, composed more clearly, and contrived more ambitious interiors comprising scenes within scenes. He must have made a close study of grisaille painting on the outer sides of the wings of altarpieces in order to be able to adopt this technique himself. These new influences are most clearly evident in the *Holy Kinship* Altarpiece of 1509 in Frankfurt. Italian art also interested him. His paintings of the Virgin and Child with the Infant John the Baptist reveal a thorough familiarity with Perugino and Raphael, obtained either by crossing the Alps himself or by seeing works which had been imported into Germany.

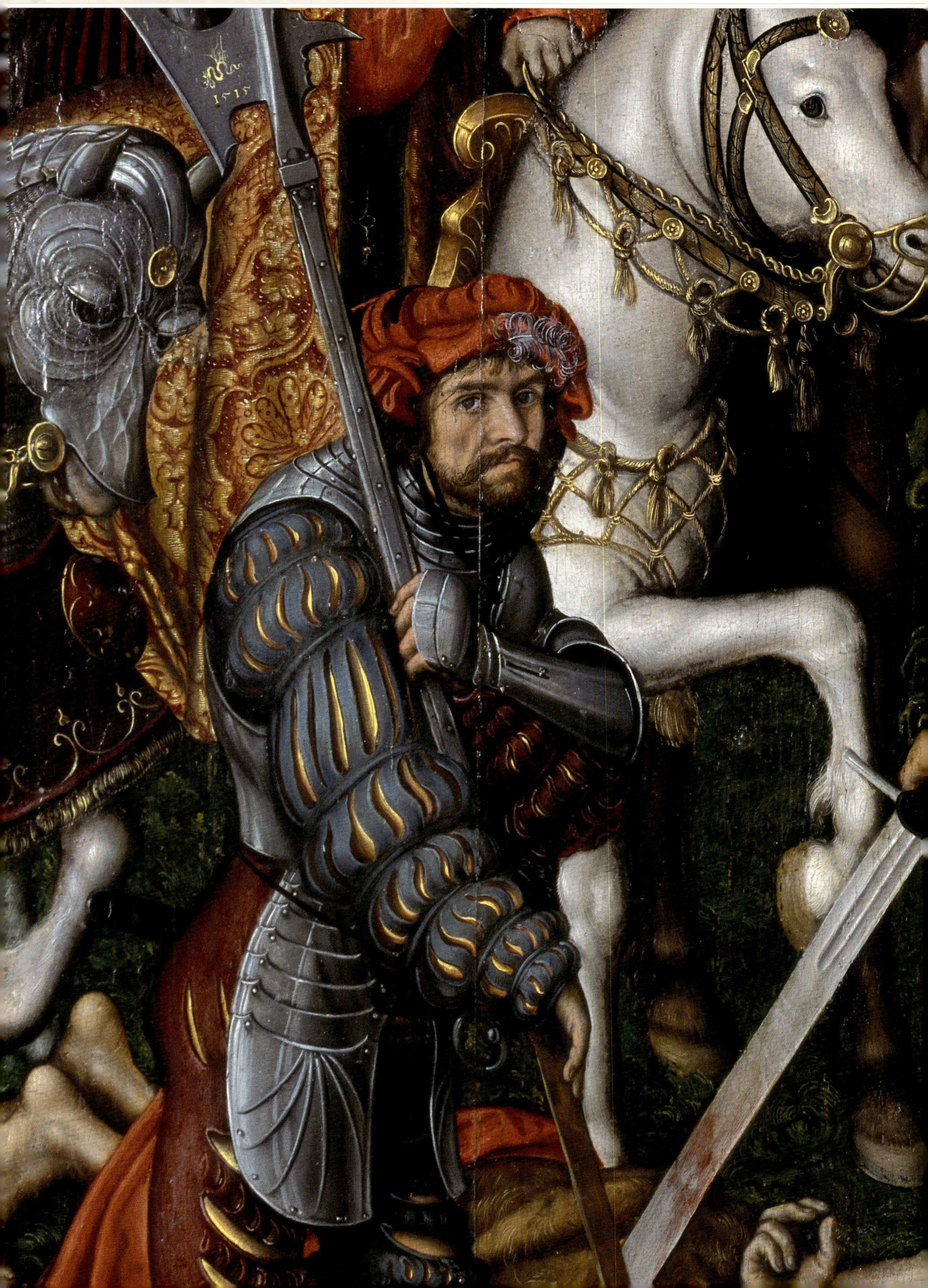
1515

The Art of Being a Court Painter

In Wittenberg in 1505 Cranach took on the wide-ranging tasks of a court painter. To the satisfaction of Elector Frederick the Wise and his brother John the Steadfast he featured both of them as donors in retables of a demanding subtlety. He worked as a court portrait painter and made contact with other lay and religious patrons. His duties also included secular projects such as decorating equipment for tournaments and hunts, recording these activities and later publicising them in woodcuts.

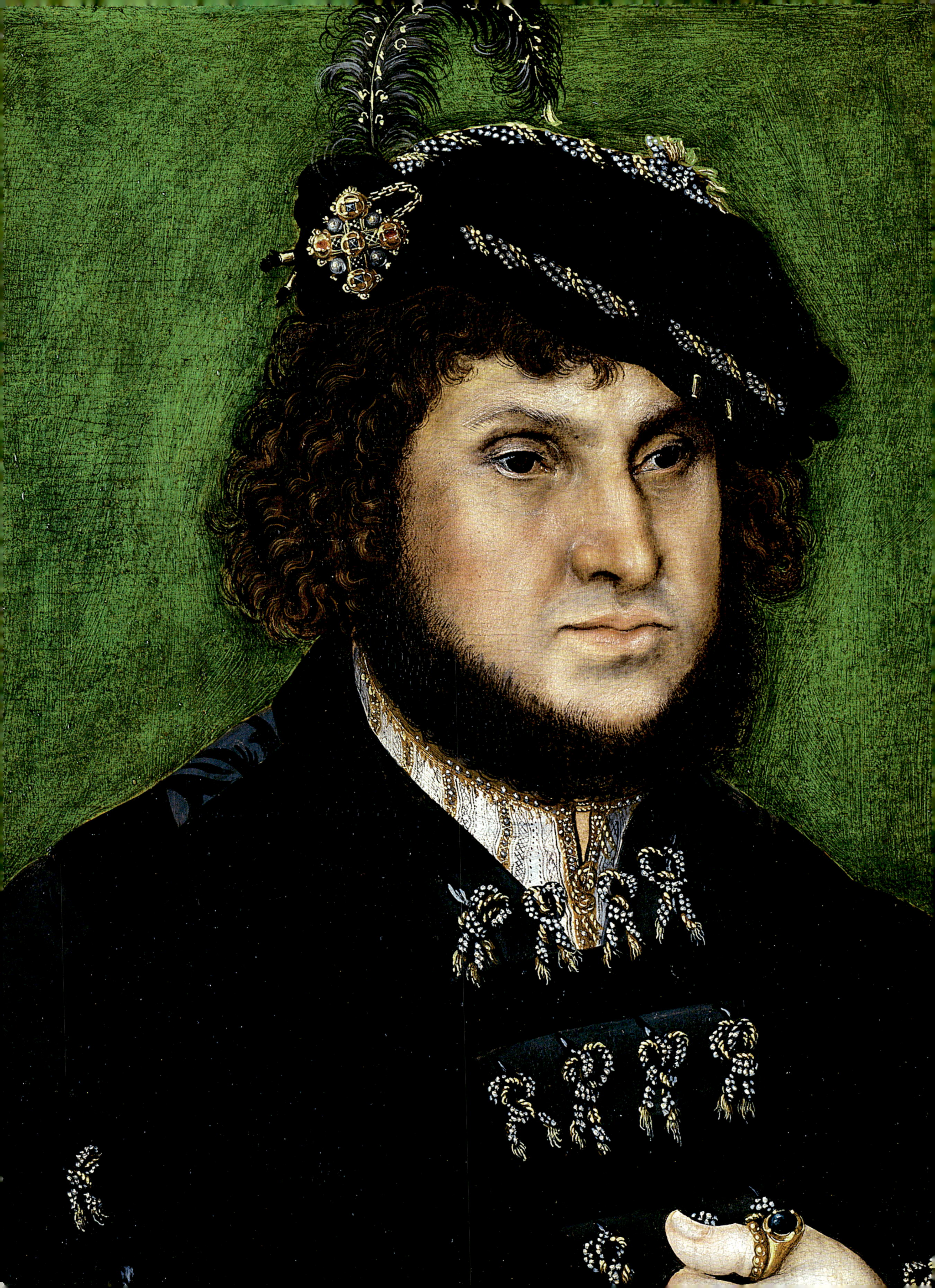

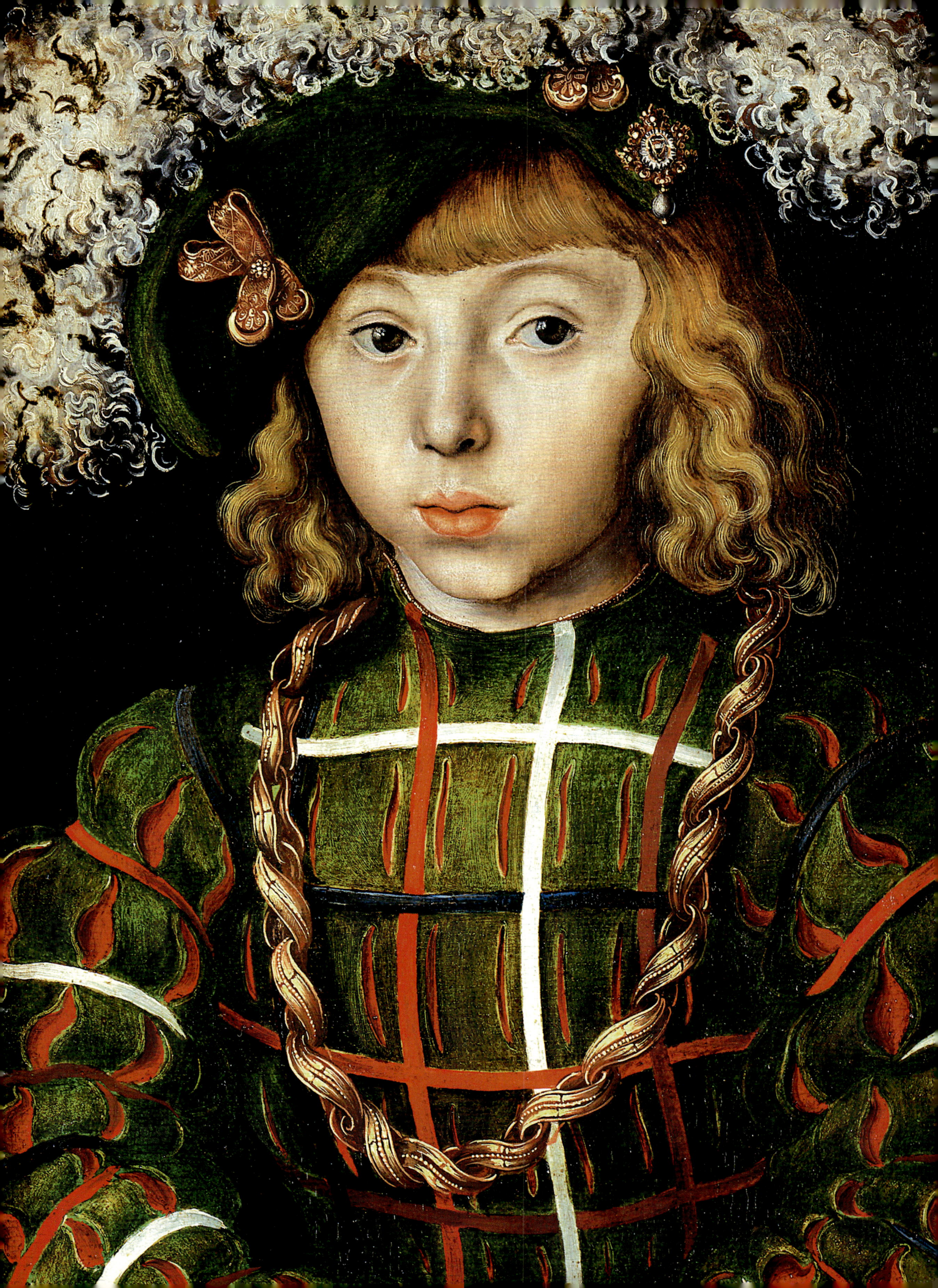

19 # Triptych with the *Holy Kinship*

Signed and dated on the column to the right of the central panel 'LVCAS CHRONVS / FACIEBAT / ANNO 1509'

Oil and tempera on limewood
121.1 x 100.4 cm (central panel)
120.6 x 45.3 cm (wings)

Städel Museum, Frankfurt, 1398

Provenance:
acquired in 1906 at the auction of the Emile Molinier Collection in Paris; apparently bought by the latter in Cadiz

Selected references:
FR 18; Schade 1974, pp. 28–30, 40, 55 f., 66; Hinz 1993, pp. 32–34; Koerner 2004, p. 73; Brinkmann/Kemperdick 2005, pp. 204–25

On the verso of the altar wings, the Madonna and Child and her mother, St Anne, announce the subject to be displayed when the wings are opened: the legendary family of Christ, derived from the idea of Anne's three marriages with Joachim, Cleophas and Salomas. In the central panel, Mary is seen with her mother tending the Infant Jesus while her husband Joseph sleeps. Mary is said to have had two similarly named stepsisters, whose marriages with Zebedee and with Alphaeus produced the Apostles John the Evangelist and James the Greater (right), and James the Less and Joseph and Simon and Jude (left and centre).

The number of children demanded by the subject inspired the artist to include delightful genre elements such as the pair of brothers in the foreground playing with their puppy and a conveyance known as a rabbit cart – a sledge made of willow shoots – and the mother on the right who combs her children's hair and searches them for fleas, while they show little enthusiasm for the process. In this way Cranach introduces a lighter note into the weightier content of his composition, which comments on a current political issue: the looming crisis between the Saxon princes and Emperor Maximilian. Elector Frederick the Wise and his brother, Duke John the Steadfast, are shown full-length in the side wings in the roles of husbands of Mary's two stepsisters (comparisons with other portraits of them confirm this (see cat. 18, 28, 29). The second and third husbands of St Anne seen in the gallery are given the features of Emperor Maximilian and one of his advisers at court. The employment of 'portraits that tell a story' – one of the earliest examples of this device – is clearly meant to suggest the loyalty of the Saxons towards the Imperial court; here they slip into the picture in the roles of sons-in-law of the two men seen above in the gallery, which is clearly marked out as Saxon territory by the frieze bearing the region's coat of arms. The message: loyalty must always be mutual.

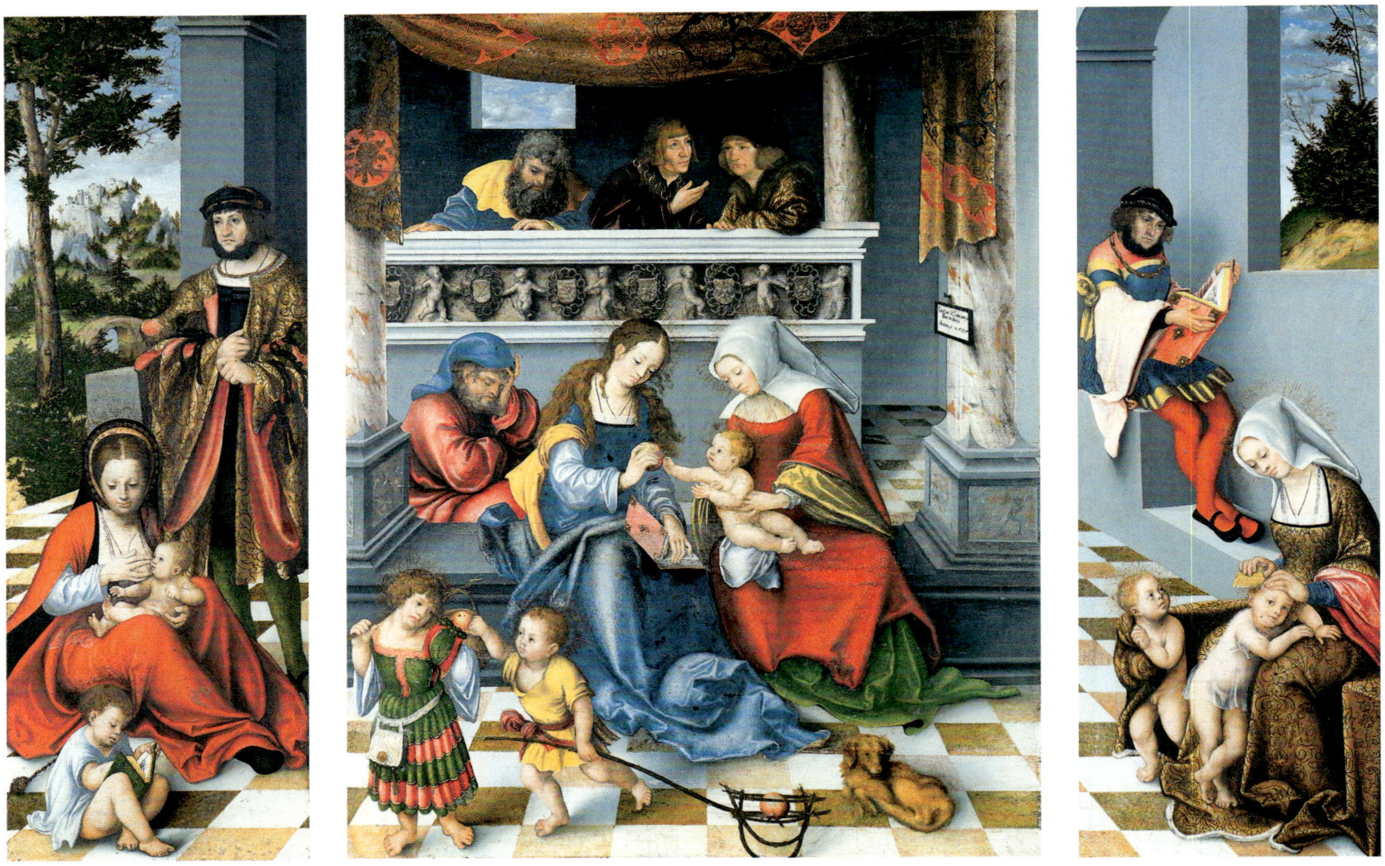

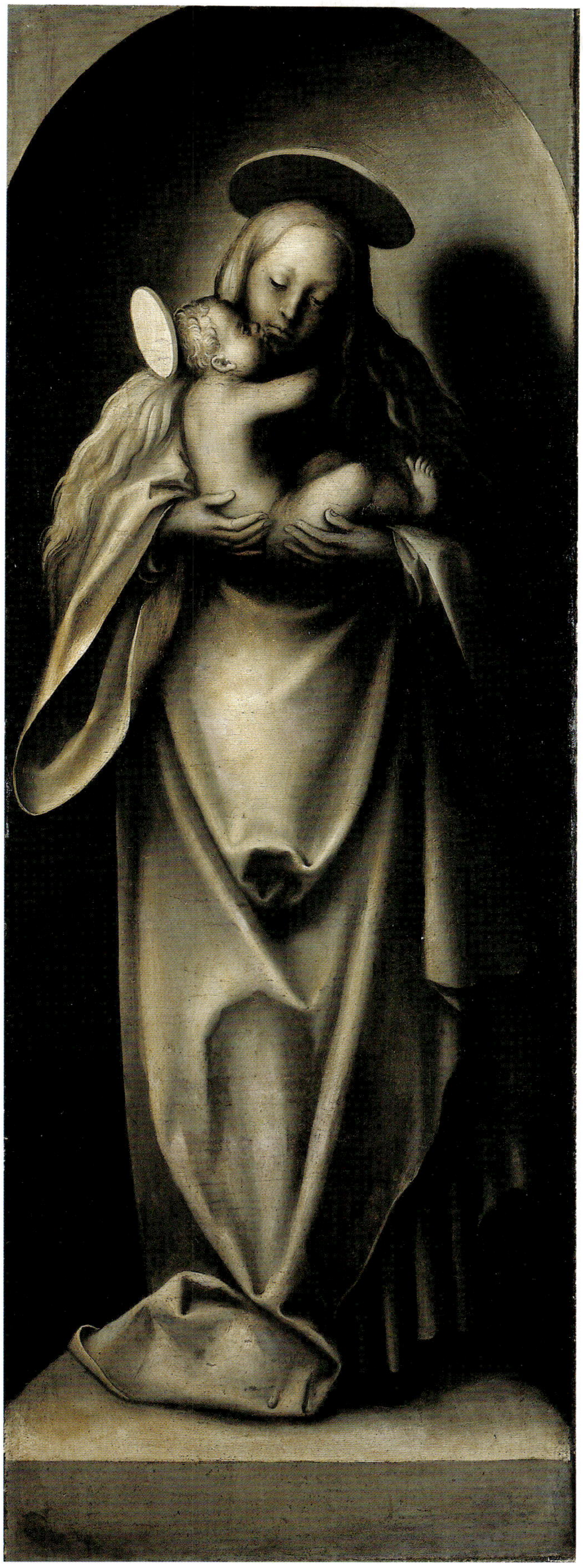

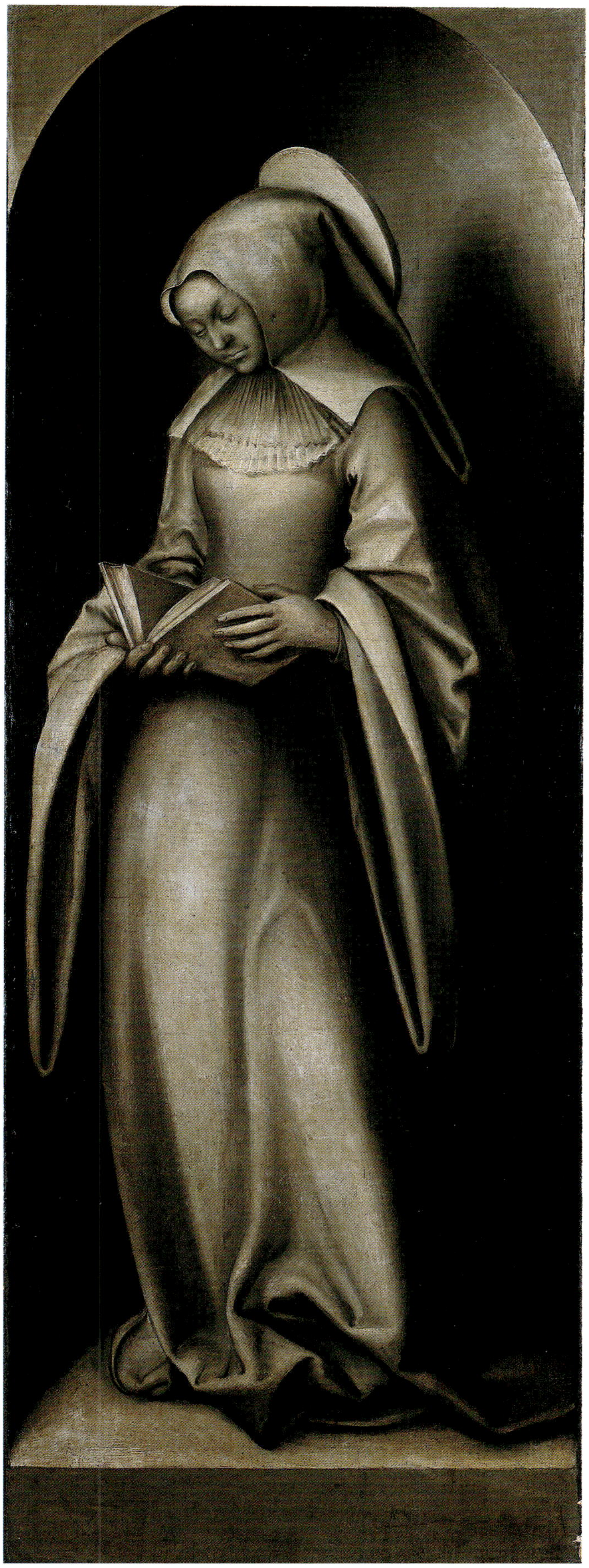

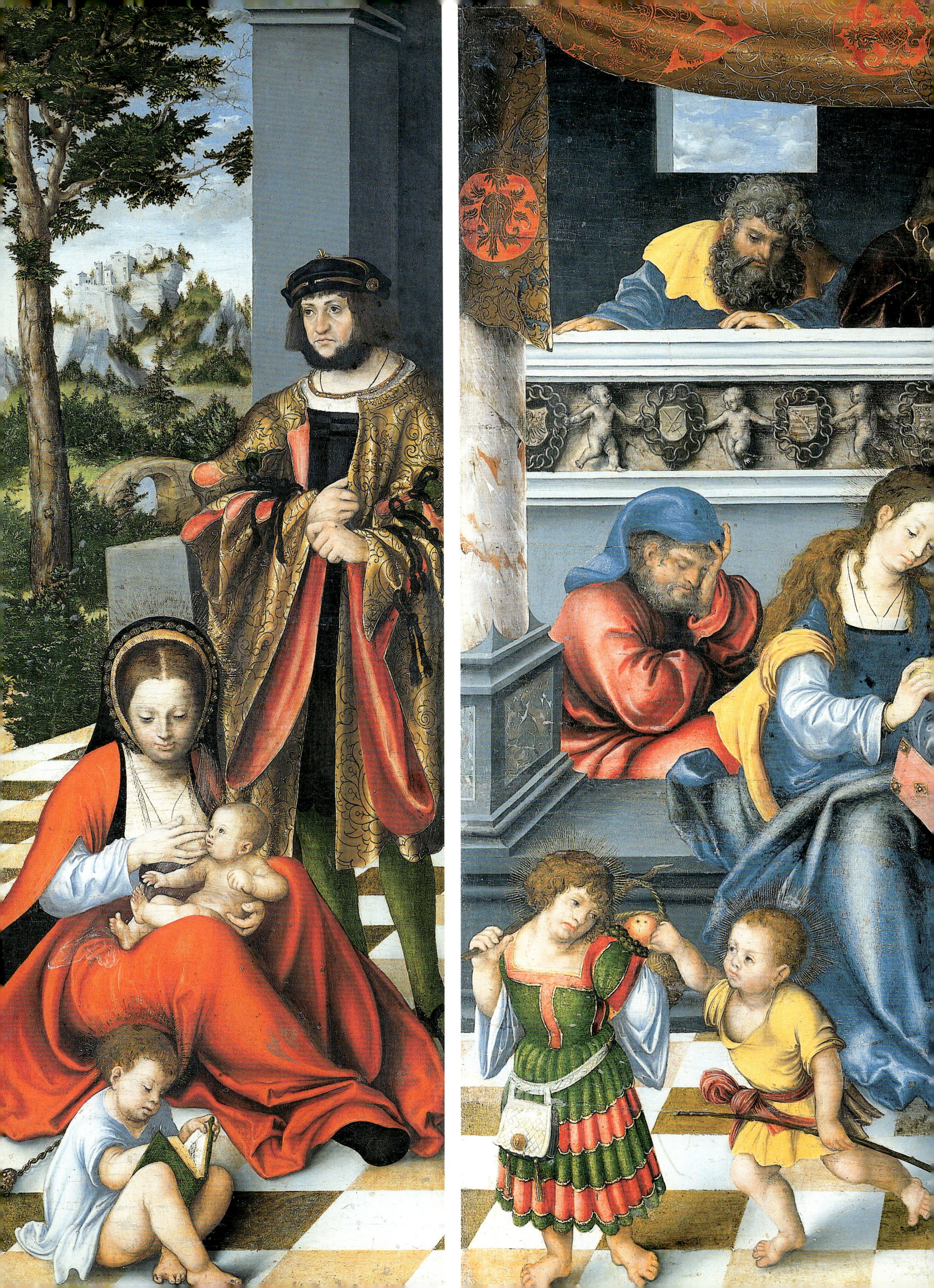

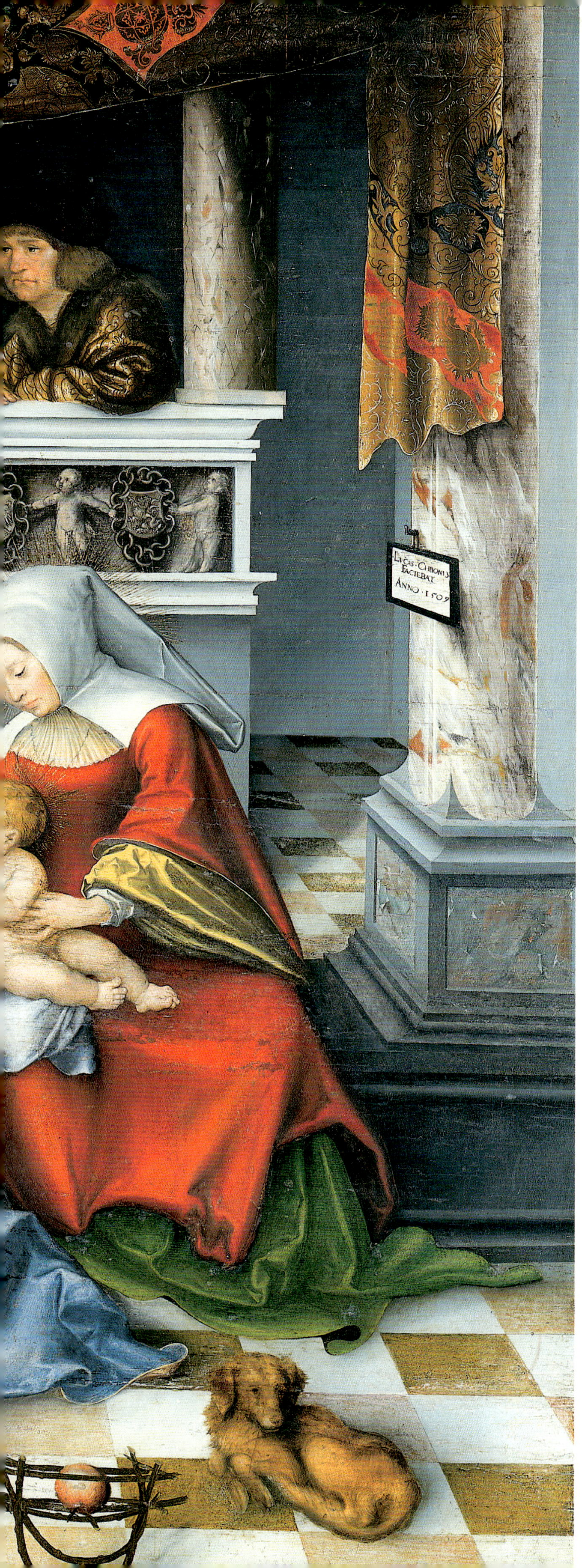
LVCAS · CHRONIS
FACIEBAT
ANNO · 1509
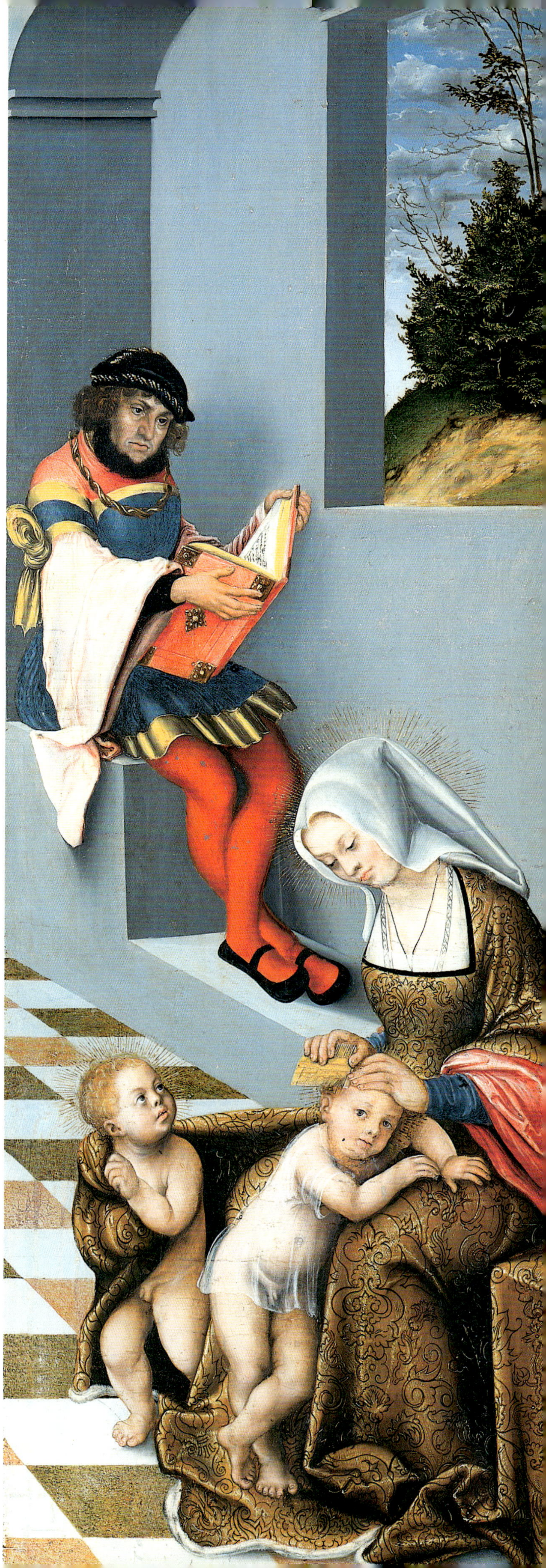

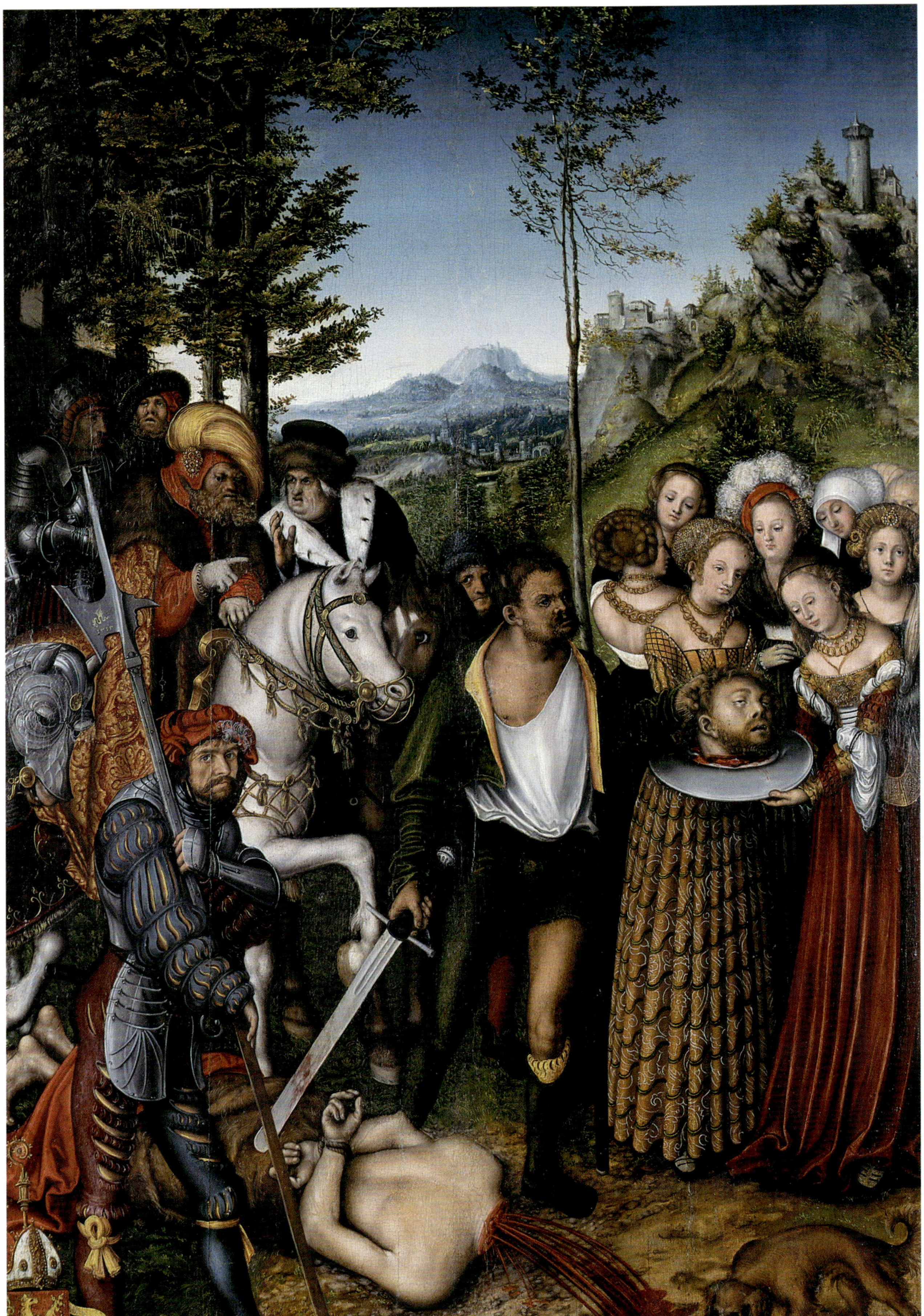

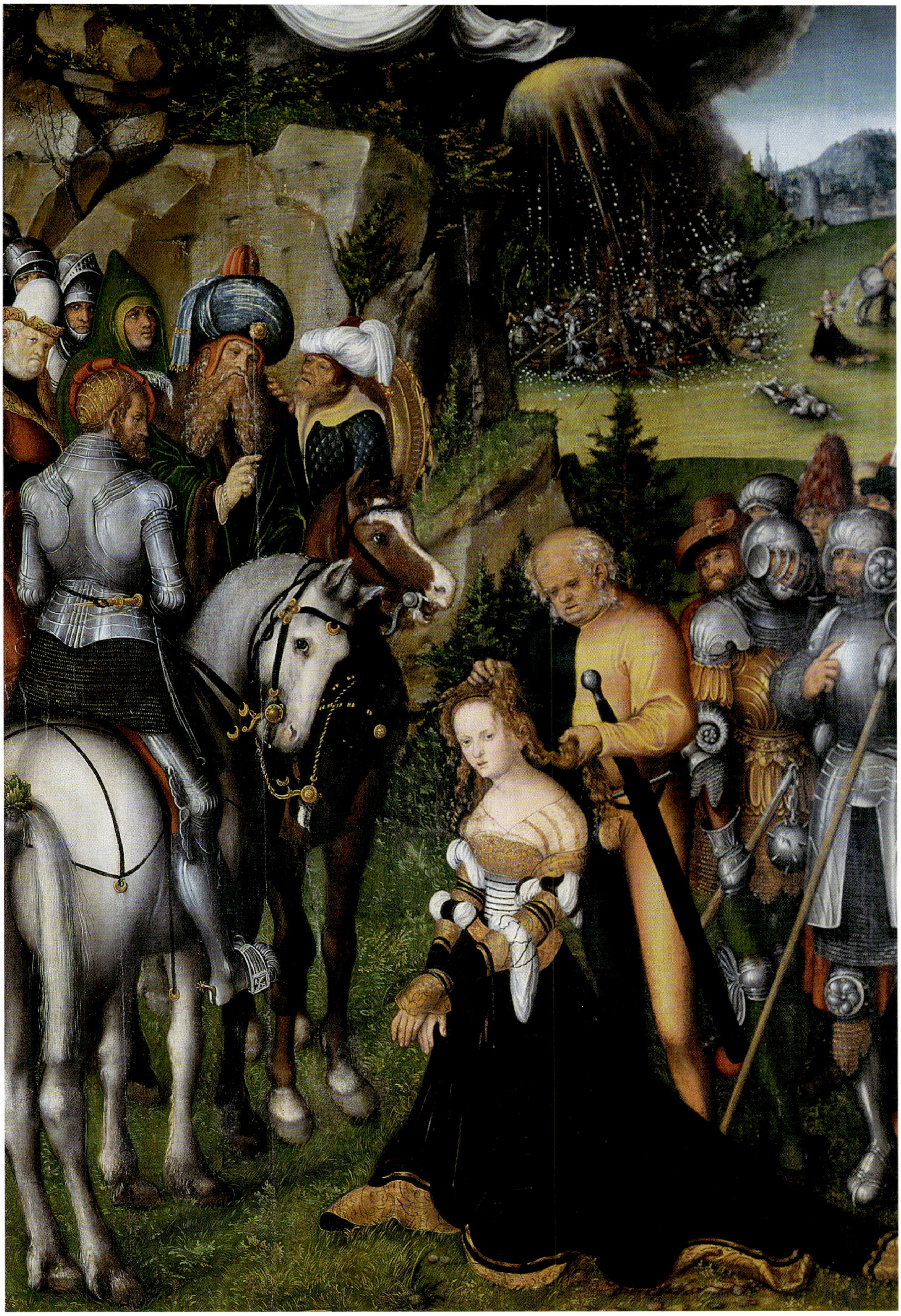

22 Christ at the Column, Adored by Saints

Wittenberg, 1515

Signed upper right in the notice on the pedestal with the serpent with upright wings facing left between the two pairs of figures bearing the date 1515

Oil and tempera on limewood
60 x 52.3 cm

Staatliche Kunstsammlungen Dresden, Gemäldegalerie Alte Meister, 1906D

Provenance:
acquired shortly after 1820

Selected references:
FR 71; Marx/Kluth/Hollberg 2004, vol. 1, no. 7; Marx/Mössinger 2005, pp. 350–8, no.25

This panel of medium size was probably intended for private devotion rather than for a public space. The format supports this idea, as does the original iconography which is so complex that it may have required theological guidance. It could be said that Cranach has created a threefold devotional picture: he begins with the pictorial formula for the Man of Sorrows, the scourged Christ whose body exhibits every trace of the Passion including death by crucifixion. Representations of the Man of Sorrows were common in the late Middle Ages because of their strong appeal to viewers. However, while the painter positions the *Man of Sorrows* in front of the column, shows him holding the instrument with which he was scourged and places the scene in a palatial setting as a reminder of the historical circumstances, he introduces at the same time moments from the theme of *Christ at Rest* – another type of devotional picture in which Christ is shown momentarily pausing to rest on the Road to Calvary. The viewer is thus similarly encouraged to share this waiting period with the Redeemer and so to take part in the Passion. Cranach allows this by directing the gaze of the Man of Sorrows towards the viewer. Christ's head and torso turn to face outwards, while at the same time his head is deliberately placed in front of the window in the room, allowing its bright light to suggest the cruciform halo and perhaps remind the viewer of the 'Light of the World' (John 8, 12). Finally, the viewer is not alone with the Messiah: John the Evangelist, the Virgin Mary and two other saints are grouped in pairs in front of the podium; a note laid on the step identifies the figure in the foreground as St Roch. His youthful beardless neighbour is probably St Sebastian, since these two generally appear together through their association with the plague. In a woodcut of 1505 (JB 320), which apparently refers directly to an outbreak of the epidemic, Cranach brings the same four saints together as they worship the heart of Jesus. Cases of the plague also appeared a decade later, and the Dresden panel may also have been created as a plea for protection against the disease. Above all, however, the four saints, each praying with their own individual gestures, served as examples for the viewer in the worship of the Lord in accordance with the contemporary doctrine of the 'Imitation of Piety', pleasing God by imitating the devout patterns of behaviour manifested in Christian iconography. In this way, by stimulating the impulse to prayer, the picture serves a further, third purpose.

The clarity of the composition is formally interesting. The right-angled podium and the way the Man of Sorrows turns towards the front, bring balance to the scene: the figures of the saints extend from the right, parallel with the podium, towards the subject of their devotion just as the viewer, emulating their example, directs his gaze forwards to the middle of the picture and then, after mounting the two steps, as it were, reaches the same level as Christ. There is little doubt that the painting was based on the title page of Albrecht Dürer's engraving of the Passion of 1509 (SMS 45), although in the latter the podium steps descend to the side. If we compare Cranach's painting with Dürer's print, it appears particularly satisfying in the tightness of its conception and the sharpness of its theological message.

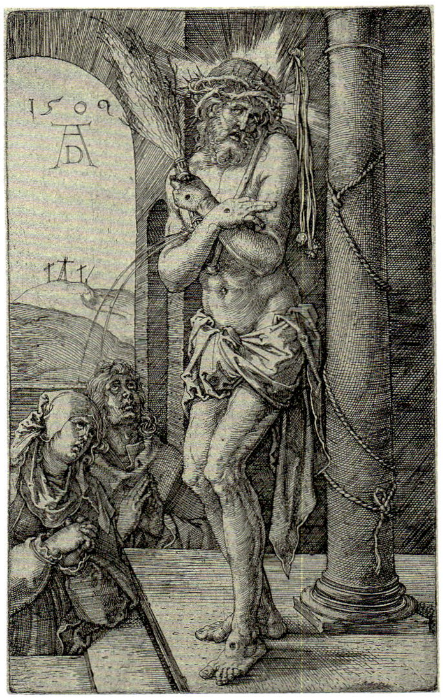

Albrecht Dürer, *Christ at the Column, Adored by the Virgin Mary and John the Evangelist*, engraving, 1509, Städel Museum, Frankfurt, Graphische Sammlung

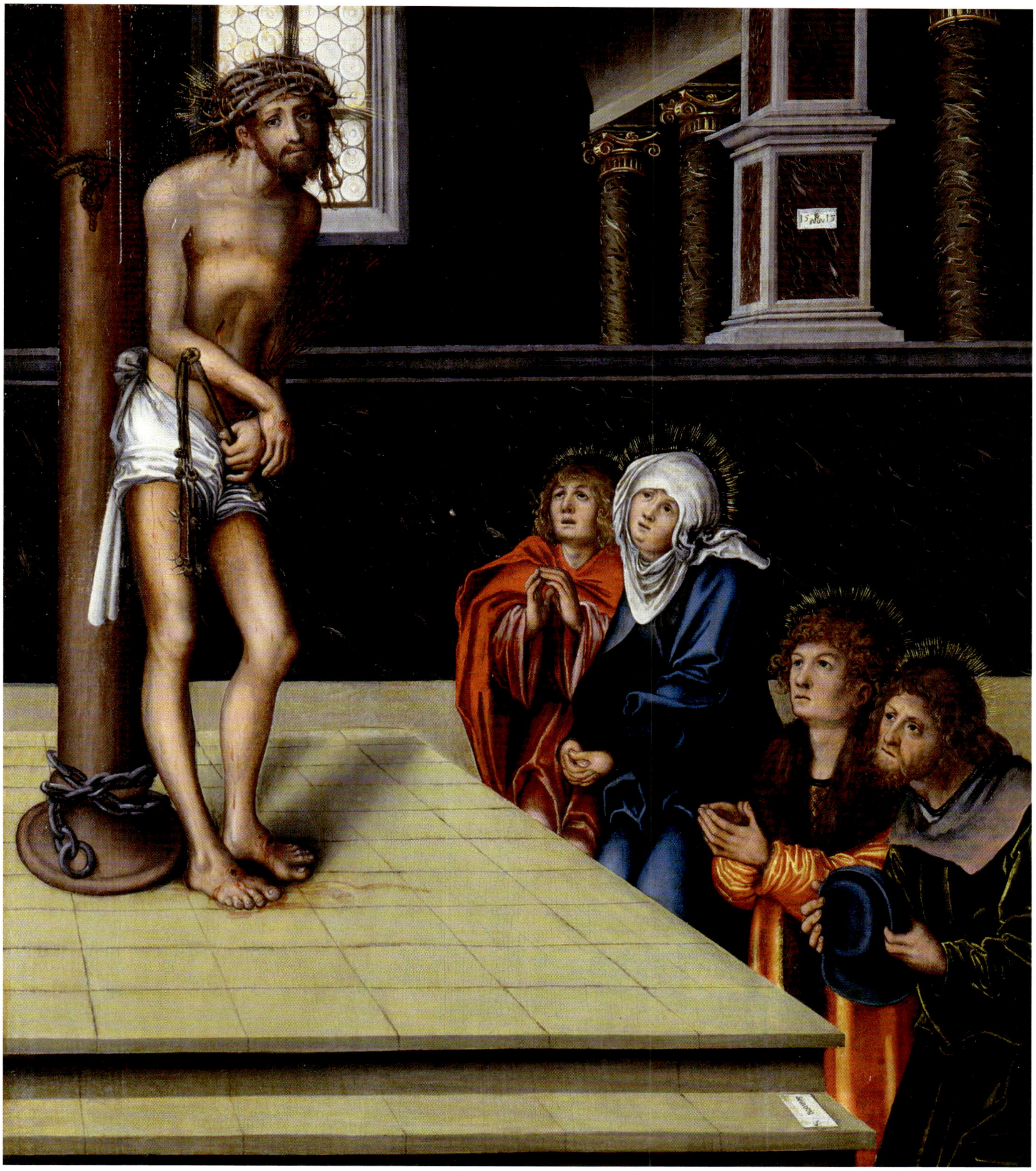

23 Small triptych with the Resurrection of Christ and SS Barbara and Catherine

Wittenberg, *c.* 1509–10

On a black background on the outer wings the arms of Hesse and Mecklenburg

Oil and tempera on wood (wood type in the original frame uncertain), 38.2 x 25.9 cm (central panel); 39 x 9.9 cm (wings)

Staatliche Museen Kassel, Gemäldegalerie Alte Meister, GK 11

Provenance:
presented in 1905 by Ludwig Mond

Selected references:
FR 17; Grimm/Erichsen/Brockhoff 1994, p. 315, no. 134; Schneckenberger-Broschek 1997, pp. 53–8; Sandner 1998, pp. 158 f., no. 17.4

In 1500, the Landgrave Wilhelm II of Hesse (1469–1509) married Anna of Mecklenburg (1485–1525); the pair of arms on the outer wings must refer to this alliance. We can thus know for whom the small altarpiece was intended, though the date of its creation remains uncertain. William contracted syphilis in 1506 and died three years later at the age of forty. These biographical facts invite speculation about the subject of the central panel, since the *Resurrection of Christ* clearly demonstrates the conquest of death by the Redeemer. In this way the work might have provided a kind of consolation, of which William and his wife must have been in need, from 1506. However, we do not know whether this message was directed specifically at the dying man or whether his wife commissioned the altarpiece in memory of her late husband; in fact, stylistic arguments support the latter theory. It is noticeable that in his treatment of the radiant sunrise on Easter Monday Cranach moved away from the composition usual in German art, placing Christ in front of the sepulchre in the rock, which had been closed with a stone slab and sealed in many places, rather than showing Christ rising from the sarcophagus. Cranach may have encountered this motif, which comes originally from Italy, during his journey to the Netherlands, perhaps in pictures by Gerard David. The idealized type of body of the risen Christ with his splendid curling hair is also somewhat Italianate, and is adapted from a copperplate engraving by Jacopo de' Barbari.

The head-dress and low-necked bodice worn by St Barbara in this small altarpiece are similar to those of Mary's stepsisters in the wings of the Frankfurt triptych of the *Holy Kinship* of 1509 (cat. 19). The artist's memory of Netherlandish costume was thus still fresh. The somewhat more painterly cloudy sky and the greater depth of the landscape on the right suggest this was painted shortly after the dated *Kinship* altar, as do the proportions given to the saints on the side wings. With their small heads and extenuated columnar bodies they correspond to an ideal shape which recurs many times in works from the years 1510–12, and even in the lifesize full-length portraits of 1514, in Dresden, of Duke Henry the Devout and his wife (Gemäldegalerie Alte Meister; FR 60, 61). If a dating of around 1509–10 is correct, then this small altarpiece of very high quality is the first of Cranach's commissions from his time in Wittenberg not to be destined for a Saxon court. In the last years of his life, Wilhelm II of Hesse was certainly in close contact with Frederick the Wise of Saxony, and it is also possible that this distinctive work could have been sent as a present from the elector to the Landgrave or to his widow.

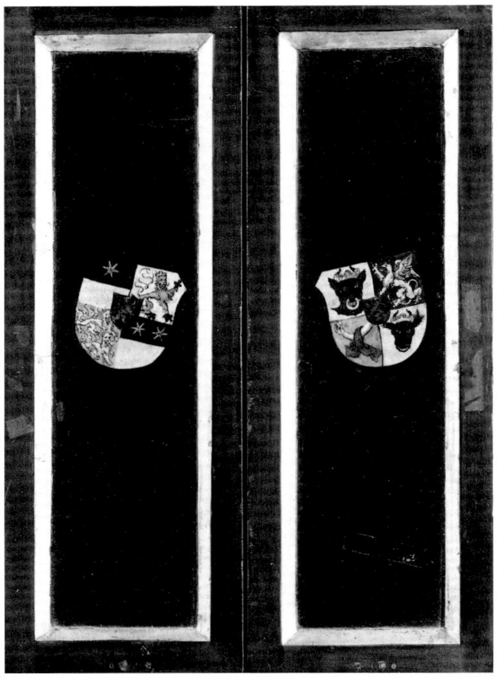

Outer sides of the wings with the arms of Landgrave Wilhelm II of Hesse and Anna of Mecklenburg

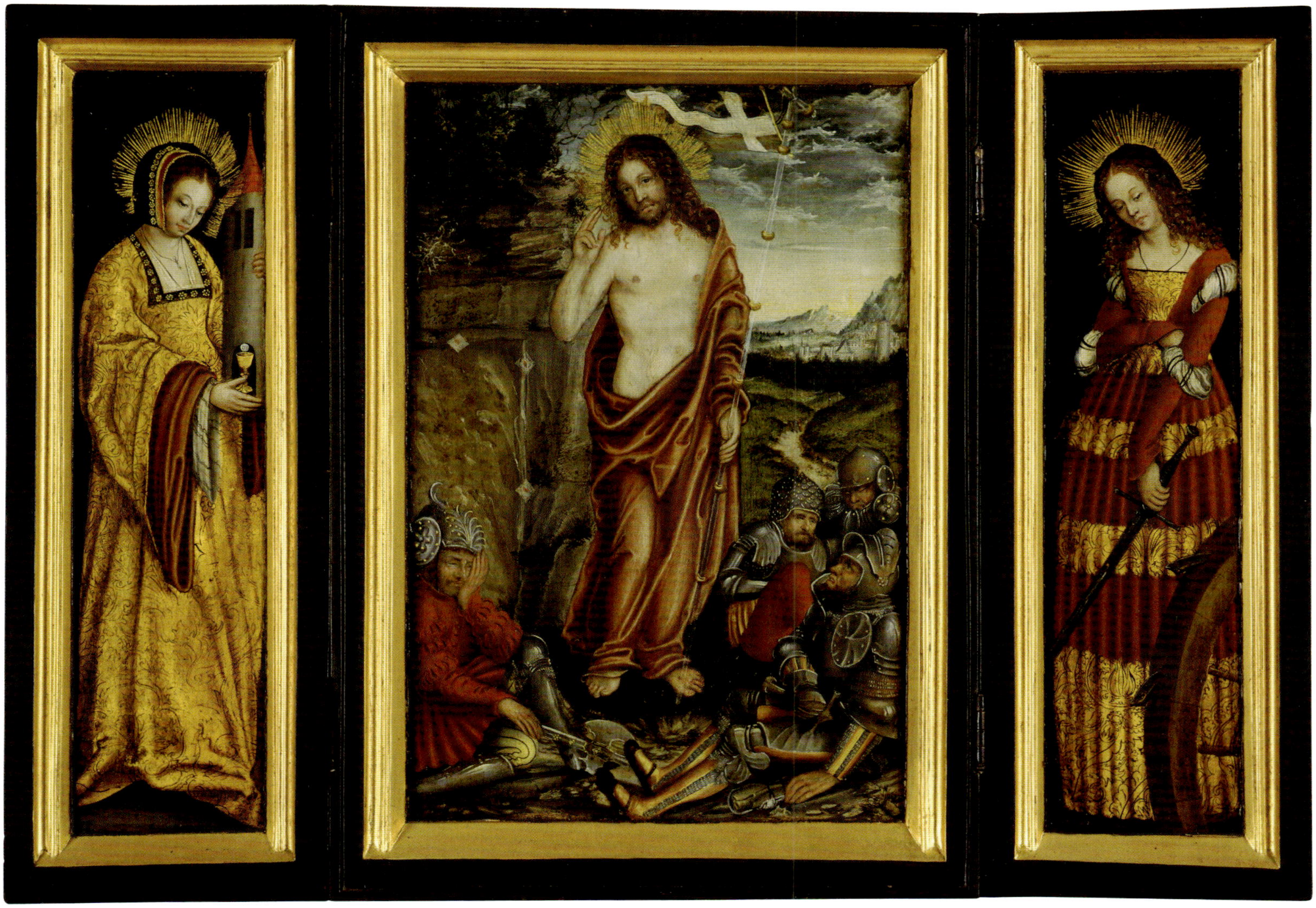

24 The Holy Family with Angels
25 The Education of the Virgin Mary

Wittenberg, *c.* 1510–12

The Holy Family with Angels

77 x 28 cm

The Education of the Virgin Mary

Oil and tempera on wood
77 x 30 cm

Anhaltische Gemäldegalerie, Dessau, 8, 9

Provenance:
since 1851 verified in the Gotischen House, Wörlitz

Selected references:
FR 35; Grimm/Erichsen/Brockhoff 1994, p. 138, no. 149; Klingen 1996, pp. 25–27

The outer sides of these wings bear the ducal arms of Saxony and Kursachsen on a grey background. The altarpiece was probably intended therefore for the private devotions of a member of the ducal family. The central panel may well have shown St Anne or the Holy Kinship; the mother of Mary was increasingly venerated in Saxony after Frederick the Wise brought back a relic of Anne from the Holy Land.

If, as seems likely, the central panel featured a large group of figures, then the lovingly portrayed and highly detailed scenes in the wings would have served as a supplement to the story. On the left, leaning against a tree, the Virgin Mary is absorbed in reading, while in the middle ground her husband is asleep against a tree stump – a motif that Cranach had already introduced in his *Holy Kinship* Altarpiece of 1509 (cat. 19), and which also appears in Dürer's early engraving of the *Madonna with the Grasshopper* (SMS 2). In front of this, a winged cherub worships the Christ Child who is covered in a thin shift. In the immediate foreground, two cherubs scoop water from the enclosed pool of a well with their hands and with a small bowl; in a beautifully observed moment, the cherub on the left is reflected in the water which he disturbs as he dips in his hand. Above, four cherubs glide towards the big tree, on which a fifth has already alighted and goes off to rob a bird's nest.

In the right-hand wing, the tree offers a perch to a cherub with bagpipes, while a second one flies down with outstretched arms. On the ground, Joachim accepts some fruit from a third cherub, and a fourth is curious about the yarn that St Anne is winding. Below on the left, Mary practises on the loom, with childish enthusiasm; for according to the apocryphal Protevangelium of James she was chosen by the priests together with other virgins to make a new curtain for the Temple. She wears the same red dress with the black edging as her grown-up self in the other panel. The two Dessau wings mark a high point in the playfulness of Cranach's pictorial invention, perhaps inspired by Dürer's similar narrative style in the woodcuts of his *Life of Mary* that appeared in 1511. The merry activities of the cherubs take over the stage, while the subject of Mary at the loom, one with a longer iconographic tradition, is forced almost into a corner.

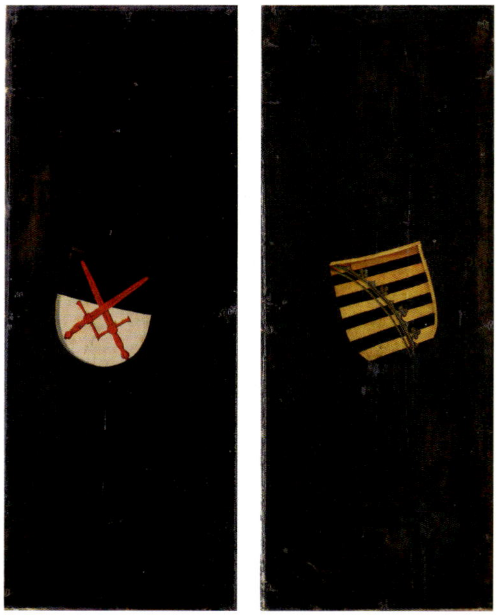

Reverse of the panels

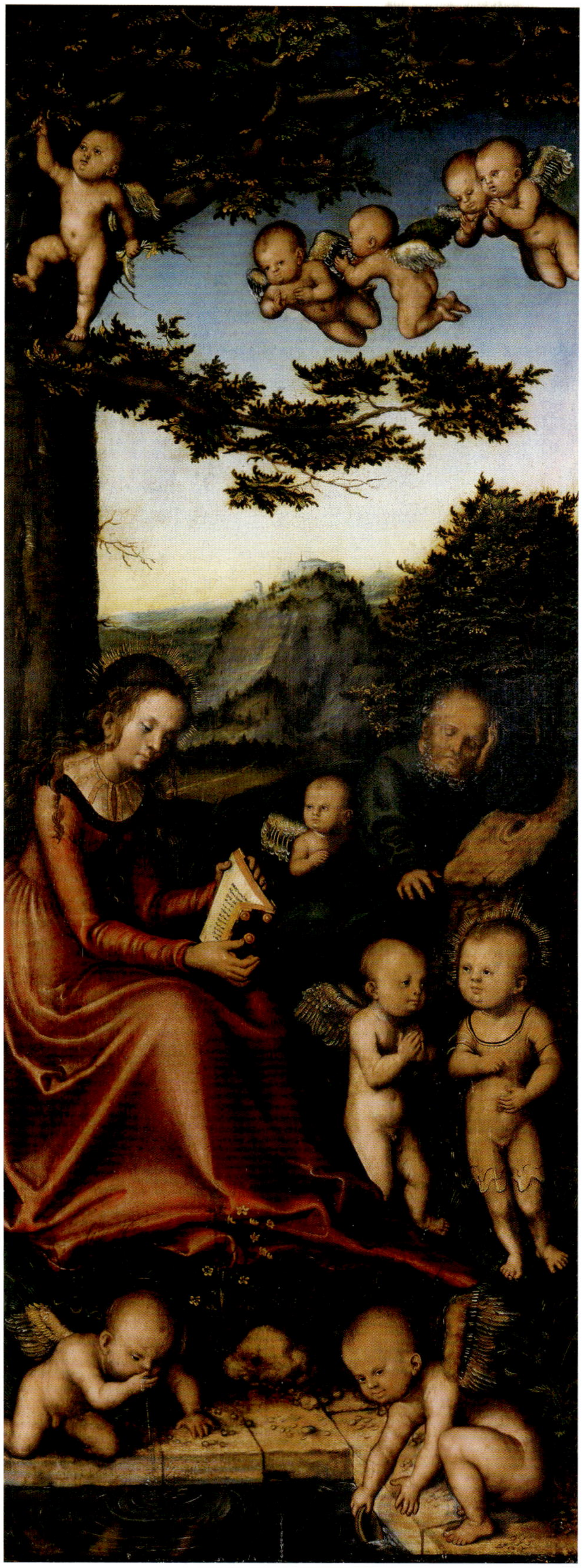

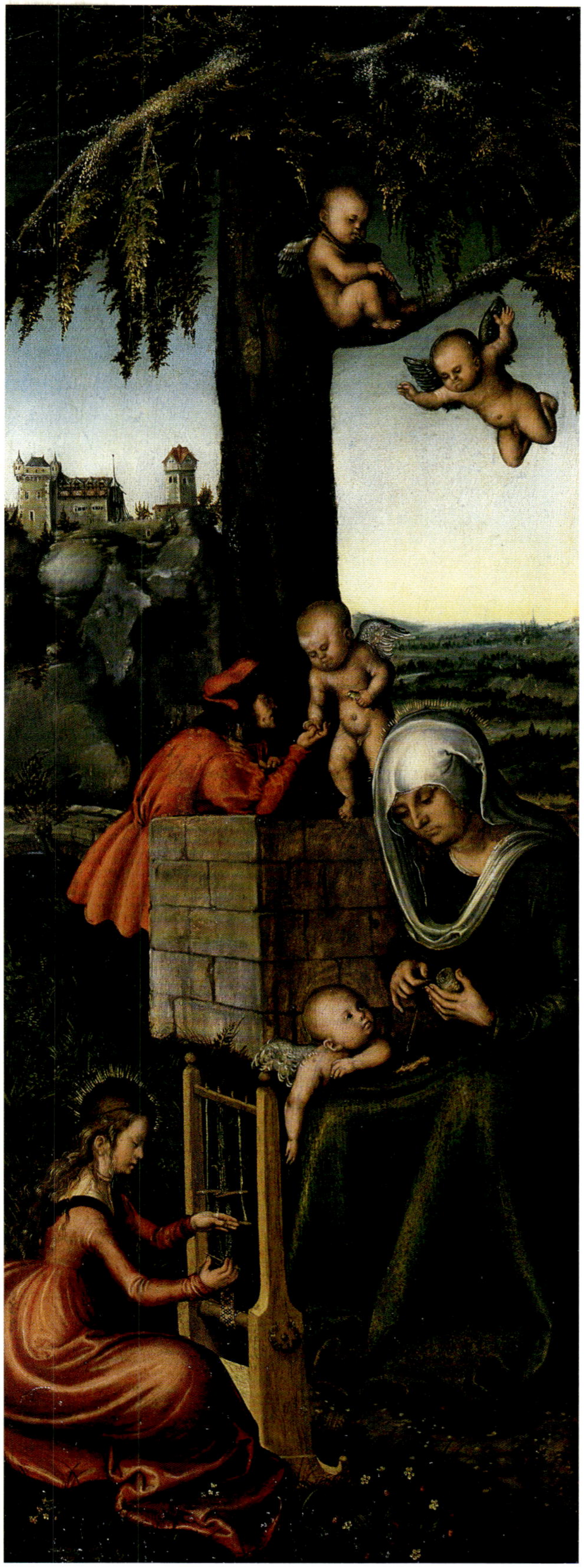

27 # The Mystic Marriage of St Catherine Accompanied by the Holy Virgins

Wittenberg, *c.* 1516–18

Signed bottom left on the wheel with the serpent with upright wings facing left

Oil and tempera on limewood
67.5 x 47.3 cm

Szépmüvészeti Muzéum, Budapest, 133

Provenance:
from the Imperial collections in Vienna: until 1848 in the Chamber Presidium

Selected references:
FR 86; Garas 1987, p. 81, no. 75; Ember/Takács 2003, pp. 29 f.

In devotional paintings such as this it was customary in the late Middle Ages to merge two themes stemming from the mystical philosophy of the fourteenth century. One of these prompted an increase in the hierarchically structured veneration of the saints by placing the emphasis on four capital virgins, the most important ones being Margaret, Barbara, Catherine and Dorothea (or sometimes just three, excluding the last-named), each of whom is indicated by her attribute: the dragon, the tower, the sword and a small basket filled with flowers. These female saints were now represented, in the style of courtly society, as the entourage of the Virgin Mary – gathered casually around her like ladies of the court out together. In German and Netherlandish painting this led to the widely adopted pictorial formula of the *Virgo inter virgines*, with the Virgin Mary as the central figure accompanied by similarly virginal female saints.

In another development, one of the four capital virgins acquired increasingly striking features and more and more popularity as her legend was constantly elaborated and embellished. According to accounts going back to the late fourteenth century, St Catherine of Alexandria, the beautiful and highly intelligent daughter of a king, would accept only a husband who was her equal in every respect, and for that reason she rejected her suitors. She then learned from a hermit that only Christ fulfilled these criteria, but in her first vision he refused her. Not until she had been baptised did he appear before her in a second vision and place a ring on her finger as a symbol of marriage. Soon afterwards, the mystic bride was martyred (cf. cats 11, 21).

The task of painting a devotional picture of the *Virgo inter virgines* type as a way of celebrating the motif of the *Mystic Marriage of St Catherine* meant that the artist had to merge two different groupings of figures, one of which was static and symmetrical , the other dynamic, and at an angle to the picture plane. To judge by his various treatments of the theme, it seems that Cranach was aware of the problem. In the panel in Dessau dated 1516 (Anhaltische Gemäldegalerie; FR 85) he resolved it with a relief-like composition featuring two rows of figures; Mary changing places with Dorothea and moving to the left side of the picture. In the painting in Budapest, the Virgin Mary is placed in the centre; the arrangement of the figures looks more evenly balanced, but at the same time the two main figures of Mary and Catherine are made more prominent and even slightly larger than the others. The background scene is both dynamic and distinctly divided. The cloth of honour which slopes downwards and is held by a row of angelic cherubs advancing from the left like a guard of honour, appears only to the side of St Catherine. The conifer behind Dorothea marks the change to a landscape view of a sloping hillside, at the base of which stands the judiciously placed tower of St Barbara. For all the artifice employed in this composition, its overall harmony and elegance are undeniable.

Both versions contain distinct Eucharistic references. The chalice in the window of the tower is one of the attributes of St Barbara, who is credited with receiving a communion of angels which was thus associated with the giving of the last sacrament. It is unusual, however, for the saint to hold grapes in a cloth, as she does in the Dessau panel, and to look out at the viewer. In the Budapest version the Virgin Mary takes over this role. She holds the grapes in her left hand, while the Christ Child touches them, and is the only figure to face the viewer.

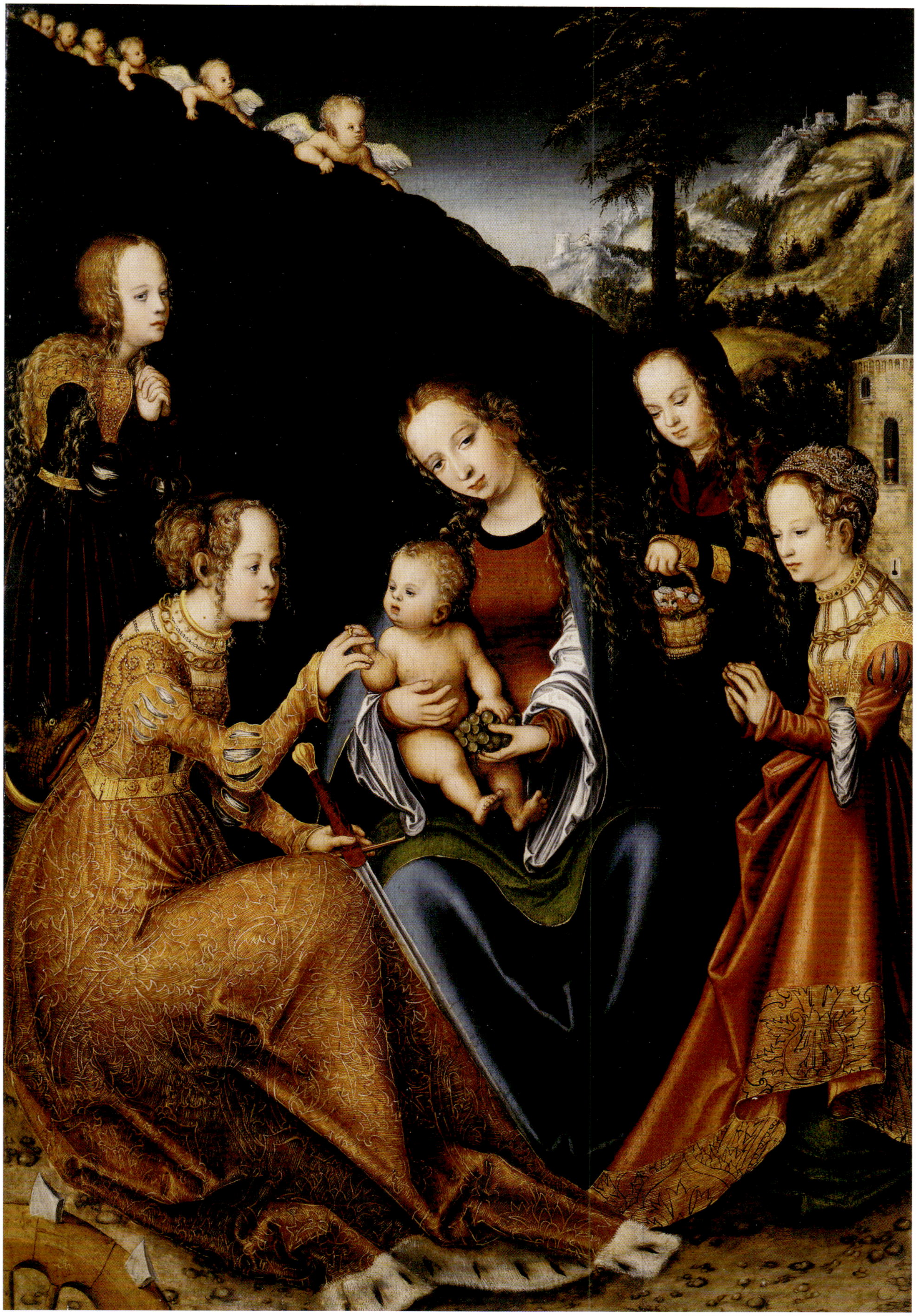

30 Posthumous Portrait of Frederick the Wise in Old Age

Wittenberg, 1527

Dated in the background at shoulder height on the left edge of the picture; beneath this the serpent with upright wings facing right

Oil and tempera on red beechwood
40 x 23 cm

Hessisches Landesmuseum
Darmstadt, GK 72

Provenance:
possibly from the estate of the old landgraviate; certainly in the museum since 1843

(Frankfurt only)

Selected references:
FR 179 ; Koepplin/Falk 1974/76, vol. 1, p. 298, no. 188; Beeh 1990, pp. 244 f., no. 71

Frederick III, Elector of Saxony (1463–1525), was honoured by later historians with the epithet 'the Wise', in recognition of his resolute, persistent and diplomatic political style. Frederick felt himself primarily committed to the interests of his own region, regarding military adventures with suspicion. The sharing of the regency with his younger brother John the Steadfast, the founding of the very successful University of Wittenberg in 1502, the refusal of the imperial crown in 1519 and the secret rescue and concealment of Luther in the Wartburg after the edict against him in 1521 are examples of Frederick's political skill. His tolerance of the Reformation is even more remarkable: he did not apparently share Luther's theological views and personally remained true to the worship of the Virgin Mary and the veneration of relics. Only on his deathbed did he accept the Protestant communion.

After Frederick's death his brother John commissioned Lucas Cranach to paint numerous portraits of the deceased, among which the Darmstadt picture is one of the best. It refers back to a portrait which must have been completed by 1522 at the latest; this is the year marked on a version of the same composition which was formerly in Gotha (FR 151) and shows the subject with characteristic beret and moustache. Until around 1533 this type was constantly reworked showing varying amounts of the bust and slightly different positions for the hands. The late Elector appears with grey hair in his posthumous portraits; although in the versions of 1522 and 1525 (formerly in Schloss Sibyllenort; FR 179) the hair of his head and beard is still dark, a small circular picture in Karlsruhe (Staatliche Kunsthalle; FR 179E), which also dates from the year of his death, and the Darmstadt panel completed two years later show him completely grey. Behind this there may have been some propagandist move to stress the dignity and wisdom of old age.

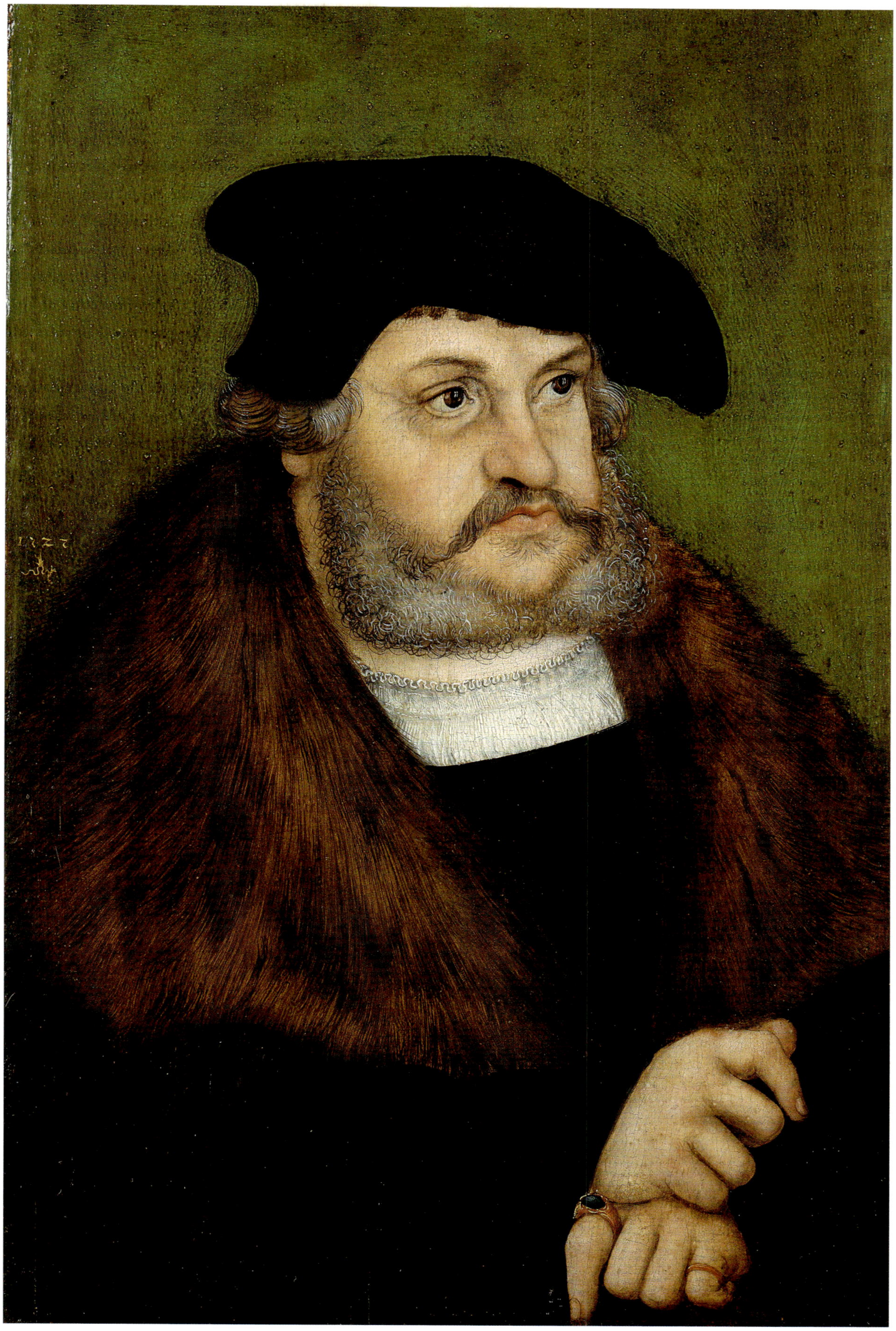

The Tournament with Lances

Wittenberg, 1509

Signed on the lower edge left of centre with the letters L and C and the year below

Woodcut, 30.5 x 42.3 cm

Städel Museum, Frankfurt, Graphische Sammlung, 31247

JB 392

The Tournament with Swords

Wittenberg, 1509

Signed on the bottom edge right of centre with the letters L and C and the year beneath

Woodcut, 29.8 x 42.2 cm

Kunstmuseum Basel, Kupferstichkabinett, Amerbach-Kabinett, Aus K.20.57

(London only, not illustrated)

Selected references:
Maedebach/Gebhardt 1972, pp. 42 f., nos 87–90; Koepplin/Falk 1974/6, vol. 1, pp. 227–9, nos 108–12; Andersson/Talbot 1983, p. 229, no. 124, pp. 320 f., no. 141 f. (Ursula Timan); Schütt/Stuffmann/Woelk p. 35, no. 20

On 15 and 16 October 1508, Frederick the Wise Elector of Saxony held another tournament in Wittenberg at which because of a bereavement his brother John the Steadfast had to represent him. The court poet Georg Sibutus described it in a long poem and Cranach commemorated the event in a series of three woodcuts published in 1509. The most original of these is the *Tournament with the Samson Tapestry*, featuring a picture of a tapestry or a cloth such as Cranach carried out by the dozen for the Saxony court. The tapestry in the woodcut bears the arms of the Electorate of Saxony and shows the Old Testament hero fighting with lions – it could equally be Hercules – and hangs over the parapet of the balcony where the Saxony court is seated. Frederick the Wise's entourage looks down with fascination at events in the sand-covered square. In the middle a joust has just finished in which the horse of the knight on the left has stumbled to its knees and in the foreground the rider's lance has fallen on the ground, whereupon the opposing knight has thrown down his lance. On both sides pairs of knights take up their positions for the next joust. In the background to the left a mounted contest with blunt tournament swords is being held in which the knights are supported by their squires armed with clubs.

The lively picture with its mass of fast-moving figures frozen in time consciously evokes the impression of a live report on the historic tournament of the year 1508. However, it is typical of this artist of early modern times that he placed more faith in a model than in the live scene. As Ursula Timann has proved, the apparently spontaneous eyewitness accounts of motifs such as the lance which is still in the air as it falls to the ground and the squire bending down towards the lance in the foreground come from a somewhat earlier engraving by the Master MZ (Matthäus Zasinger). Unlike the joust in the Samson tournament, in which two single opponents face each other, the second sheet from 1509 shows a tourney in which two knights chosen by lots compete against two others. When the musicians in front of the wall above left sound their trumpets, the contestants attack each other with their lances, fighting until one side has no rider capable of fighting left in the saddle. In the second part of the tourney they fight each other on horseback with swords. This is the scene in the third woodcut from Cranach's tournament series of 1509, where the broken weapons from the previous contest still lie on the ground. It follows closely a tapestry in the Musée des Beaux-Arts in Valenciennes which bears the arms of the Electorate of Saxony and which probably belonged to Frederick the Wise.

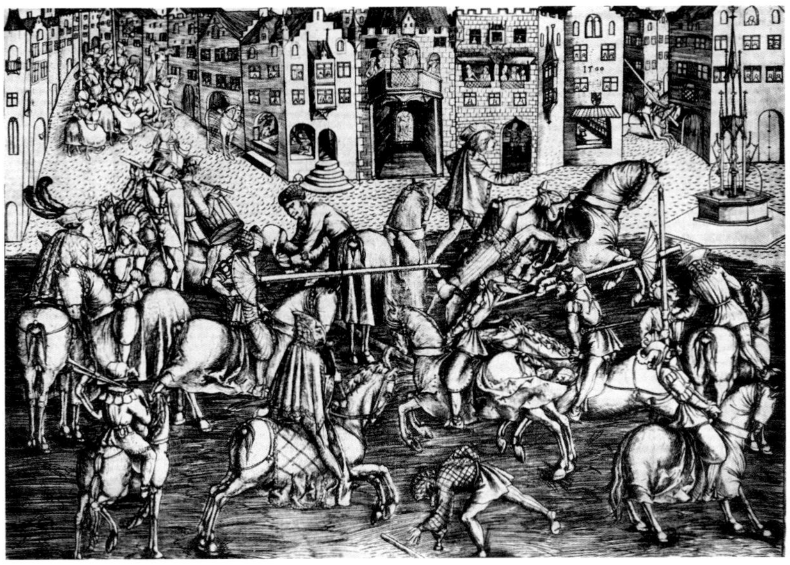

Master MZ (Matthäus Zasinger), *Tournament*, engraving

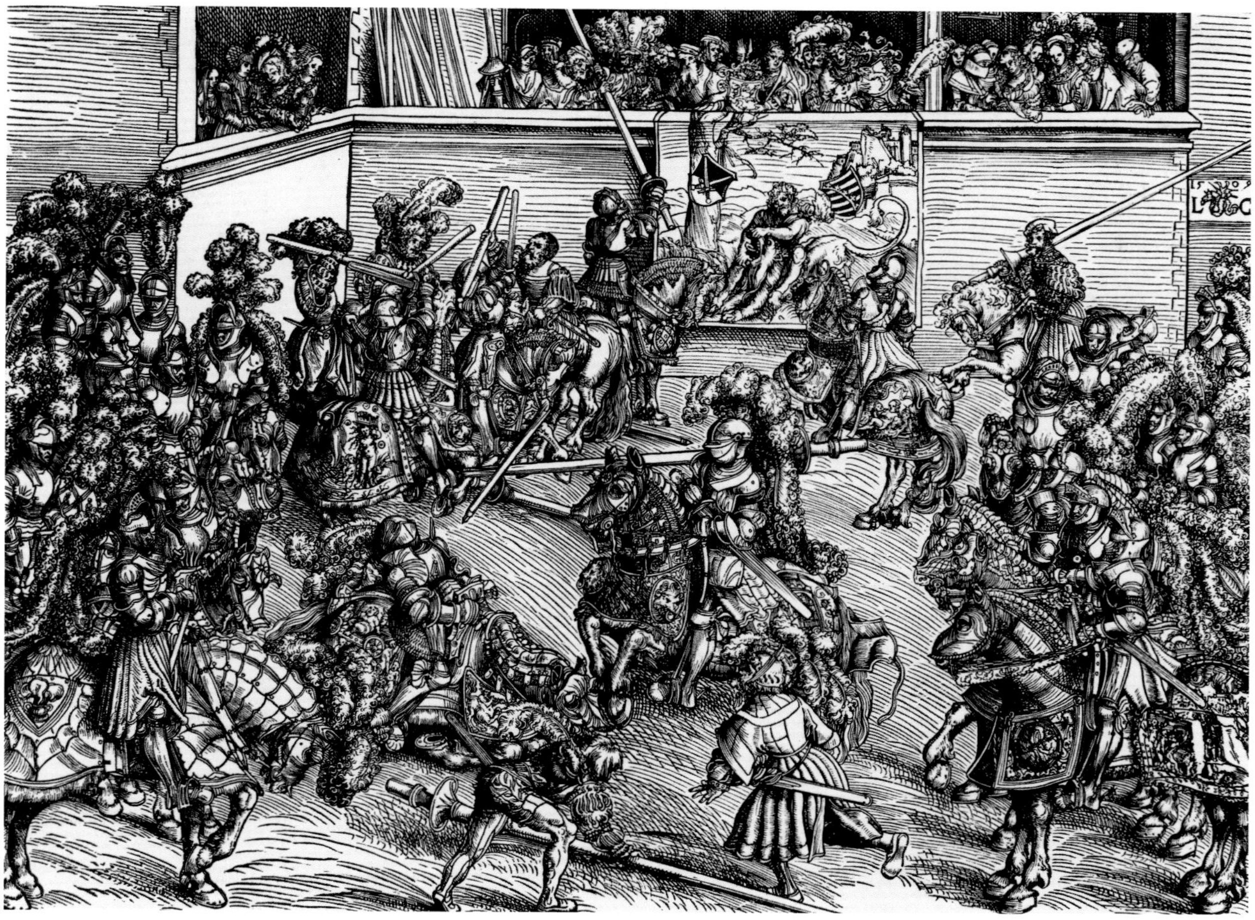
L C

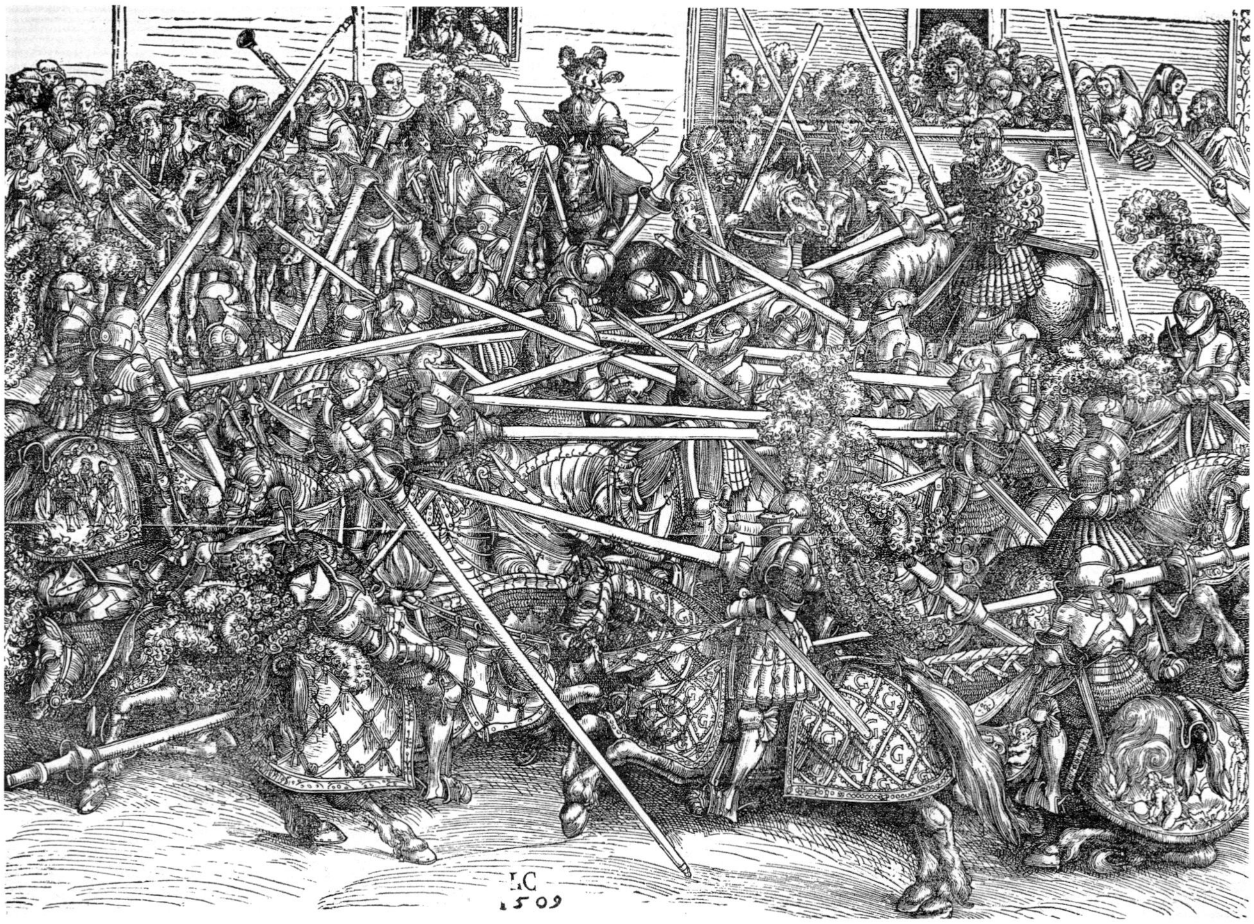
LC
1509

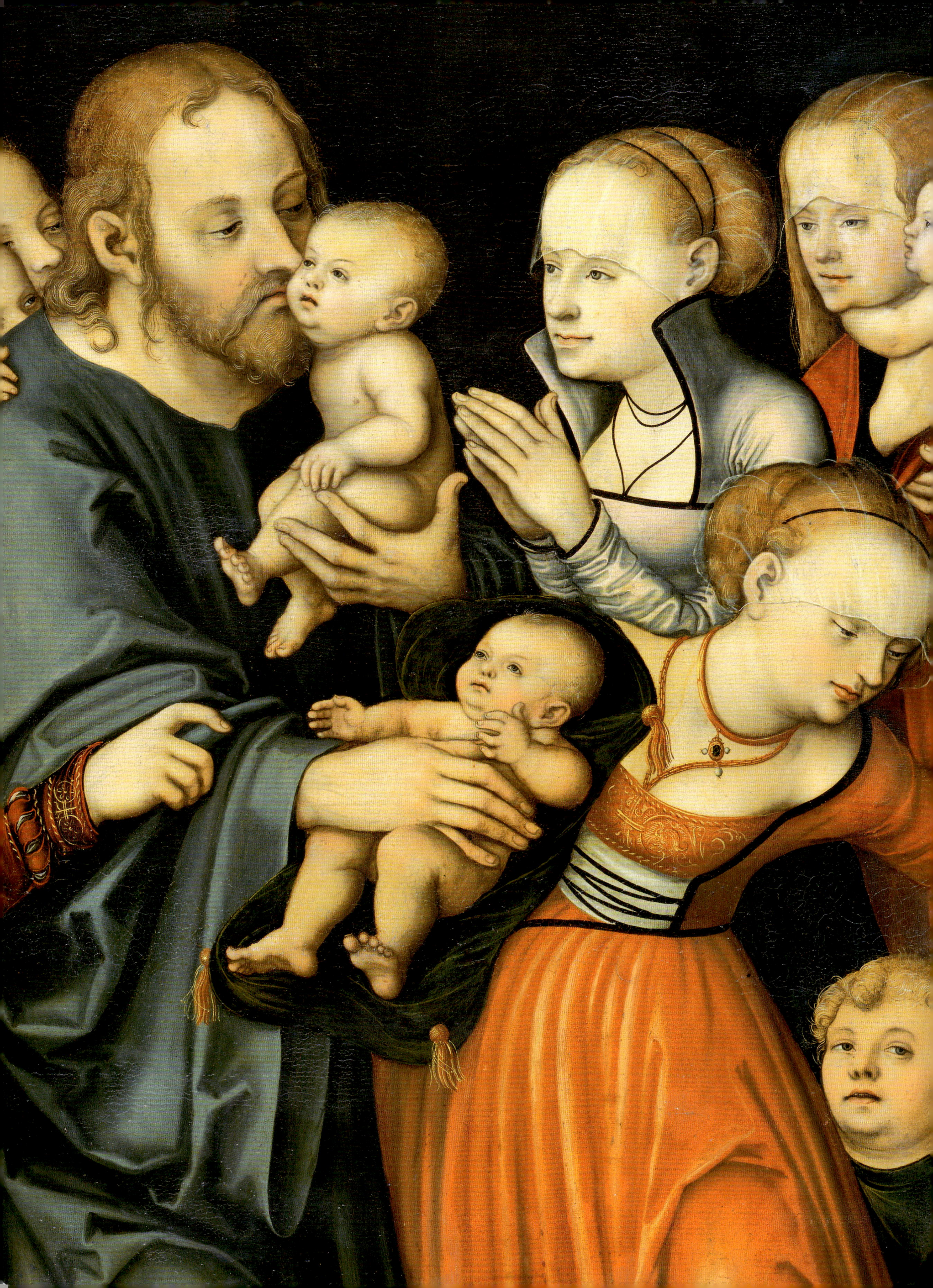

The Pictorial World of the Protestants

Lucas Cranach developed a close friendship with Martin Luther. From the beginning he shaped the public image of the Reformer both in prints and in painted portraits, of which the workshop produced entire series from the third decade of the sixteenth century onwards. He accompanied Luther's tracts against Catholics with a number of particularly cutting illustrative schemes. As a canon of preferred pictorial subjects slowly emerged and took definite form on the Protestant side, it was Cranach who found suitable artistic formulations for them. At this point he produced allegories of Law and Justice and paintings of Christ summoning the children, or showing mercy to the adulteress, each of which was produced in large numbers.

38 Martin Luther as an Augustinian Monk in a Doctoral Hat

Wittenberg, 1519–20

Signed with the serpent with upright wings facing right, to the far left of centre; beneath this the remains of a date; in the top left corner the year 1517, added later

Oil and tempera on wood
40.3 x 26.5 cm

Private collection

(Frankfurt only)

Selected references:
FR 147; Koepplin/Falk 1974/76, vol. 1, p. 100, no. 43; Schade 2003, p. 175, no. 43

The costume in this portrait combines the monk's habit of the second engraved portrait of Luther in front of a recess (JB 210) with the doctoral hat of the engraved portrait in profile of 1521 (JB 208–209). Only the first two numbers of the date beside Luther's shoulder are readable. If the more conspicuous date given at top left is the same, then it is probably 1517 – or possibly 1519. A damaged nine may easily be mistaken for a seven, but not a figure one for a figure two, so the painting must date from the first decade of the sixteenth century. It is also conceivable that the author of the dating at top left simply adopted the most famous date in Luther's life, the year in which he nailed up his Theses.

In any case, a dating of about or before 1520 seems possible. The picture is close to the portrait of Luther in front of a recess both in its framing and its pose, but deviates slightly in individual details. The nostrils are more visible and the arches of the brows more strongly defined. The underdrawing is extremely detailed, suggesting that it was drawn directly from the subject during a portrait sitting; it is still partly visible to the naked eye, beneath the layer of paint now transparent as a result of the saponification of pigments. Luther's features seem somewhat more rounded and less ascetic than in the first two engravings, and his hair is longer. As Werner Schade observed: 'When he is painting, Cranach sees things differently from when he is drawing. He develops his shapes more gradually, whereas in his drawings he looks for the quickest way to a solution. [...] In its objectivity the present picture clearly stands out from the later run of Luther portraits. In the earliest of the surviving paintings we feel the rawness of the early Luther.'

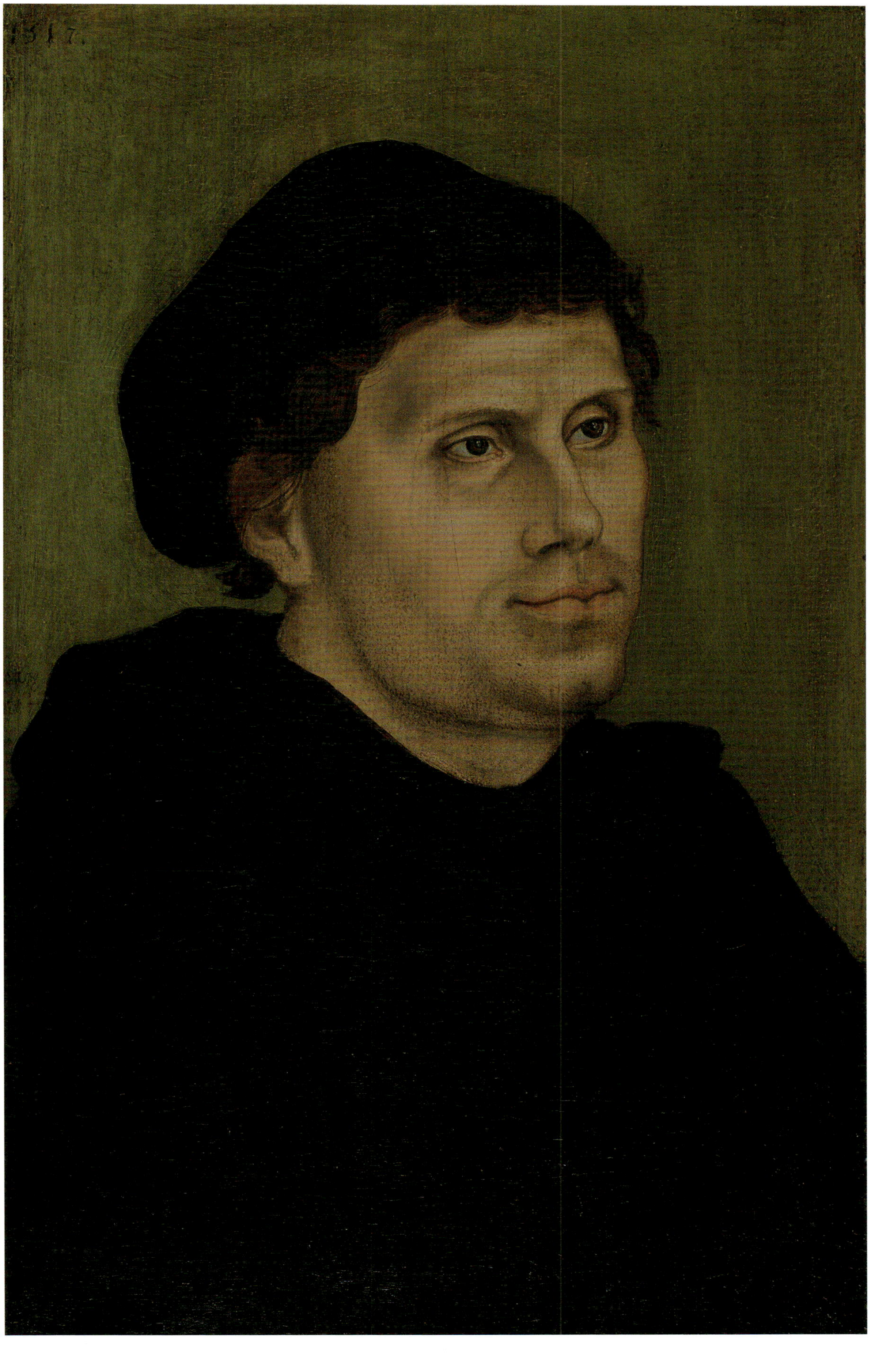

39 Portrait of Martin Luther as Junker Jörg

Lucas Cranach the Elder
(and workshop)

Wittenberg, 1521 or 1522

Oil and tempera on red beechwood
33.5 x 25.3 cm

Museum der bildenden Künste,
Leipzig, 566

Provenance:
Transferred in 1921 from the Leipzig City Library, where it was recorded in 1761 but not rediscovered until 1883

Selected references:
FR 148; Schade 1974, pp. 52 f.; Koepplin/Falk 1974/76, vol. 1, p. 98; Gurasch1994, pp. 41, 45; Martin Luther, exh. cat. 1983, pp. 204 f.; Warnke 1984, pp. 49–51; Von Lucas Cranach bis Caspar David Friedrich, exh. cat., 1994, p. 63, n. 13

Luther's life was in grave danger after his appearance at the Diet of Worms on 17 April 1521, where he was again and for the last time ordered to repudiate his Theses – already in January that year he had been excommunicated by a bull issued by Pope Leo X – but he had persisted with his views, declaring that his conscience was clear. Emperor Charles V then placed him under the imperial ban, and from then on he was regarded as an outlaw. To protect him from the threat of arrest and murder, Elector Frederick the Wise had him abducted on his way home and held captive at Wartburg, where he remained incognito as the aristocratic Junker Jörg until early the following year, and there among other activities began his translation of the New Testament into German, which appeared in print in September 1522 (cat. 44).

In the course of his trial and through his extensive published writings the Reformer had become immensely popular, but the general public knew nothing of these latest events and believed that he was dead. To prove that he was still alive and to return their 'hero' to his public, Lucas Cranach completed a woodcut dated 1522 and several paintings of the 'disguised' Luther, of which two have survived (the other is now in Weimar, FR 149); there are also at least two other versions, though not painted until 1537 (in the church in Penig [FR 149A] and in a private collection in Switzerland). The portrait on which the very popular woodcut and also the paintings were based could have been made as early as December 1521, when Luther went to stay in Wittenberg for a few days. It remains unclear whether the Leipzig portrait was painted at this time or not until Luther's official return to the city in March 1522. It shows the Reformer in three-quarter profile facing right in a head-and-shoulders format filling the entire width of the panel. In keeping with his role as a supposed aristocrat he is dressed in a dark robe with a high collar and wears a carefully trimmed beard in the fashion of the day; his partly cropped right hand holds the just recognisable pommel of a sword. The facial features are rendered in a very fluid, plastic manner – the firm cheekbones, bulging brows and the broad, bulbous nose lend Luther an energetic, aggressive air as he looks intently upwards out of the picture, his expression very much that of a man who insists on maintaining his own point of view. The impression of forcefulness is helped by the tight framing of the picture, leaving no space above the head and creating a monumental atmosphere.

Certain deficiencies in the painting and the comparatively summary treatment of many areas, for example in the nose, ear and hair, have led Schade to see the Leipzig version as a repetition by the workshop, modelled on the Weimar version which shows Luther in a slightly different pose, seen at half-length with his right hand raised as though he is speaking. It could also be that these deficiencies were at least partly caused by hasty execution – possibly just after Luther's stay in Wittenberg in December 1521. Although we can only speculate about this, Cranach himself seems to have considered the tight framing, on the lines of a classical bust, more effective for the general public than the half-length figure; a comparison with the successful woodcut of 1522 shows that in this respect the two are similar. GD

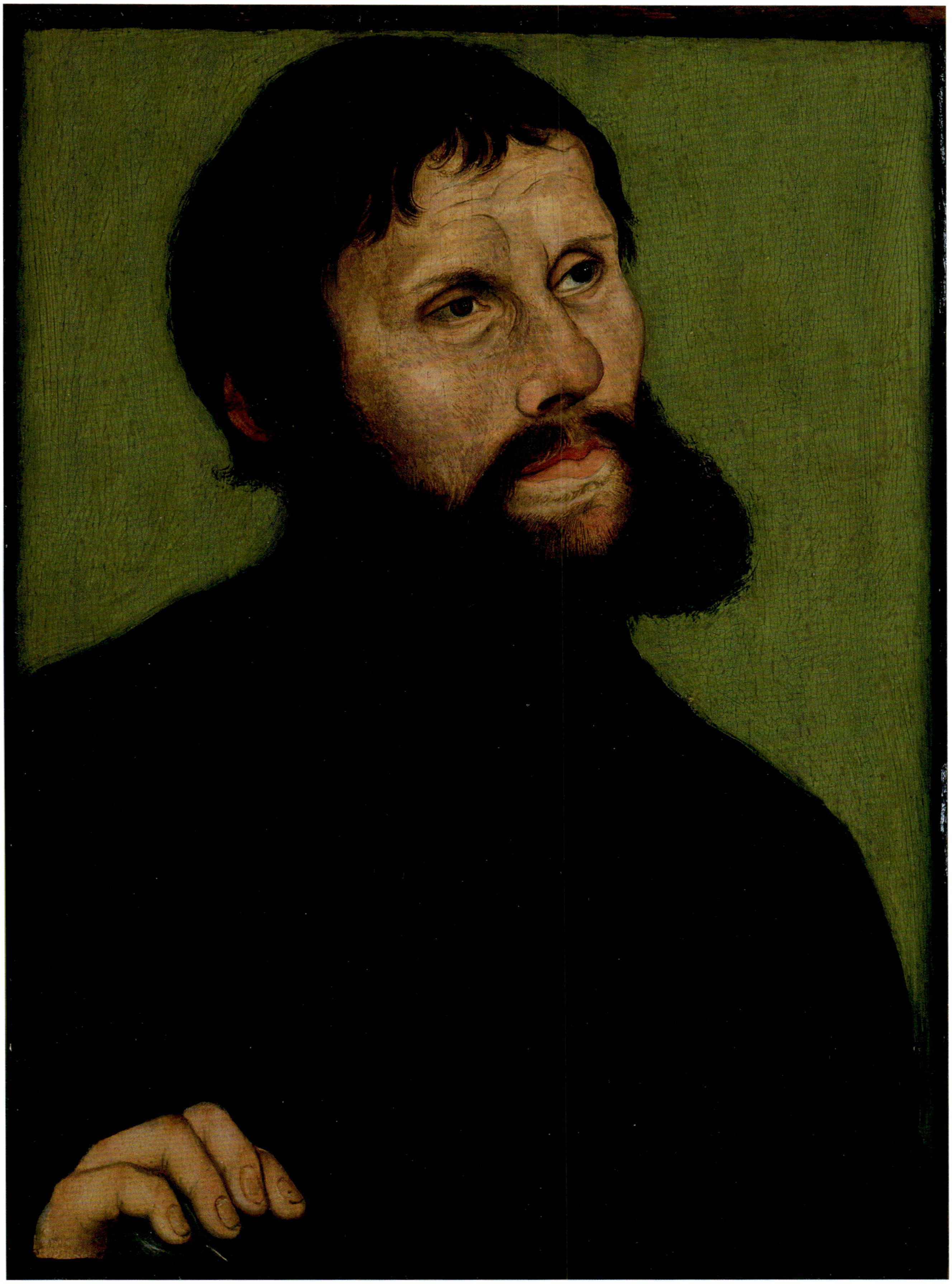

45 Judith Dining with Holofernes
46 The Death of Holofernes

Wittenberg, 1531

Judith Dining with Holofernes

Signed on the tree trunk with the serpent with upright wings facing right between the two pairs of numbers denoting the year 1531

Oil and tempera on limewood
98.5 x 72.5 cm

The Death of Holofernes

Signed on the drum with the serpent with upright wings facing right beneath the date 1531

Oil and tempera on limewood
98 x 76.3 cm

Stiftung Schloss Friedenstein, Gotha, Schlossmuseum, collection of the Duke of Sachsen-Coburg und Gotha's Foundation for Art and Science

(Frankfurt only)

Selected references:
FR 214; Schade 1974, p. 56; Schade 2003, p. 172, nos 36, 37; Schuttwolf 1994, pp. 22-4, nos 1.4, 1.5

Only one book, one of the Apocrypha, celebrates the heroic deed of Judith, the rich and beautiful widow from Bethulia. Holofernes, head of the army of the Assyrian king Nebuchadnezzar, was besieging the city of Bethulia, where the supply of drinking water was running out. In order to help, Judith set out with her maid for the Assyrian camp, passing herself off as a deserter. Holofernes submitted to her charms, invited her to his table and then took her to his bedchamber. Since he was drunk, he immediately fell asleep, whereupon Judith took his sword and cut off his head.

Cranach often portrayed his heroine as a single figure with the severed head of her adversary; the narrative cycle from Gotha is unique in his work. The first panel shows the general entertaining his guest. Wearing a splendid hat, he sits on the left of the table, tasting the food and holding some out to his beautiful guest, while in the foreground the cupbearer busies himself with a goblet.

Judith's maid stands behind her. A small scene in the background indicates what is about to happen; in the general's tent the maid takes his severed head and hides it in a sack. This scene is then depicted in enlarged form in the left foreground of the second panel. While camp life is still in full swing on the right, Judith and the maid complete their assassination, and immediately afterwards leave the camp, undiscovered.

Two 'secret' portraits are included in the composition of the first panel. The man in the dark fur coat at the extreme left edge of the picture, pointing at Holofernes, bears the features of Cranach himself, as is confirmed out by comparison with a self-portrait of the artist in middle age (Burg Stolzenfels; Schade 2003, No. 37a). The sharply defined features of the clean-shaven young nobleman who stands in the foreground in front of the table, may be identified as those of the Landgrave Philip I of Hesse, known as Philip the Magnanimous (1504–1567). In 1531, the year in which the Holofernes panels were painted, Philip, together with other Protestant rulers and Imperial cities, had formed the Schmalkaldic League as a pact of solidarity against the Emperor Charles V's threat to persecute their faith. It can therefore be presumed that Philip the Magnanimous not only commissioned the two panels, but also seems to have wished them to include a hidden political programme. The biblical event depicted here is also an example of the death of a tyrant. The facial features of Holofernes follow the general outlines of a Cranach type; it would have been going much too far to have portrayed the Emperor himself in this role.

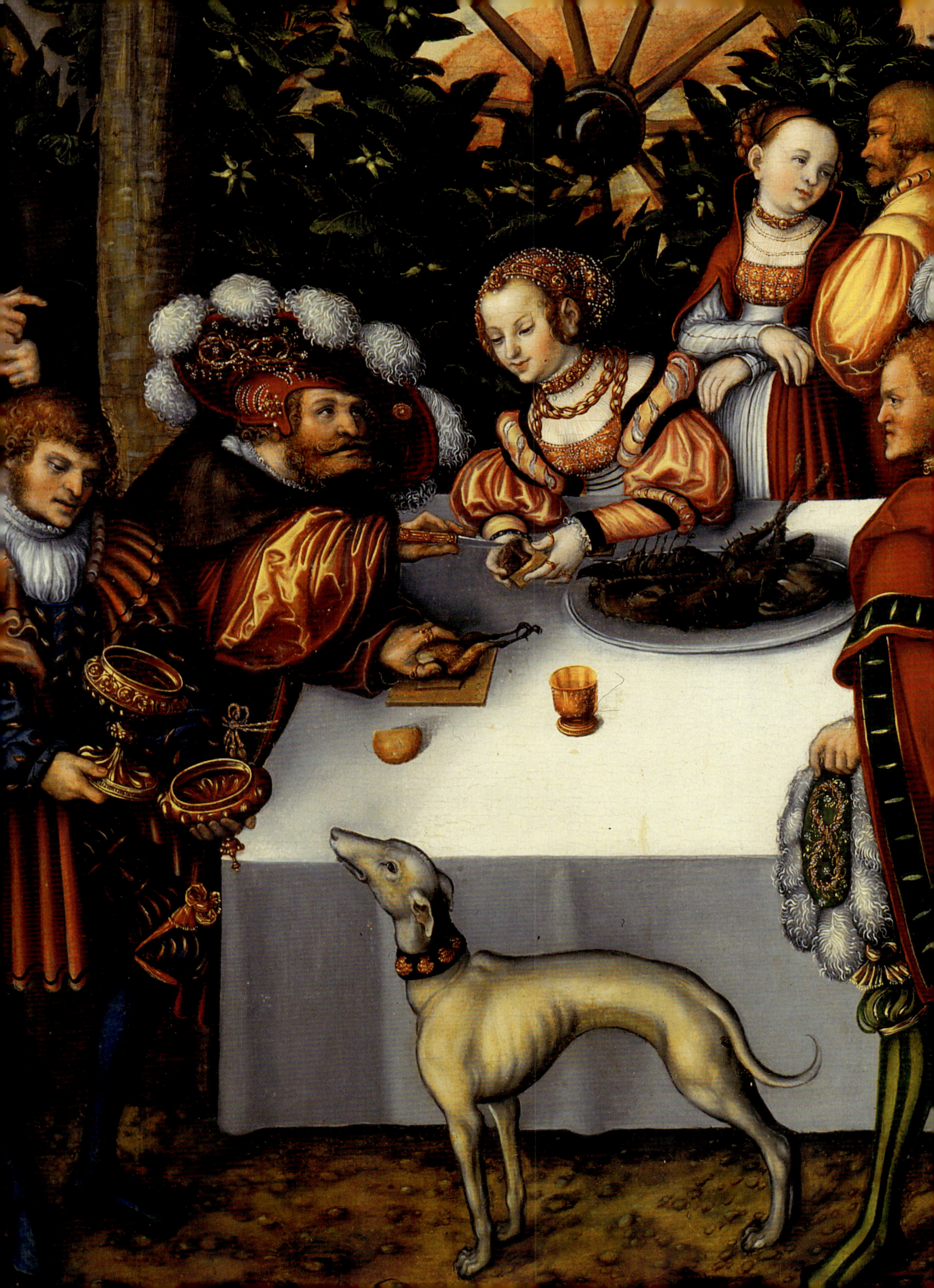

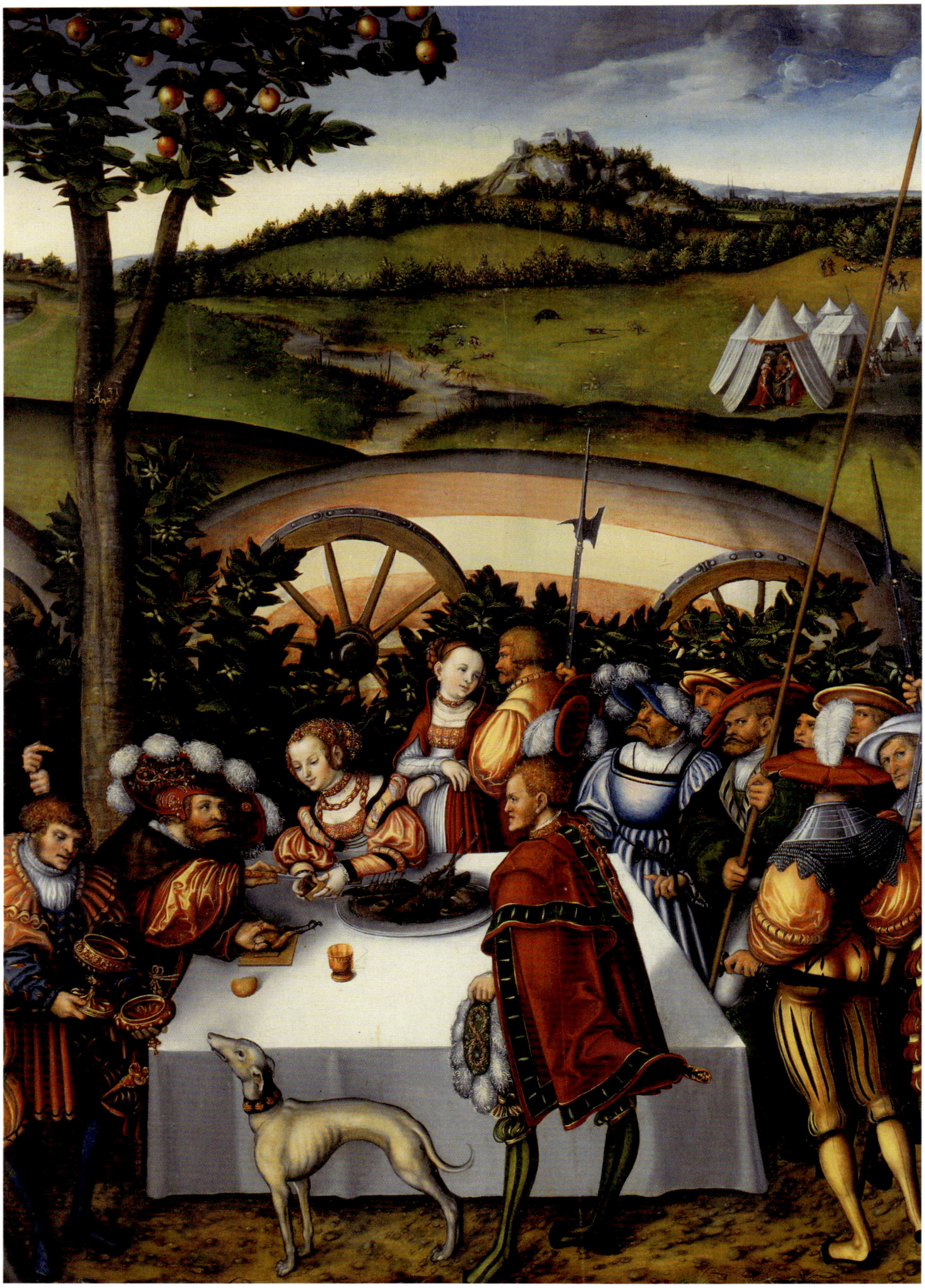

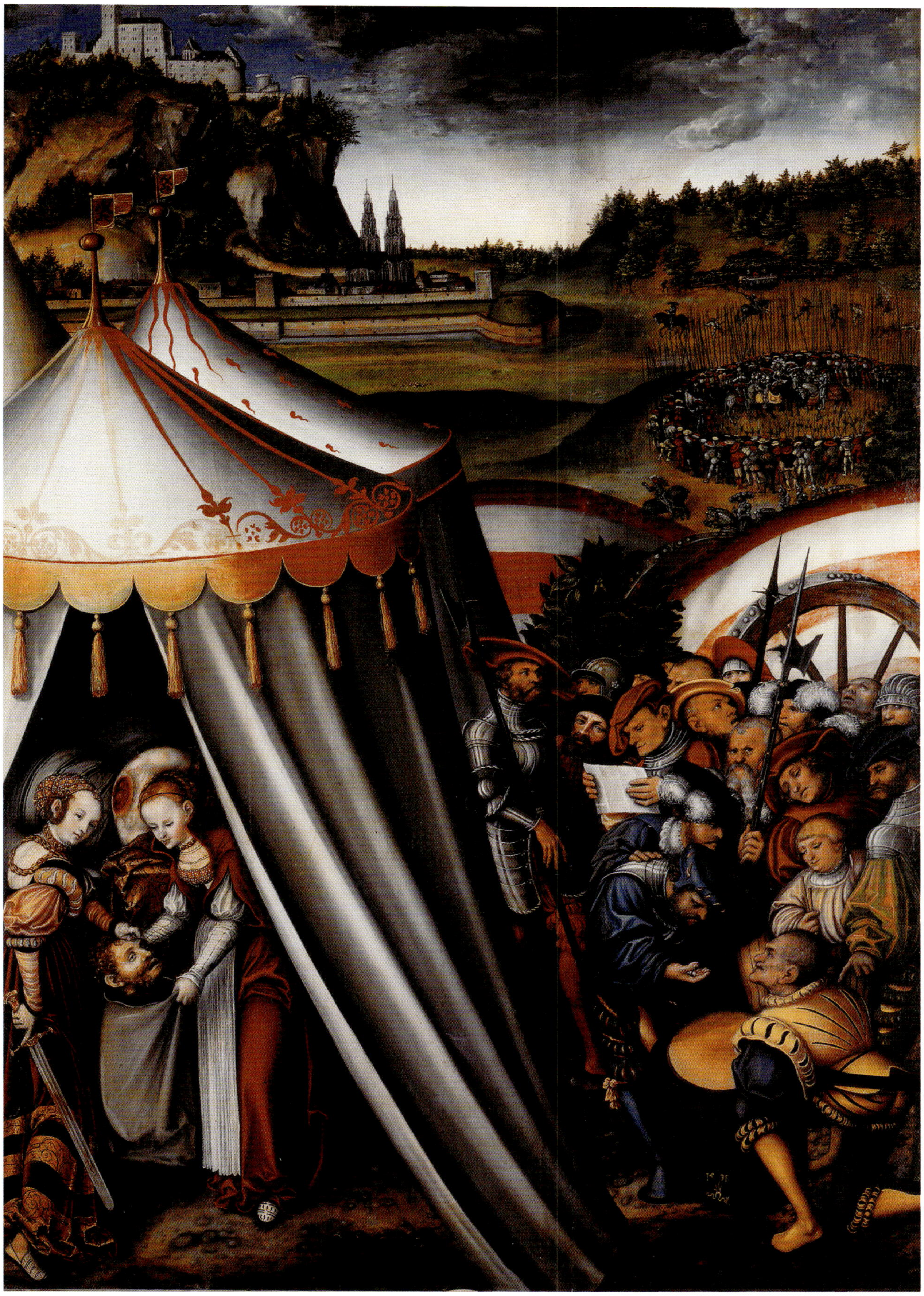

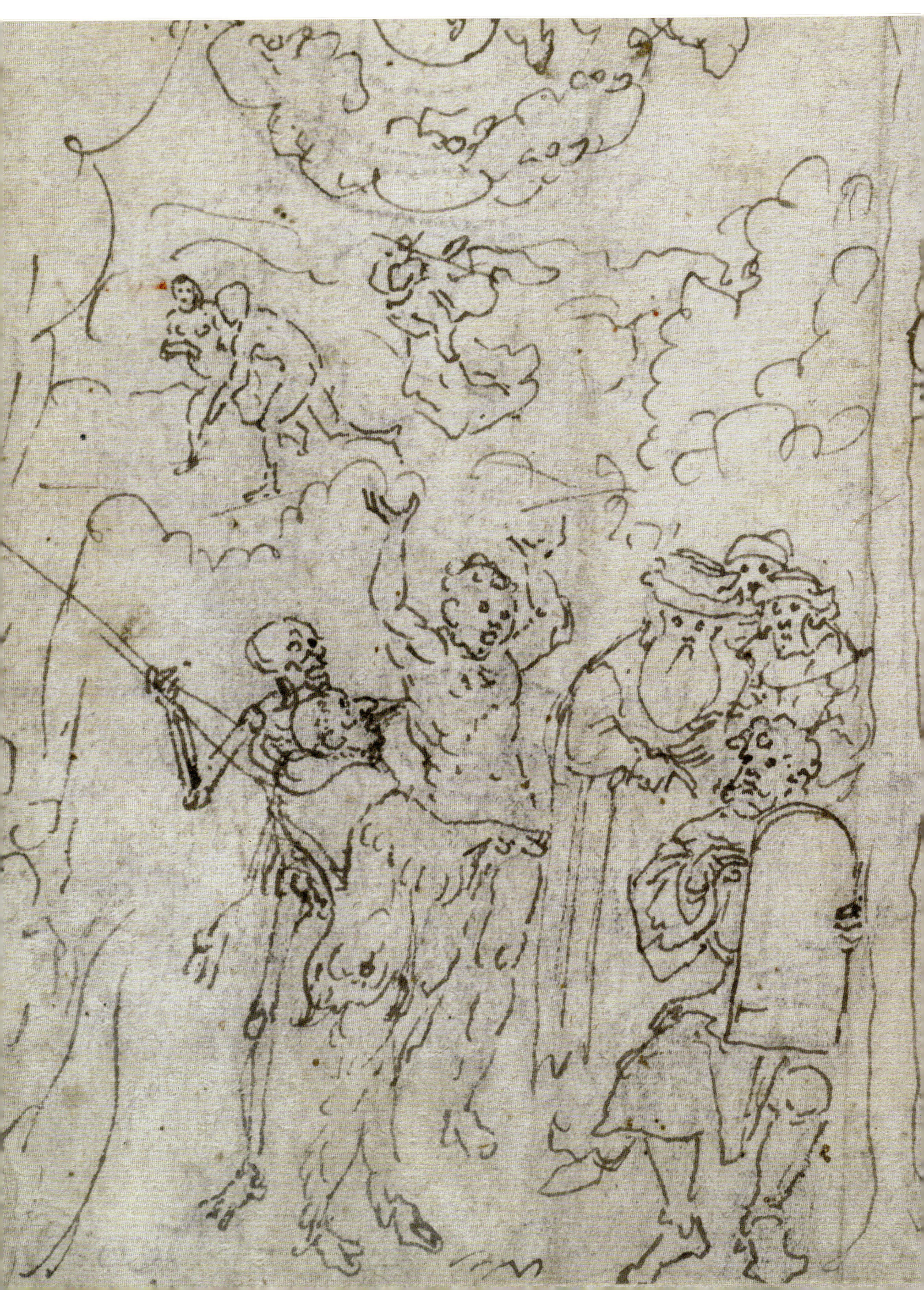

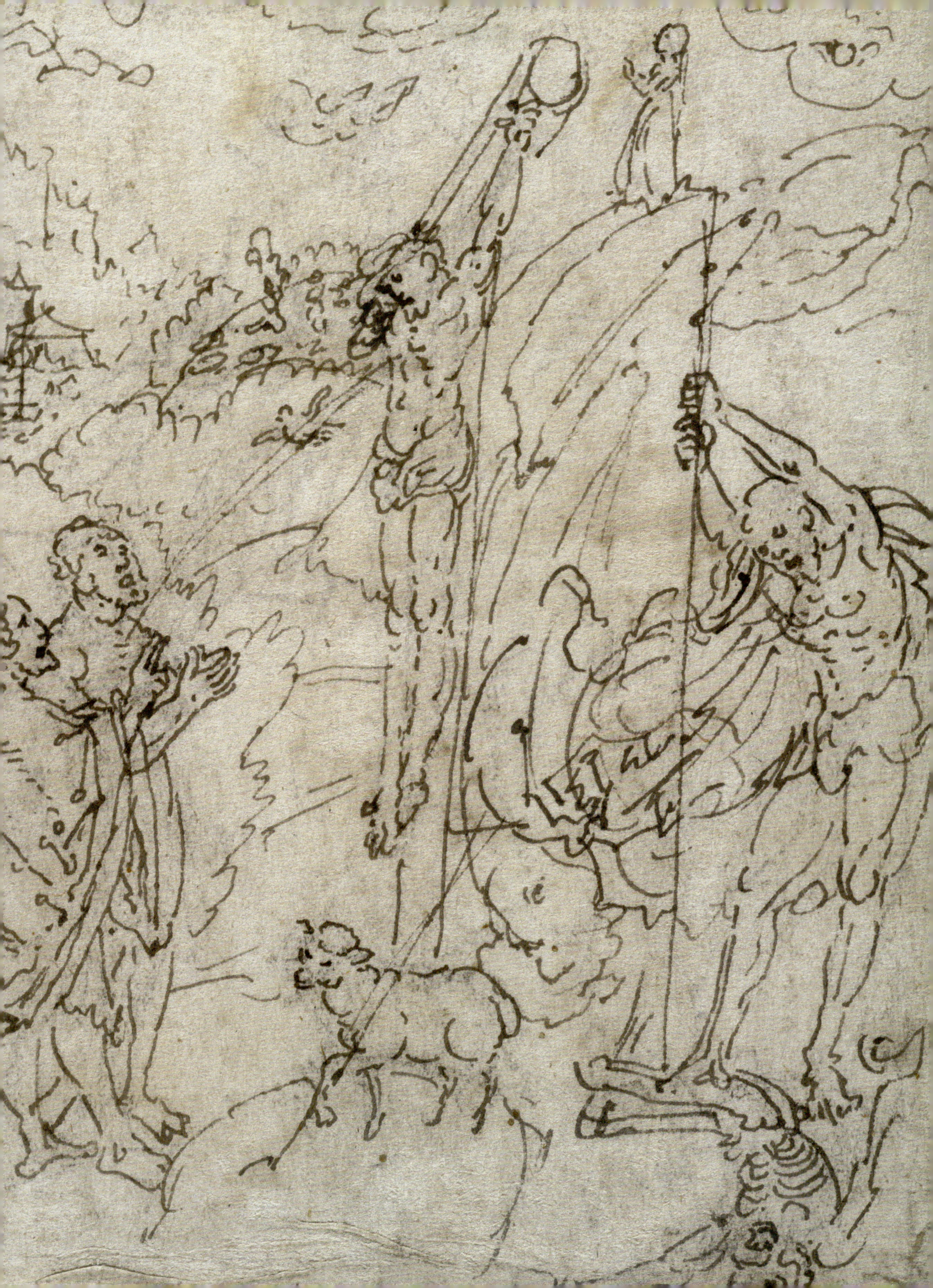

49 Christ and the Woman Taken in Adultery

Wittenberg, *c.* 1530

Pen and dark-brown ink over black pencil

Städel Museum, Frankfurt, Graphische Sammlung, 15666

Provenance:
collection of J. F. Lahmann, Dresden, from whom acquired in 1935

(Frankfurt only)

Selected references:
R A8; Schilling 1925, no. 35; Schilling/Schwartzweller 1973, vol. 1, p. 25, no. 79; on the theme generally: Koepplin/Falk1974/76, vol. 2, pp. 363–65; Martin Luther, exh. cat. 1983, pp. 380 f.; Ermischer/Tacke 2007, pp. 278 f., no. 20, p. 293, no. 37

The Gospel of St John tells the story of an adulteress taken in the act by scribes and Pharisees and brought before Jesus (John 8, 3–11). Mosaic Law demanded the death penalty, and the mob called for her to be stoned; but Jesus countered this, saying: 'He that is without sin among you, let him first cast a stone at her,' whereupon her persecutors, reminded of their own fallibility, were filled with shame and went away. This pen drawing portrays Jesus addressing the crowd. Against a background of two round-headed arches, Christ is seen at full length, like all the other figures, in the central axis of the composition, his left hand holding that of the penitent sinner. Her dress has slipped down, baring her left breast, and she lowers her eyes in shame, while Christ turns to the Pharisees and raises his other hand to capture their attention. They are placed symmetrically on each side of the central group, forming a semicircle round Christ and the woman; their angry faces clearly reveal their fierce determination, particularly the two in the foreground on either side, one of whom clutches a bag full of stones, while the other grips the adulteress by the arm.

Representations of this subject, with its didactic and moralising content, were clearly popular among Protestants, and the number of variants on the theme is correspondingly large. The Cranach workshop produced them mainly from the mid-1530s, though the earliest dated version is from as early as 1520. It is not yet clear whether the Frankfurt drawing was made as a study for a later panel painting or whether it merely demonstrates one of the many compositional options open to the workshop; so far no suitable painting has been found to match it. It has also been suggested on several occasions that it might be a later copy, carried out by Cranach himself.

Although it looks like a pictorial version of Lutheran views – all people are sinners; only through Christ, through unconditional belief in him and through the granting of God's grace, can the road to redemption be found, nor will he be influenced by the performance of good deeds – the subject was in itself neither new nor specifically Protestant. As early as 1509 Cranach himself had completed a drawing of it, and in about 1525 Cardinal Albrecht commissioned a full-length version from an artist in Cranach's circle, for his collegiate church in Halle. As often happened with Protestant pictorial themes, existing treatments were taken up and reinterpreted to fit the new requirements. In the present case, the best solution, which is basically comparable with the painting of *Christ Blessing the Children* (cat. 50) was to take a half-length composition against a neutral background, probably influenced by Venetian models.

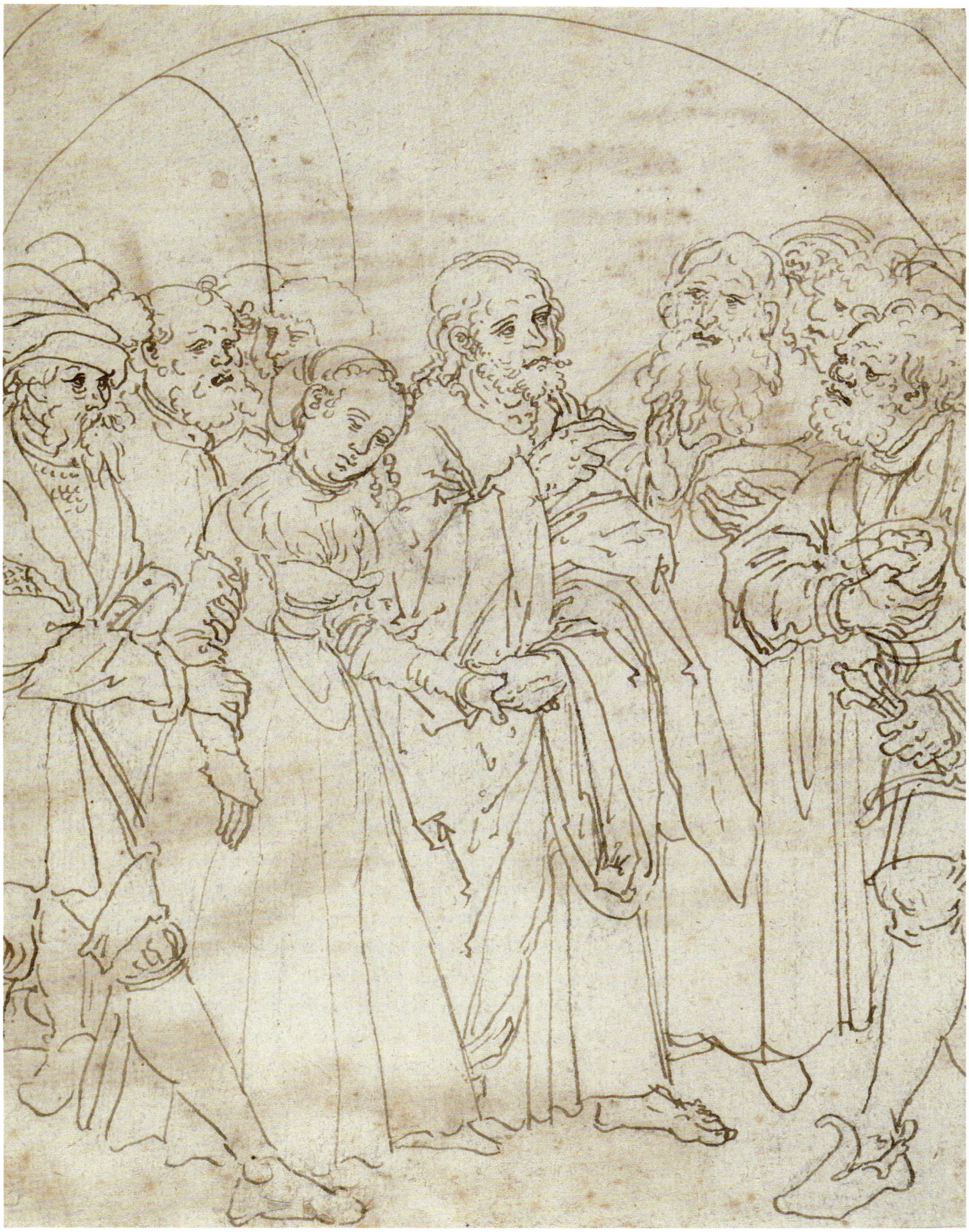

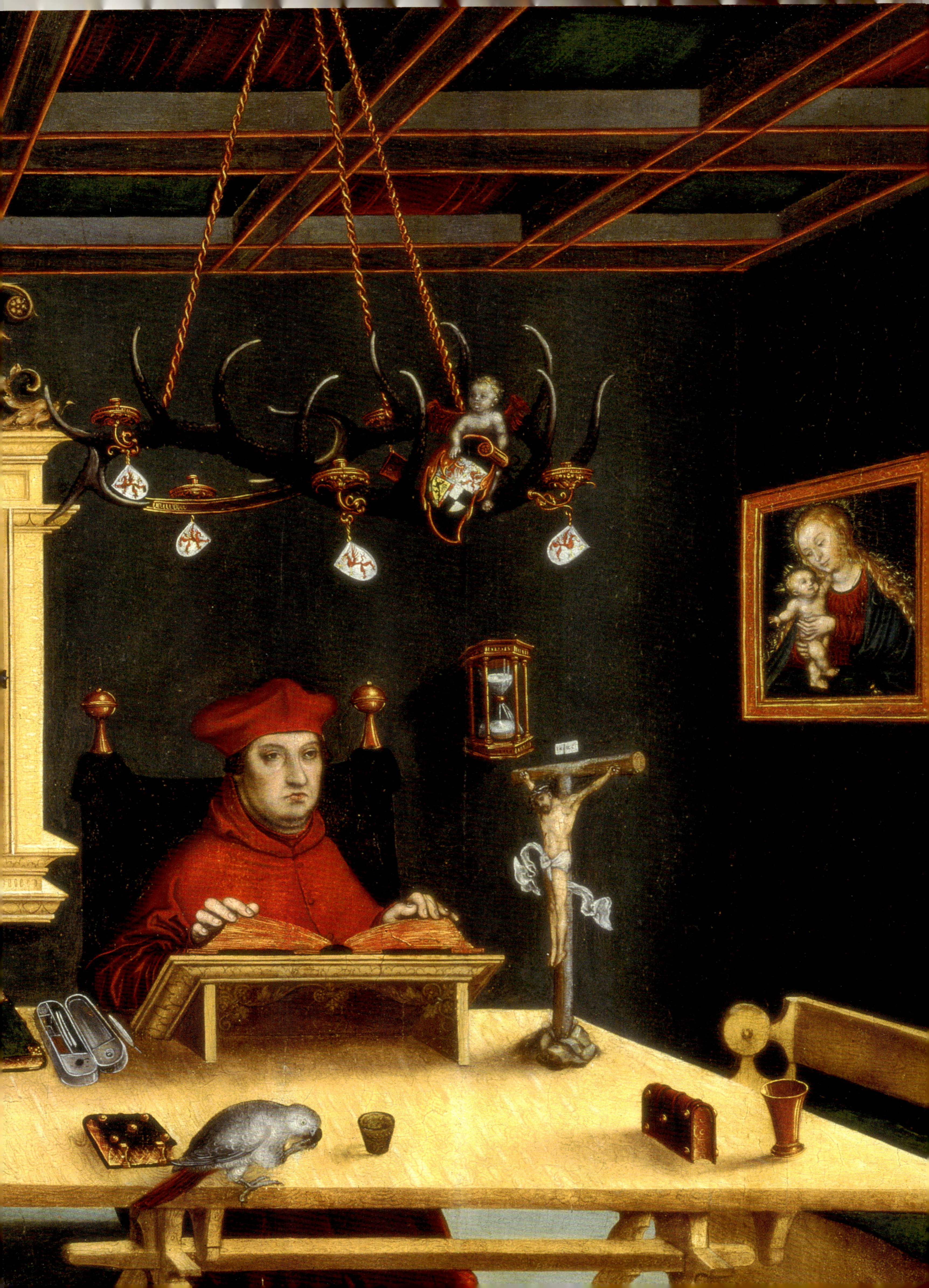

The Tradition of the Sacred

When Lucas Cranach began his career, the Reformation was still far in the future. At first he treated the same subjects as all other artists of his time, painting pictures of the Virgin and the saints, and he continued to do so after the onset of the clearly irreversible religious schism. However, it seems to have been quite acceptable for him to continue to fulfil his commissions from Catholic patrons, including even the most important opponent of the Reformation, Cardinal Albrecht of Brandenburg, in spite of Cranach's close relationship with Luther and Melanchthon. He portrayed Albrecht several times in works of great subtlety and significance, in which the Catholic ruler took on the role of St Jerome.

51 The Temptation of St Antony

Wittenberg, 1506

Signed in the bottom left corner with the monogram LC surrounded by the individual numbers denoting the year; at upper right two shields hang in the tree with the arms of the Electorate of Saxony

Woodcut
40.6 x 27 cm

Städel Museum, Frankfurt, Graphische Sammlung, 53362

(London only)

Selected references:
JB 322; Maedebach/Gebhardt 1972, p. 32, no. 59; Grimm/Erichsen/Brockhoff 1994, pp. 324 f., no. 147

The hermit is lifted into the air by at least a dozen fantastic chimeras, and tormented. Giant insects, bizarre birds and flying dragons leap on him, tug at his habit and threaten him with clubs and stones. A beaked goblin standing on two legs dances on his chest and seizes his beard. The calm landscape immediately beneath makes a complete contrast with the diabolical chaos of this aerial battle. Cranach drew upon an engraving by Martin Schongauer for his depiction of the vision, but used it only as a starting point. In Schongauer's version the monsters form a ring around the upright figure of the saint, but in Cranach they mass together in a menacing jungle of outlines. Antony has been tipped on to his back, making him look even more helpless; with his robe in disorder and his arms stretched out to the side he resembles a caricature of Christ on the Mount of Olives, often depicted in the Garden of Gethsemane stretching out his arms to form a cross, as he also appears in Cranach's woodcut of the Passion which he completed three years later.

From careful study of Albrecht Dürer's *Apocalypse*, carried out between 1496 and 1498, Cranach would have seen how effective a turbulent aerial scene would look compared with Schongauer's empty space set against a distant landscape, something on the lines of Archangel Michael's battle with the dragon (SMS 122). Dürer's famous series had a lasting influence on Cranach's early woodcut style from his Vienna period onwards.

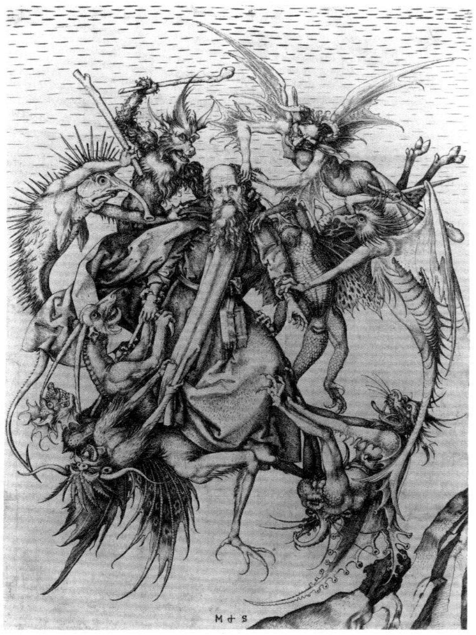

Martin Schongauer, *The Temptation of St Antony*, engraving, Städel Museum, Frankfurt, Graphische Sammlung

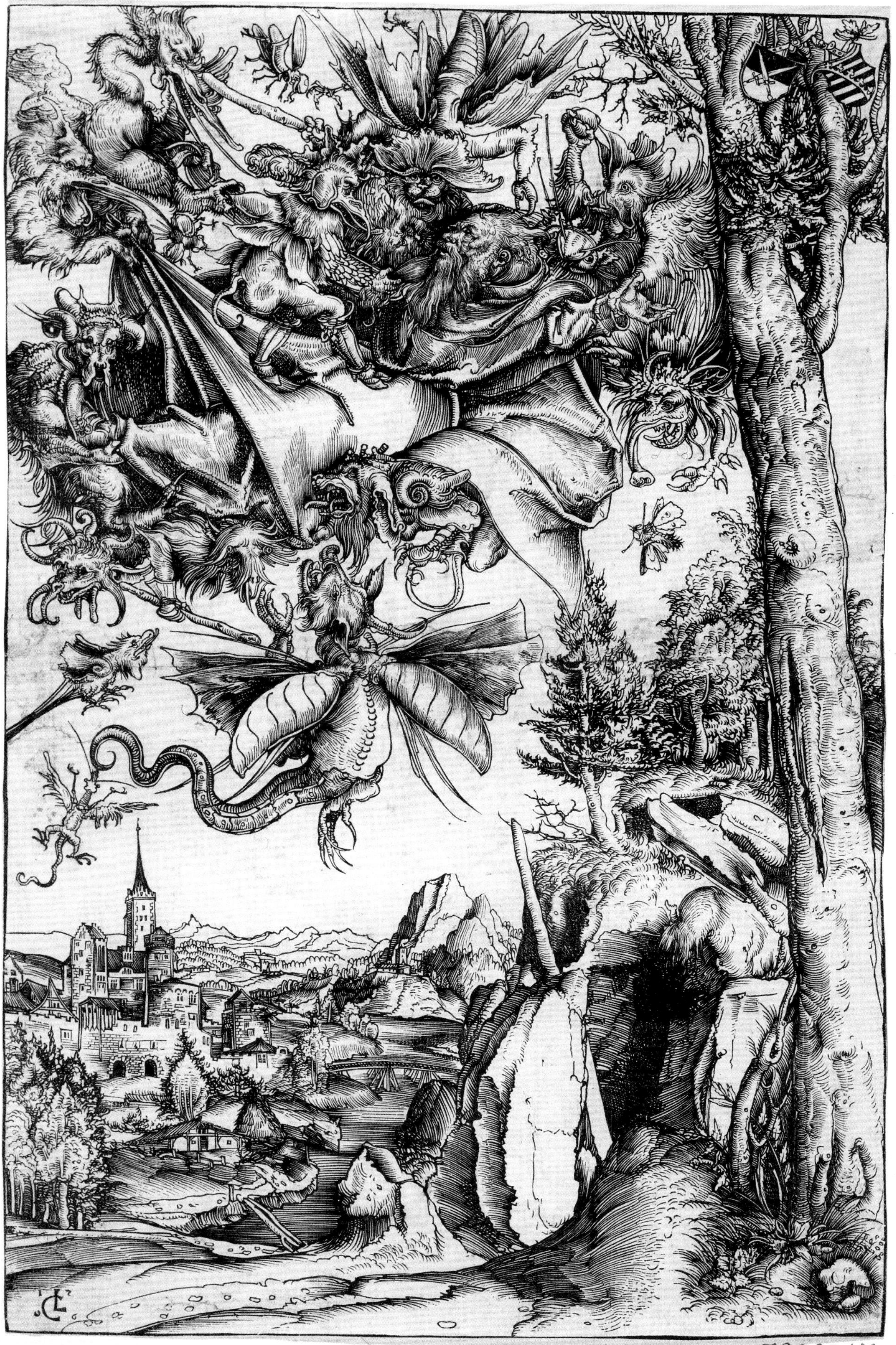

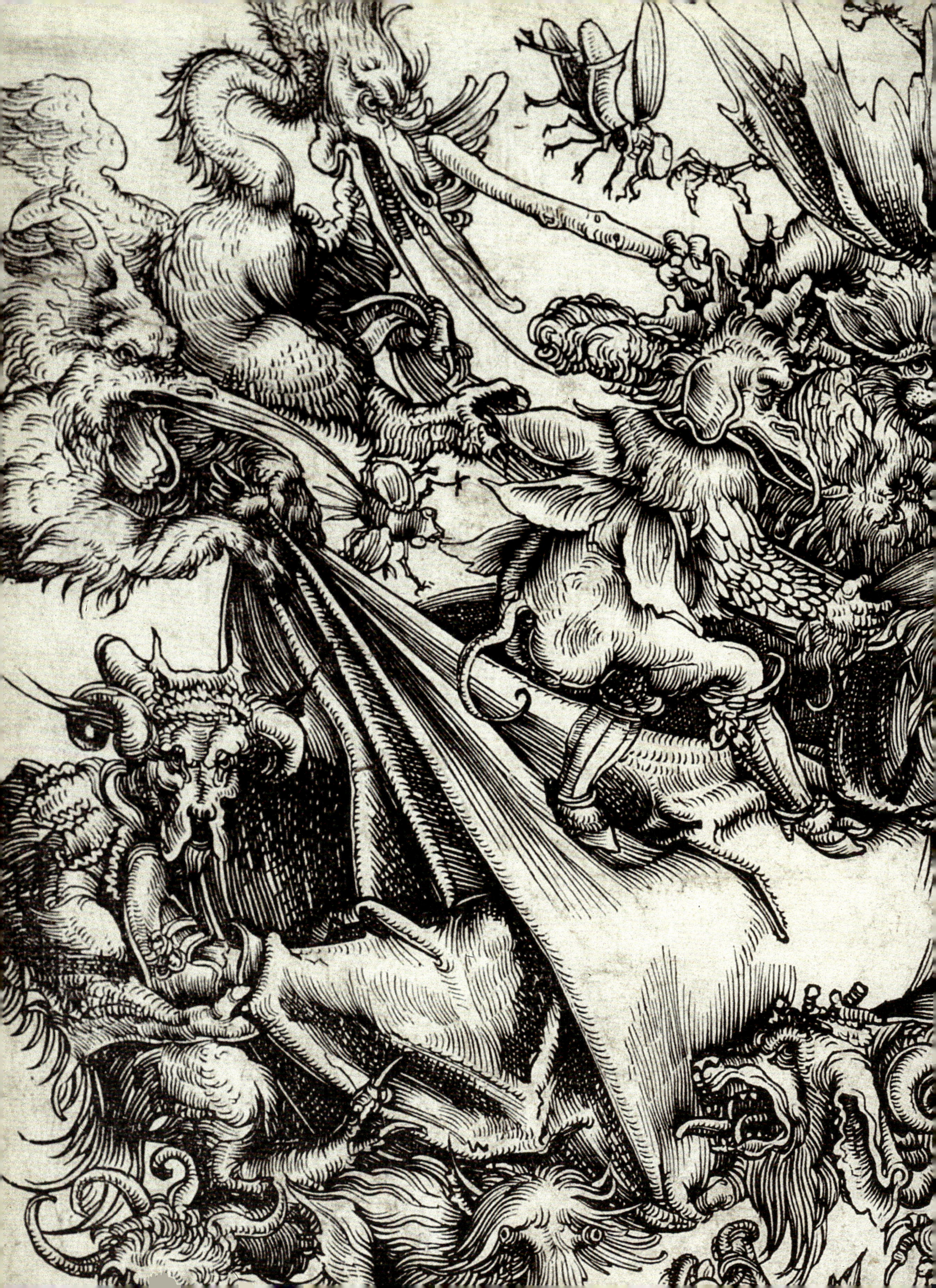

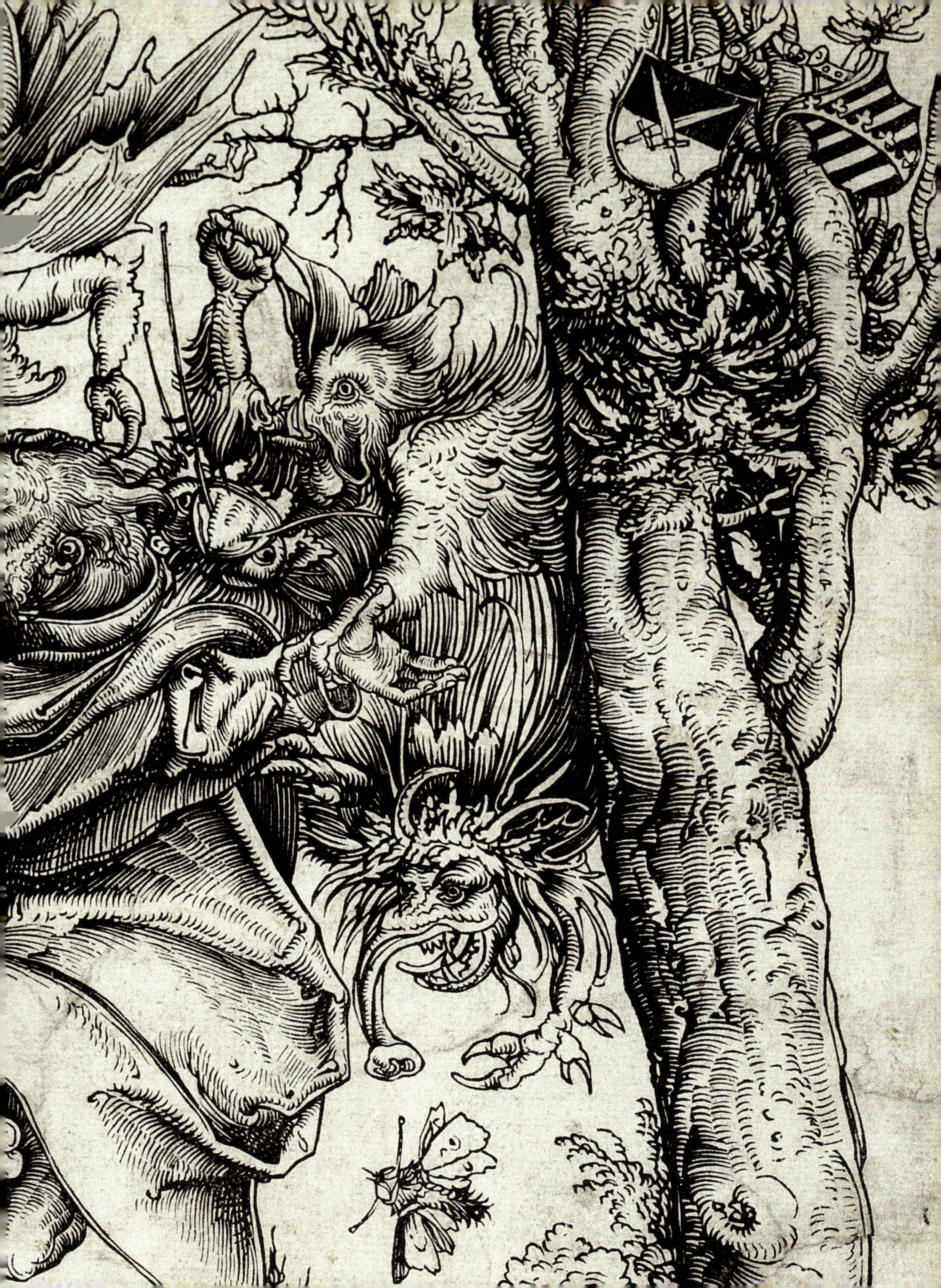

52 The Penitent Magdalen in Ecstasy

Wittenberg, 1506

Signed on the stone at bottom right with the monogram LC , surrounded by the individual numbers denoting the year; in the top corners the arms of the Electorate of Saxony

Woodcut
24.4 x 14.2 cm

Städel Museum, Frankfurt, Graphische Sammlung, 31241

(London only)

Selected references:
JB 326; Maedebach/Gebhardt 1972, pp. 37 f., no. 75

According to legend, after an adventurous voyage across the Mediterranean the remorseful sinner Mary Magdalen committed herself to spend 30 years as a penitent in the wild, somewhere near Aix-en-Provence. She survived her rigorous fasting with the help of angels who carried her up to the heavenly spheres and refreshed her with heavenly foods. The pictorial representation of this event is relatively fixed; in the small panel showing the standing figure of Mary Magdalen, which Cranach painted a good ten years later, her ecstasy in heaven can be seen in the background, the naked penitent's pose, her legs slightly bent, corresponding with the early woodcut (cat. 56). The landscape too, with its steep cliffs, is also very similar to that of the print. One characteristic peculiar to Cranach, in which he departs from pictorial tradition, is the saint's complete nakedness: in the late Middle Ages the saint was usually shown with long hair covering her whole body.

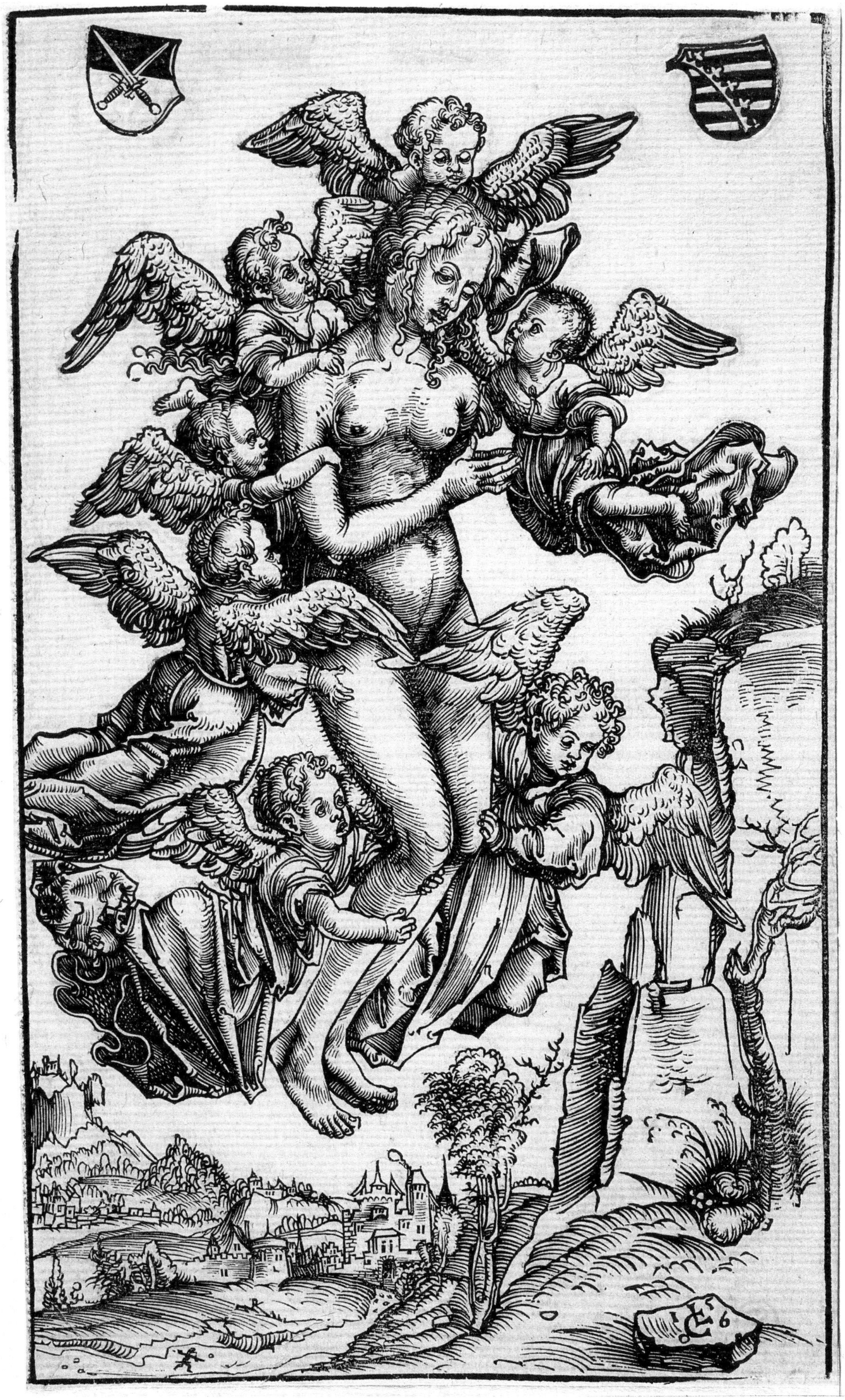

53 St Stephen of Hungary (?)

Wittenberg, *c.* 1510–15

Oil and tempera on limewood
101 x 30.2 cm

Germanisches Nationalmuseum, Nuremberg, Gm 1666

Provenance:
acquired in 1967 from the collection of Walter Bremen, Krefeld

(Frankfurt only)

Selected references:
not in FR; Löcher 1997, pp. 128–30; for Frederick the Wise with the Imperial crown: Koepplin 2007

A haloed sovereign appears facing right against a black background and standing on stony ground, with an executioner's sword, imperial apple and crown, and surmounted by a painted arch of luxuriant foliage. Two saints come immediately to mind: Charlemagne (747–814), canonised in 1165, and St Stephen of Hungary, canonised in 1083. King Stephen I (969–1038) is the Hungarian national hero whose missionary projects among the heathen Magyars completed the conversion of the country to Christianity. The fact that the sovereign wears a king's crown makes the latter the more likely subject: Cranach would probably have shown Charlemagne with an imperial crown and at an advanced age, just as Albrecht Dürer did in his painting, also in the Germanisches Nationalmuseum. The idealised imperial crown, which Frederick the Wise holds in his hand in a picture type often used by Cranach, shares with the real model the important features of the lower jewelled crown and the upper cruciform cap. Although the imperial apple would not have been part of King Stephen's regalia, the globe and cross are found among his attributes, reflecting his services to Christianity.

Originally, the medium-sized panel with the saintly king formed the left wing of an altar retable in several sections. This is confirmed by a pendant of St Jerome with the same format and structure in the Bavarian Staatsgemäldesammlungen in Munich. As the Jerome figure is facing in the same direction as King Stephen, it is unlikely that the former occupied the opposite right-hand wing. This rather suggests a double folding retable with two pairs of side wings.

The Nuremberg wing can be compared stylistically with the outsides of the Dresden *St Catherine* Altarpiece of 1506 (National Gallery, London; FR 15). There the saints also appear against a black background beneath luxuriant garlands of foliage, and the strip of ground has a similar, marble-like appearance. The haloes consist in both cases of a circle of rays with a very short radius, while the brocade material in both is covered with a decorative pattern. All these details justify an attribution to Lucas Cranach. The saintly king is much sturdier than the very slender female saints in London, however, which makes it likely that they were painted a good five years apart.

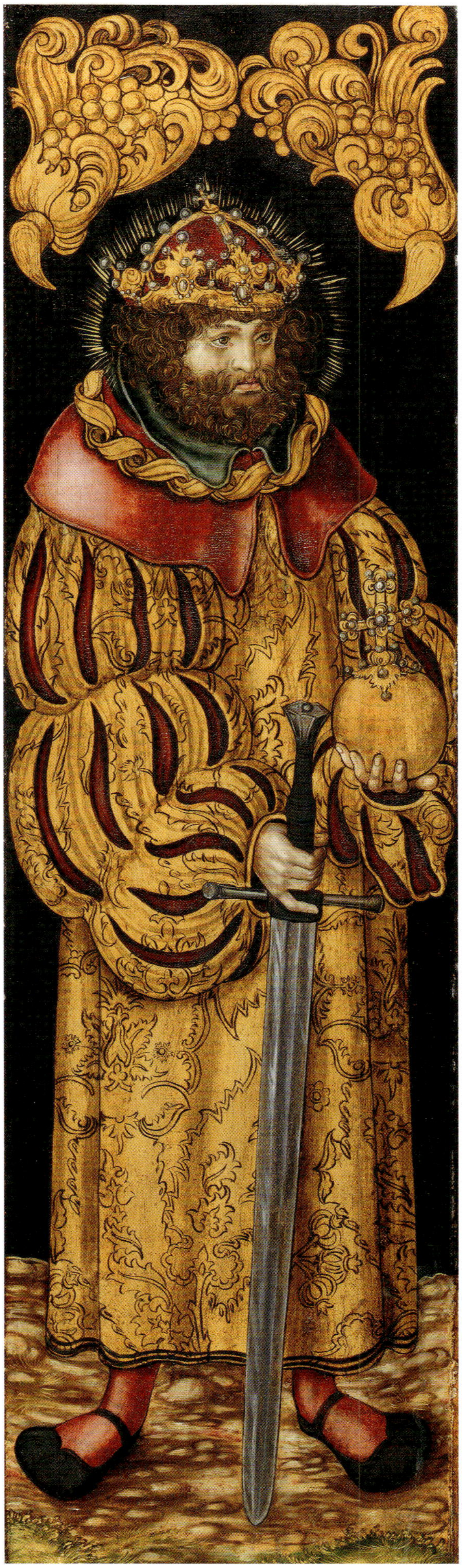

55 St Jerome in the Desert

Lucas Cranach the Elder

Wittenberg, *c.* 1525

Signed on the tree trunk with the serpent with upright wings

Oil and tempera on firwood
89.8 x 66.5 cm

Tiroler Landesmuseum Ferdinandeum, Innsbruck, GEM 116

(Frankfurt only)

Selected references:
FR 169; Koepplin/Falk 1974/1976, vol. 2, pp. 548 f., no. 409; Marx/Mössinger 2005, pp. 16, 604; Stadlober 2006, pp. 204–20

This representation of the Church Father doing penance alone in the wilderness might be called Cranach's *Jerome with the Many Animals*, in allusion to a famous drawing by Dürer. The later gather round in a friendly way, companions of the lonely man. It was painted a good two decades after the Vienna panel of 1502 (cat. 3) which treats the same subject. Since the compositions look very similar (almost a mirror image of each other) and the scales of the figures also come close, a comparison of the two is extremely instructive. The dynamism of the self-punishing action in the Vienna picture has given way to a more relaxed pose, a moment of pause and reflection. The sinewy swinging movement, so full of energy, has become more low-key, even fragile; the motifs from nature, there shuffled rather stagily together, have become a variegated landscape which stretches more convincingly into the distance, the individual shapes no longer merging into one ornamental pattern but clearly outlined and set apart from each other with plenty of contrast. Although the later work may lack painterly verve, it has acquired its own distinctive aesthetic quality, combining gracefulness and precision.

Above all, however, the artist clearly enjoyed filling out his works with attractive details which, although not essential, significantly heighten the viewer's visual pleasure. Cranach spreads these almost evenly over the picture surface. On the right, a wide river flows past a chalk cliff and beneath a bridge, in front of which red deer browse in a clearing, a stork searches for food in a meadow, and in the foreground the main figure is framed by a whole menagerie, including a peacock, a tortoise, an eagle, a small amphibian, a beaver and even two harpies (a hybrid creature with a bird's body and a human head). In the tree on the left edge of the picture, two squirrels leap, and at its top perch two more birds. The sky, too, is not left empty: a flock of birds salute us on their travels. Amid all this lively movement, even the lion cannot be left inactive, although according to legend he was meant to follow the saint everywhere he went, after the latter had extracted a thorn from his paw. He leans over the little pond in the foreground and laps up water with his parched tongue. The harpy-woman too stoops over the water and catches sight of her reflection. Her little male companion is also mirrored in the water, sinister expressions on both their faces.

The fauna of the Middle Ages, unlike those of Greek mythology, included harpies of both sexes. Jacob van Maerlant reports in the third book of his encyclopedia *Der naturen bloeme*, published in 1270, that they inhabit the desert and, as soon as they meet a human being, try to kill him. However, if after murdering her victim a harpy glimpses her reflection in water, she is seized by bitter remorse and may die of grief. The mythical hybrids are thus in the same position as the saint kneeling above them: they too are remorseful sinners in the desert. But the small pond they are looking into seems to continue beyond the bottom edge of the picture and into the real world. The viewer can also look into it, and must then, like the mythical creatures, contemplate his own sinfulness. In this way the harpies make an important contribution to the pictorial message. Even the beaver can be seen as the symbol of the renunciation of worldly pleasures in order to escape from the Devil, since it is alleged to have bitten off its own genitals while fleeing from hunters (for whom these parts were a most desirable delicacy), and by leaving them behind escaped with its life. The distinctive two-coloured markings of the stork led to its being seen as a symbol of the dual nature of Christ. It is difficult to say, of course, whether each animal depicted does in fact bear a specific meaning.

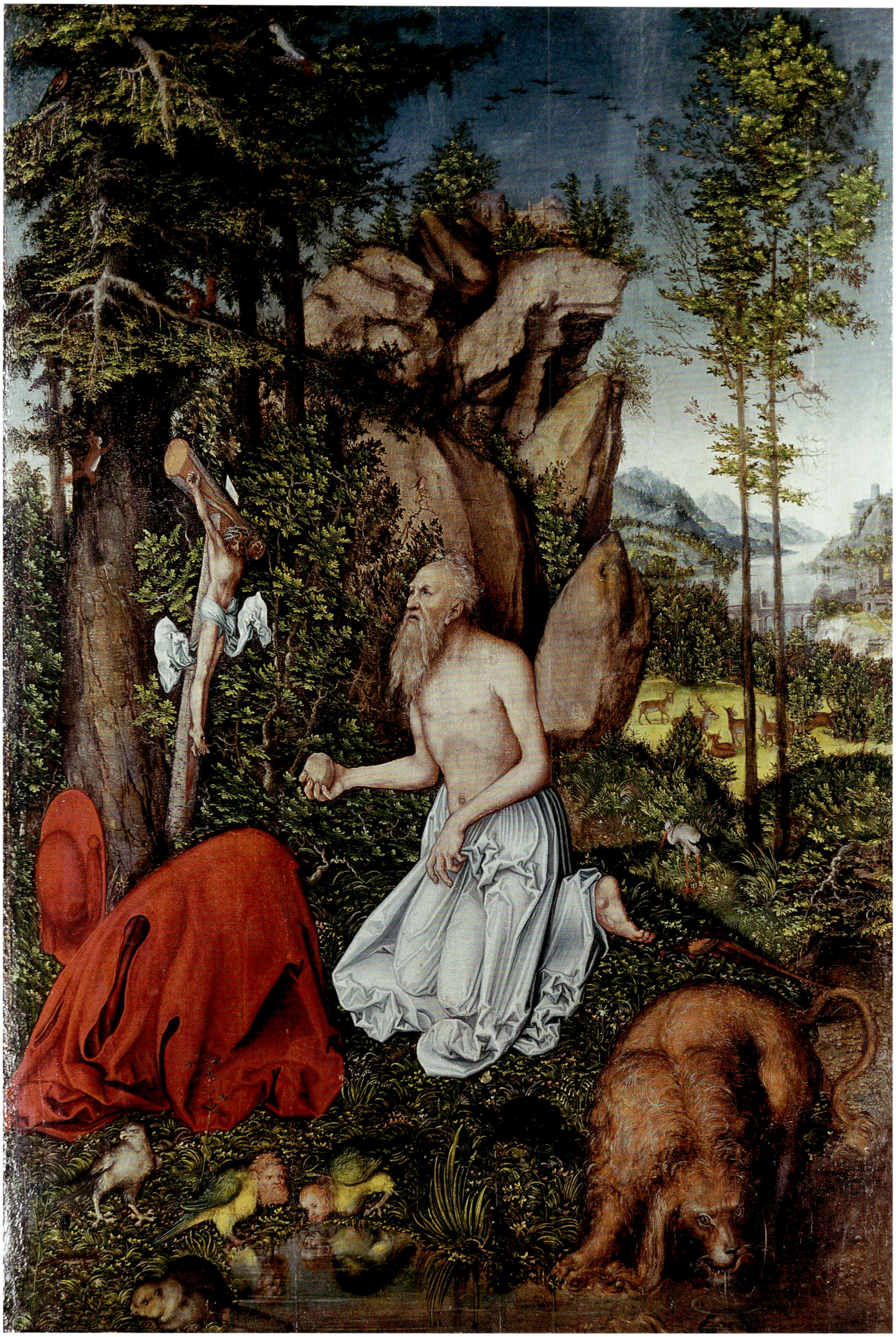

56 St Mary Magdalen

Wittenberg, 1525

Dated 1525 in the sandy ground at bottom left, and signed below with the winged serpent facing right

Oil and tempera on beechwood
47.8 x 30 cm

Wallraf-Richartz Museum/Fondation Corboud, Cologne, WRM 390

Provenance:
Frau Therese Schaafhausen; acquired as a gift from her in 1867

(Frankfurt only)

Selected references:
FR 168; Hiller/Vey 1969, pp. 43 f.; Krischel 2003, pp. 6 f.

Mary from Magdala (situated on the Sea of Galilee) has always been associated with the unnamed sinner who anointed the feet of Christ in the house of Simon (Luke, 7, 37–50), and for this reason she is often portrayed as a converted prostitute wearing fashionable clothes adorned with expensive jewellery. She was one of the three women said to have gone on Easter Monday to Christ's tomb to anoint his body. Her attribute is thus the jar of ointment which she carries, in Cranach's panel: a costly piece of faience in the slightly conical form of the *albarello*, a pharmacist's receptacle. According to legend, Mary was driven out of the Holy Land and withdrew to the wilds of southern France to do penance by rejecting any form of clothing. As a reward for her willingness to repent she was carried up to heaven by angels where she could listen to the heavenly choirs. In the halo in the upper-left background, Cranach repeats the motif of this legend, which he had already used in one of his earlier woodcuts (cat. 52). Cranach's Cologne composition offers an interesting combination of the two types of picture of the saint. On the one hand, the panel can be seen as portraying a scene from her life, showing the moment when Mary Magdalen sets out for Christ's tomb. On the other hand, the figure, with her strict frontality, corresponds to the normal type of isolated image of a standing saint, as could have been seen in abundance on contemporary altarpieces. This reading is supported by the presence of the tree behind the saint; it surrounds the contours of her body with its strangely dense foliage and almost shields her from the background landscape. Thus the saint might appear, with her upright stance, as closely tied to her role as a Gothic portal figure. Even the sandy ground at her feet separates her from the idyllic landscape, populated by red deer, in the middle ground and background.

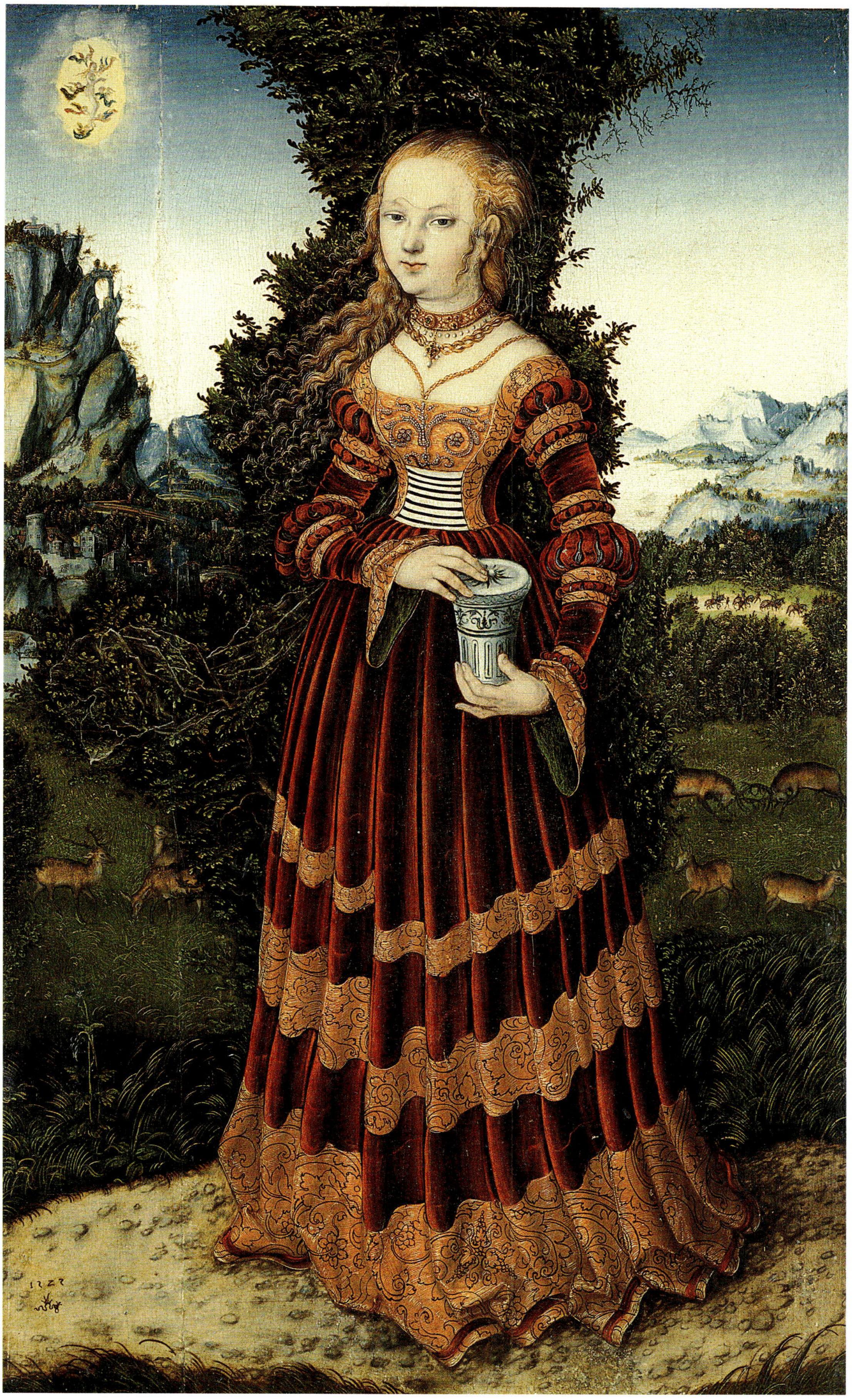

57 St Helena

Wittenberg, 1525

Signed upper right on the black background with the serpent with upright wings facing left between the pairs of numbers denoting the year

Oil and tempera on red beechwood
40 x 27 cm

Cincinatti Art Museum, Cincinatti
1927.387

Provenance:
in 1851 in the gallery of the Princes of Liechtenstein in Vienna; acquired in 1927, the bequest of Mary M. Emery.

Selected references:
FR 164; Scott 1987, pp. 45 f., no. 14

St Helena (*c.* 255–330) is a historical figure, wife of Emperor Constantius I and mother of Constantine the Great, who in 313 introduced Christianity as an official religion into the Western Roman Empire, which he ruled. According to legend, when over 70 she was ordered by God in a dream to go to Palestine to find the Holy Places and to have them restored in a worthy manner. She went immediately on a pilgrimage to Jerusalem, where she had the Hill of Golgotha excavated for the cross of Christ. The excavation uncovered three crosses, corresponding to those of Christ and the two Thieves crucified with him, one of which proved to have miraculous properties. The discovery of the crosses was certified by the bishop of Jerusalem and led to the building of the burial church and other memorials; in Rome, Emperor Constantine had the Basilica of Santa Croce in Gerusalemme built for the relics of the cross brought back by his mother.

Lucas Cranach depicts the saint against a black background, wearing a red velvet dress with gold brocade insets, adorned with fashionable chains and a typical contemporary necklace, and on her head a cruciform crown. The figure's angled pose and her attribute, the cross, which she holds with her right arm, suggests the picture's original function as the wing of a medium-sized triptych intended for private devotions. Although the cult of St Helena north of the Alps is mainly associated with her residence in Trier, she may also have been popular in Saxony since she was regarded as the patron saint of miners, in reference to the excavation of the crosses at Golgotha. At that time silver mining flourished in the Erzgebirge (The Ore Mountains). As patron saint of donatrixes she also appears in a *Lamentation* panel by Cranach in Budapest (Szépmüvészeti Muzéum; FR 76).

The foreshortening of the perspective also includes the saint's face, which thus appears a little broader than usual. Although this view does not seem quite correct in terms of mathematical perspective, together with her fresh complexion it does lend the young empress a soft, girlish charm. More surprising is the uninhibited way in which Cranach chooses to dress the figure of a saint like the young ladies in his courtly portraits, down to the last detail (cf. cat. 78).

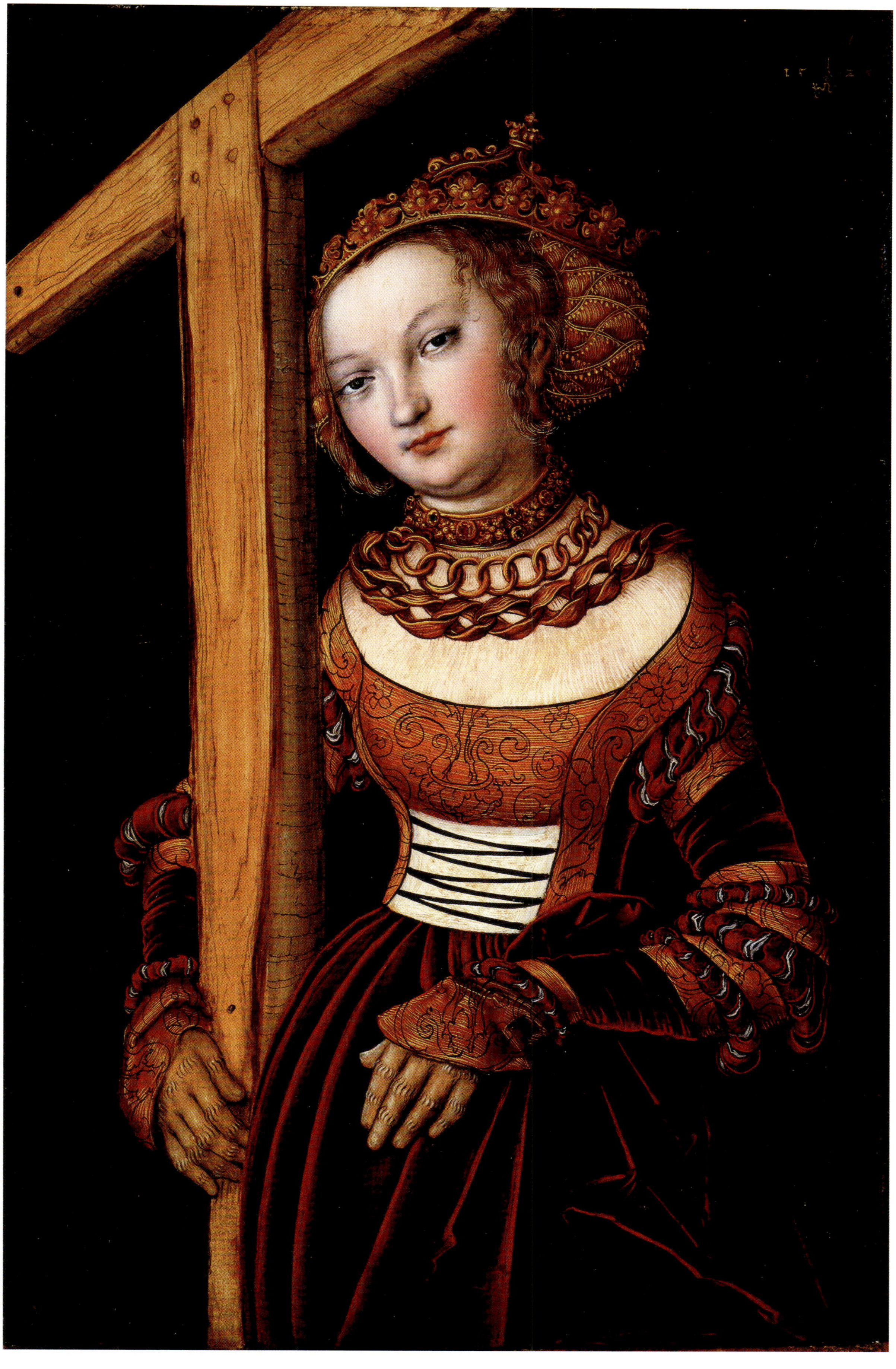

58 Plague Picture

Wittenberg, *c.* 1516–18

Oil and tempera on limewood
74.5 x 56 cm

Szépmüvészeti Muzéum,
Budapest, 128

Provenance:
until 1848 in the Chamber Presidium

Selected references:
FR 134 D; Hagemann 1982, pp. 17–19; Ember/Takács 2003, p. 32; on the concept of type transference in Cranach: Koepplin 2003

'God is a just God who threatens us every day. If we refuse to turn, he has whetted his sword and bent his bow and loaded it with deadly missiles; he has directed his arrows to destroy.' (Psalms 7, 11–13) So states Luther's Bible, which appeared in 1545. Yahweh (Jehovah), the God of the Old Testament, is an angry God who in many places in the Bible, dating from the time of the Tribal League, is connected metaphorically with punitive arrow shots. This kind of thirst for revenge is sometimes transferred in medieval thought to the Saviour, motivated as much by the unity of the Trinity as by the role of Christ as Judge of the World. Thomas Aquinas himself, the great theologian and Dominican (1225–1274), saw in a vision the angry Christ sending plague, hunger and war down in the form of arrows upon men who had fallen into sinful ways, and by so doing aiming to annihilate the whole world. Plague pictures from the late Middle Ages did indeed show the Son of God (at least as often as his father) hurling or firing down arrows symbolising the threat of death – one need only mention the famous right upper half of the outside of the *Barfüsseraltar* of 1424, named after the Franciscan Barefoot Church in Göttingen (Niedersächsisches Landesmuseum, Hanover). A woodcut from around 1460–70 attached to the lid of a medicine box shows this ambivalence directly: on the left, Christ as the Man of Sorrows kneels on a T-shaped cross, while on the right God the Father fires three arrows together at mankind; both figures wears cruciform haloes.

At the same time, comparison with the woodcut makes it clear that Lucas Cranach returned once more to simple forms of art to find sources for the painting now in Budapest,and transferred them to the medium of the panel picture. This was a basic principle of his picture making, as Dieter Koepplin has frequently pointed out. In this composition Cranach repeats the formula almost exactly: God the Father, this time without a halo, aims his bow with three arrows downwards and, on the left, is watched by the kneeling Man of Sorrows. In the right half of the picture, however, he replaces tormented mankind with a more encouraging motif, depicting humanity gathered together beneath the protective cloak of the Mother of All or the *Madonna of Mercy*. In the iconography of plague pictures, Mary the Madonna of the Protective Cloak functions as the second significant advocate seeking the grace of God for sinful humanity. Lucas Cranach was not the first to combine Jesus and Mary in this context. Around 1490–95 a figure group from the workshop of Michel Erhart, the woodcarver from Ulm, shows precisely this pairing of the *Man of Sorrows* and the *Madonna of the Protective Cloak* beneath a God the Father firing arrows (from the Benedictine convent, Urspring; now in the Diocesan Museum, Rottenburg). However, Cranach's painted version of the subject remains a highly original devotional picture.

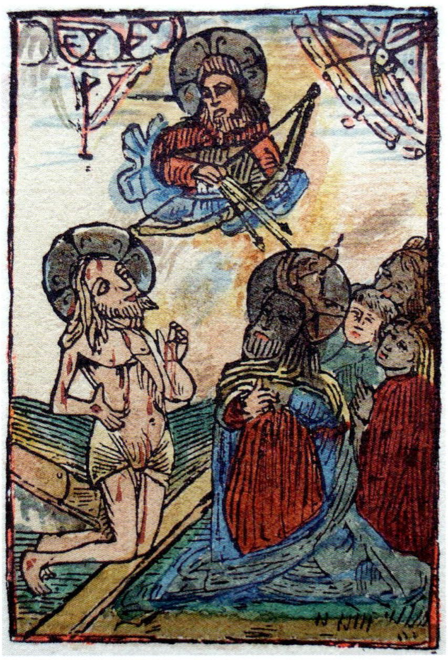

South German *c.* 1460–70, *Plague Picture*, woodcut

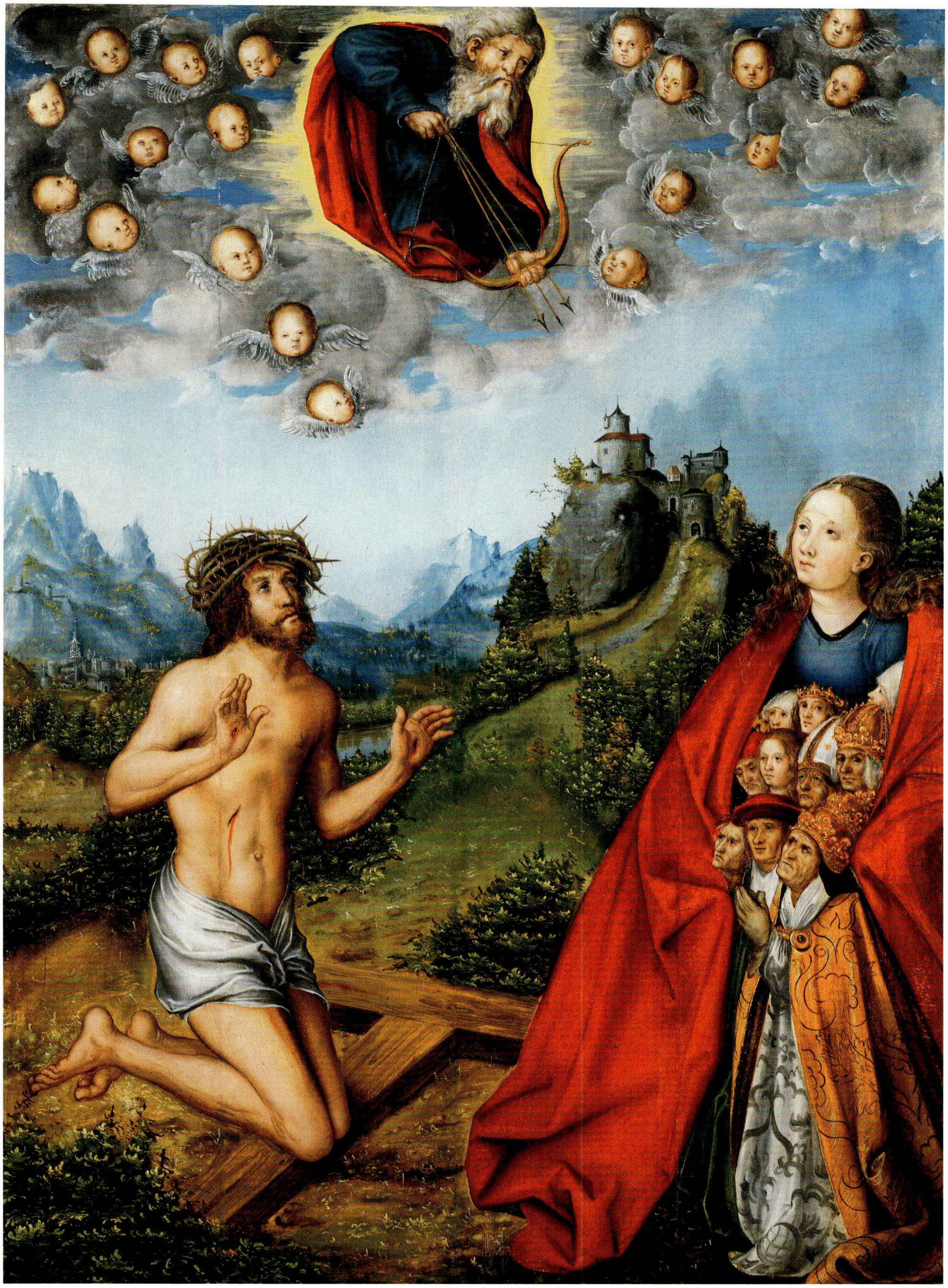

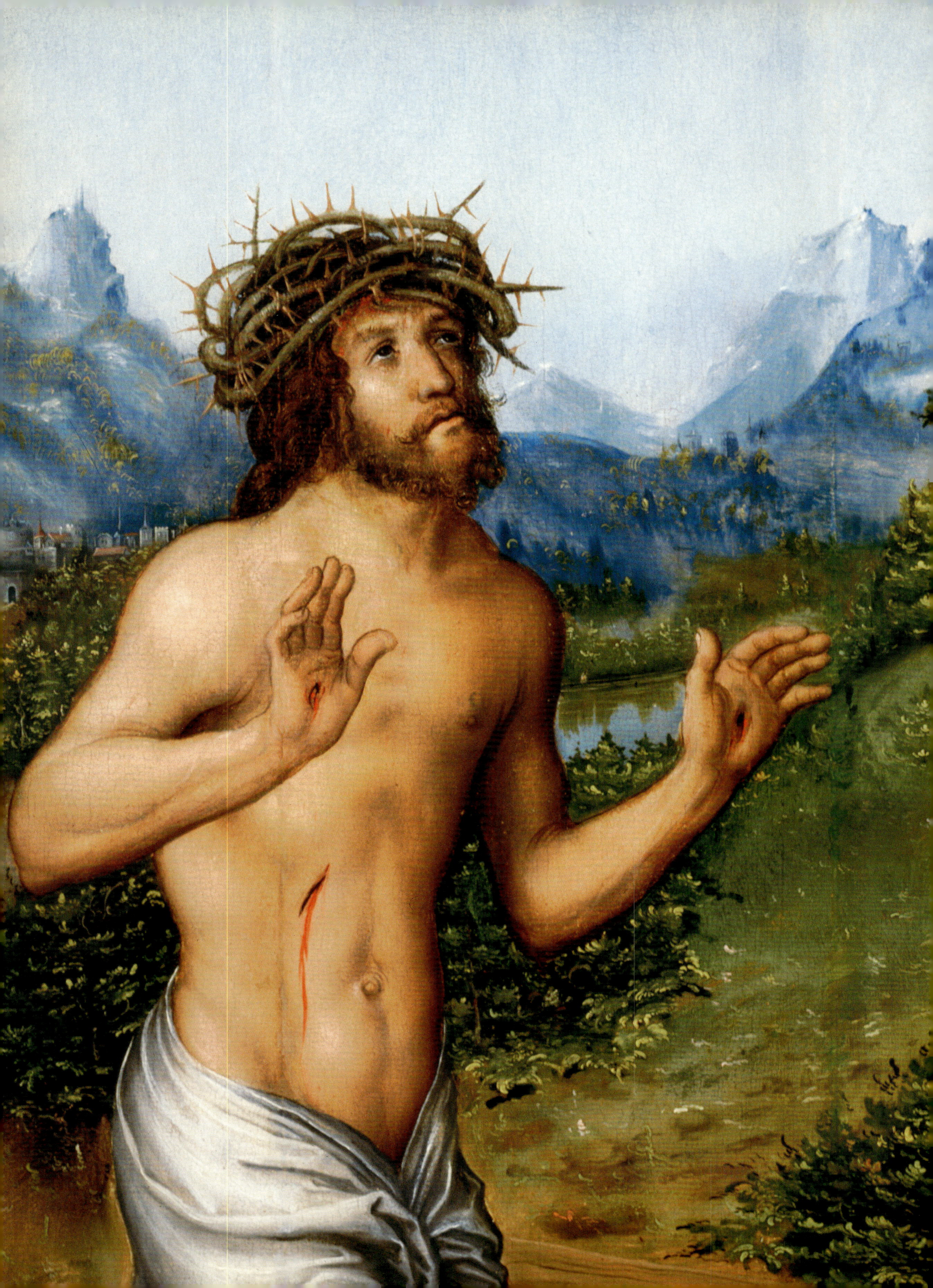

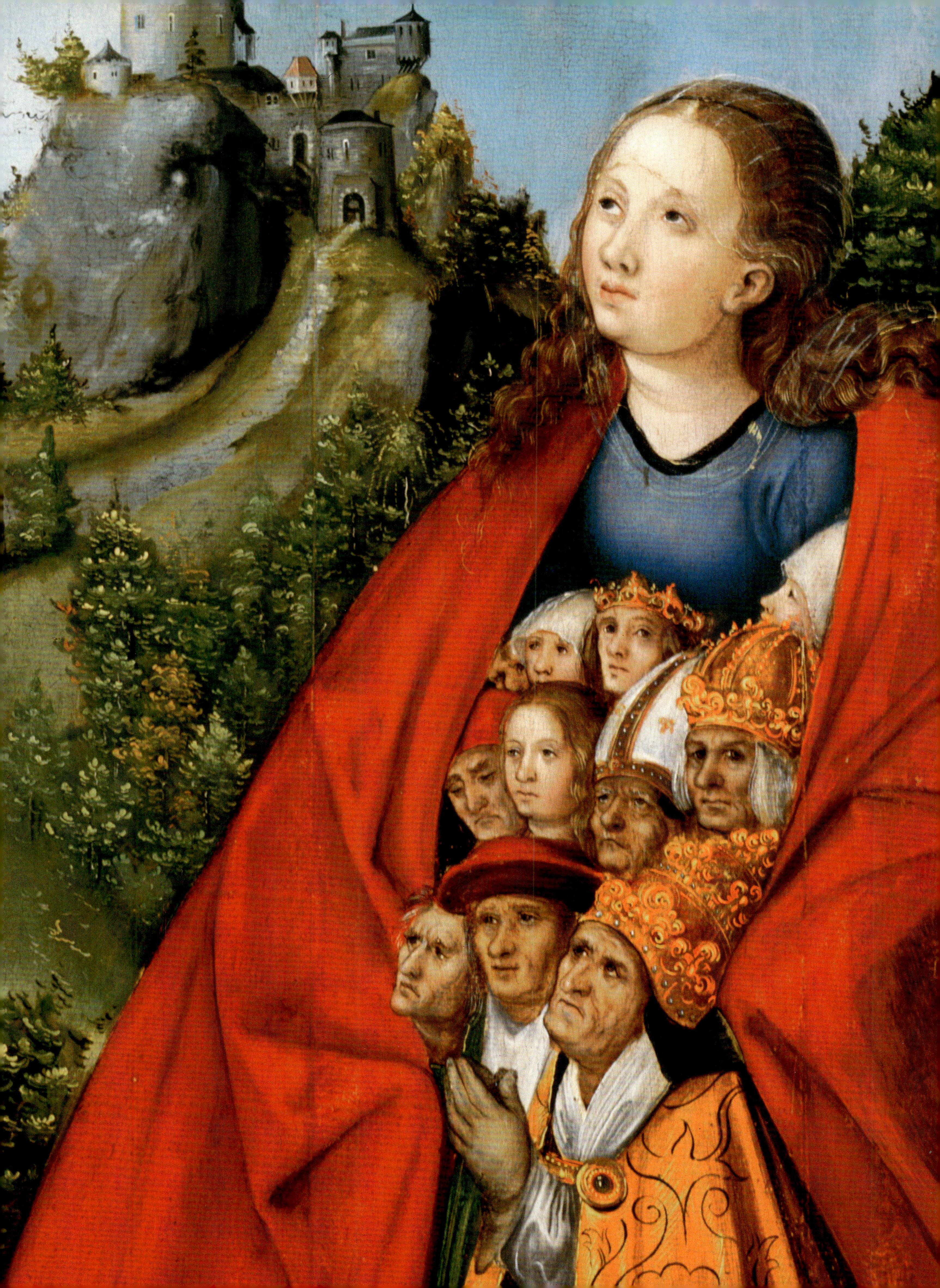

59 Christ's Head with Crown of Thorns

Wittenberg, *c.* 1520–25

Oil and tempera on limewood
27.5 x 20.7 cm

Private collection

(Frankfurt only)

Selected references:
not in FR; Sotheby's 7.7.2004, pp. 108–11, lot 31

This small panel is in excellent condition: it shows the head, neck and shoulders of the Redeemer on a black background, the head crowned with an extensive wreath of branches with long thorns and lit from behind with a cruciform halo indicated by beams of light at the top and on both sides. The representation is based on the *vera ikon*, the true face of Christ. According to a legend popular since the twelfth century, this likeness appeared in a miraculous way on St Veronica's veil after the devout companion of Mary had used it to wipe the blood and sweat from the Lord on the Road to Calvary. The *vera ikon* is revered as a relic in St Peter's, Rome, and was a favourite subject of paintings and graphic works in the late Middle Ages.

Cranach's version differs in crucial ways from the traditional treatment. The black background extinguishes any sign of the veil bearing the likeness, which is usually indicated in other works. The facial type no longer corresponds to the traditional picture of Christ with a separate beard and moustache. Examples of frank realism such as the wide-open eyes containing reflections of light and the mouth opened in pain, in which even the lower teeth can be seen, are far removed from the conventional formula. Nevertheless, some graphic versions of the head of Christ do follow this mode. An engraving by the Master B M and a woodcut from Dürer's circle (SMS A 18) include the open mouth, the latter also featuring a head of curls which is so similar as to suggest itself as a possible model for this small panel. However, the painting differs from the graphic works in two aspects: neither of the latter shows more than Christ's face, which is logical and consistent with traditional representations of the legend, according to which Christ wipes his face with a cloth. By including the upper body, Cranach merges the pictorial scheme of the *vera ikon* with a second idea, that of Christ as the Man of Sorrows, here presented in extreme close-up and tightly cropped. Cranach also veers away from the strict frontality and symmetry of the *vera ikon* by shifting the head slightly to the left and away from the axis, and moving the Redeemer's gaze to the right in the opposite direction. The impression of movement thus conveyed serves to stress that the picture should be seen as a representation of the real Messiah and not simply His image.

The crown of thorns also departs from convention, being not just unusually large but also placed more to the centre of the picture rather than following the sideways alignment of the head. Although it seems to hover over the head, its thorns have left wound marks from which ooze drops of vermilion-coloured blood, some of them containing pinpoints of light which help to lend the painting its very painterly atmosphere. The prominence of the crown and the length of the thorns leads us to share Werner Schade's view that the most precious relic in the *Wittenberger Heiltum*, a book of relics which Frederick the Wise went to great lengths to reproduce and publish, was a thorn from the crown of thorns presented by the king of France in the fourteenth century. This impressive painting was clearly intended to remind people of the presence of the relic in Wittenberg.

Cranach's small panel was also the subject of an astonishing discovery after infra-red photography uncovered the preparatory underdrawing on the ground, revealing two much smaller male heads in profile. They indicate that the limewood panel was originally intended to depict a completely different subject.

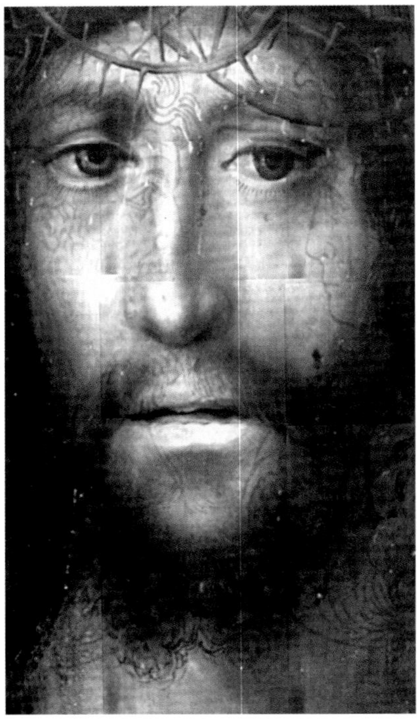

Infra-red reflectograph

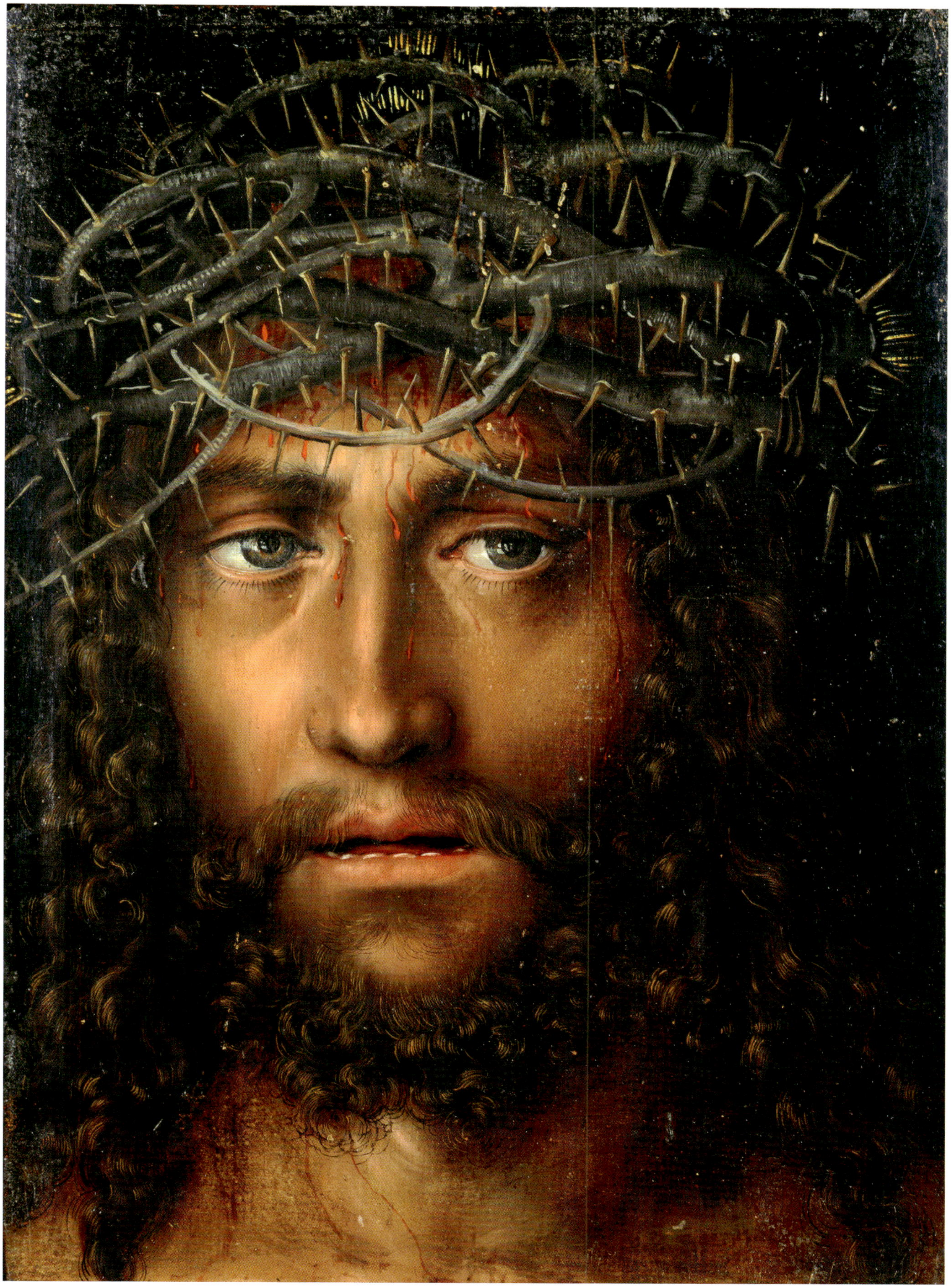

60 Christ as the Man of Sorrows

Lucas Cranach the Younger (?)

Oil and tempera on red beechwood
51.2 x 34.5 cm

Museum im Roselius-Haus, Bremen,
B 56

Provenance:
acquired in 1928 through
Arthur Hauth: 1919 in Flechthein,
both Düsseldorf

(Frankfurt only)

Selected references:
FR 381 F; Stamm 2003, pp. 62–8,
no. 14

The inscription in the top right corner reads: *'JESUS / [...] / come and simply drink [...] or / come, come and give your heart to me / my blood shall refresh / and bring you to heaven's splendour'*

'MAN / Jesus's side is wide open / to me. His blood that cries / whoever thirsteth come to me. / Jesus! I too am very thirsty, / and drank from the hollow in your side / your wounds touch my soul / which I summon your blood to refresh.'

As Harold Hittenbeck of Bremen discovered, the second stanza quotes word for word from Song XIV of the religious songs of Countess Ludämilia Elisabeth von Schwarzburg-Rudolstadt (1640–1672), which were published posthumously in 1687 in Rudolstadt under the title *Die Stimme der Freundin.*

Although the verses were added towards the end of the seventeenth century, they show the function of this devotional painting: the beholder (Man) enters into a direct dialogue with the Redeemer about the wound in his side and the blood flowing from it. In a characteristically expressive proto-baroque gesture from the pictorial repertoire of the late Middle Ages, the Christ figure is drawn into the centre of the composition to show both the nail wounds in the back of his hands and the wound in his side caused by the piercing from Longinus's lance, the wound in the side now gaping wide, held there by the fingers placed on the chest. Jesus's side is indeed opened wide before us. The painter also meticulously depicts the spiny crown of thorns and the wounds caused by them, as well as countless wound marks all over the body which stem from the scourging suffered in the palace of Pilate (cat. 22). Even the implements used appear in the picture: in his right hand Christ holds a bundle of rods and at the same time shows the nail wound; behind the rods are two scourges to indicate that several of Pilate's assistants were involved. Christ's body writhes to one side as though from the torture he suffers. The dislocated appearance of the right shoulder is intended to recall the overstretched arms on the cross. The beholder gradually becomes aware of all these signs of the Passion as the Redeemer looks directly at him.

It is therefore easy to understand why this representation of the half-length Man of Sorrows was seen as the epitome of the 'Image of Piety', a devotional picture that commands compassion. It confronts the devout viewer both as a speeded-up succession of images and at the same time as a close-up account of the entire Passion sequence. It also recalls that powerful eucharistic moment when Christ, according to the legend of Pope Gregory the Great (*c.* 540–604), appeared above the altar in precisely this form when the Pope was celebrating Mass while holding secret doubts about the doctrine of transubstantiation.

The pictorial formula had been very popular since the fourteenth century. The great achievement of the Cranach workshop was to sharpen it by summarising the story while retaining a consistent pictorial logic. In their version of the subject they achieved this not with the help of angel figures and gestures of grief or a complete collection of the 'arms of Christ', the instruments of his suffering, but through an exact rendition of the martyred body, evoking each aspect of the Passion.

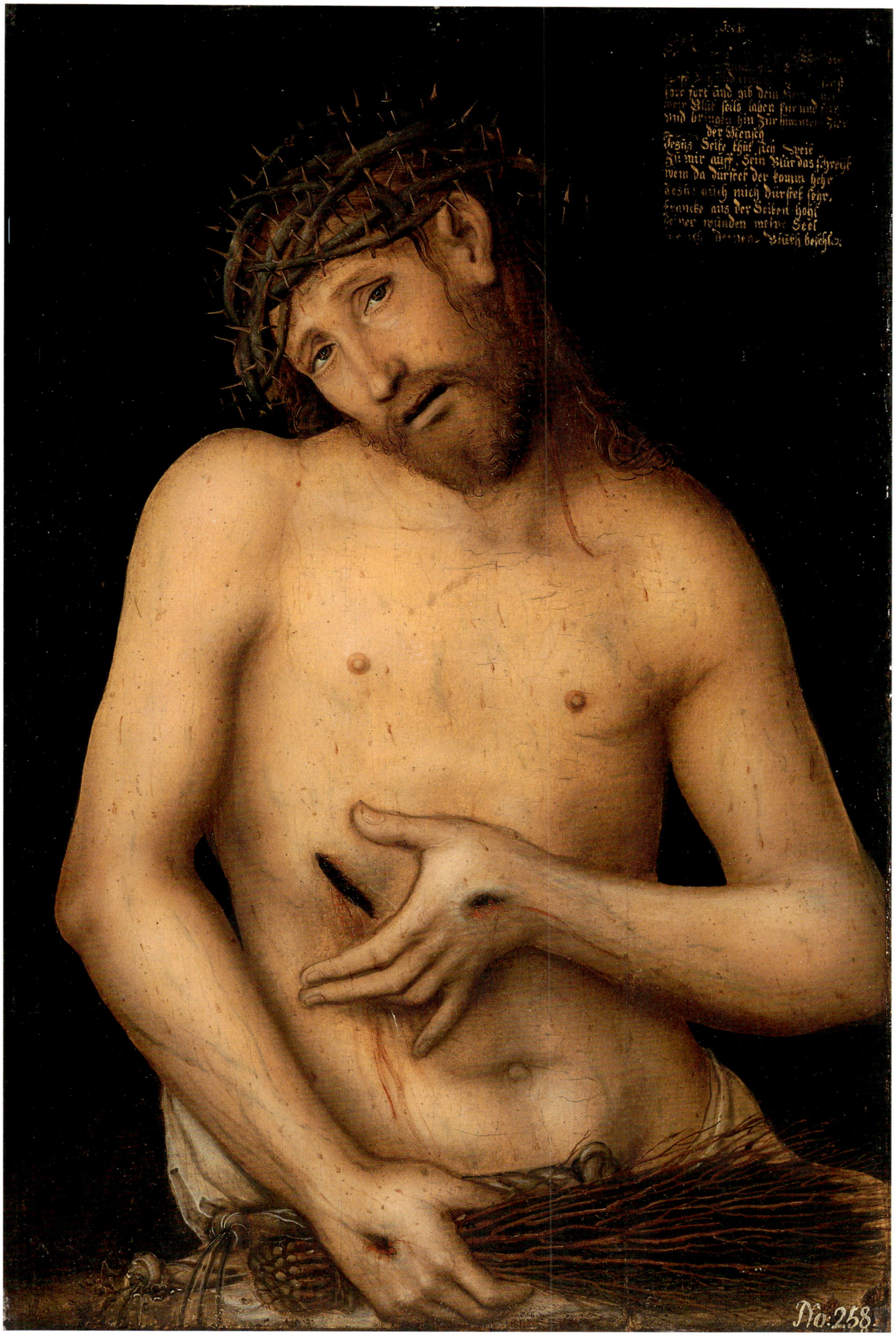
No:258.

62 Virgin and Child

Wittenberg, *c.* 1518

Signed in the bottom left corner with the serpent with upright wings facing left

Oil and tempera on limewood
40.7 x 31.2 cm

Staatliche Kunsthalle, Karlsruhe, 108

Provenance:
acquired in 1691 in the collection of Margravine Sibylla Augusta von Baden-Baden from the estate of the Dukes of Sachsen-Lauenburg in Schloss Theusing

(Frankfurt only)

Selected references:
FR 87; Lauts 1966, vol. 1, p. 89; Koepplin/Falk 1974/76, vol. 2, pp. 532 f., no. 382; Dresel/Lüdke/Vey 1992, pp. 64–7, no. 10

This small picture sparkles like a jewel, the result of extremely fine handling of paint, applied with great confidence in every area to produce the appropriate effect. This applies equally to the porcelain-like smoothness of the flesh tones, created by delicate varnishes, to the architectural clusters in the background landscape and the tiny nuances in the finely shaded folds of the Madonna's dress. The landscape, in the background on the left and above on the right, is developed in a calm and convincing manner – the fantastic shapes of earlier years have given way to scenery that is closer to nature but no less impressive. These culminate in the soft yellow of the sunrise (?) on the horizon, whose light from below meets the painterly cloud forms above and illuminates their rounded, cottonwool shapes. To the front of this, the Virgin Mary appears, entering from the right so that the Christ Child, held sideways in her arms, is in the central axis of the picture. She is placed so subtly within the composition that the asymmetry is hardly noticeable: the strands of hair covering her right shoulder continue the descending line of the built-up hill crest and lead it into the contours of her cloak, finally running out near the bottom left corner of the picture. She holds the child securely in her right arm, though without cramping him, while her left hand is laid like a cushion over his thigh. The large oval sweep of the Child's cloth and, the sleeve of the Virgin's dress and cloak lend optical support like a pile of cushions. Comfortably lodged in his mother's arms, the Infant Jesus reaches up with both hands towards his mother's face, which is inclined sideways. The tips of the child's fingers almost touch her cheek. The old pictorial formula of the Christ Child nestling against his mother's neck and cheek, as seen in the Byzantine Madonnas of the *Eleousa* and the *Glykophilousa* types, is here refined through the artist's observation of a child's rather awkward efforts to touch his mother.

It is a mark of the quality of this Cranach Madonna, perhaps the finest to have survived, that, according to the former restorer Paolo Cadorin of Basel, lapis lazuli was used for Mary's cloak instead of the usual azurite. Lapis lazuli was so expensive that painters generally only obtained it on request for specific commissions, whereas for pictures destined for the open market they used cheaper blue pigments. Lapis lazuli blue is also delicate, and here ageing has proved somewhat detrimental; the cloak is the only part of the picture not to have been perfectly preserved.

The painting may be dated by comparing it to dated works such as the Cologne *Madonna* of 1518 (Wallraf-Richartz Museum, FR 89). This shows how the Karlsruhe figure, with its high, spherical forehead above the dainty doll's face, which looks as if it has been pushed downwards, has already acquired the features which in Cranach's later works became the hallmark of his ideal of feminine beauty.

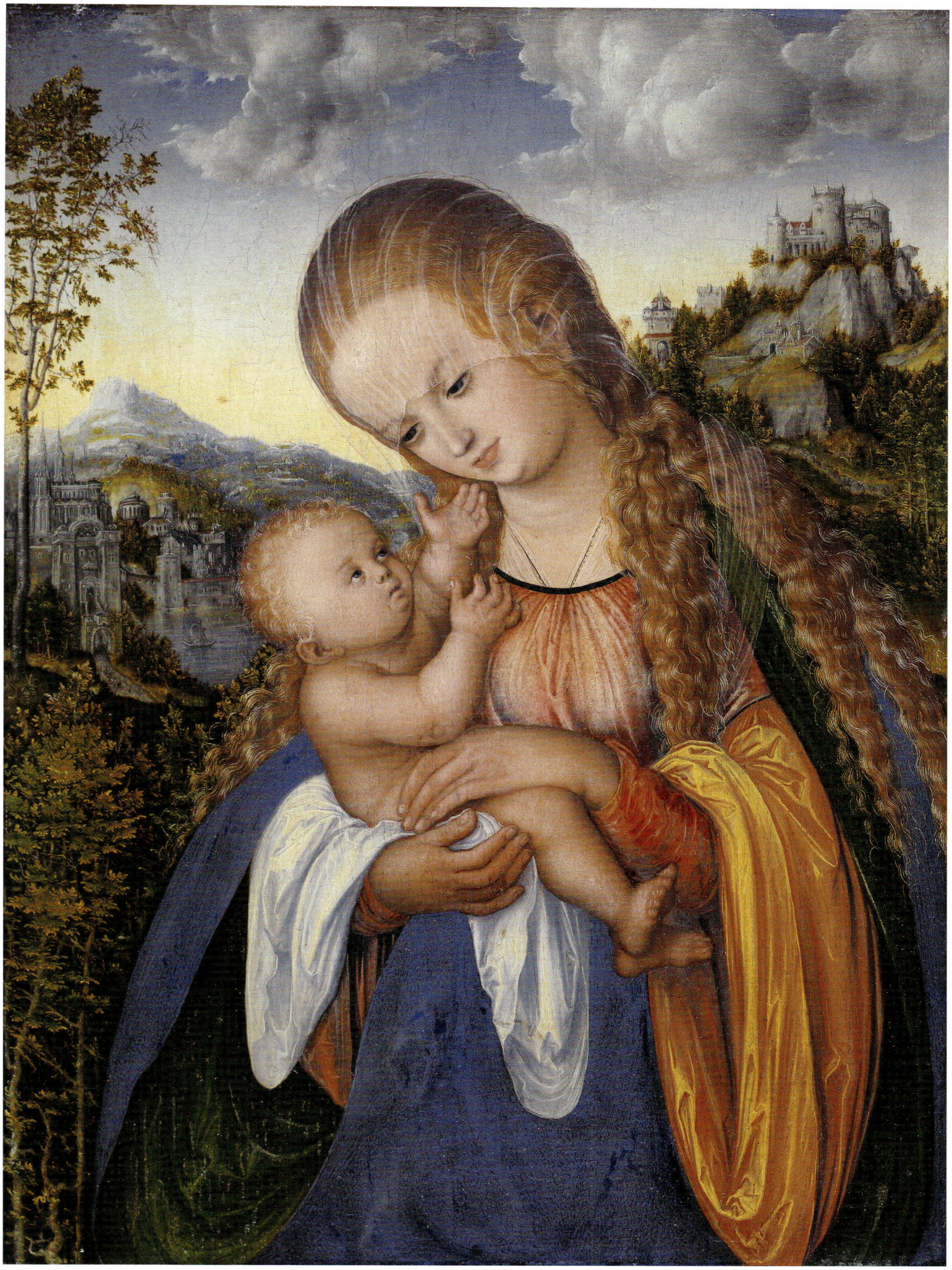

63 The Virgin of the Grapes before a Hanging held by Two Angels

Wittenberg, *c.* 1520–1525

Signed bottom left with the serpent with upright wings facing right

Oil and tempera on beechwood
60 x 42 cm

Bayerische Staatsgemäldesammlungen, Munich, Alte Pinakothek, 1023

Provenance:
formerly Fugger family collection; gift of King Ludwig I of Bavaria, 1824

(Frankfurt only)

Selected references:
FR 163;Von der Osten 1965, pp. 182–4; Koepplin/Falk 1974/76, vol. 2, pp. 522–6; Alte Pinakothek, München, 1983, p. 150; Grimm/Erichsen/Brockhoff 1994, pp. 331 f., no. 153; Sandner 1998, p. 142, no. 16.2; Wittmann 1998, pp. 176–80

The Virgin Mary is seated with the Child on her lap in front of a cloth of honour held by two winged putti. To the right of the hanging is a view of sky, and a landscape reaching into the distance. The Virgin is seated slightly to the right away from the central axis but leans to the left while at the same time inclining her head and shoulders in the other direction so that her head is in the middle of the panel. Thus she creates a space for the Christ Child who stands on a diagonally arranged moss-green silk cushion with a tassel on the front corner. The Virgin wears a conventional red dress fastened at the top with a clip; beneath the turned-back sleeves is a dark undergown. Over the dress she wears a dark-blue coat with yellow lining which lies in folds above her knees. The outline of the coat on the left continues the line of her head and combines with that of the hanging on the right to enclose the two figures in a triangular composition. With her left hand she carefully supports the small child while he balances on one leg and raises his arm to offer his mother a grape. He has clearly picked this from the bunch that the Virgin holds in her right hand, and which he holds with his left hand to support himself. The relationship between mother and child reveals a special warmth and harmony. While the Child presents the grape with a touchingly portrayed expression of childish accomplishment, the Virgin looks mildly down at him with a pensive air – though it almost seems, from the angle of her head, that she is about to draw back instinctively from the fruit.

Portrayals of the Virgin and Child were among the favourite themes of the Wittenberg court painter from an early stage. Although the number of surviving pictures shows that this was an extremely successful commercial product, he carried out the many versions with great care (cat. 16 [Florence], cat. 62 [Karlsruhe]). Even after the beginning of the Reformation, his pictures of the Virgin were bought not only by Old Believers; we know that Luther himself took a comparatively liberal view of devotional pictures and might very well have owned an image of the Virgin, as one of his recorded conversations of 1532 suggests. It is thus hardly surprising that this panel from Munich, completed towards the middle of the 1520s, should be of such high quality, and may have been painted largely by Cranach himself. It follows the popular type of the Virgin of the Grapes, which appeared relatively early in Cranach's repertoire, as we know from two that were painted around 1510 (FR29, formerly in Breslau (Wroclaw) and FR30 in the Thyssen-Bornemisza collection in Madrid). The bunch of grapes has numerous symbolic meanings, relating both to the Virgin Mary and to Jesus. To interpreters of the Scriptures the Virgin is seen as the noble vine on which the divine grapes of Christ were nurtured; at the same time, by analogy with the grapes crushed in the winepress, it refers to Christ's forthcoming sacrificial death, as well as to the image of Christ as the true vine and his believers as the branches (John 15, 1–17). Not least, it indicates the sacrament of the Eucharist; against the background of the controversy over the practice of Holy Communion, which according to Luther should not be the sole preserve of priests but available to all believers; this panel could also have been suitable for a Protestant public for whom such paintings would not be objects of veneration but pictures reminding and teaching their viewers of God's mercy. GD

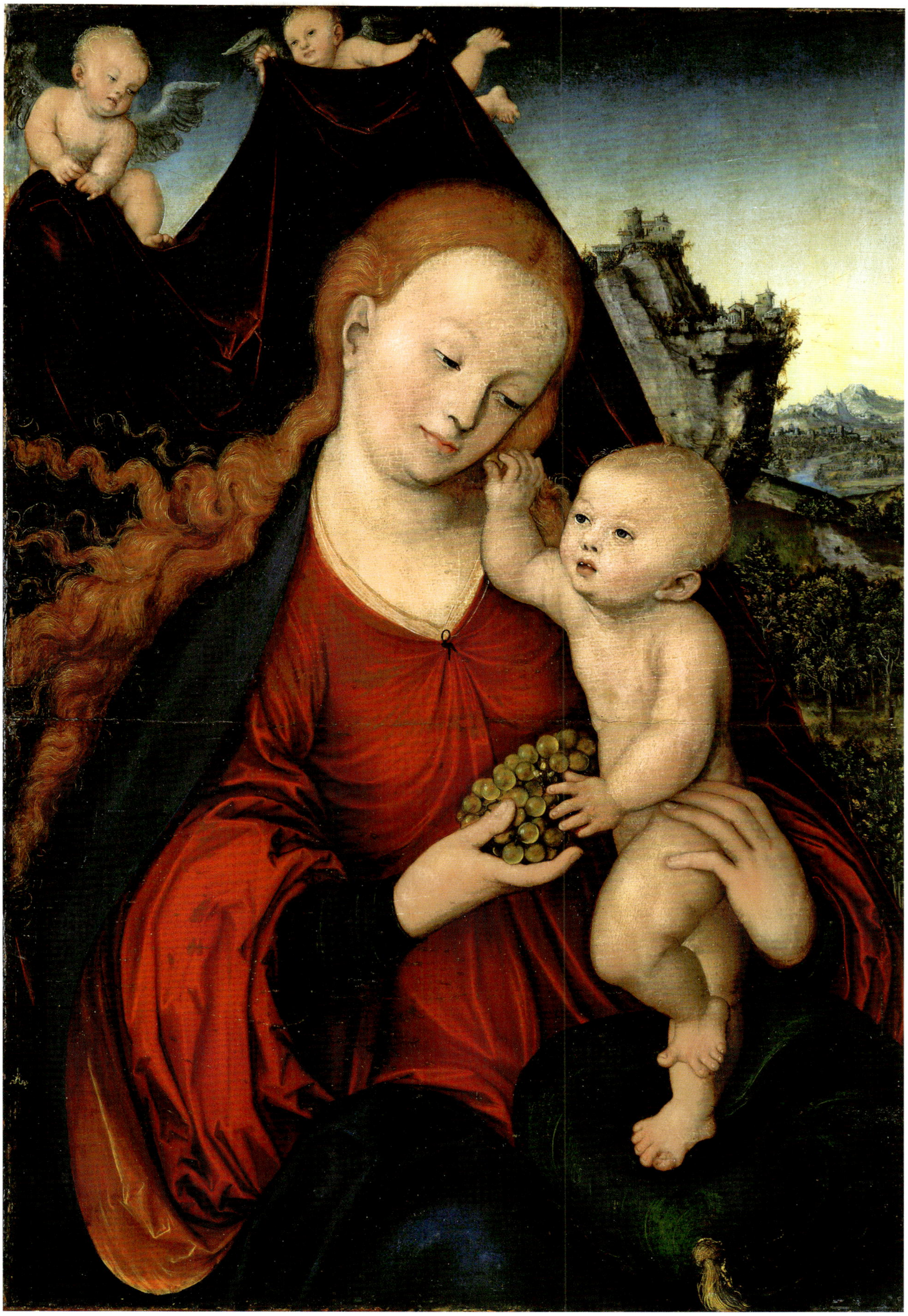

The Virgin of the Grapes before a Hanging held by Two Angels |

64 Virgin and Child with Grapes

Lucas Cranach the Elder (?)
(and workshop)

Wittenberg, after 1537

Signed beside the Virgin's shoulder with the serpent with folded wings facing left

Oil and tempera on wood
77.3 x 56.7 cm

Dr. Karl Graf von und zu Eltz-Kempenich, Burg Eltz

(Frankfurt only)

Selected references:
not in FR; Koepplin/Falk 1974/76, vol. 2, pp. 522 f.; Hinz 1993, p. 118 f.; Wittmann 1998, pp. 176–80; Ritzenhofen 2002, p. 52

This panel has been in private ownership for generations and can usually be seen in the Rübenacher Untersaal in Burg Eltz. Like the version in the Alte Pinakothek in Munich (cat. 63) it belongs iconographically to the type of the Virgin with Grapes, but this comparison reveals a radical change in its composition. Behind the Virgin there is no curtain, held by angels and serving as a cloth of honour, and no view of the landscape typical of Cranach's earlier depictions of the Virgin (cf. cats 16 [Düsseldorf], 17 [Florence] and 62 [Karlsruhe]). Instead, the Virgin and Child are placed against a neutral, almost black background and seen closer up, as a result of the picture's tight framing – the top of the panel is just above the Virgin's head and the Christ Child occupies at least two-thirds of the picture's height. As in Munich, the two are arranged in a triangular composition, broken by the inward movement of the Child's leg. Everything seems designed to give a soothing character to the painting. The folds in the robes are sparingly depicted and have a metallic hardness, and the Virgin's long hair is tied in parallel strands. Instead of climbing upon his mother, full of childish curiosity, the Infant Christ stands, safely supported, with both feet in her lap and is just about to put a grape in his mouth; meanwhile he looks serenely past the viewer and out of the picture; the Virgin observes all this, keeping her thoughts to herself. Even the colour scheme is simplified: the Virgin's cloak and robe are painted in intense but muted tones of red, blue and green to harmonise with the background, making the pale flesh tones stand out.

There are several isolated examples from the late 1520s of the Virgin depicted against a neutral background, but nonetheless these were unusual. On the other hand, the Cranach workshop produced a whole series of Virgins with Grapes, some of them including John the Baptist as an infant, which are comparable with our panel in their basic features; these are listed in Friedländer and Rosenberg as nos. 386 to 389. They are not dated, and offer few clues as to when they were painted. Many of them, however, like our panel, are signed with the device of the serpent with folded bat's wings which, with few exceptions, was not used until 1537; so a dating after that year seems plausible. In many cases they were series products of only moderate quality, but the panel from Burg Eltz stands out from these by virtue of its particularly successful, sensitive composition and the high standard of its execution.

From the large number of surviving variants it is clear that even as late as 1540 the Cranach workshop was producing devotional pictures of the Virgin on a large scale. Even though the tight framing of the compositions, making them easier to read, the focusing on Christ as the Redeemer and the references to the Eucharist (cf. cat. 63 [Munich]) make these pictures seem better suited to Protestant tenets, in most cases they were intended for supporters of the Old Belief. Once more this shows that Cranach's reputation in Wittenberg did not suffer when he continued to fulfil the demands of this clientele, neither does there seem to have been any resentment concerning his work for Luther and the Reformers. A particularly interesting example of this is a Virgin panel by Cranach now in Innsbruck Cathedral and which was apparently a present from the Elector George of Saxony to Archduke Leopold V, and then donated by the latter's son to Passau. It now attracts great admiration as an image of mercy, and is frequently copied and sold in the form of reproductions (cf. figs 80, 82).

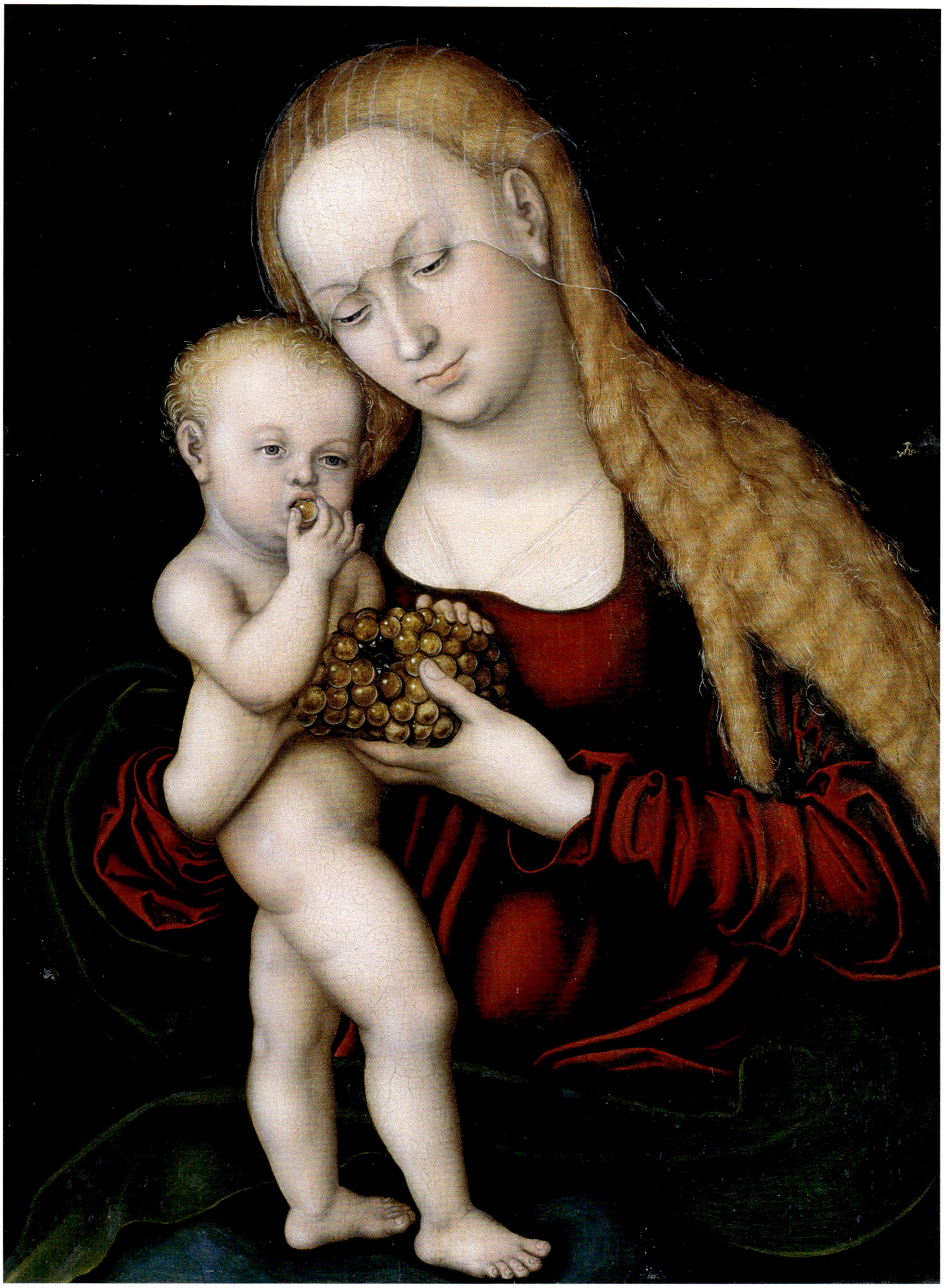

65 The Virgin and Child on a Crescent Moon with the Donor Hieronymus Rudelauf

Lucas Cranach the Elder (workshop)

Wittenberg, before 1523

The figure of the donor is accompanied by the Rudelauf family arms. Until a restoration in 1991 a damaged inscription was emblazoned over the arms: *HIERONYMVS RVDELLANT. AETATIS SVAE 74 JAHR ANNO 1500*

Oil and tempera on limewood
89.9 x 60.3 cm

Städel Museum, Frankfurt., 1731

Provenance:
acquired in 1923 as a bequest from Freiherr Adolph von Holzhausen

(Frankfurt only)

Selected references:
FR sup. 6 H; Tacke 1991; Brinkmann/Kemperdick 2005, pp. 235–42; Koepplin 2006, pp. 157 f.

Next to the bearded and hooded figure of the dignitary who, as donor or patron, kneels at bottom left in front of the apparition of the Virgin Mary, appears an allusive, or canting coat of arms: the figure portrayed with two oars in his hands is a play on the name of Hieronymus Rudelauf (*c.* 1450–1523). Rudelauf was one of the first students to matriculate in 1502–03 at the newly founded University of Wittenberg. After graduating, he made his career in the administration of the Electorate of Saxony and finally became chancellor and advisor to Frederick the Wise. He remained a lifelong and aggressive champion of the Old Faith, on one occasion, for example, refusing to consent to the marriage of a priest who had become a Lutheran.

The choice of subject for the panel commissioned from Lucas Cranach, possibly in connection with his tomb, is therefore fitting. It shows not just any image of the Virgin but one which is the epitome of the Catholic Mary, hundreds of which are still to be found in the churches and chapels of South Germany: the *Madonna of the Crescent Moon*. Stemming from the Mariological interpretation of the woman mentioned in Revelation 12, who is 'clothed with the sun, and the moon under her feet', there developed in the late Middle Ages one of the most compelling and popular pictorial formulae for Mary, Queen of Heaven, a symbol, as it were, of the worship of the Virgin Mary. The emphasis in this picture is further strengthened by the angels in liturgical dress, adoring the Virgin Mary with various gestures of prayer and in some cases with song, suggesting an association with a Marian litany. At the same time the apple in the Virgin's hand is a reference to the 'New Eve', who overcomes the original sin committed by her ancestor. Rudelauf could hardly have found a clearer expression of the veneration of the Virgin Mary. As well as its confessional dimension the panel may also have a political one. In about 1516 Cranach's regional overlord had ordered a splendid *Virgin Mary on the Crescent Moon* (FR 83; Karlsruhe, Staatliche Kunsthalle), the basic features of which are repeated in the Frankfurt picture, though without the patron saint who accompanies the donor. Although Rudelauf ordered a somewhat more modest interpretation of the same pictorial idea, he might claim to have emulated the Elector without actually competing with him. The Chancellor seems also to have followed this principle in choice of dress and style of beard; with a differently shaped nose and chin, he might easily have been confused with Frederick the Wise.

The quality of the painting also reflects the more modest nature of Rudelauf's Virgin Mary. While the Karlsruhe painting is unquestionably by Lucas Cranach the Elder, scholars are unanimous that the Frankfurt panel must have been executed by an artist in his workshop. Although it incorporates Cranach's formal properties, it interprets them in a somewhat rough manner. The faces look a little frozen and the expression of the heads is rather schematic. It seems plausible to date the panel to the last years of Rudelauf's life, in other words between 1520 and 1523.

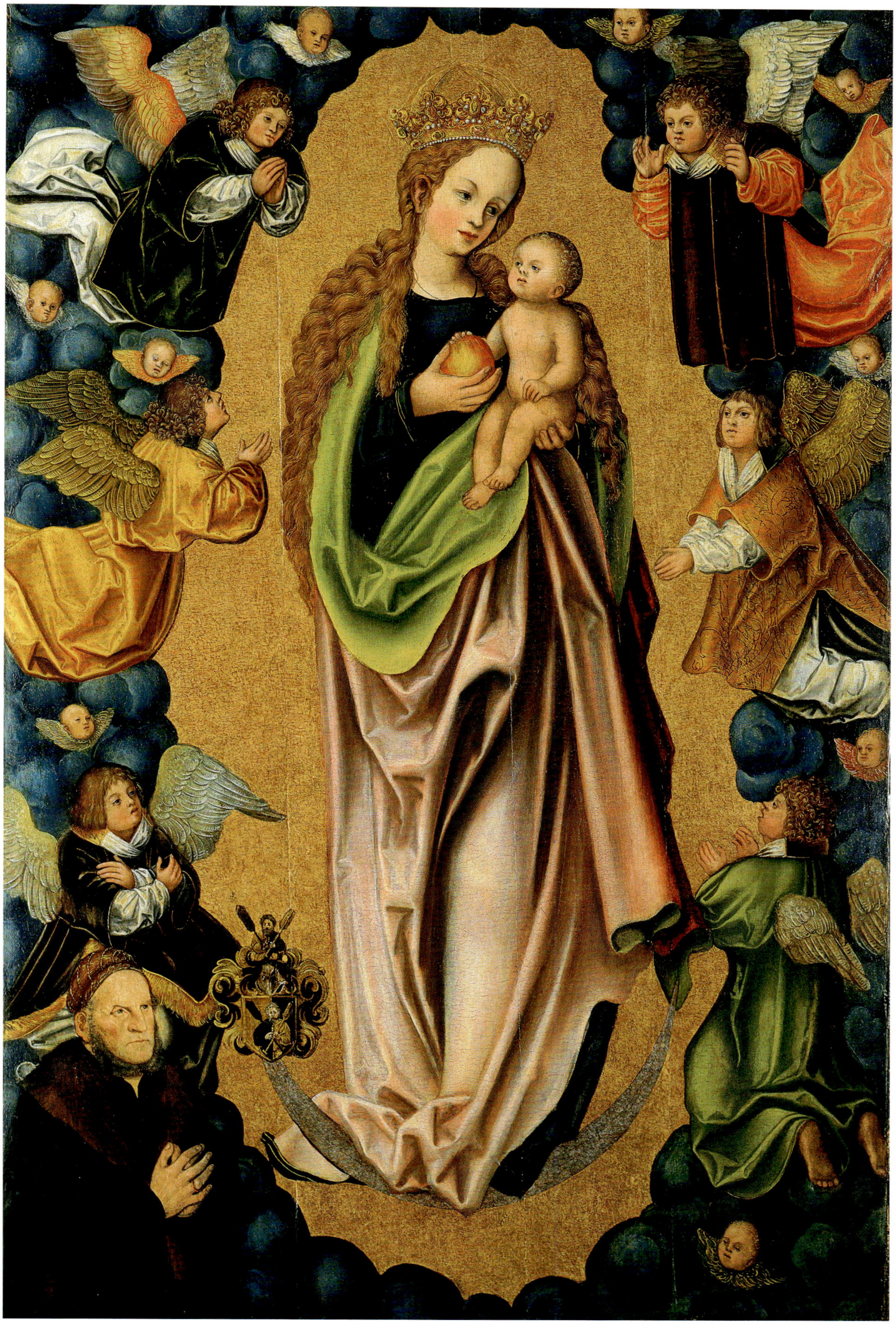

66 Cardinal Albrecht of Brandenburg as St Jerome in His Study

Wittenberg, 1525

Signed at bottom left on the front of the chest with the serpent with upright wings facing right between the two pairs of figures indicating the year

Oil and tempera on limewood
116.5 x 77.5 cm

Hessisches Landesmusum
Darmstadt, GK 71

Provenance:
acquired before 1820, possibly from the estate of the old landgraviate

(Frankfurt only)

Selected references:
FR 185; Beeh 1990, pp. 241–43, no. 70; Tacke, Albrecht, 2006; see also Andreas Tacke's essay in the present catalogue, pp. 81–9

In the late Middle Ages the Church Father Jerome, whose Latin translation of the Bible from early Hebrew and Greek texts is still in use and is known as the 'Vulgate' (the generally familiar version), became one of the most prominent saints. One particular pictorial type was formulated, emphasising his philological work and making him a role model, even among humanists: it shows Jerome as a cardinal in his study, working on texts.

This is how Cranach too portrayed him, in a comfortable room with wooden beams equipped with a water container and pewter dishes and furnished with bookshelves, a chest, tables and a bench. The Church Father's enormous work table occupies the centre of the composition, which is lit by bright daylight coming through the large window with crown-glass panes. The spatial organisation is undoubtedly drawn from Albrecht Dürer's masterly engraving of *St Jerome in His Study* of 1514; this is clearly reflected in Cranach's painting. It is possible that he used a reversed copy by Daniel Hopfer, though the quality of the painting suggests that it was Dürer's original that he sought to surpass by painterly means. The grain in the table surface and the reflections of light on the sides of the window recess are unusually detailed and naturalistic.

Cranach was trying to outdo his famous model for the good reason that his work was destined for Cardinal Albrecht of Brandenburg (1490–1545), an important client and a great patron. The figure of Jerome the Church Father is thus given the unmistakeable facial features of the Cardinal. The Darmstadt panel was one of the first examples of a new pictorial genre, the 'portrait historié', or historiated portrait, in which the person portrayed takes on the role of a historical, biblical or mythological figure.

Political circumstances gave rise to this development – whether they stemmed from within the sphere of the painter or that of his subject; these have been persuasively documented by Andreas Tacke. At the time the Darmstadt panel was being painted, Cardinal Albrecht, the most powerful ecclesiastic in the Holy Roman Empire and the most important opponent of Luther, was occupied with a project that makes his association with St Jerome particularly apposite: the translation of the Vulgate into the native language. Albrecht had clearly recognised that a German Bible with a Catholic bias had to be produced to counter the Lutheran translation which appeared in 1522–24. His Catholic translation was published in 1527.

Cranach places his Jerome (or Albrecht) in precisely this role. Unlike Dürer's engraving, in which the cardinal is seen writing at his desk, bent deep in concentration, here he leafs through a volume and gazes at the window, in front of which a wooden crucifix – much more prominent than in the Dürer engraving – stands on the table. Albrecht seems to hope it will give him inspiration as he searches his mind for the correct translation. The prayer books, which lie ready to hand on the table, indicate that such inspiration can only come from deep devotion and from true belief in the Holy Church. Philology also has a role here: in the bookcase on the wall, also within easy reach, are large volumes of reference, stacked with the cut edge forward according to the custom of medieval libraries. All this very clearly evokes the atmosphere of a period when, for example, Hieronymus Emser (1478–1527), a theologian from Dresden, chaplain to the court of Duke George the Bearded of Saxony and a bitter opponent of Luther, wrote to the Reformer to point out 400 mistakes in his translation of the Bible.

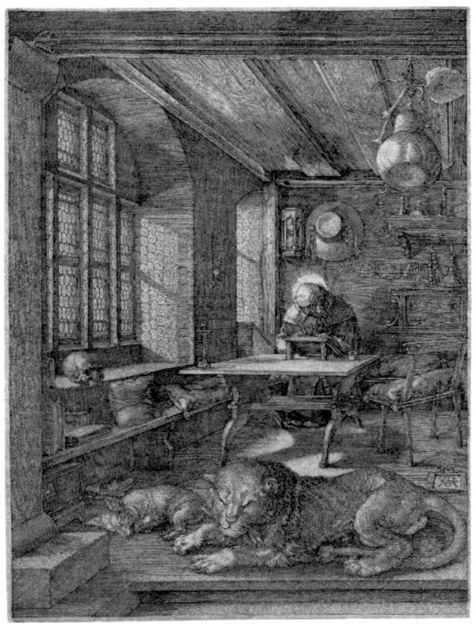

Albrecht Dürer, *St Jerome in His Study*, 1514, engraving, Städel Museum, Frankfurt, Graphische Sammlung

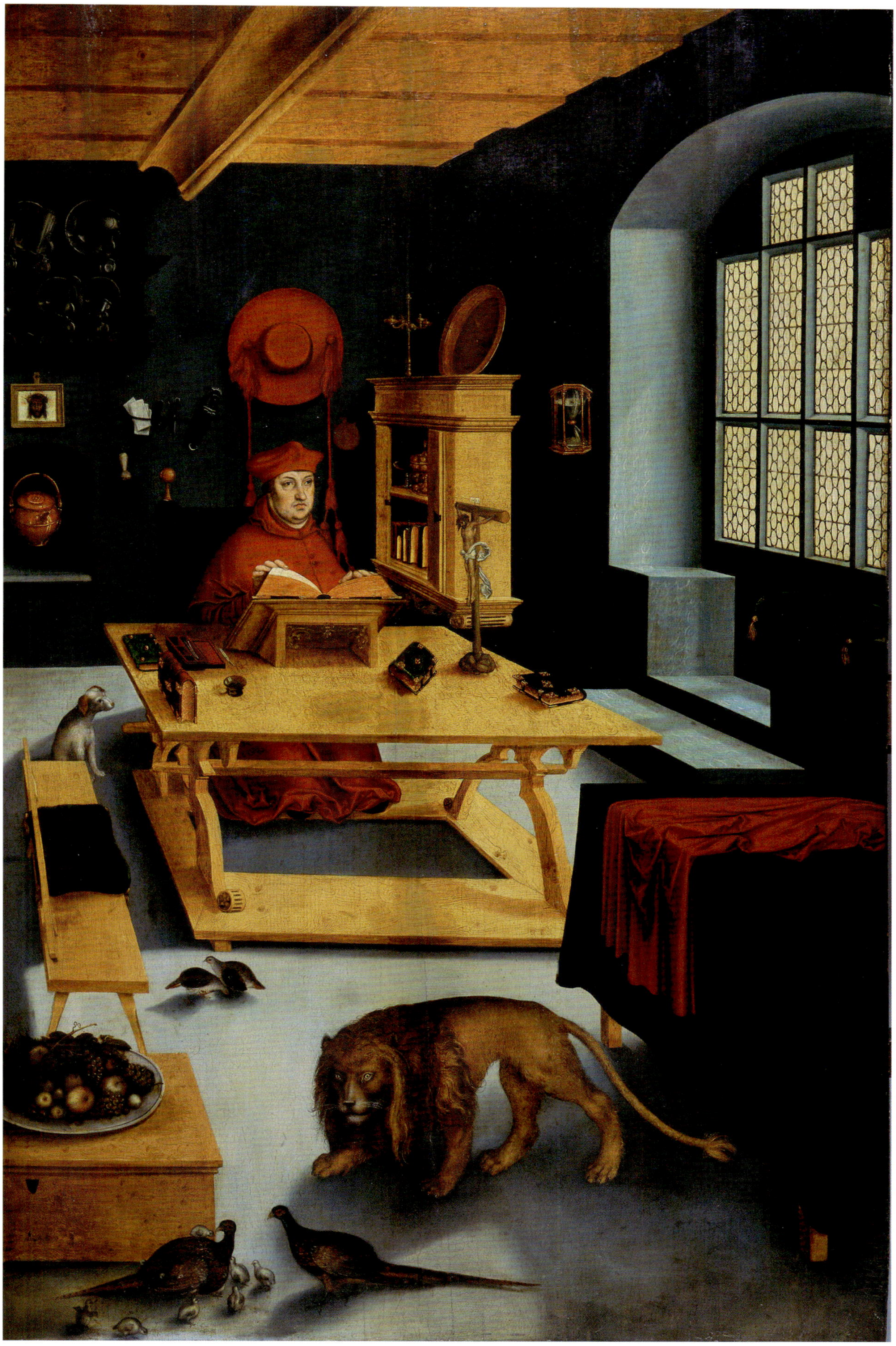

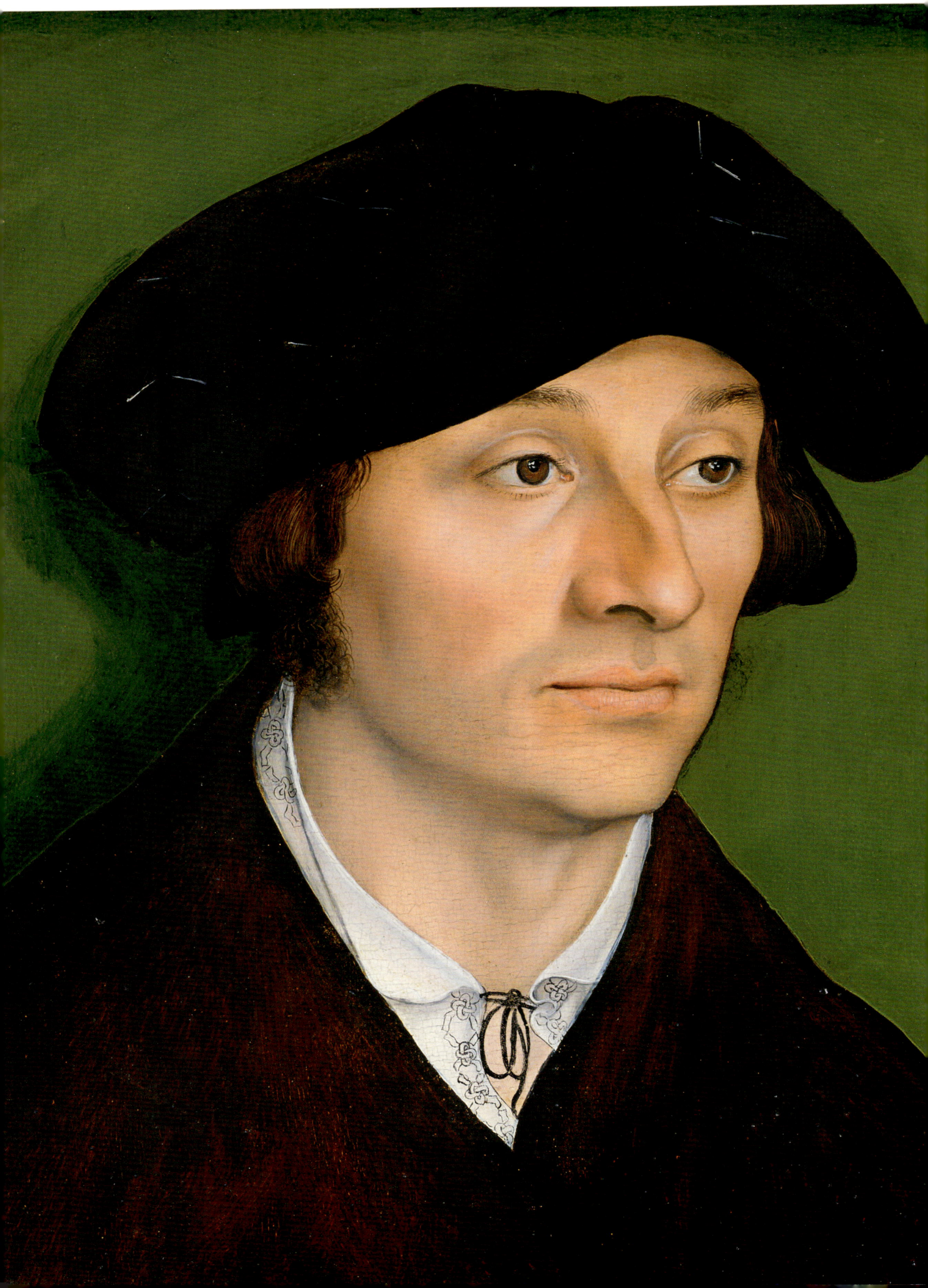

The Observer of People

Lucas Cranach was an excellent painter of portraits. He perfected a technique which was then very seldom used: the oil sketch on prepared paper. His clients came from the Wittenberg court and from other royal houses nearby, as well as from the patrician classes in the cities of Saxony; occasionally he made sketches of simple peasants. He portrayed children with a special understanding. However striking his studies may appear, the meticulous reproduction of external appearances was not his chief aim; he was much more concerned to breathe life and expressiveness into his subjects.

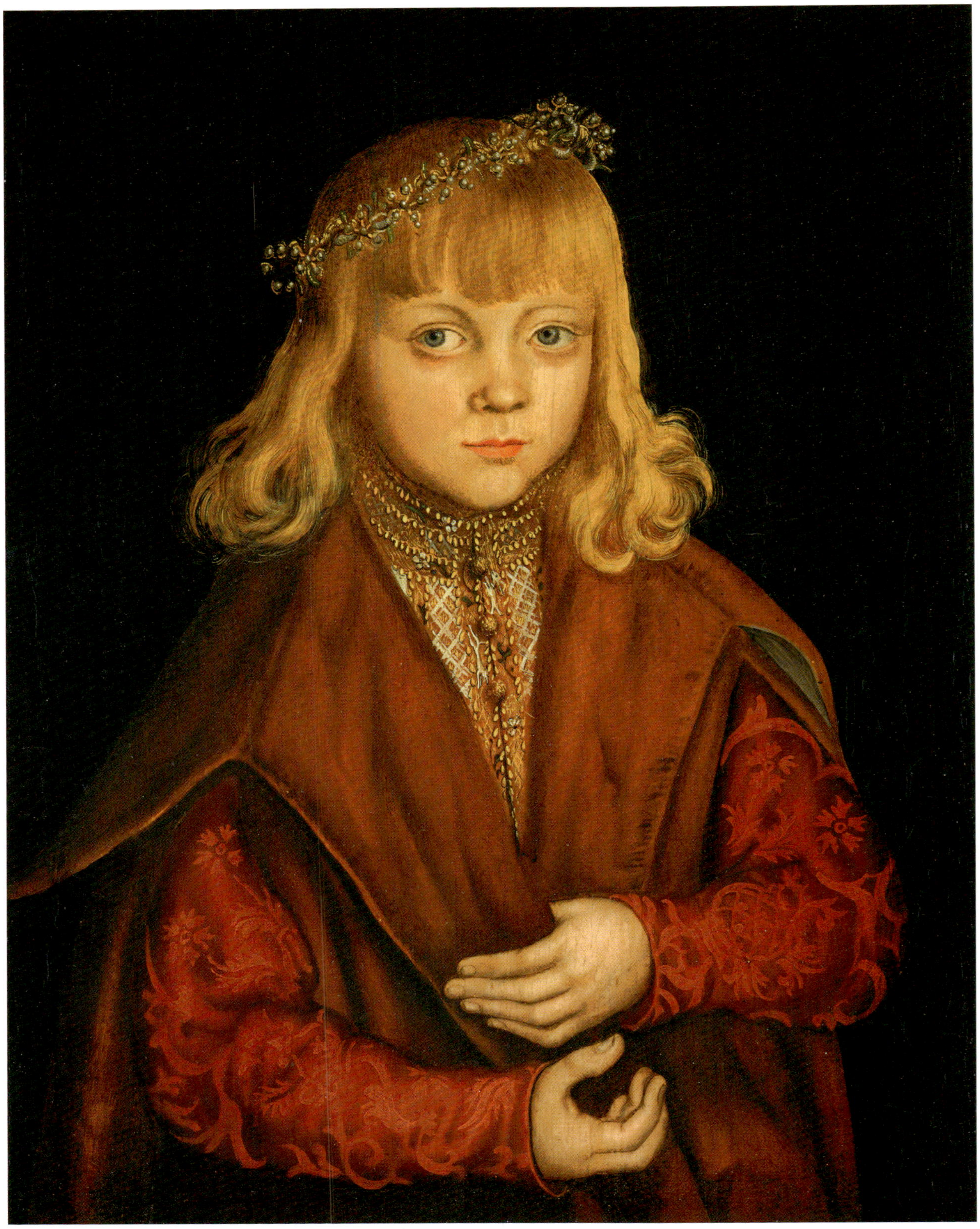

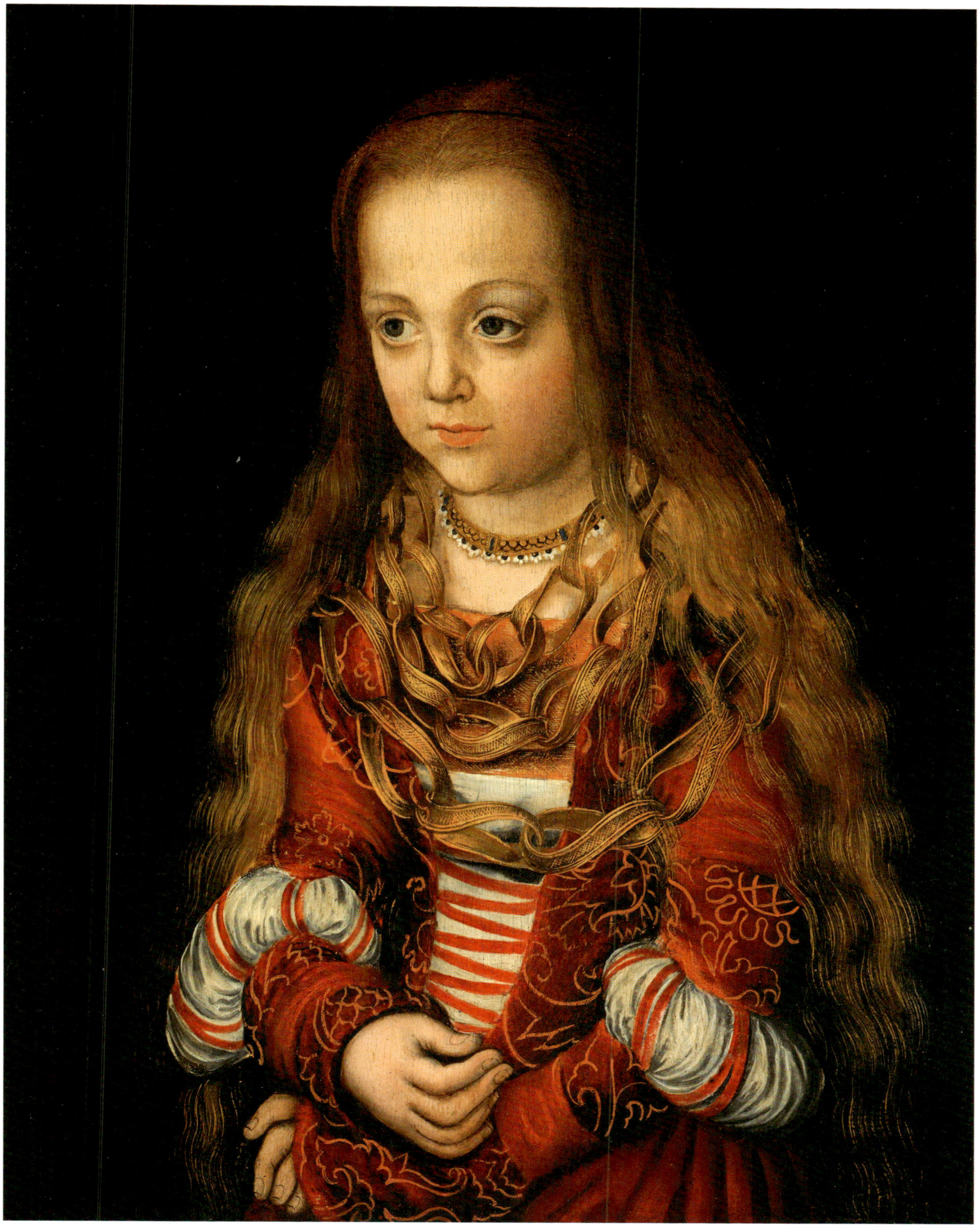

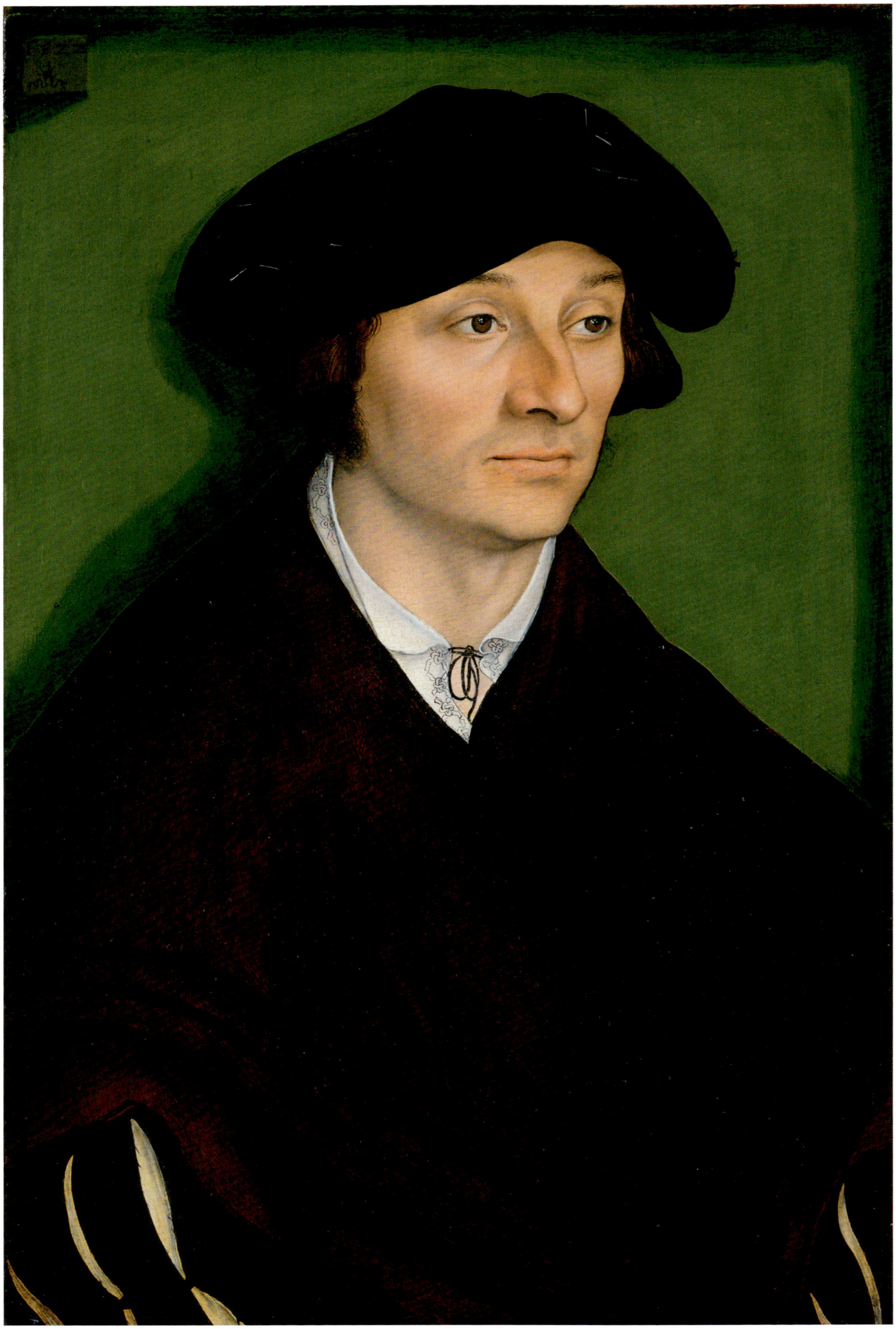

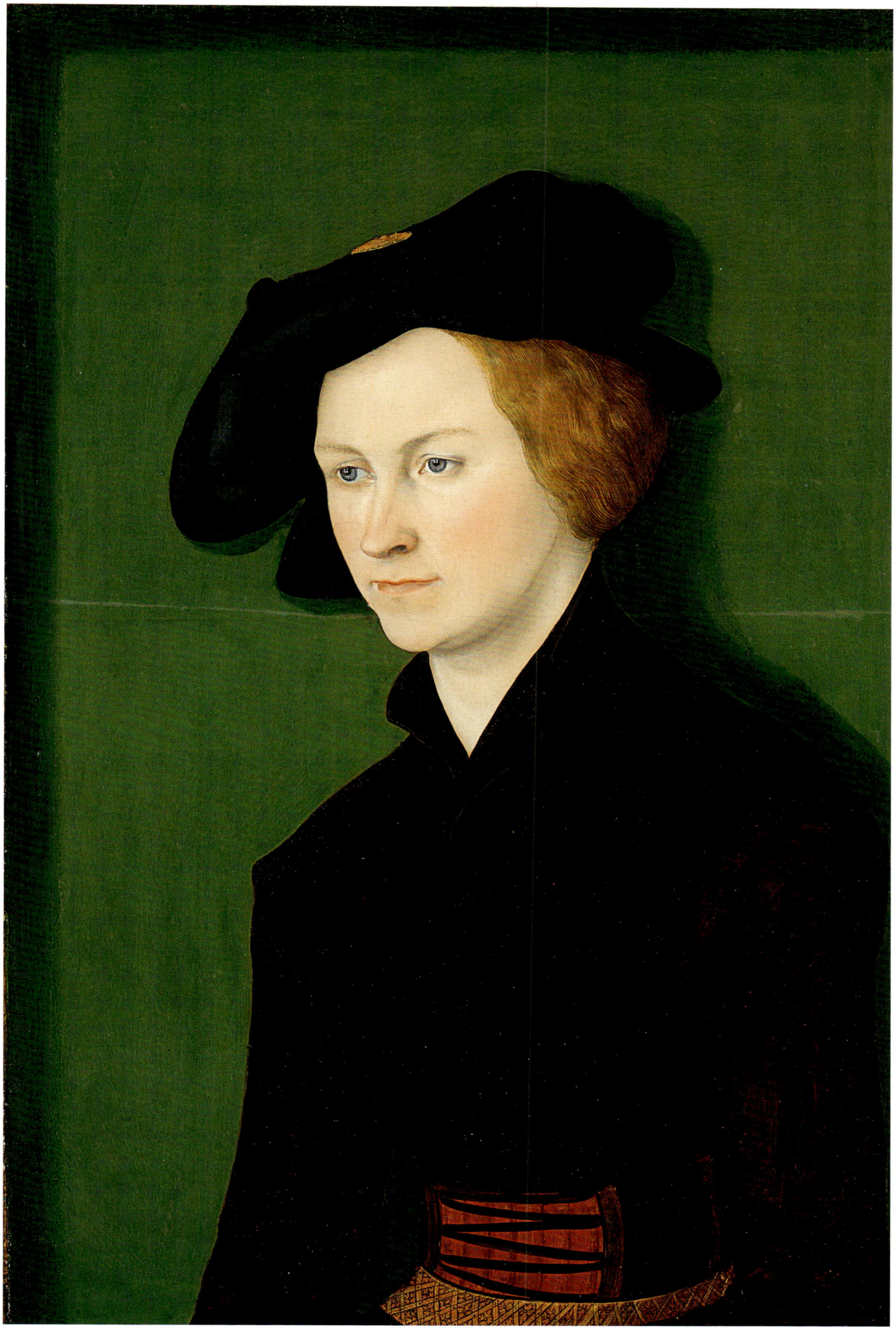

72 # Portrait of Hans Luther
73 # Portrait of Margaretha Luther

Wittenberg, 1527

Portrait of Hans Luther

Dated in the background to the left above the shoulder; beneath this the serpent with upright wings facing right. At the top the inscription added later: *ANNO . 1530 . AM . 29 . TAG . IVNY . IST . HANS . LVTHER : D . MARTINVUS . VATER . INN . GOTT . VERSCHIEDENN*

Portrait of Margaretha Luther

At the top the inscription added later: *ANNO. 1531. AM. 30. TAG. IVNY. IST. MARGARETA. LVTHERIN: D. MARTINVUS. MUTTER. INN. GOT. VERSCHIEDEN*

Oil and tempera on red beechwood 37.5 x 24.5 cm each

Wartburg-Stiftung, Eisenach, M 69, 70

Provenance:
acquired for the Wartburg in 1841 from the Grand Duchess of Saxe-Weimar through the Cologne art dealer Heberle

Selected references:
FR 316/317; Schade 1974, p. 54; Koepplin/Falk 1974/76, vol. 2, p. 693, nos 613, 614; Martin Luther, exh. cat. 1983, p. 18; Grimm/Erichsen/Brockhoff 1994, pp. 339 f., nos 160, 161; Sandner 1998, pp. 15, 130 f., no. 15.1

Hans Luther (1459–1530), the father of Martin Luther, was the eldest son of a farming family from Möhra near Eisenach. After the birth of his eldest son he moved from Eisleben to nearby Mansfeld, where he ran a copper works which he made modestly prosperous. His wife Margaretha (1460–1531) came from Eisenach, and after the birth of the future reformer brought at least eight more children into the world. Treasury records in Kursachsen list an honorary gift of red wine to Hans Luther in the year 1528, which suggests that in the previous year the parents went to Wittenberg to visit their son, now famous, and who had also recently married. On this occasion the parents may have sat to Lucas Cranach; the portrait sketch on paper of the father is held in the Albertina in Vienna (see below).

A comparison between the portrait pair of Martin Luther's parents and the portrait diptych of the reformer himself and his wife (cat. 41) clearly shows the extent to which artistic form serves function. Unlike the numerous versions of portraits of the reformer, the portraits of the parents are unique items, not intended for distribution as propaganda but as purely personal mementoes. Their originality is immediately expressed in the unusual format which is highly imposing and in its extreme simplicity lends the upright figures a special dignity. Cranach portrays the successful 68-year-old entrepreneur, who at that time was withdrawing from his somewhat erratic business, as an assertive, rather mischievous person who is rightly pleased with what he has achieved. Three years later, Hans Luther was to leave in his will the proud sum of 1250 florins. Although his wife shows the strain of having raised nine children, she seems equally comfortable with herself and presents a dignified, more relaxed pendant to Albrecht Dürer's expressive 1514 charcoal drawing of his sick mother, now in the Kupferstichkabinett in Berlin.

With powerful, sure and economic brushstrokes Lucas Cranach paints in the fur, clothing, hair and wrinkles which convincingly give shape to the thin, flat underpainting. The paintings express an unmistakeable sympathy with the parents of his friend.

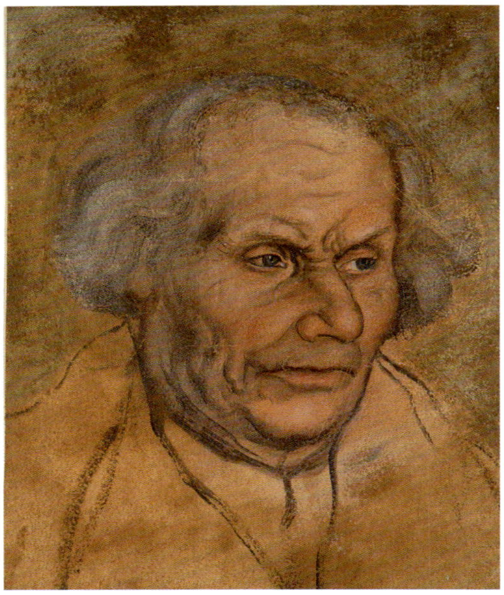

Portrait Study of Hans Luther,
oil on paper, Albertina, Vienna

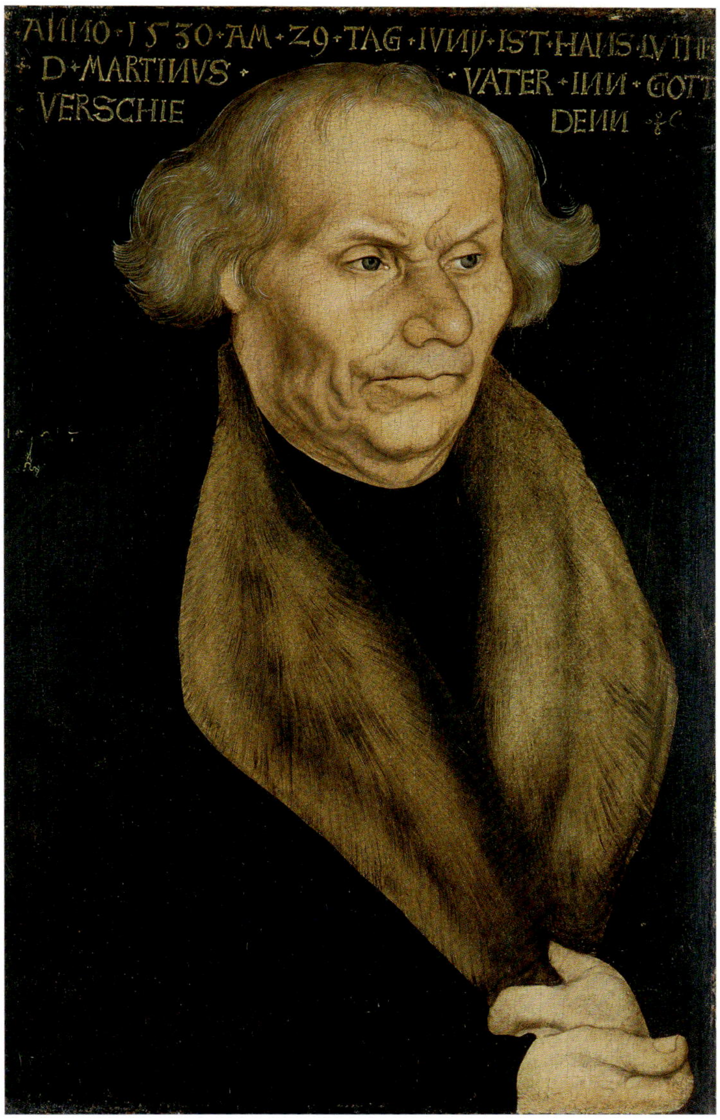

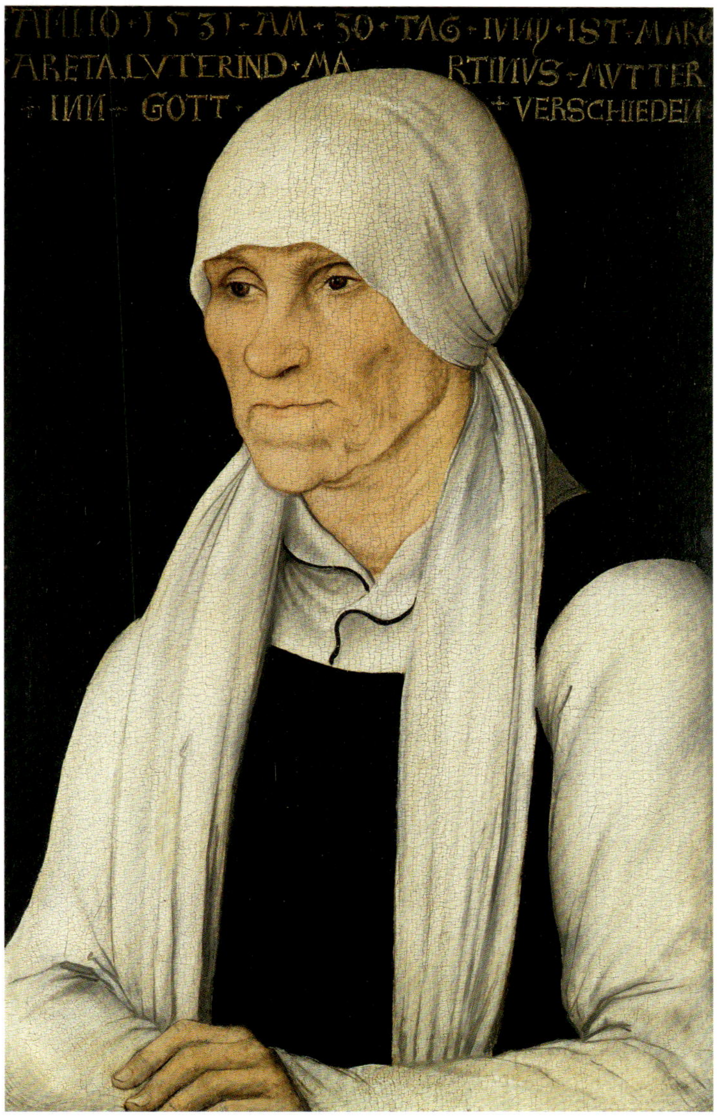

Portrait of Hans Luther / Portrait of Margaretha Luther

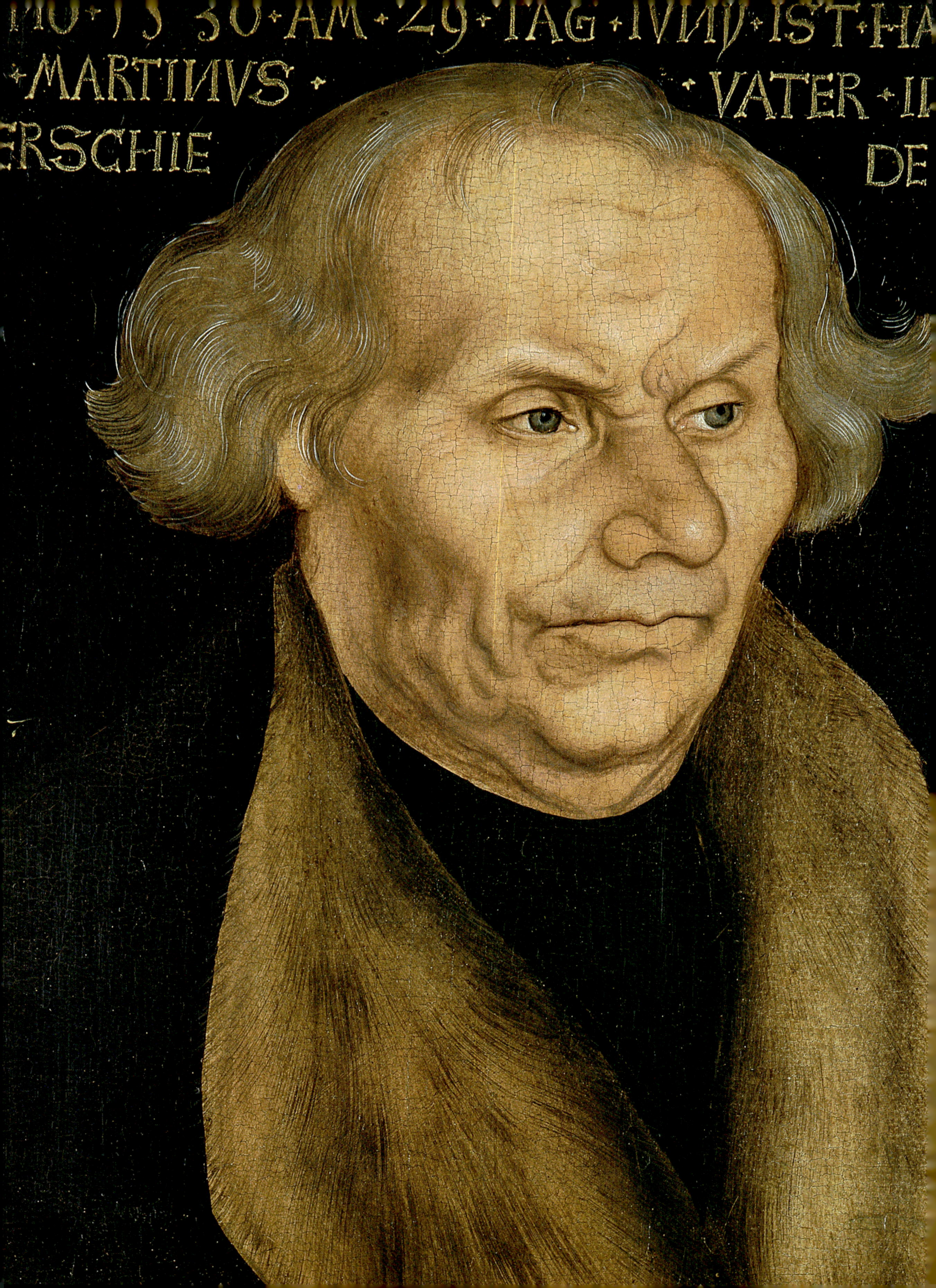
15 30 · AM · 29 · TAG · IVNII · IST
MARTINVS · VATER

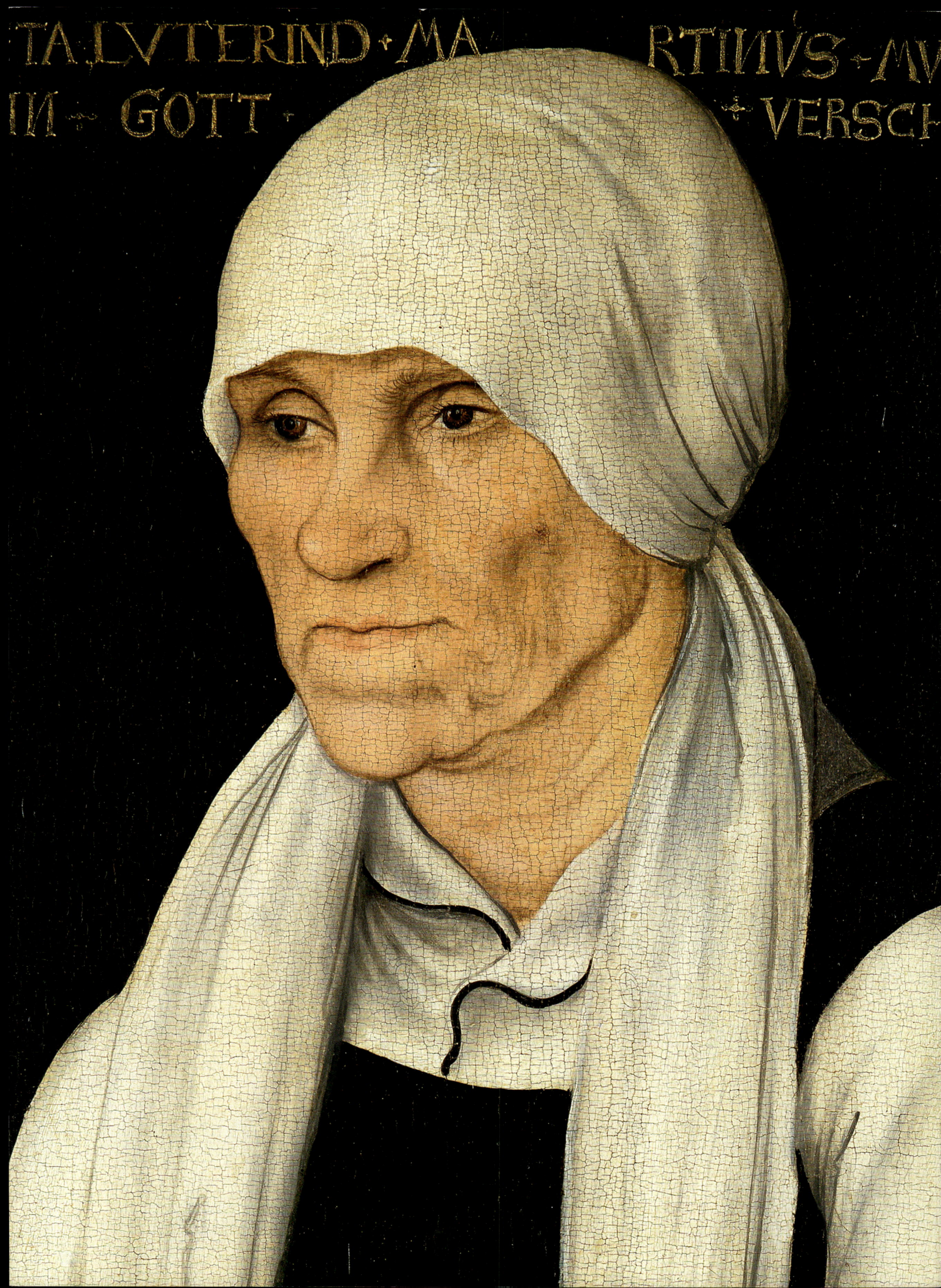
TA.LVTERIND MA
RTINVS MV
IN GOTT
VERSCH

74 Portrait of Margaret of Austria

Wittenberg, *c.* 1520–30

Signed in the black background on the left edge of the picture two-thirds up with the serpent with upright wings facing right

Oil and tempera on red beechwood
50 x 34.7 cm

Anhaltische Gemäldegalerie, Dessau, 13

Provenance:
since the 1780s in the Gothic House in Wörlitz

Selected references:
FR 321; Schade 1993, pp. 32–37; Klingen 1996, p. 29; see also Werner Schade's essay in the present catalogue, pp. 91–7

While staying at Wörlitz in 1786, Caspar Lavater (1741–1801), the founder of physiognomics, remarked, in a note stuck to the back of the panel: 'Gentle, receptive child, born to devotion and humility/by Lucas Cranach [...] L.[avater].' The 'gentle, receptive child' is Margaret of Austria (1480–1530), the daughter of Emperor Maximilian I from his first marriage with Maria of Burgundy. Lavater was not completely wrong in his estimation. After the failure of a first marriage plan that would have made Margaret queen of France, she was twice widowed in quick succession before her father appointed her Governess-General of the Netherlands at the age of 27, and two years later Regent – a role in which she very quickly proved herself. Margaret was in fact one of the most significant female figures of the sixteenth century, and won the respect of her contemporaries by the conduct of her life and office. Her punning motto, 'Fortune. Infortune. Fort Une' (a strong woman in good fortune and bad), and the fact that she had herself portrayed by her court painter Bernard van Orley (1491/92–1542) in the plain black and white dress of a widow, reflect her disciplined outlook.

Lucas Cranach's portrait, probably painted in the third decade of the sixteenth century, refers back to Orley's work, although he did not use any of the painted versions of the official portrait (for example those in the Koninklijke Museum voor Schone Kunsten, Antwerp, in the Musées Royaux des Beaux-Arts, Brussels, and in the Royal Collection at Hampton Court), which all show the regent facing in the other direction, and with her hair completely concealed beneath her hood. Werner Schade has discovered Cranach's probable source (cf. his contribution, pp. 91–97): a chalk drawing attributed to van Orley in the Kupferstichkabinett, Berlin. The arrangement of the half-length figure is similar, as are the hair drawn back on either side of the forehead, the broader and more oval shape of the face and the complete concealment of the neck. The similarities between the two must indicate a close connection between the two works.

It was probably the Berlin drawing that Cranach used for his presentation model, or at least another version of the same portrait type. The hands were not to be shown in the presentation picture, and were added later at Cranach's suggestion. The supple, boneless fingers and the round whirlpool of creases in the inner lining of the glove in Margaret's left hand correspond to the artist's formal canon. The original source from the Netherlands stimulated the Wittenberg master to exceptional heights in his handling of the face: his *Margaret of Austria* surpasses by far van Orley's somewhat chilly and unapproachable state portrait both in its soulfulness and in its lively expression.

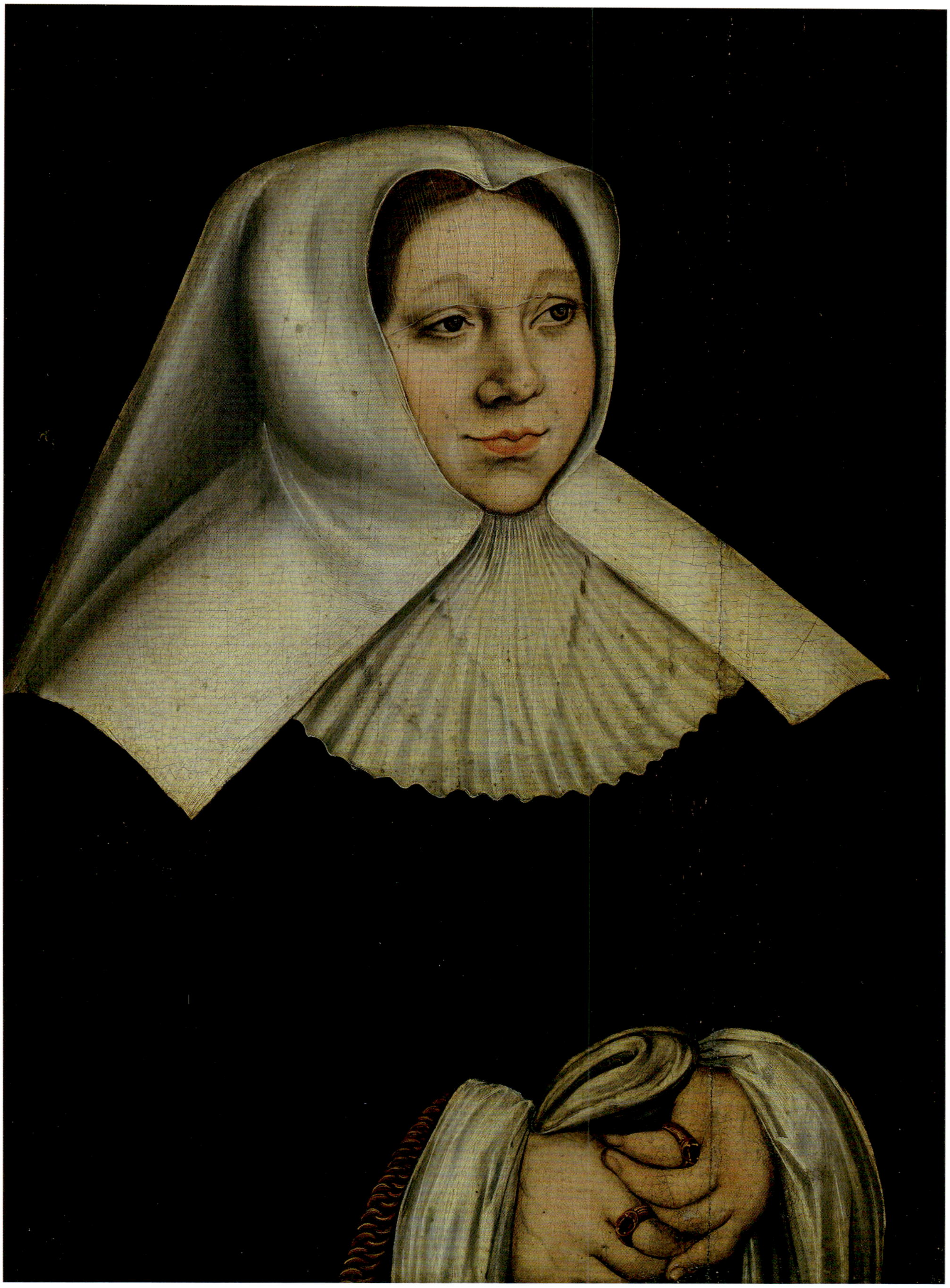

76 # Portrait of Princess Maria of Saxony

Lucas Cranach the Elder (workshop)

Wittenberg, 1534

Dated bottom left: beneath this the serpent with upright wings facing right

Oil and tempera on red beechwood
51 x 36 cm

Hessisches Landesmuseum
Darmstadt, GK 76

Provenance:
acquired in 1805 through Herr von Perglas

(Frankfurt only)

Selected references.:
FR 348 A; Zimmermann 1942, pp. 26–8; Koepplin/Falk 1974/76, vol. 2, p. 708, no. 627; Beeh 1990. pp. 250 f., no. 74

The daughter of Elector John the Steadfast – from his second marriage to Margaret of Anhalt – was born on 15 December 1515 and died on 7 January 1583; she outlived her husband Duke Philip I of Pomerania-Wolgast by 23 years. They were married on 27 February 1536.

As Duchess of Pomerania, Maria of Saxony appears in the famous Croy tapestry of 1554, which can be seen in the Pommerschen Landesmuseum in Greifswald. However, the identification of this panel rests chiefly on the account in the so-called Dresdner Stammbuch (Sächsische Landesbibliothek, MS R 3). According to this, the eighteen- or nineteen-year-old princess is probably shown here in a bethrothal picture; her hair is drawn up beneath a hood crowned by a golden bridal chain trimmed with pearls. On the band of the hood the letters *EWRH* are also picked out in pearls, possibly the initials of a motto or device. The medallion with the profile portrait of a man, which the sitter wears on a long gold chain, can be identified by the circumscription *HANS FRIDRICH HERZOG VON SACHSEN* as a memento of Maria's stepbrother John Frederick the Magnanimous.

The princess is portrayed half-length, almost knee-length, against a pale blue background in a black skirt with a top worked in gold and puff sleeves with multiple slashes. Fashion and the stylistic development of Cranach's workshop seem here to go hand in hand: the restless curving shapes of the costume – even the cuffs are slashed and their slashes curved – correspond to the flatness and nervous stylisation which lend a noticeably mannerist tone to pictures of the 1530s. The face seems abstracted and flat. The palette is concentrated on two strong contrasts only: the pale blue and the gold ochre tone which is set against pure black and white.

There is another version of the painting in Lyons (Musée des Beaux-Arts; FR 348). This also bears the serpent emblem and the year, 1534, and one is left with the strong impression that it was painted by another artist in the workshop working from a common source, probably a preparatory portrait drawing, though without this affecting the quality of either. The body in the Lyons portrait is more slender and pointed, as are the facial features and even the proportions of the earlobes. In its stylised curves it goes a step further, noticeably in the more arched and at the same time more asymmetrical lines of the standing collar. The more decisive arrangement of the hands and the way the left arm rests directly on the bottom edge of the picture lend greater tension to the arms as they frame the picture space. The most striking difference is in the direction of the head: the Lyons figure looks directly out of the picture, and her almond-shaped eyes slope more sharply. It seems as though the painter of the Lyons panel kept more closely to the model, while the painter of the Darmstadt portrait was making an interpolation when he turned the head slightly to the left. The nose slips a little in the process, but altogether his more relaxed feeling for form allows him to produce facial features that are more regular and natural in appearance.

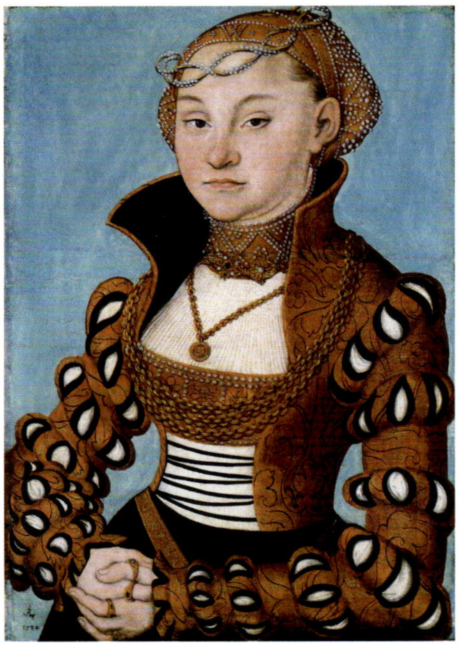

Portrait of Princess Maria of Saxony, 1534,
Musée des Beaux-Arts de Lyon

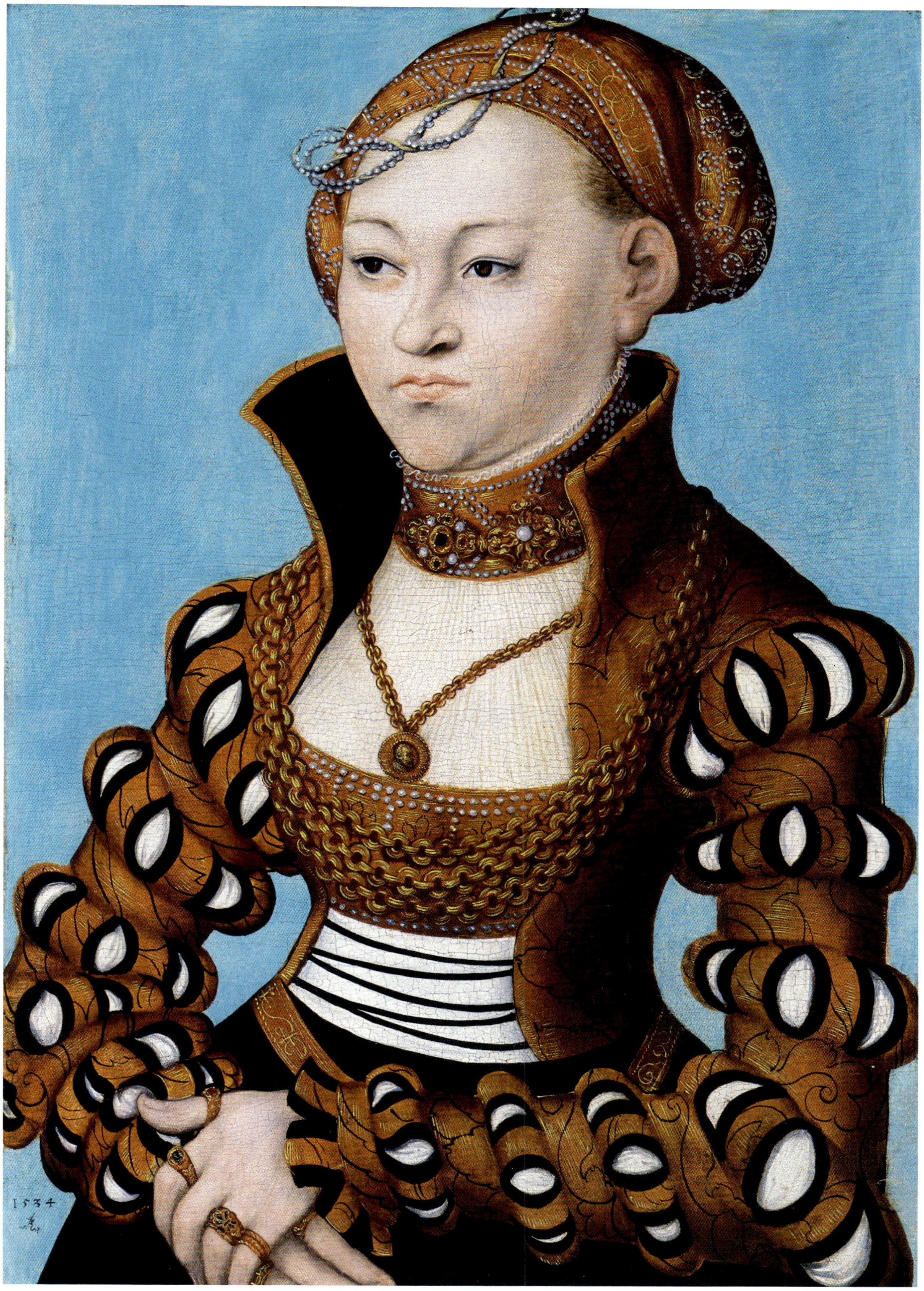
1534

77 The Princess and the Legend of St John Chrysostom

Wittenberg, *c.* 1520–30

Signed on the bottom edge on the left near the child with the serpent with upright wings facing right

Oil and tempera on red beechwood, transferred to canvas and plywood
60.5 x 37.5 cm

Wartburg Stiftung, Eisenach, M 2

Provenance:
*until 1901 with Cou*nt Einsiedel; acquired from the estate of the Oberburghauptmann von Cranach

Selected references:
FR 170; Schade 1974, p. 61; Koepplin/Falk 1974/76, vol. 1, p. 166, vol 2, pp. 593 f.; Sandner 1998, pp. 15, 143, no. 16.3; Marx/Mössinger 2005, pp. 60, 604; for the iconography: Wind 1937

A very young woman, rather pale, stands, with a grave expression on her face, in front of a tree in a hilly landscape. She is wearing a velvet dress trimmed with gold brocade and sumptuous jewellery. In her hands she is carefully holding a tiny new-born baby lying on a napkin. Clearly she is a woman of rank who while still very young has recently become a mother.

The panel might easily be seen as the portrait of an unknown lady connected to the Saxon court, had not Werner Schade's sharp eye recognised a tiny detail in the background. Following the path immediately above the child's head to where it bends to the right, a figure is visible, barely the size of a fingernail; a bearded and naked man crawling on all fours among the bushes and trees. This most unlikely secondary scene fits a legend concerning St John Chrysostom (*c.* 344/354–407), one of the four Church Fathers of the Eastern Church, whose Greek name *Goldmouth* refers to his exceptional rhetorical talent. Before he joined the Church, Chrysostom lived for four years as a hermit in the wilderness. At that time, so runs the legend, a king's daughter wandered into his cavern while on a walk in the forest. The saint was immediately overcome by the temptations of the flesh and raped the girl. Becoming aware of his guilt he then threw his victim over a cliff to conceal the cause of his sin. At the same time he vowed that from then on he would live like an animal, crawl naked on all fours through the forest and feed himself on grass. His readiness to atone for his sin was rewarded: one day as he was crawling along he saw a young naked woman sitting on a rock in the distance, suckling a new-born child, and recognised her as the princess whom he had made pregnant.

Johann Güldinmund (John Goldenmouth), as he was called in German tracts of the fifteenth century, was one of the most widely-read and venerated theologians of the late Middle Ages; people marvelled both at his rhetorical skills and at his pitilessness. The crude legend eloquently bears out the saint's harshness towards himself. The subject was engraved in copper by Cranach, Albrecht Dürer and Hans Sebald Beham (1500–1550). In all the graphic versions, the young mother appears in the foreground with her child, while the saint on all fours is seen much smaller in the middle ground – a pictorial convention that possibly indicates a confusion of the subject with the *Temptation of St Jerome*. Although the graphic works point the way to Cranach's panel, the latter is nevertheless unique in its departure from convention; one has almost to search with a magnifying glass for the saintly penitent, since with the naked eye he is barely visible. The concealment of the real subject is reinforced by a further departure from the legend and its pictorial tradition: in the panel painting the young mother is dressed like a lady of the court, while in the prints she is always shown naked. These observations have led Dieter Koepplin to the idea that the picture could not be a role-portrait of a lady at the Saxon court. Several of Cranach's works for Frederick the Wise (cat. 19) and also for Albrecht of Brandenburg (cats 66, 67) show that he contributed to the development of the historiated portrait, and that secondary figures could be used in order to portray contemporaries; one example is his self-portrait in the *Beheading of John the Baptist* of 1515 (cat. 20). However, it is difficult to imagine that a noble lady of the early sixteenth century would willingly be portrayed in the role of a rape victim with a bastard child. Whatever may be concealed behind the apparently straightforward panel in the Wartburg, it shows once again Cranach's skill in generating radically new pictorial ideas out of elements of traditional iconography.

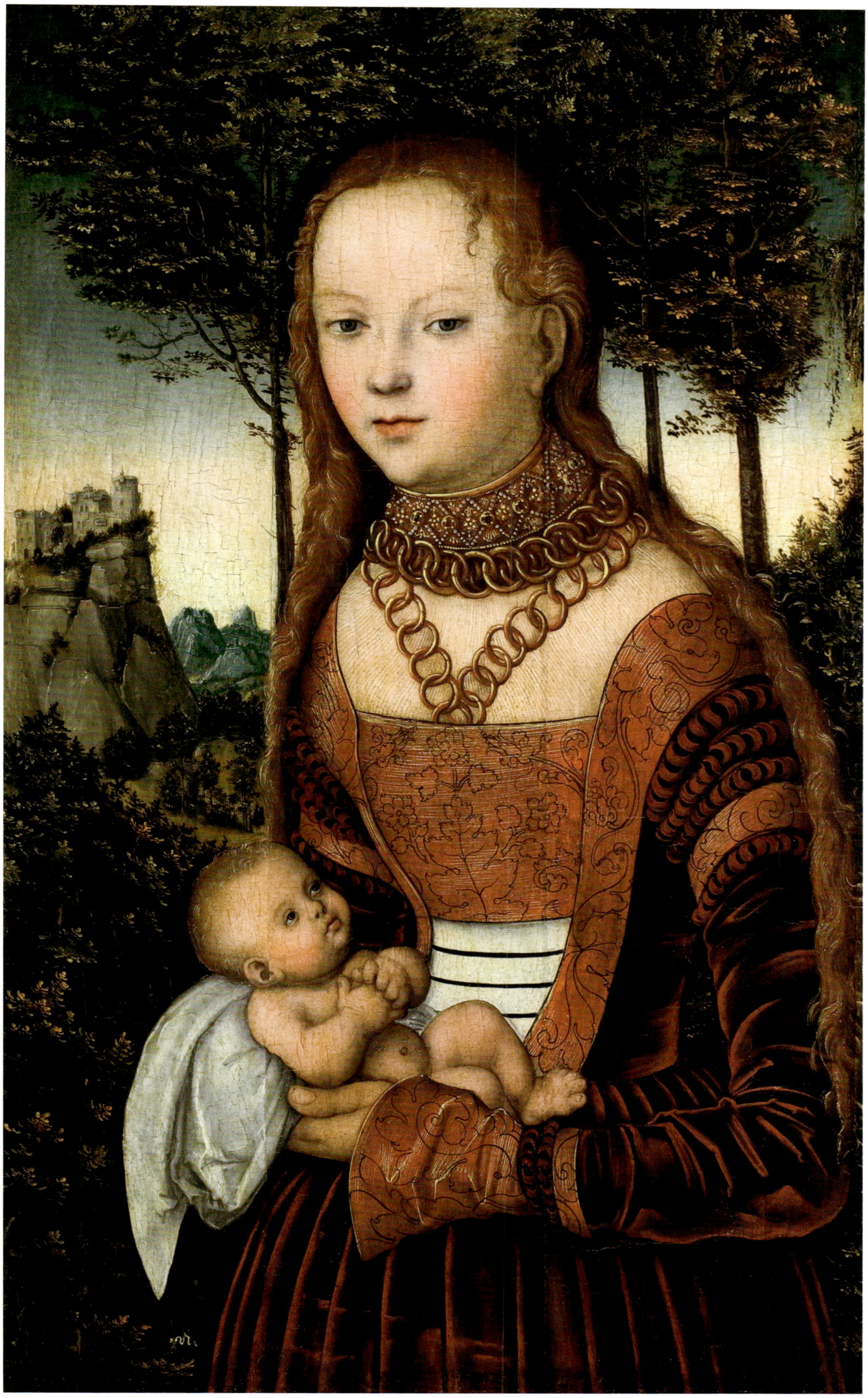

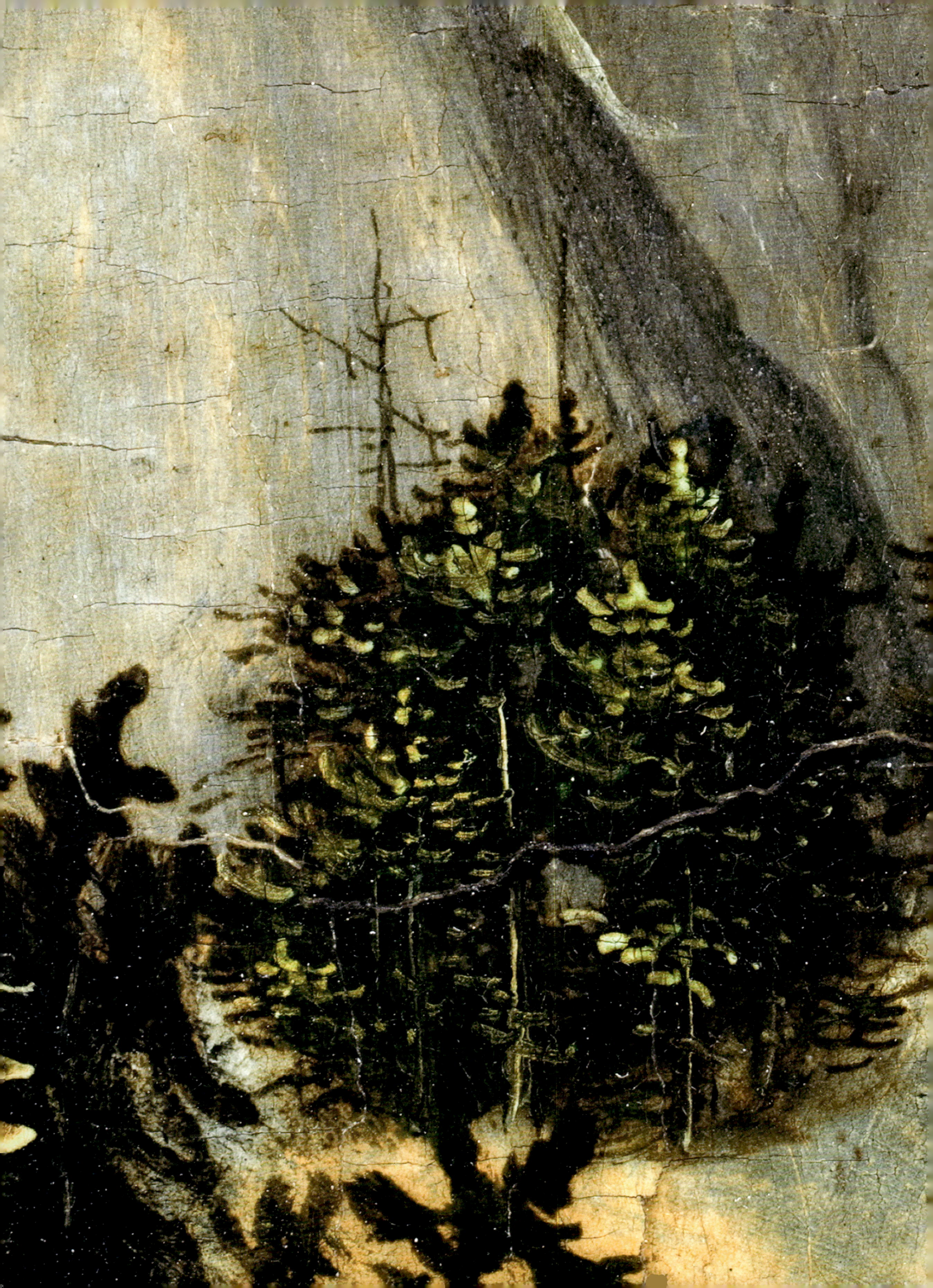

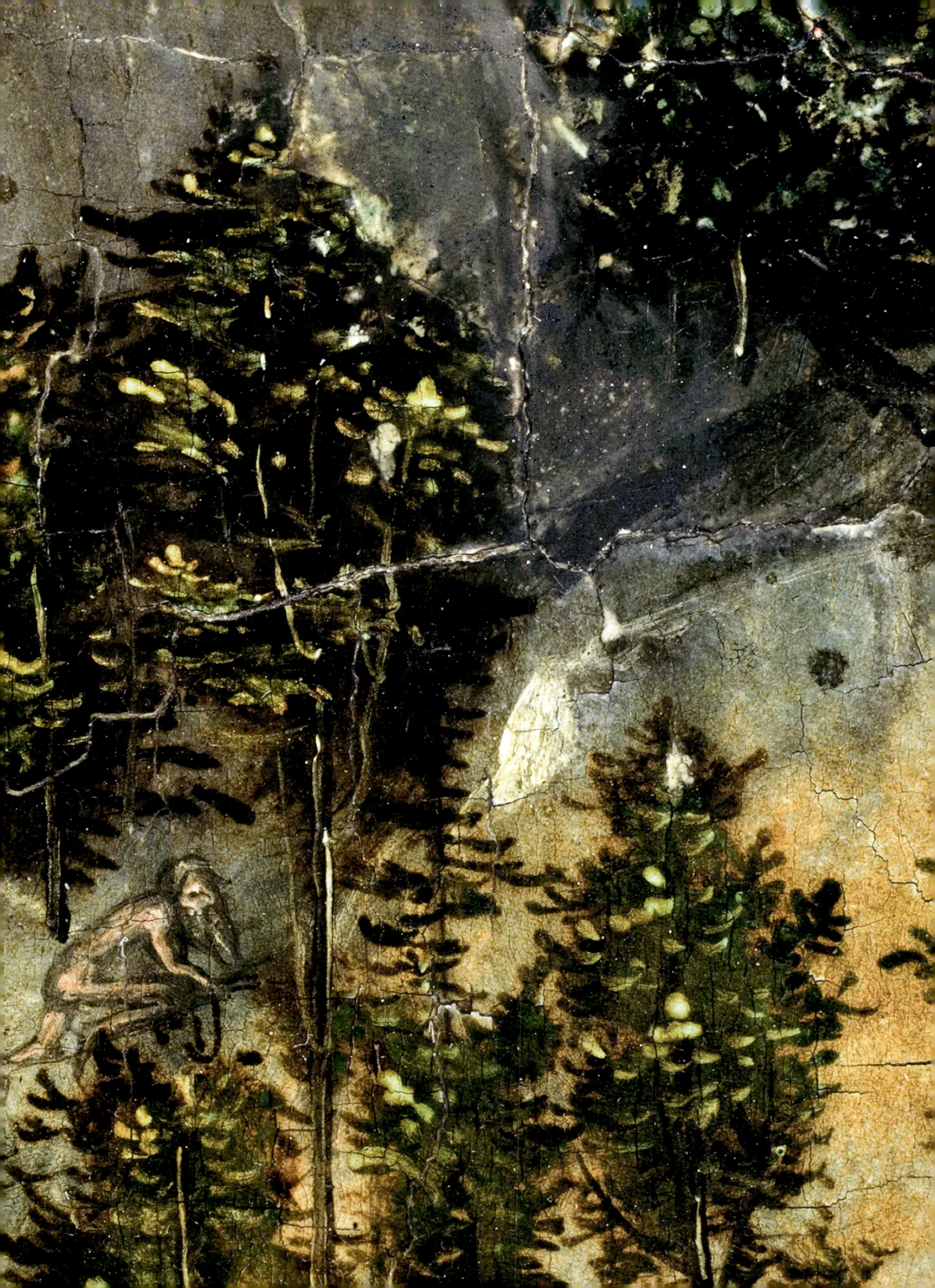

78 A Generalised Portrait of a Woman

Wittenberg, *c.* 1525

Signed at bottom left in the background with the serpent with upright wings facing right

Oil and tempera on red beechwood
37.6 x 26.6 cm

National Gallery, London, 291

Provenance:
acquired in 1857

Selected references:
FR 172; Smith 1985, pp. 96 f.; Hinz 1993, pp. 89–91; Baker/Henry 1995, p. 157; Dunkerton/Foister/Penny 1999, p. 148; for Albrecht of Brandenburg: Tacke, 'Alles besiegt Amore', 2006

Towards the middle of the third decade of the fifteenth century, the Lucas Cranach workshop formulated a new picture type. It consisted of a series of portraits of young women against a black background, not the usual head and shoulders portraits but half-length, three-quarter-length and sometimes even full-length figures (National Gallery, Prague, FR 178; National Museum, Warsaw, FR 296), notable for their minutely observed courtly dress and the lack of individualism in the facial features. The formats are around 40 x 25 cm and thus unusually small for portraits depicting such a large proportion of the figure. We can only speculate about the function of these clearly popular small panels: perhaps they were idealised portraits, half contemporary, half mythological, historical or biblical forms like those commonly found in Italy from the early Renaissance onwards. What makes this unlikely is that Cranach's portraits from this period offer no suggestion of identification with, for example, a goddess of antiquity, or an Old Testament heroine. If they do embody an ideal, then it is the ideal of a lady of the Saxony court, or even of a courtesan. It has also been proposed that portraits of mistresses are concealed within these works, their personal features consciously understated so that in each case only the lover (who presumably ordered the picture) can recognise her. This idea suggests the world of light opera, but is by no means absurd when one thinks of the pictorial hide-and-seek that Albrecht of Brandenburg played with altar retables, and which Andreas Tacke has recently investigated.

The picture from London, with its astonishingly fashionable details, fits in seamlessly with other portraits in the series: the silk dress tied at the waist and the puffed sleeves, the inset embroidered with pearls, the necklace and chain, the gloves slit to allow space for rings worn underneath, though this has not prevented the wearer from wearing additional rings on top – which actually was technically impossible. Her rounded face might well be compared with the studies of heads from Truro (cat. 85), and in turn contrasted with the portrait of a young woman in Copenhagen (Statens Museum for Kunst; Fr 173) which shows much more individual character in the facial features. However, with her sleepy eyes, cool smile and low-cut bodice revealing the tops of well-formed breasts, her erotic effect on the beholder is undeniable. One should also bear in mind that from the early fifteenth century the pictorial tradition for portraits of women called for much greater regularity of features than those of men, and this led to a great deal of uniformity. The clearest indication that a real person may be concealed behind this small figure is perhaps provided by the costume and the letter M repeated in the pattern of the bodice, which may stand for a first name or personal motto.

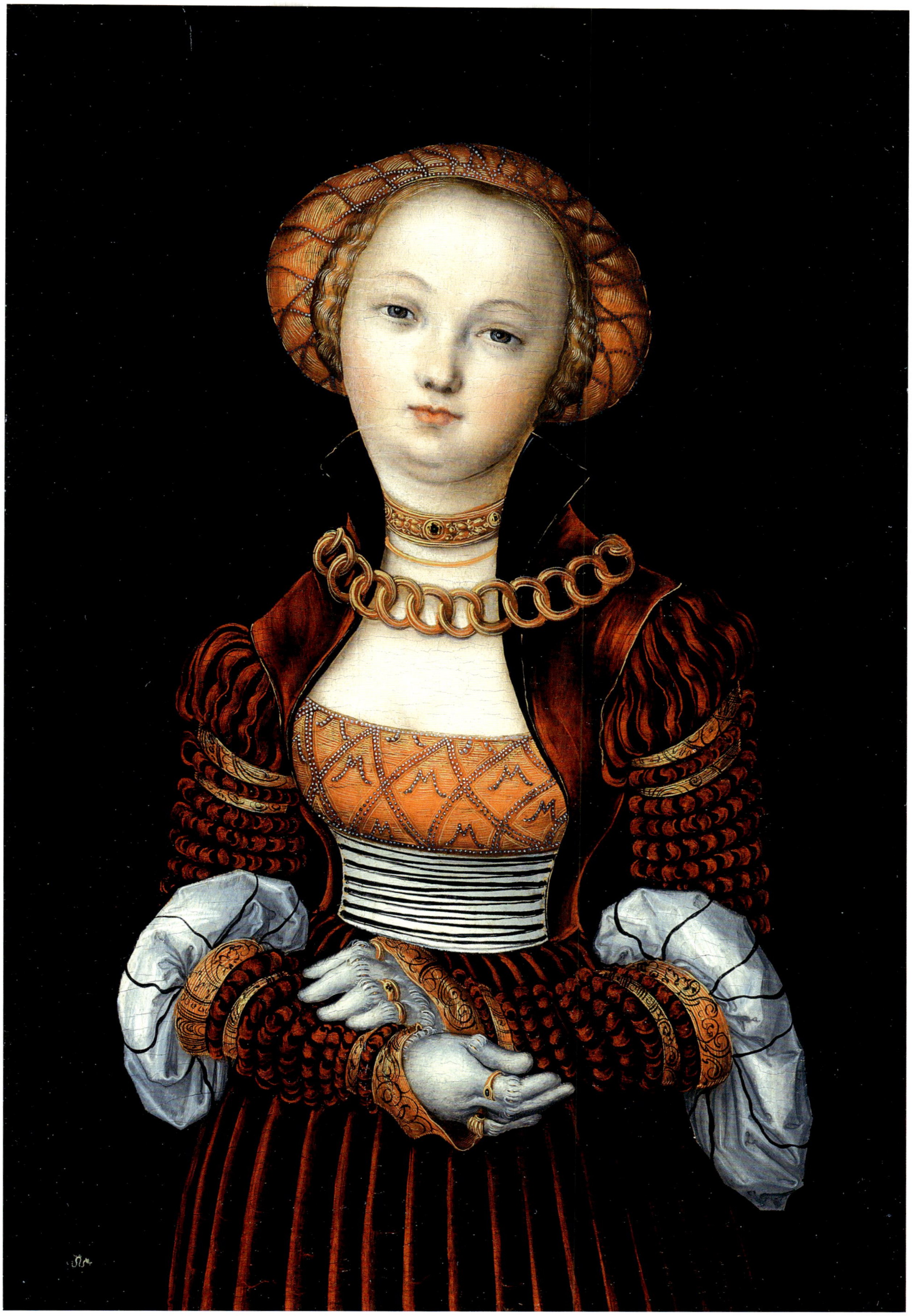

79 Study of the Head of a Peasant

Wittenberg, *c.* 1520–25

Watercolour with opaque white highlights, with additional pen for the beard
19.3 x 15.7 cm

Öffentliche Kunstsammlungen Basel, Kupferstichkabinett, 1937.21

Provenance:
acquired in 1937; from the Wittenberg family register of a certain Herr von Goldbeck, kept between 1590 and 1593

Selected references:
R A9; Koepplin/Falk 1974/76, vol. 2, p. 688, no. 607; Dürer Holbein Grünewald exh. cat. 1997, pp. 257–9, no. 17.4; cited in Heinz, 1993, p. 25

Lucas Cranach's finest portrait study was carried out in watercolour on a paper whose watermark suggests a date between 1519 and around 1525. However, it conveys a wonderful impression of complete spontaneity which, on material and technical grounds, makes a somewhat later date seem likely. Perhaps it is indeed the work of the experienced painter rather than the young artist, someone capable of employing such emphatic brushstrokes as these to capture an unusual subject, the expressive face of a simple man of the people. According to Dieter Koepplin's attractive suggestion, Cranach may have taken as model a beater at one of the hunts organised by the Saxon court. In his speech in praise of Cranach's sketches carried out on such occasions, printed in 1509, the jurist Christoph Scheurl reported, perhaps with a certain professorial exaggeration: 'Whenever the princes take you out hunting, you bring a drawing-board with you.'

There is another version of this study in London (British Museum, Department of Prints and Drawings, Sloane 5218–19). Opinions on the Basel work, which came to light only in the 1930s, were at first entirely negative, as so often happens in the world of art history when a previously unknown work appears and is compared with one widely known and long familiar. The London drawing, is, however, much softer and more painterly, and at the same time more finicky and pedantic in its execution. Since its basic outlines coincide precisely with those of the Basel version, even where these are applied several times in a rather indecisive manner, to the right of the chin, for example, it is clear that one of the sheets is a copy of the other. The quite different handling rules out any thought that they were produced by the same artist. The most likely answer is that a colleague, possibly Lucas the Younger, copied his father's masterly Basel work to create the London version.

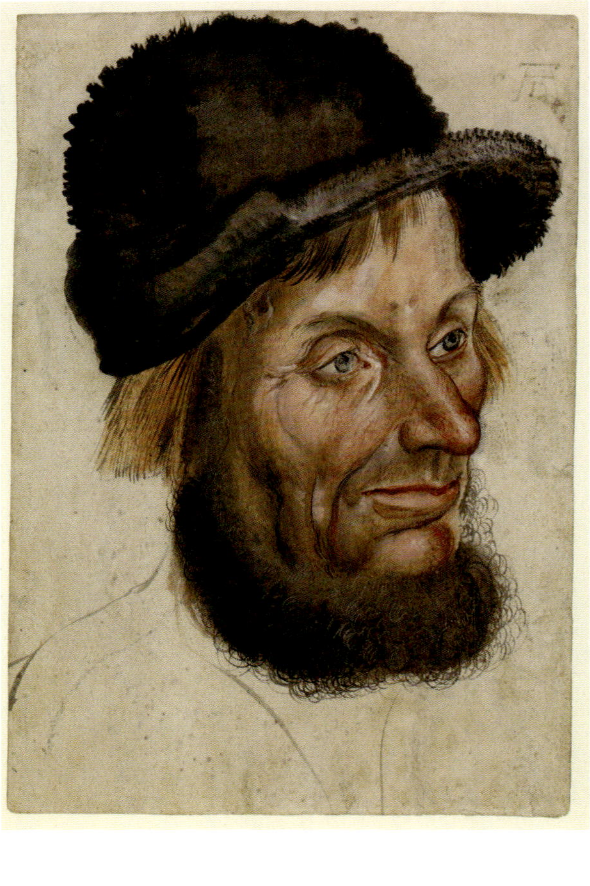

Study of the Head of a Peasant, The British Museum, London, Department of Prints and Drawings

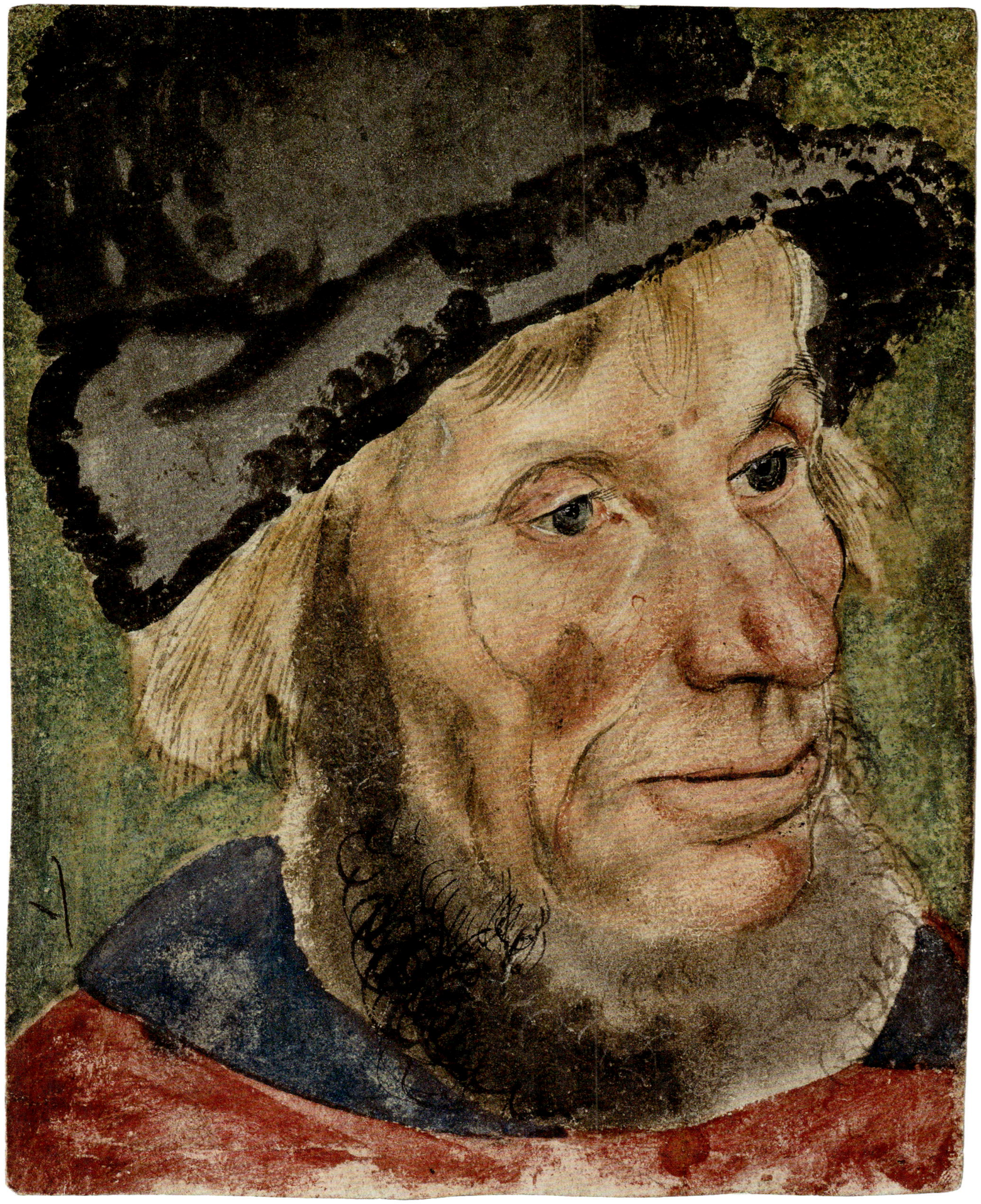

80 Portrait Study of Philipp of Solms-Lich

Wittenberg, *c.* 1530

At upper right a later inscription *FRANCESCO COMES ... F DU ... DE*

Oil on lightly primed paper
17.9 x 13.2 cm

Stadtmuseum, Bautzen, L 83

(Frankfurt only)

Selected references:
Schade 1974, pp. 49, 64; Koepplin/Falk 1974/76, vol. 2, pp. 689 f., no. 609; Grimm/Erichsen/Brockhoff 1994, pp. 342 f., no. 164

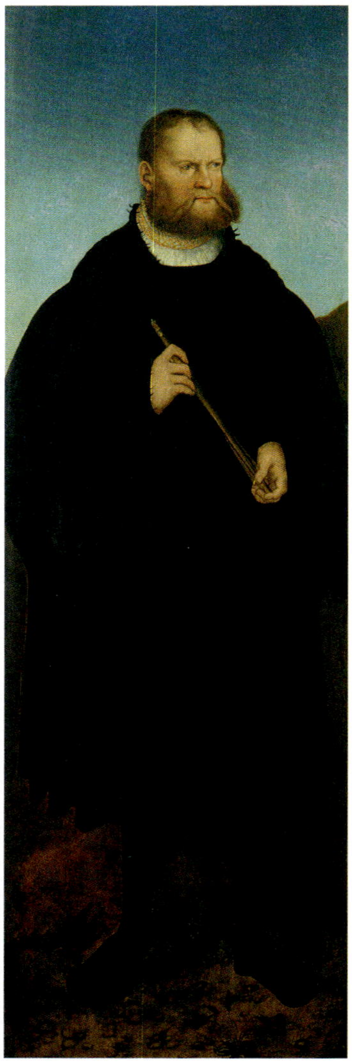

Unknown master from the Cranach workshop, *St Sebastian*, with the facial features of Philipp of Silms-Lich, inner side of the left wing of an altarpiece, Bischöflicher Stuhl, Eichstätt

Count Philipp of Solms-Lich (1468–1544) was an imperial councillor not only under Maximilian I and Charles V but also served in this office between 1506 and 1514 at the electoral court of Frederick the Wise, for whom he administered the Veste Coburg. He would have met the painter Hans Döring (*c.* 1483–1559) in Wittenberg, where at the time he was very probably working in Lucas Cranach's studio. Philipp made Döring his court painter, whereupon the latter moved to Wetzlar to be nearer the courts in Solms and Dillenburg. On the basis of a portrait of Philipp painted by Döring in 1520, now in Schloss Laubach, Werner Schade has been able to identify the subject in this fine oil study – a further example in Cranach's oeuvre of the sensitive empathy he deployed so well to bring out the character of his subjects.

The dating of *c.* 1520 stems from the fact that this is also the date of an altar triptych which the Cranach workshop produced for the Bishop of Eichstätt, Gabriel von Eyb (1455–1535), bearing Saxon arms on the central panel and which was a gift from the Saxon princes (FR 133). The local patron saints Willibald and Walburga, adored by the bishop, occupy the central panel, which in the nineteenth century was transferred from Eichstätt to the Historical Museum of the city of Bamberg. The side wings with SS Sebastian and Roch on the inner sides are still in the possession of the diocese. While the treatment of the latter follows pictorial tradition, St Sebastian is only recognisable in the general iconographic context and from the arrow, his attribute, which he holds in his hands; otherwise, his contemporary dress and facial features, which are exactly like those in the Bautzen study, suggest a portrait of the count as a historiated portrait (cf. cats 66, 67, 77). Werner Schade has offered some conjectures about the accompanying circumstances, and wondered whether the Saxon prince may have sent his confidant to the Bishop of Eichstätt to mediate in the dispute with Martin Luther, for Professor Johannes Eck (1486–1543) of Ingolstadt, Luther's adversary in the Leipzig debate of 1519 and his most important opponent in the following years, was under the control of Bishop Gabriel von Eyb in his roles as a university teacher and canon of Eichstätt. The gift of the altar retable may have had the political function of providing a lasting reminder of this meeting. It is still unclear, however, why the retable contains the characteristics of a plague programme, Sebastian and Roch being the most important patron saints of victims of the plague.

The close connection between the Saxon prince and Philipp of Solms-Lich was never broken. As late as 1543 the electoral treasury of Kursachsen settled an account with Cranach for a Lucretia panel which was sent to the count.

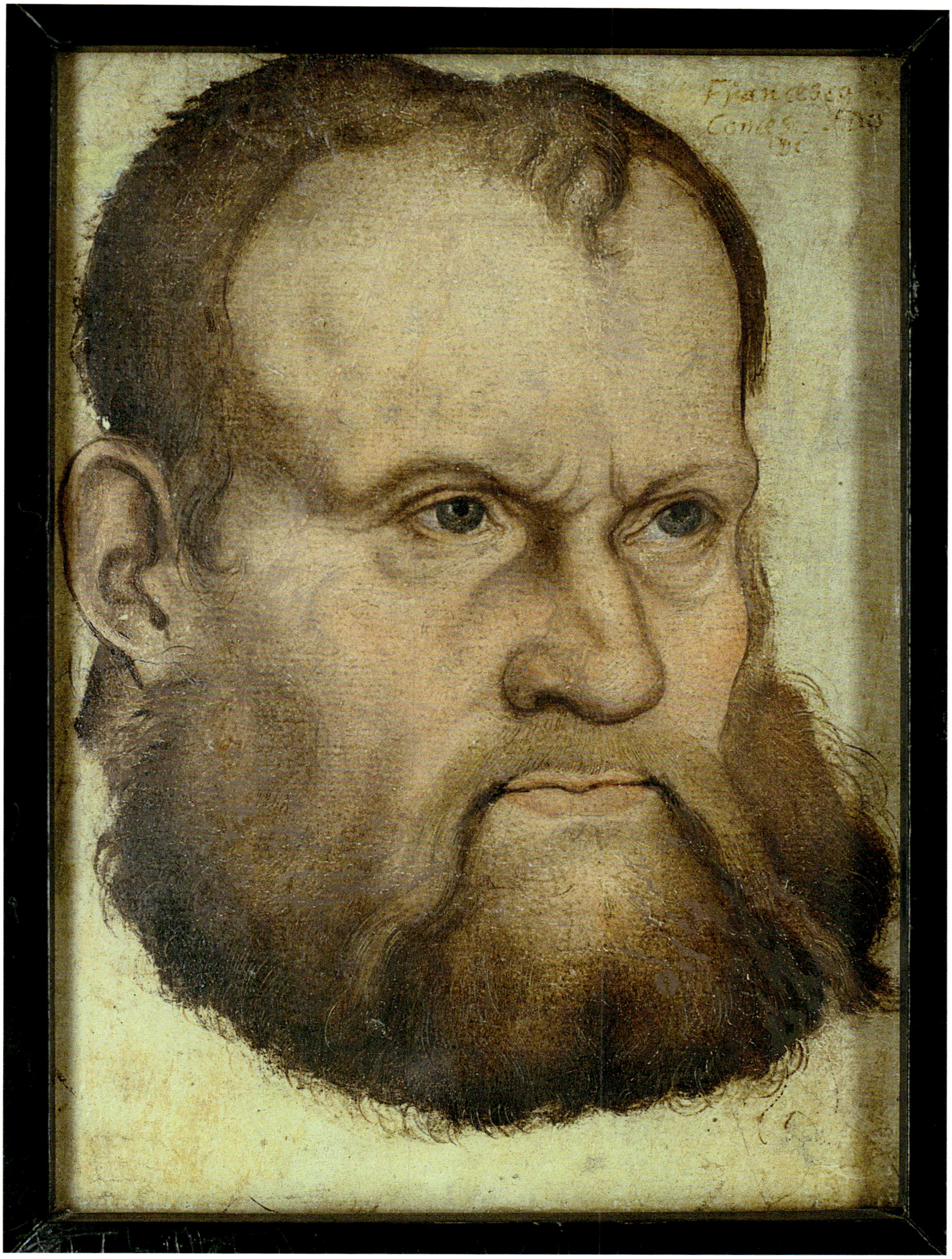

81 Portrait Study of a Clean-Shaven Man

Wittenberg, *c.* 1520

Oil on paper primed with brownish colour, over preliminary drawing with pen and chalk, mounted on canvas
22.3 x 16 cm

Staatliche Museen zu Berlin PK, Kupferstichkabinett, KdZ 4478

Provenance:
acquired 1855

Selected references:
R 73; Schade 1974, p. 49; Grimm/Erichsen/Brockhoff 1994, p. 342, no. 163

The subject of this portrait study fixes the viewer with a steady gaze. Werner Schade has deemed it Cranach's finest achievement in this genre. The portrait shows a middle-aged man who dispenses with the beard usual for someone of his age. The picture shows some damage to the lower half, but even in its present condition Schade's assessment is thoroughly justified. The curling brown hair is built up with lively brushstrokes in a summary but striking way. White highlights are added here and there, and harsh shadows are mostly omitted; some asymmetry in parts of the eyes and mouth contribute to the picture's liveliness. The contours of the nose and cheeks are somewhat angular and lend the subject an air of determination and resolution – an impression emphasised by the compression of the lips. It is hardly surprising that this portrait was later mounted on canvas, clearly so that it could be constantly on show.

The similarity noted by Jakob Rosenberg between this and a panel painting belonging to the Gemäldegalerie, Berlin, possibly the portrait of a mayor from Weissenfels (FR 63), has more to do with the facial type of the subject than his character. This portrait is more closely related in terms of expressiveness and liveliness to the *Head of a Peasant* in Basel (cat. 79), and may be dated to *c.* 1520.

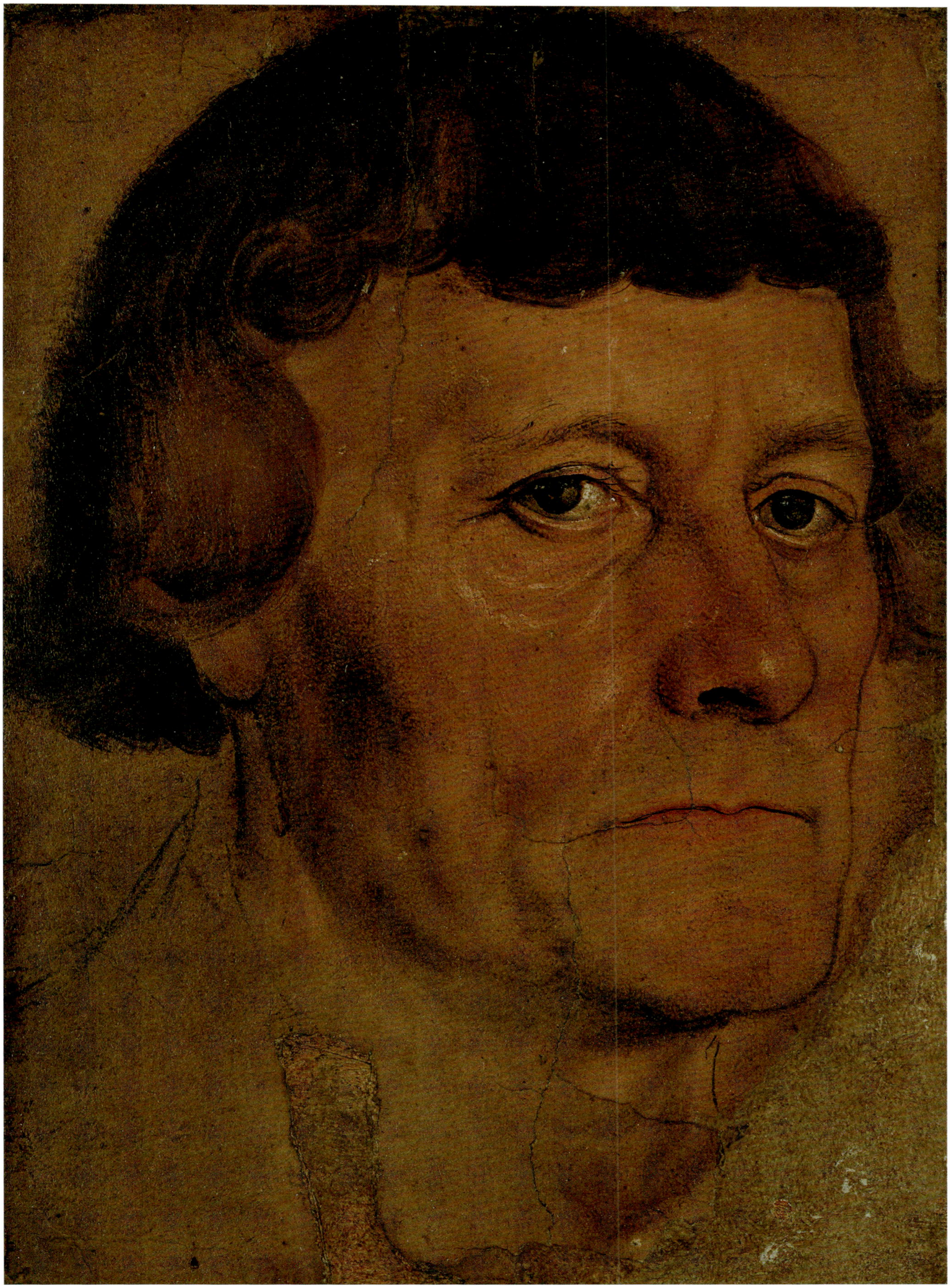

82 Portrait Study of a Young Man

Wittenberg, *c.* 1530

Pen, black chalk and oil on paper primed in brownish colour
26.2 x 19.9 cm

J. Paul Getty Museum, Los Angeles, Dept. of Prints and Drawings, 92.GG.91

Provenance:
acquired in 1992; previously in the J. Pzn: Zoomer Collection, Amsterdam

(Frankfurt only)

Selected references:
R 90; The J.Paul Getty Museum Journal 21, 1993, p. 123, no. 28; Grimm/Erichsen/Brockhoff 1994, p. 343, no. 165

The head of a young man is shown turned slightly to the right; this seemingly accidental viewpoint contributes to an appearance of spontaneity, as does the subject's piercing gaze into the distance. Here Lucas Cranach concentrates with great economy on the essentials: the cap, shoulder and the lower part of the shirt are merely outlined in chalk; the surface of the hair and the stand-up collar are indicated with just a few brushstrokes, the thin layer of colour allowing the lines of the preparatory drawing to come through. In contrast, the facial features are carefully modelled with fine brushwork. The shadows of the beard are indicated in a different shade from real shadow, and special care is given to the eyes with their finely delineated brows and eyelids, the detailed treatment of the edge of the lower lid and the moist corner of the eye, the two-coloured iris and the dark pupil and the light reflected in them.

The selective use of fine detail in this drawing from the Getty Museum forms a link between the more strongly delineated portrait heads of the 1520s and a series of portraits in the Musée des Beaux Arts in Rheims, some of which are attributed to Lucas Cranach the Younger. This portrait of a young man may thus be dated to the 1530s; it is considered one of the most absorbing and lively portrait studies by Cranach the Elder.

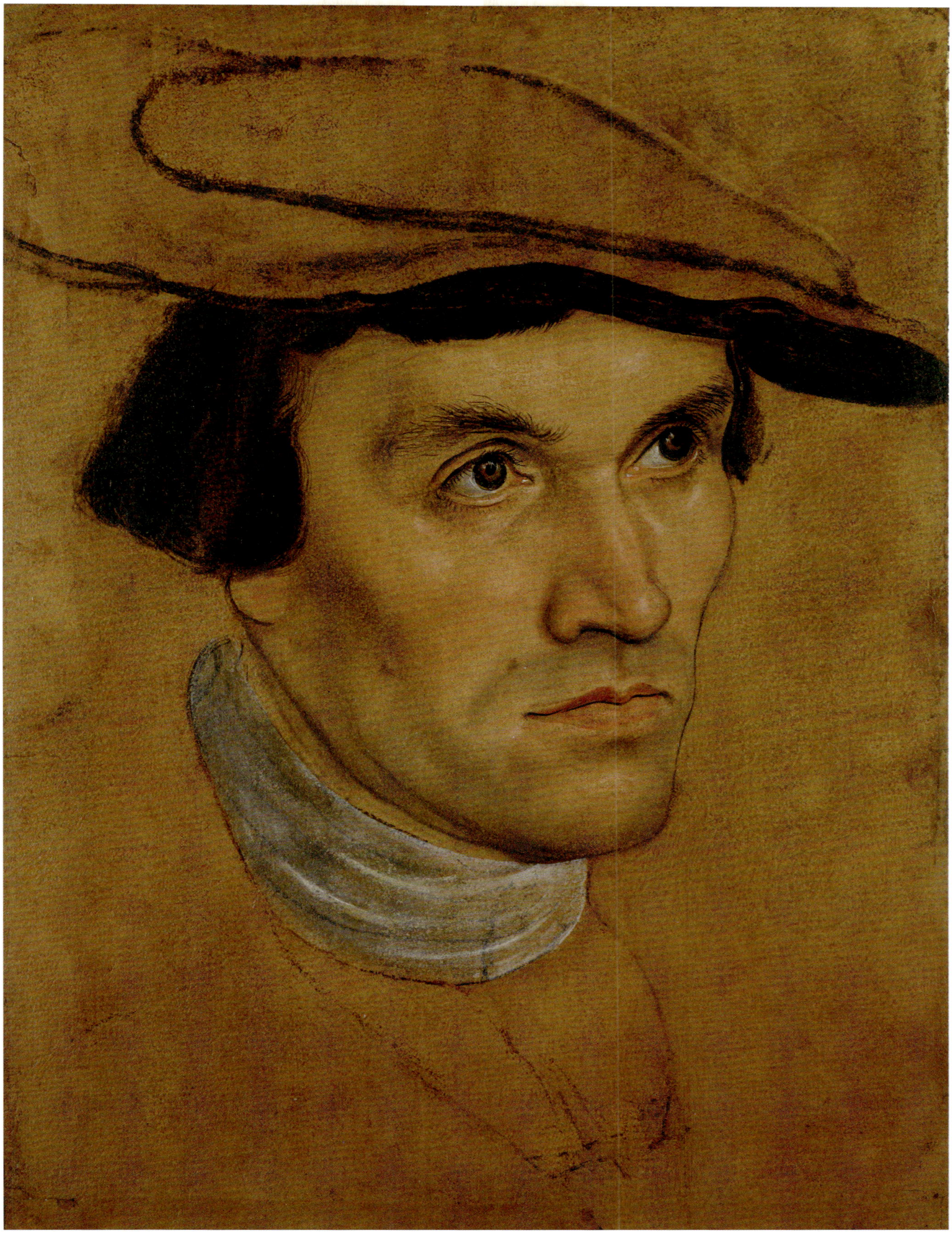

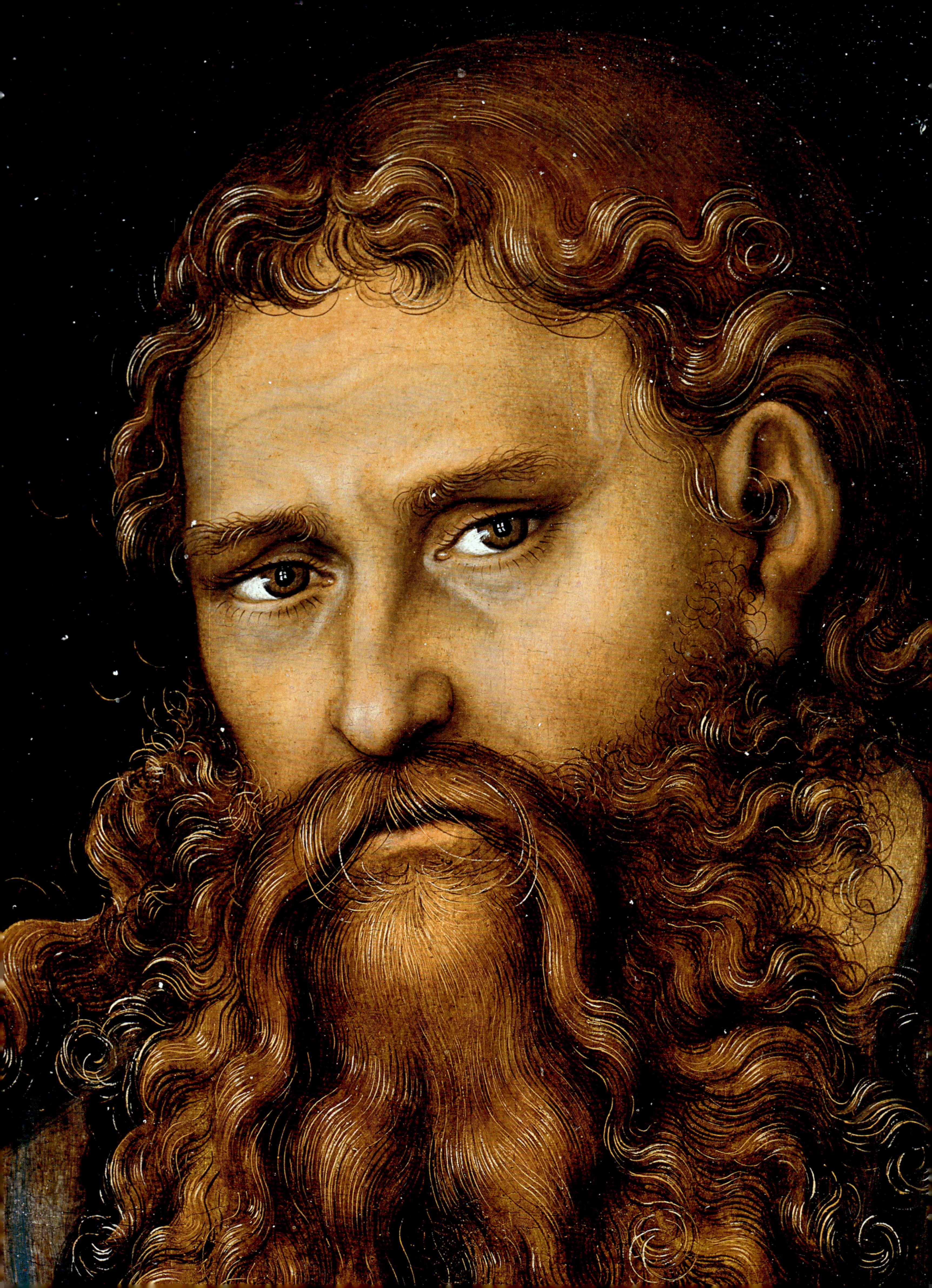

Models for Mass Production

A productive studio on the scale of the Cranach workshop created a large store of pictorial models with attractive details such as heads and animals that could be copied as required and included in new paintings. Very little of this workshop material has survived, but there are some studies of exceptional quality which clearly suggest they were made by the master alone.

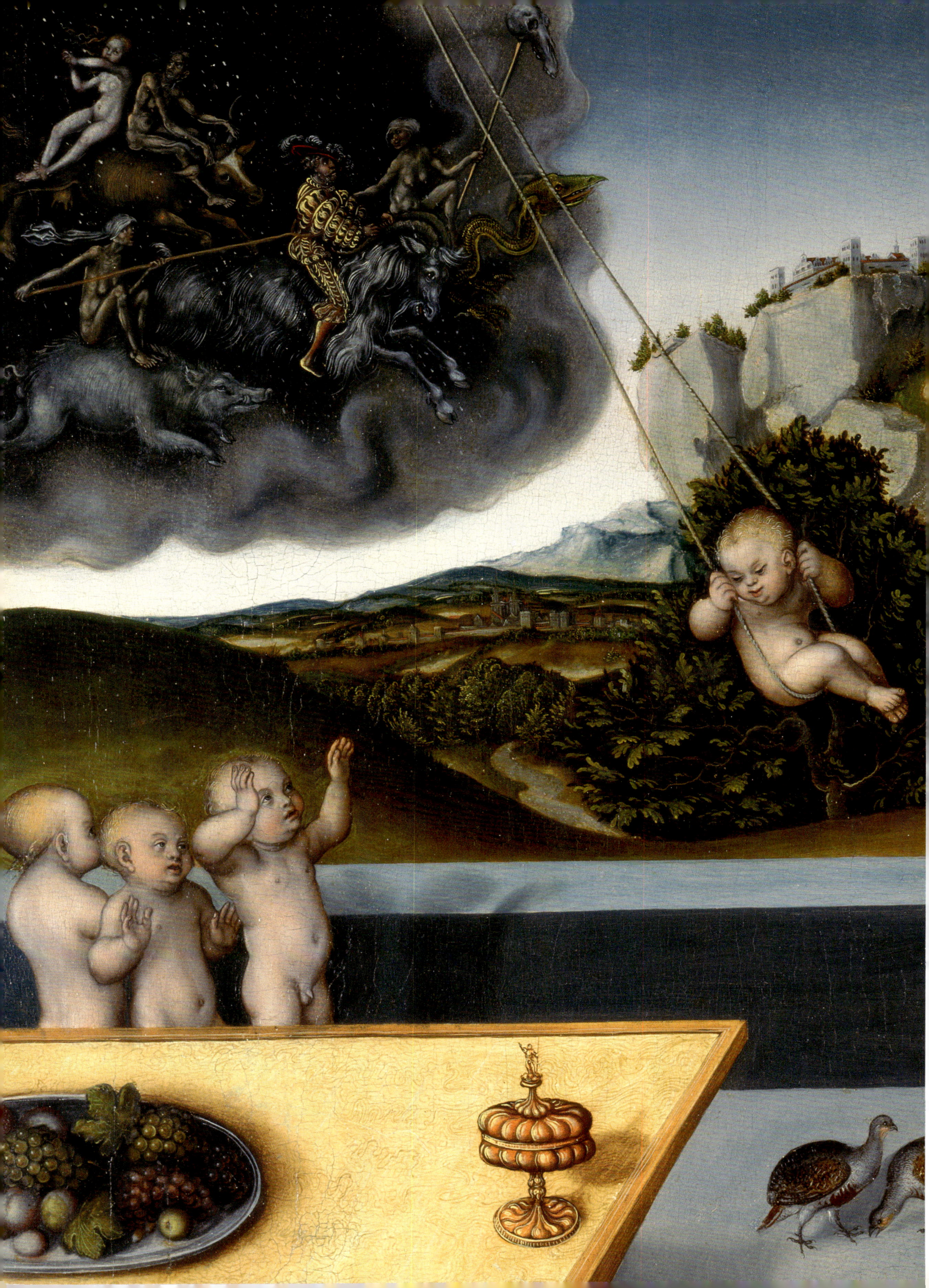

Entertaining and Teaching

The narrative richness of stories from the Old Testament and ancient mythology, and from time to time an ironic perception of the everyday world of his times, offered alternative subjects when sacred themes became difficult. At this point Cranach began to paint cunning young women such as daughters of Lot, heroines such as the virtuous Lucretia and the courageous Judith, and capturing the antics of anonymous old men in pursuit of pretty girls. In pictorial inventions of this kind he smoothly combined entertainment and humour with serious didactic elements, producing important seminal works which were to enable the new category of genre painting to gain acceptance.

87 Lot and his Daughters

Wittenberg, *c.* 1528–30

Marked on the brown jar on the right of the picture with the serpent with upright wings facing left

Oil and tempera on red beechwood
57.3 x 38.5 cm

Provenance:
since 1819, at the latest, in the collection of the monastery Premonstratensian monastery of Nová Říše, on loan to the Moravian Gallery, Brno

Selected references:
not in FR; Koepplin/Falk 1974/76, vol. 2, p. 566; Lucas Cranach, exh. cat., 2006, pp. 80 f., no. 13

The Book of Genesis describes the downfall of the sinful cities of Sodom and Gomorrah in a rain of brimstone and fire which the Lord sent down from heaven (Genesis 19, 24). To save the righteous, he sent two angels who took Lot, a nephew of Abraham, and saved him from being raped by his fellow citizens (hence the old use of the word Sodom to mean homosexuality). Before Sodom was destroyed, the angels brought Lot and his wife and two daughters out of the city and sent them to the nearby town of Zoar with the instruction not to look back. Lot's wife disobeyed this order and was turned into a pillar of salt; her husband fled with his daughters to Zoar and then on to a cave in the mountains. There his daughters grew afraid that in their lonely state they would never have children, so on two consecutive nights they got their father drunk and became pregnant by him. Each of them bore a son, who became the ancestors of the Moabites and the Ammonites.

In the early sixteenth century the subject enjoyed great popularity as an example of female cunning; Lucas Cranach painted at least eight versions of the Old Testament scene. The panel from Nová Říše reveals the closest parallels to a version dated 1528 in a private collection (Koepplin/Falk 1974/76, no. 460) and another from the following year in the Alte Pinakothek, Munich (FR 204). In both of these the daughter on the left pours wine from a clay wine jug with a chain, which in our picture is placed on the far right. The father receives the wine in a drinking bowl which he holds out, as he does in the picture in the private collection. In another version in an American private collection (FR 205), the daughter pours the wine with a great flourish, as in our picture, from a pewter jug, but this time into a tumbler. The path in the middleground with the mother turned into a pillar of salt is closest to the Munich version.

A singular feature of the panel from Nová Říše is the design of the background, which in all the other versions is framed by an arch of grey cotton-wool smoke clouds, which look highly artificial. These are not present in our picture, for which Cranach took a very different approach. On the deep black background he used a fine brush and a single colour, a bright red, to pick out the contours of an extensive landscape with trees, hill slopes and the two cities condemned to destruction, also some low threatening clouds from which – here for once breaking into monochrome – dazzling white strokes of lightning spear downwards. The depiction of this part of the picture recalls a coloured woodcut seen in negative; it is one of the most impressive scenes of nocturnal catastrophe in sixteenth-century painting. The red dresses of the daughters, with their deep black shadowy areas, harmonise with the triangular area in the upper-right background; even the foreground seems to have been caught by the pale light of the lightning flashes from the scene of the catastrophe.

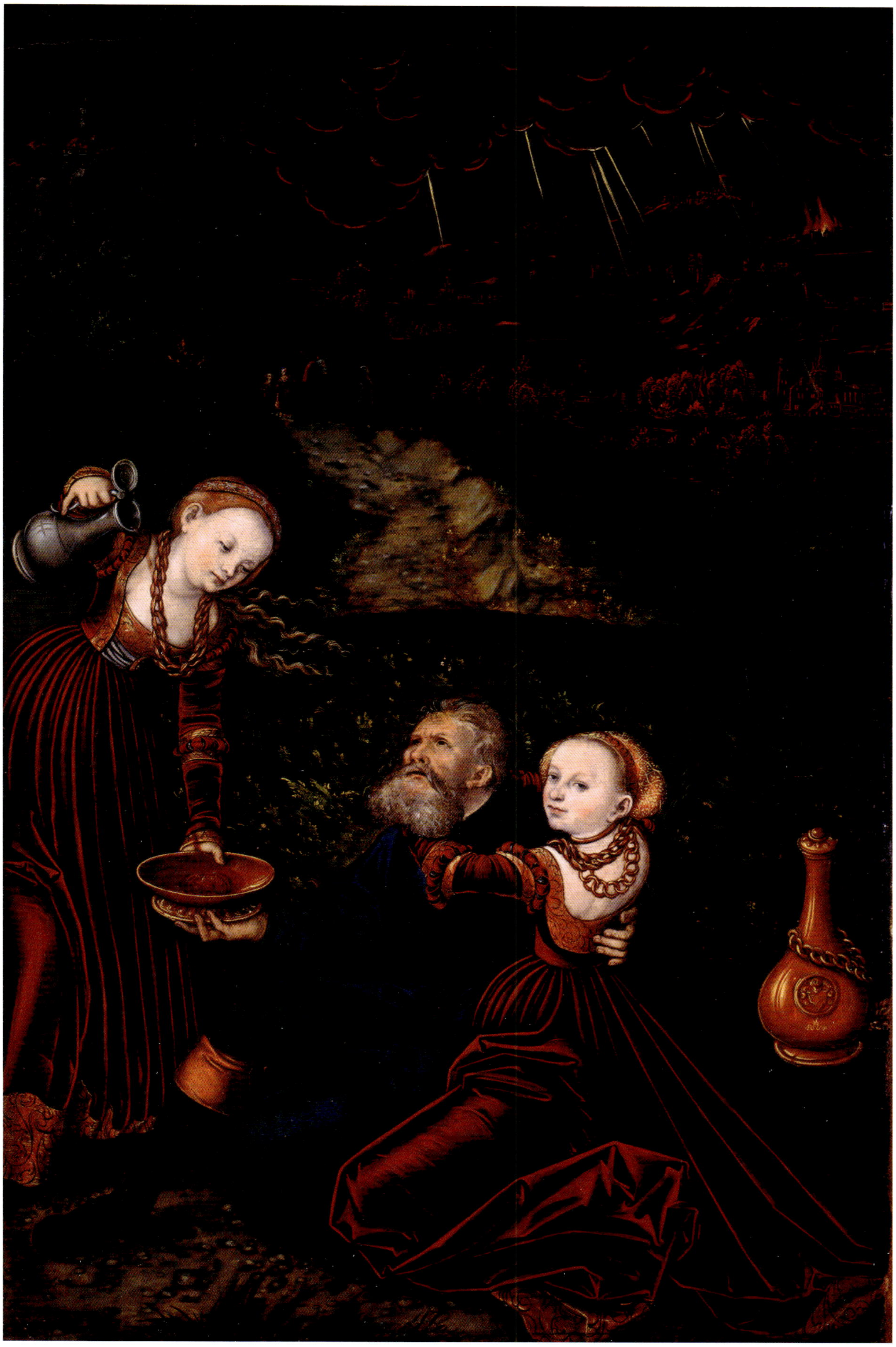

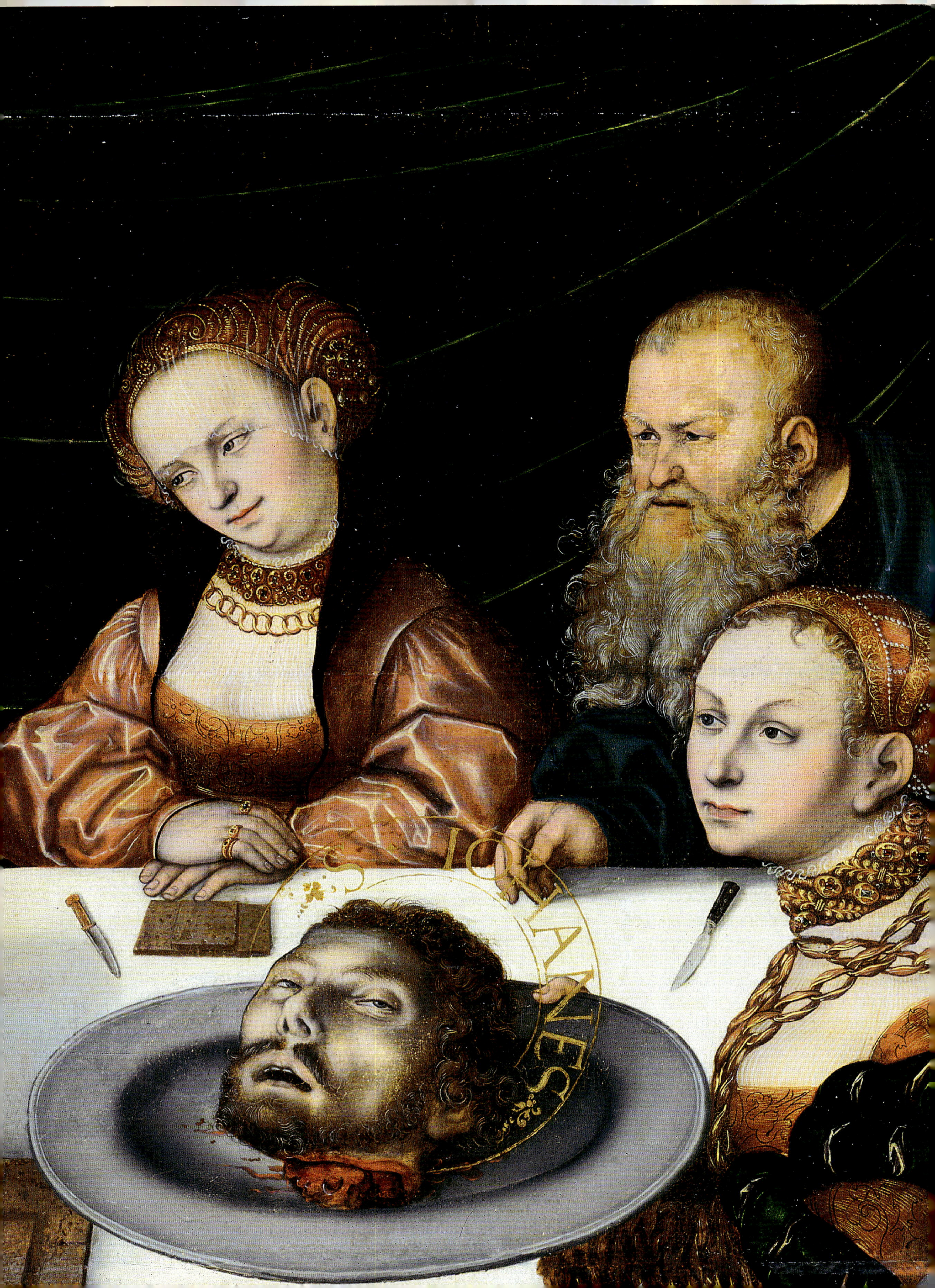

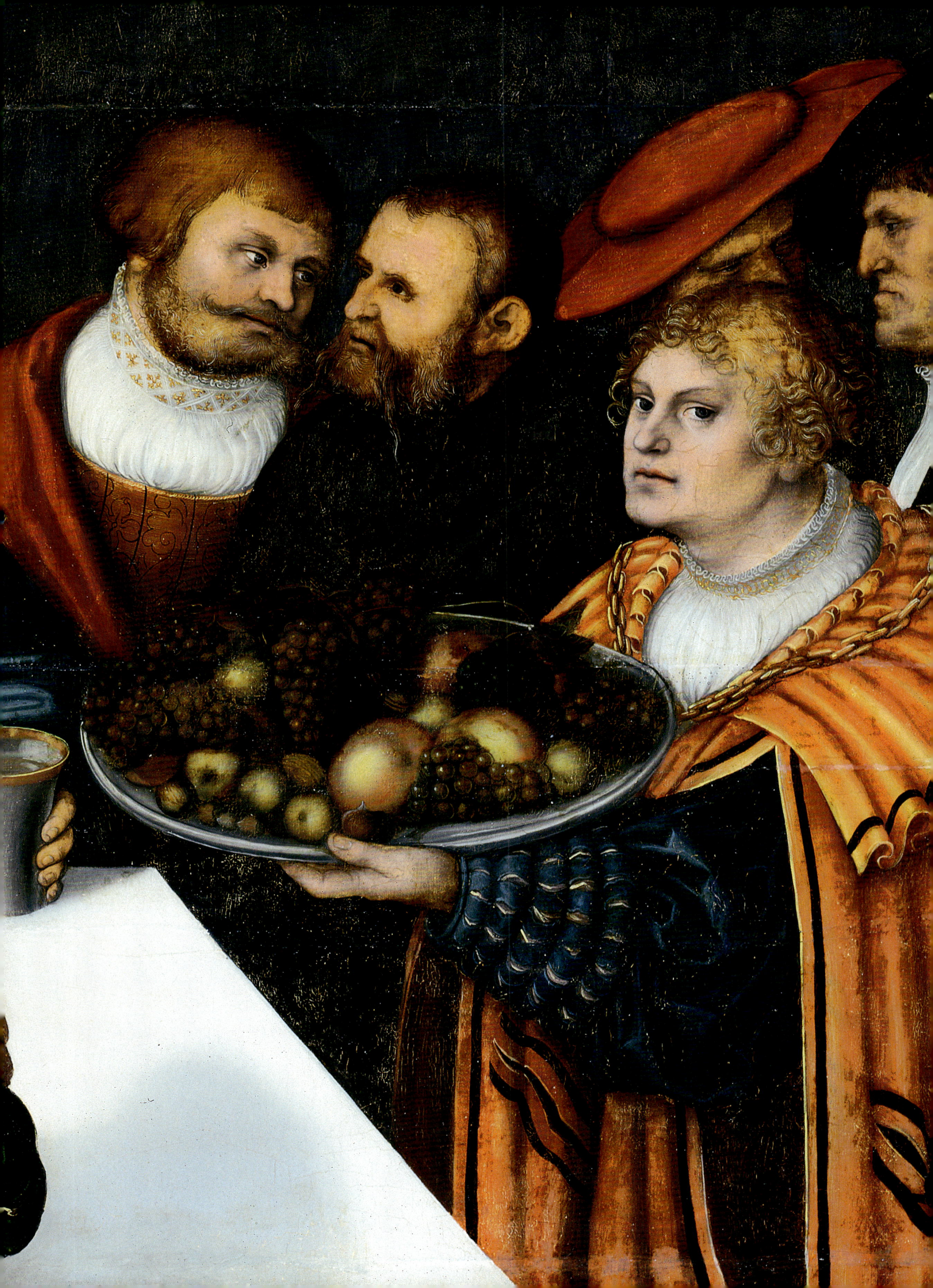

90 Salome with the Head of John the Baptist

Wittenberg, *c.* 1509–10

Signed in the top right corner with the serpent with upright wings facing left

Oil and tempera on oak
61 x 49.5 cm

Lisbon, Museu Nacional de Arte Antiga, 738 Pint

Provenance:
presented in 1872 by Conte de Cavalhido

(London only)

Selected references:
FR 33; Koepplin/Falk 1974/76, vol 2, p. 660; Museu National de Arte Antiga, exh. cat. 1999, p. 166, no. 60; cited, with a discussion of the formation of the legend: Panofsky 1969, p. 44

Late medieval representations of the New Testament account of the death of John the Baptist occurring at the request of Salome, the beautiful step-daughter of King Herod (cat. 89), often isolated the protagonists and placed them in independent scenes. This led on the one hand to some strange paintings and reliefs of John the Baptist's head on a charger, as Salome had expressly demanded according to the Gospels (Matthew 14, 8; Mark 6, 25). On the other hand, the young woman became the subject of closer, almost portrait-like half- or three-quarter-length pictures.

Lucas Cranach's earliest surviving interpretation of this scene is his most impressive. There is no balustrade or other impediment to separate the viewer from the figure of Salome, nor is there anything in the black background to divert attention from her. In the bottom left corner she presents the head on the charger, itself painted with such delicacy as to recall the individual studies mentioned above. As she looks past us into the void, the sumptuously dressed princess wears a grave expression, as though she were now being tormented by doubts about her gruesome deed, the consequences of which she carries literally in her hands. According to gospel accounts, Salome was urged to make her request by her mother Herodias and acted 'more with imprudence than evil intent', as Jacob Grimm put it, which partly accounts for the legend that grew up in the Middle Ages, of her secret love for John the Baptist. Salome's stern, slightly androgynous features are reminiscent of the young page on the far left of the middle panel in the Dresden *St Catherine* Altarpiece (Staatliche Kunstsammlungen, Gemäldegalerie; FR 14).

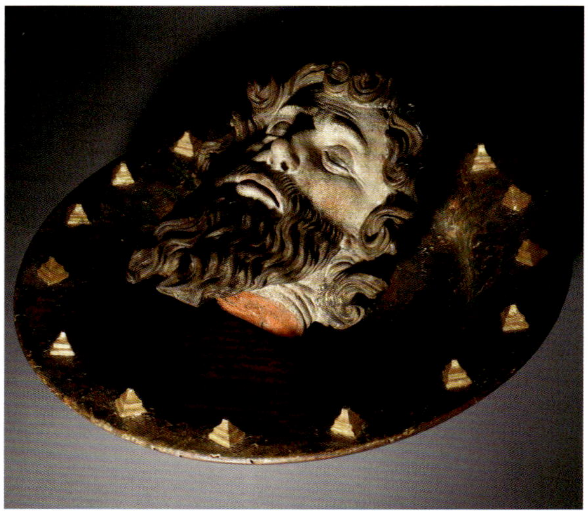

Austrian, *c.* 1490, *Charger with the Head of John the Baptist*, Liebighaus Skulpturensammlung, Frankfurt

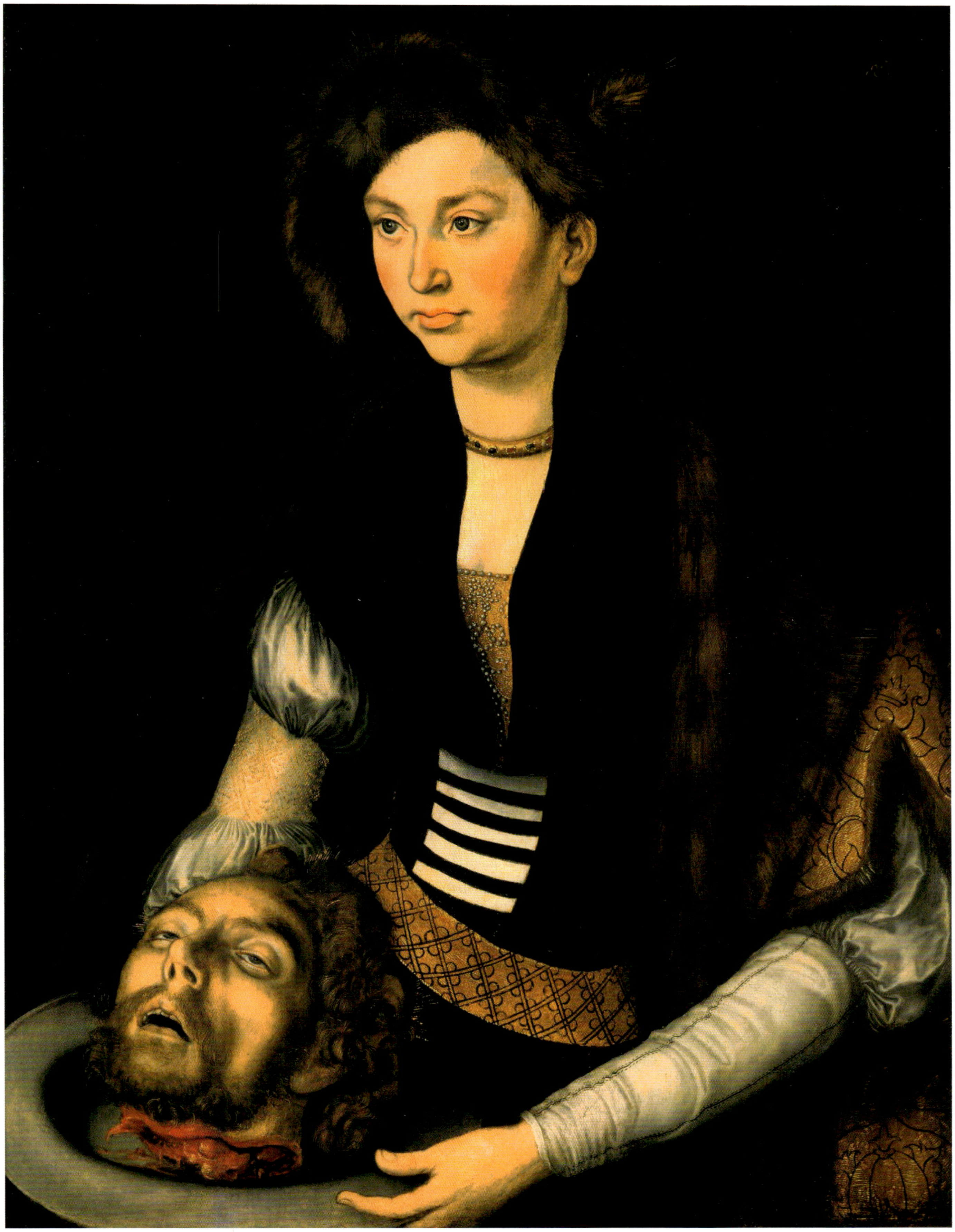

95 The Ill-Matched Couple: a Young Man and Old Woman with a Maid

Lucas Cranach the Younger (?)

Wittenberg, *c.* 1540–50

Oil and tempera on pine
91 x 61 cm

Art collections of the Veste Coburg, M 10

(Frankfurt only)

Selected references:
not in FR; Weschenfelder 2004, pp. 34 f.

The relatively smooth treatment of the faces and the somewhat stiff structure of the feather and hood suggest that this is the work of Lucas Cranach the Younger. The energetic underdrawing that shows through the flesh tones in places certainly rules out the possibility of its being a copy. It is, nevertheless, the only known version of a highly original composition. At first glance it shows an ill-matched couple consisting of a young man and an old woman. The latter's lascivious leer and the youth's tender fondling of her shoulder repeat the corresponding motifs in the small panel in Budapest (cat. 93). In addition, the way she caresses the young man's beard may have been inspired by the much-copied *Ill-matched Couple* by Quentin Massys (National Gallery of Art, Washington, Ailsa Mellon Bruce Fund, 1971.55.1).

Another element connects the Cranach panel from Coburg with the Dutch model: the introduction of a third figure. In the Washington picture this is merely a fool enacting a supporting role in the background, but in the Coburg panel the protagonists are standing or sitting behind a table, towards which a young woman advances from front left holding a large pewter wine jug and offering a freshly filled glass. On the right a tall *Krautstrunk*, a special kind of glass with a knobbled surface, stands on the table.

Although the young man and the old crone completely ignore the serving maid, she looks up at them full of expectation, a knowing smile playing on her lips. The direction of her gaze creates an ambivalent situation which, in the way her head is placed immediately next to the bulging money bag, suggests an equivalence between these two similarly shaped forms. The viewer can no longer be quite sure whether the scene in the upper half of the picture actually portrays the two partners in the transaction or whether the old woman is not rather acting as a procuress, joyfully congratulating her best customer on the pleasure that lies ahead, or whether the young man is just pretending to make up to the old crone in order to be close to the younger woman. Evidence that it is he, rather than the old woman, who is on the lookout for a conquest, is provided by his elegant clothes which in their opulence far outstrip the costume of the young man who offers himself for sale to the old woman in the Budapest picture.

At all events, this late work from the Lucas Cranach workshop presents for the first time the cast of figures featuring the trio of client, procuress and young prostitute (though the latter is often not immediately recognisable as such) that was to appear in numerous brothel scenes from the sixteenth to the eighteenth centuries. The most famous example is Gerard Terborch's picture in Berlin, which Goethe misinterpreted as *The Fatherly Admonition* (Gemäldegalerie SMBPK, 791). Also prominent in this scene are the ever-present elements of every brothel painting: wine and money.

In its later years, the Cranach workshop employed constant adaptation and artful psychology, a proven recipe for success, to produce remarkable new works. Innovation is best brought about through the simple combination of known elements: an *Ill-matched Couple* is here extended downwards by one-third to form a kind of proscenium for a figure placed in front of the table in the extreme foreground, just as the Salome figure takes on a central significance in the different versions of *The Feast of Herod* (cat. 89). Psychological penetration is used to strengthen the relationship between the figures in their new positions.

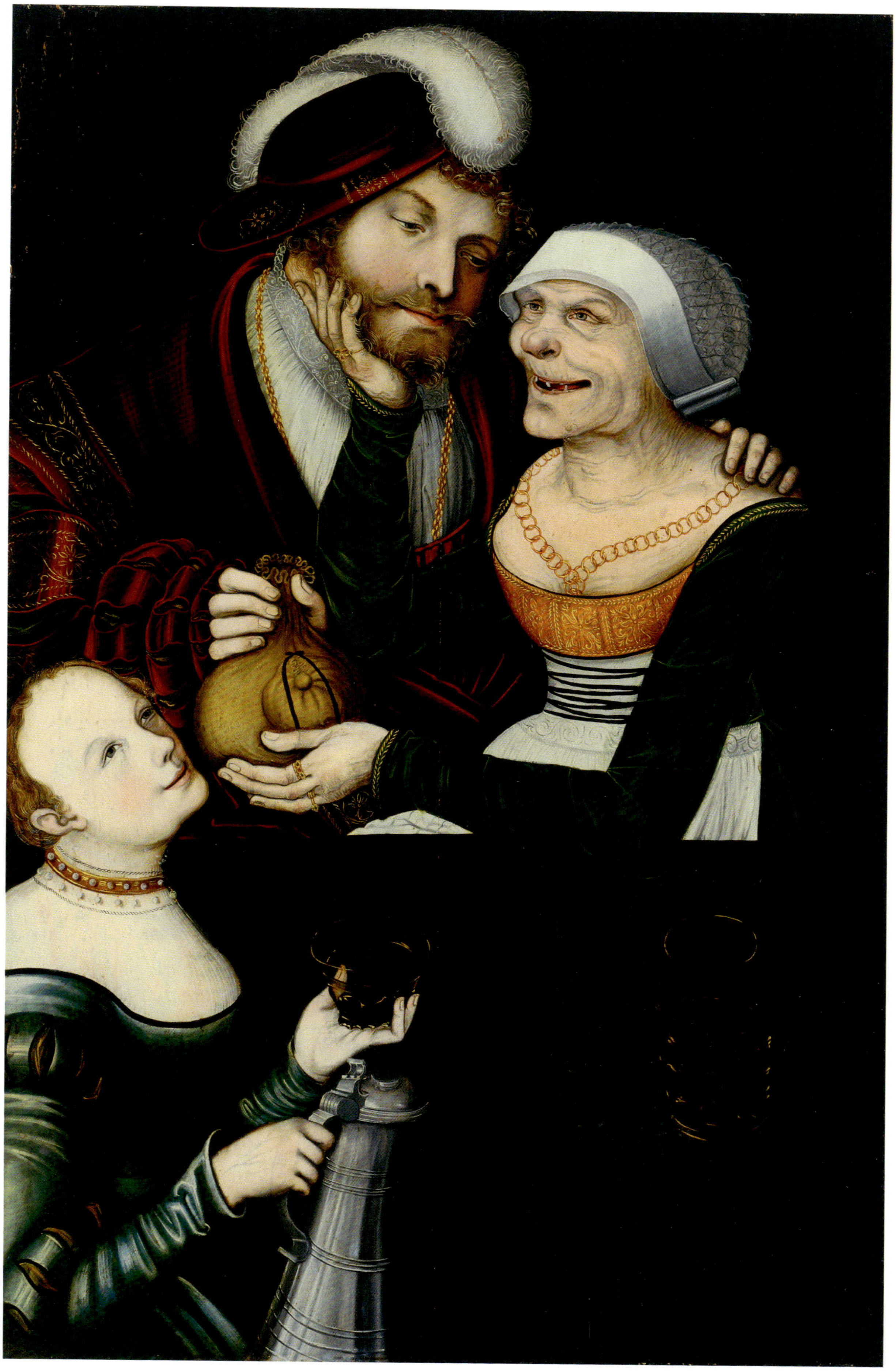

The Ill-Matched Couple: a Young Man and Old Woman with a Maid | 313

100 # Lucretia

Wittenberg, *c.* 1525–30

Oil and tempera on limewood
41.5 x 28 cm

Staatliche Museen Kassel,
Gemäldegalerie Alte Meister
GK 14

Provenance:
acquired in 1885 on the Stuttgart art market

(Frankfurt only)

Selected references:
FR 122; Scheckenburger-Broschek 1997, pp. 65–9; on Netherlandish representations: Schubert 1971

Lucretia, wife of a noble army chief in Ancient Rome, and as beautiful as she was virtuous, was fiendishly blackmailed by Sextus Tarquinius, the eldest son of King Tarquinius Superbus, and thereby compelled to sleep with him. When she at first refused, he threatened to kill both her and a slave and then to claim he had caught the two of them in *flagrante.* Shamed by the loss of honour she would suffer, Lucretia stabbed herself to death, having first informed her husband and father by letter of what had happened. The family swore revenge, and staged a rebellion which led finally to the dissolution of the monarchy in favour of the Roman republic.

Contemporary historians such as Johann Carion (1499–1537), scientist and astrologer to the court of Brandenburg, whose portrait was painted by the Cranach workshop, saw in this episode, originally described by Livy (Titus Livius) in his *History of Rome* I (57–59), an example of the punishment and overthrowing of a tyrant through the intervention of God.

Lucretia is portrayed three-quarter length in front of a landscape. She has bared her upper body, pushing back the fur-lined *Schaube* and pulling down her fashionable chemise. Her bare skin is adorned with sumptuous jewellery, a gold necklace with a pendant, a second necklace and a wide ornamental chain. Her hair is pinned up and crisscrossed with strings of pearls. Even in death she retains the insignia of her patrician status, as she uses both hands to hold the handle of the dagger which in a moment she will plunge into her heart. The tip of the weapon has yet to scratch the smooth skin of her beautiful body. It would be more precise to say that the painting shows Lucretia's decision to take her own life rather than the deed itself, and portrays her with a suitable facial expression, that of composure in suffering.

The closest parallels to this composition come from the Netherlands. Quentin Massys, circle of, (Museum of Fine Arts, Budapest) and Joos van Cleve (Kunsthistorisches Museum, Vienna, see below) also portrayed Lucretia at half- to three-quarter length in very similar ways: with the upper body bared to reveal her breasts spilling from precious fabrics and with jewellery draped across her naked skin; both female figures convey an immediate impression of beauty and luxury. Characteristic features of these creations include the head leaning reflectively to one side and the way in which the hands clasp the handle of the dagger.

The two Netherlandish works date from about 1520–25. As Dietrich Schubert has pointed out, the Netherlandish tradition of treating the subject of Lucretia constantly inspired German artists, among them Ulrich Apt of Augsburg (*c.* 1460–1532; *Lucretia*, 1523, Alte Pinakothek, Munich, 1431) and Cranach's pupil Hans Döring (*c.* 1483–1559; *Lucretia*, 1514, Wiesbaden Museum, 26). In view of the close parallels between them, it is hardly likely that Cranach could have painted this monumental image, as of a patrician's daughter, now in Kassel, without any knowledge of her Flemish sisters, and this suggests it should be dated somewhat later than hitherto. The foreshortening of the face, which makes it broader, seems to fit better with the period around 1525–30; comparison with the *St Helena* from Cincinnati (cat. 57), dated 1525, shows that this too employs the same device.

Lucas Cranach's composition seems to be unusual in two respects: it omits the actual stabbing and the blood on the dagger, and clearly shows Lucretia seated. The positioning of the body about the knees is not entirely clear. The knees themselves look as if they have been copied from a representation of a seated Virgin, which suggests that the artist himself modified the Netherlandish type in this respect. Both elements, the seated pose and the lack of a stab wound, lend the figure a truly majestic calm and composure almost at odds with the drama of the events.

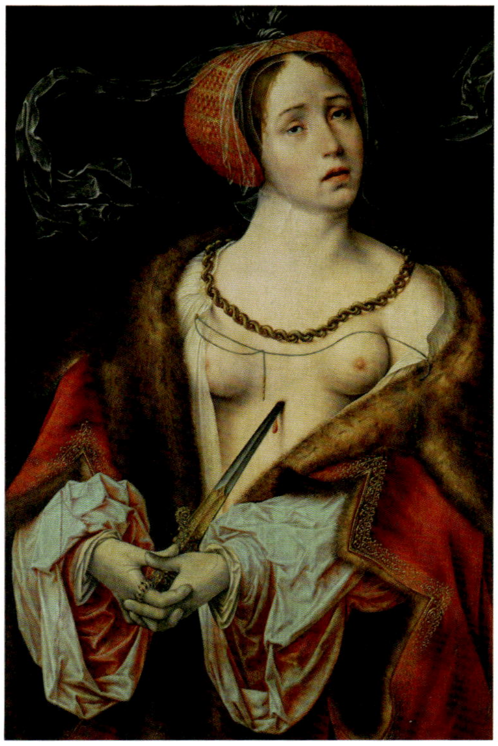

Joos van Cleve, *The Suicide of Lucretia*,
Kunsthistorisches Museum, Vienna

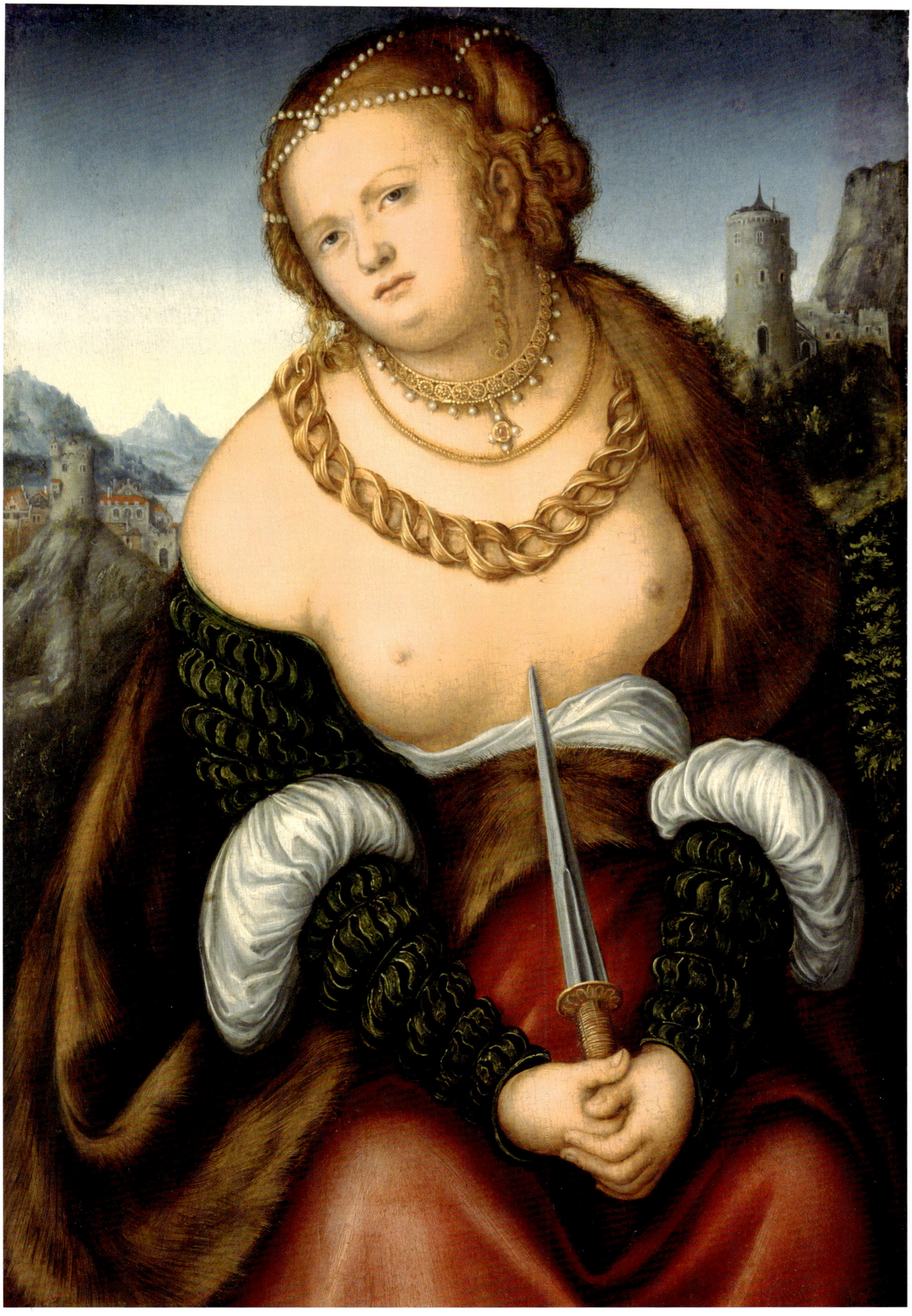

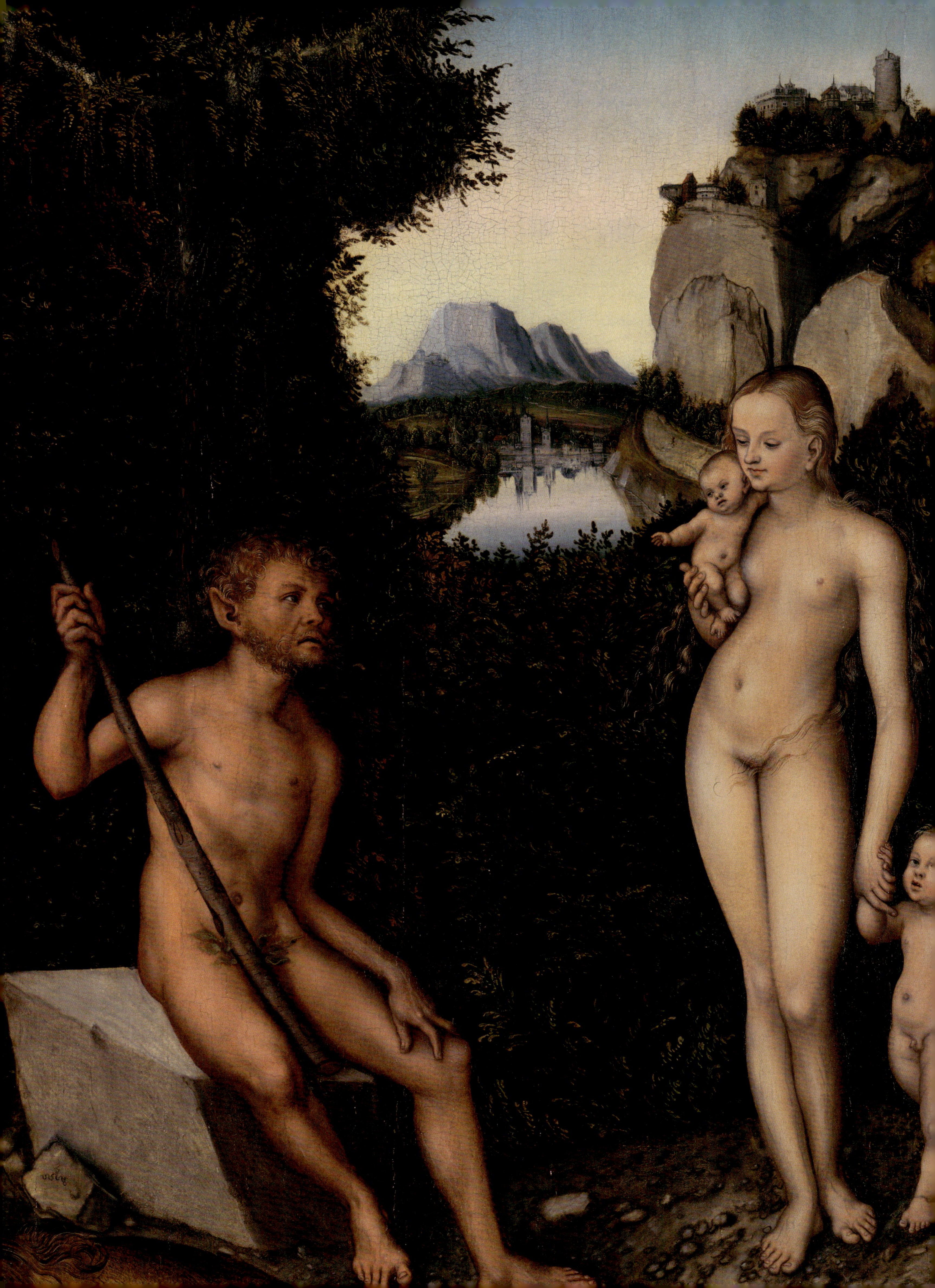

The Flowering of the Nude

Encouraged by the interest of the Wittenberg humanists, Cranach soon found that pictures from classical mythology took first place among the new subjects. This enabled him to apply his skill at painting nudes, in particular depictions of the female body, to heathen goddesses such as Venus, Diana and the Three Graces. Eroticism and sensual pleasure are essential to the appeal of these works, though they are seldom without a didactic or philosophical message. One of the most popular subjects was *Venus with Cupid Stealing Honey*, showing the pleasure and pain of love in the person of the child Cupid, who was stung by bees because he stole their sweet honeycomb.

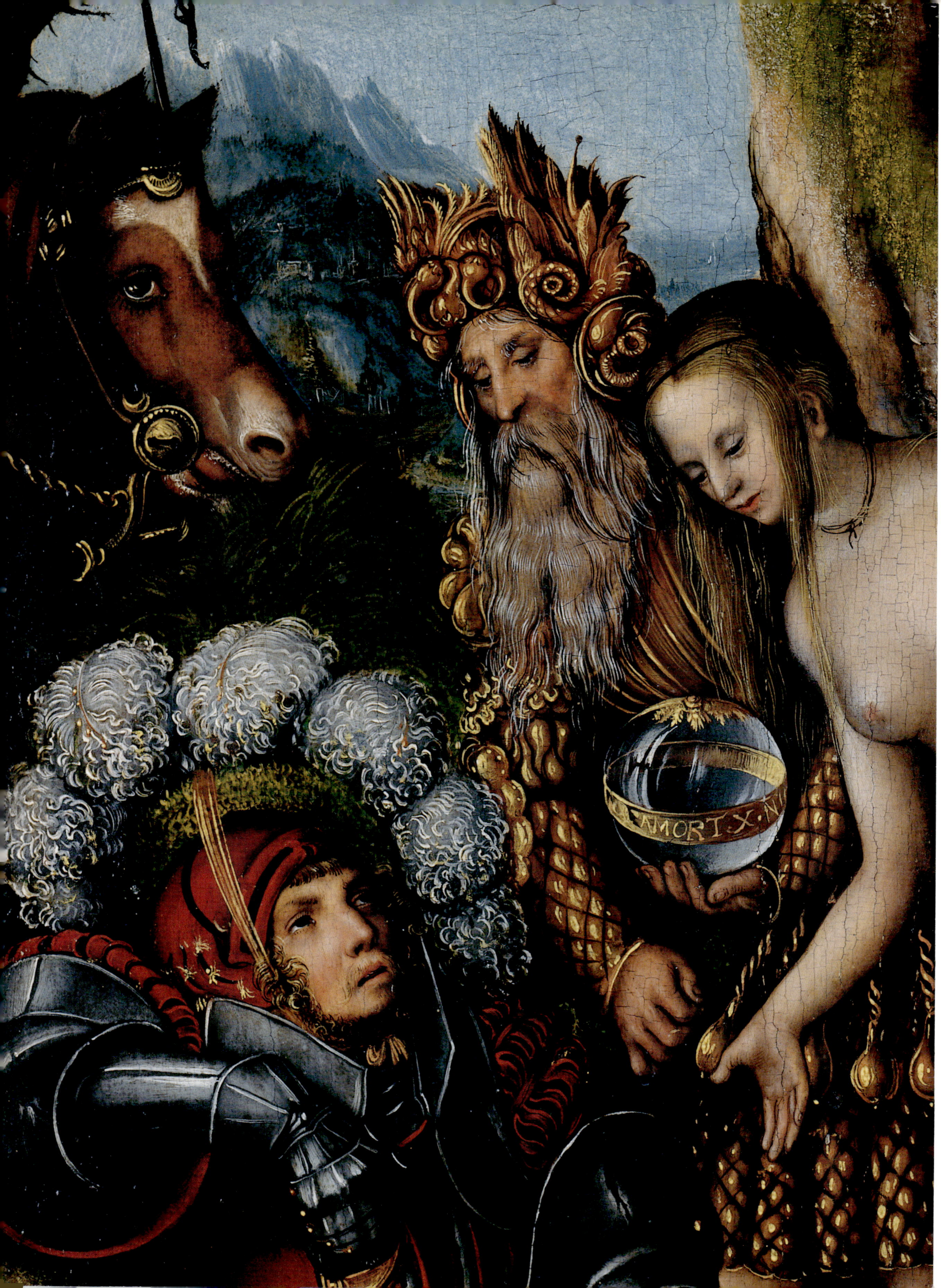
AMORT·X·N

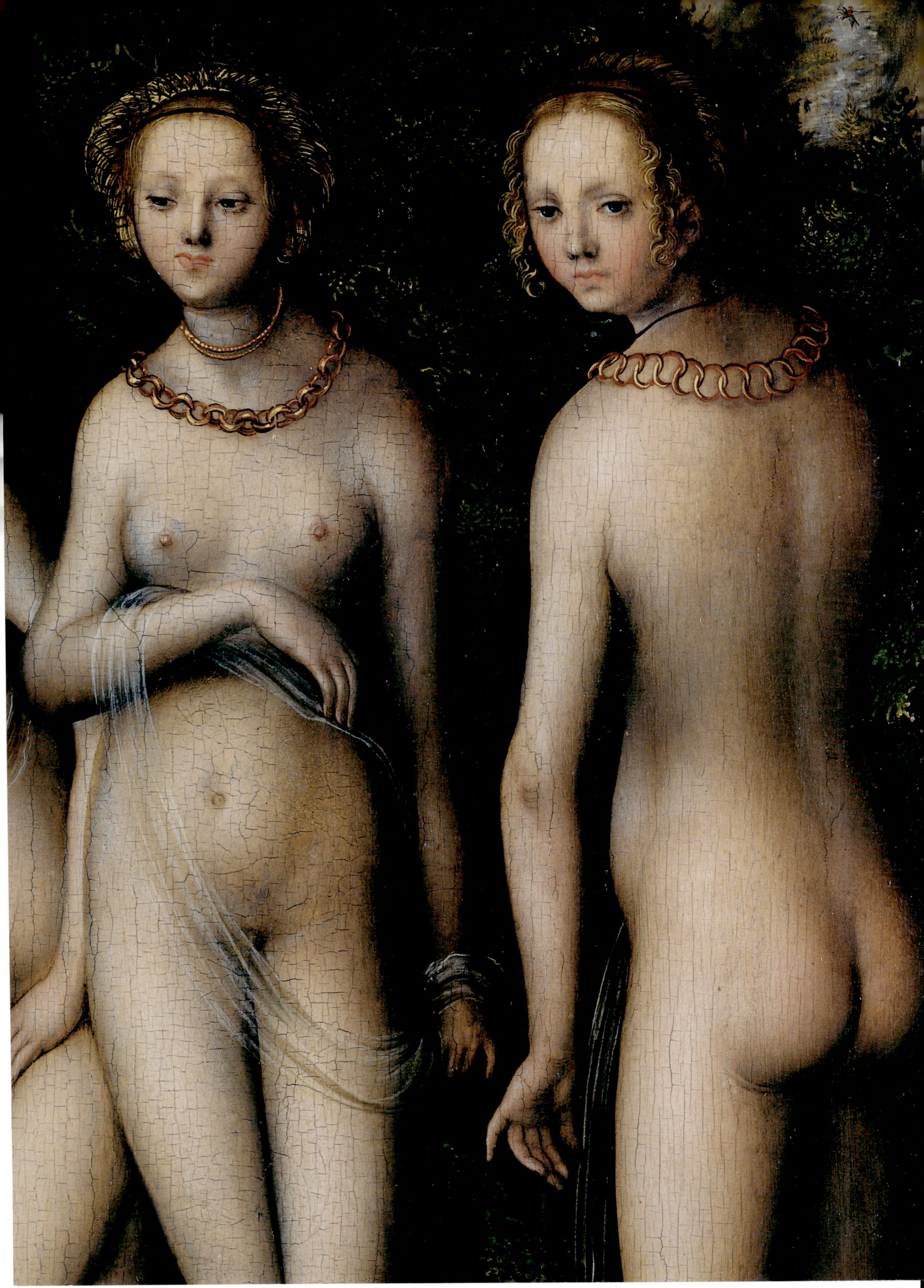

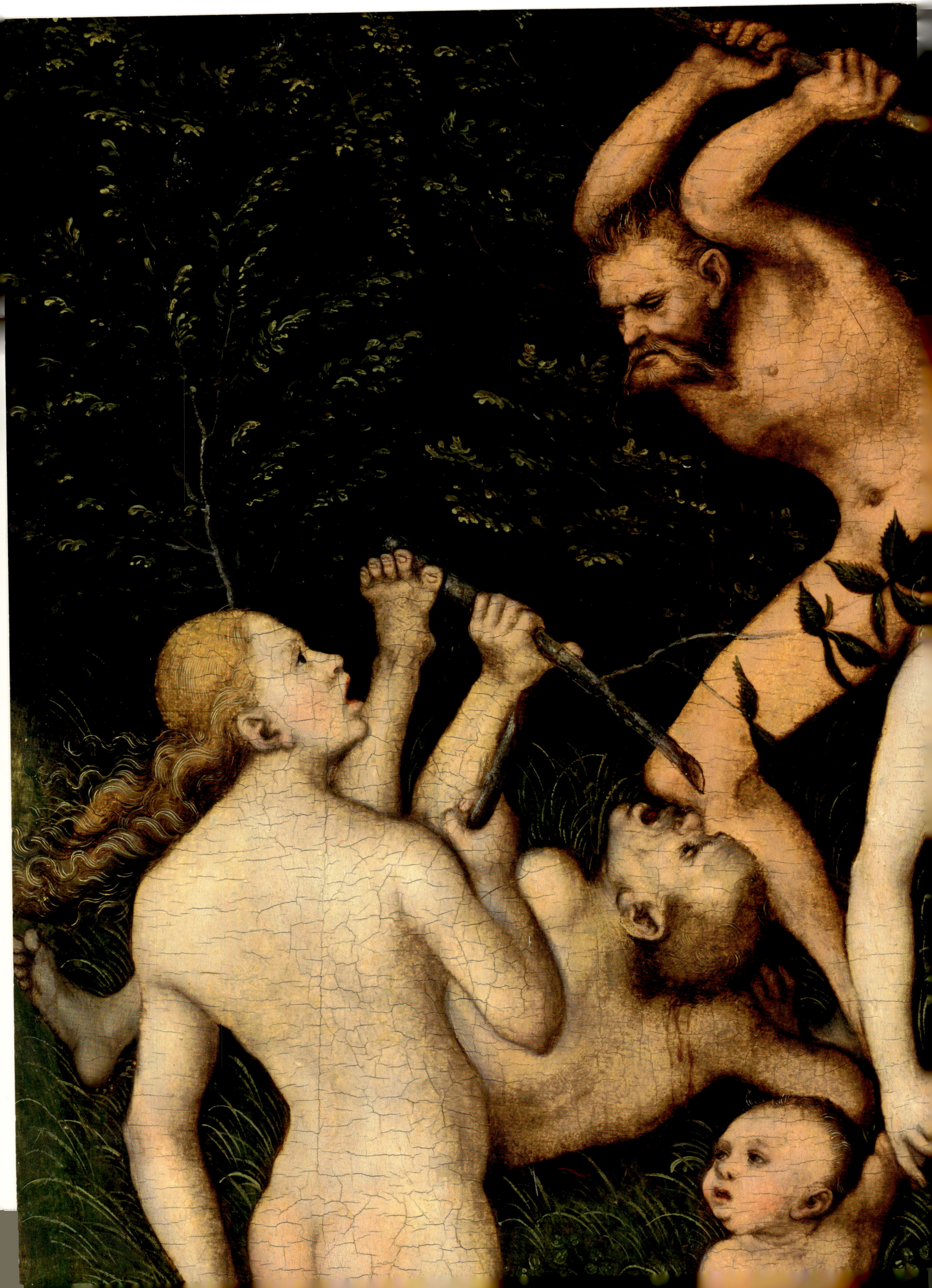

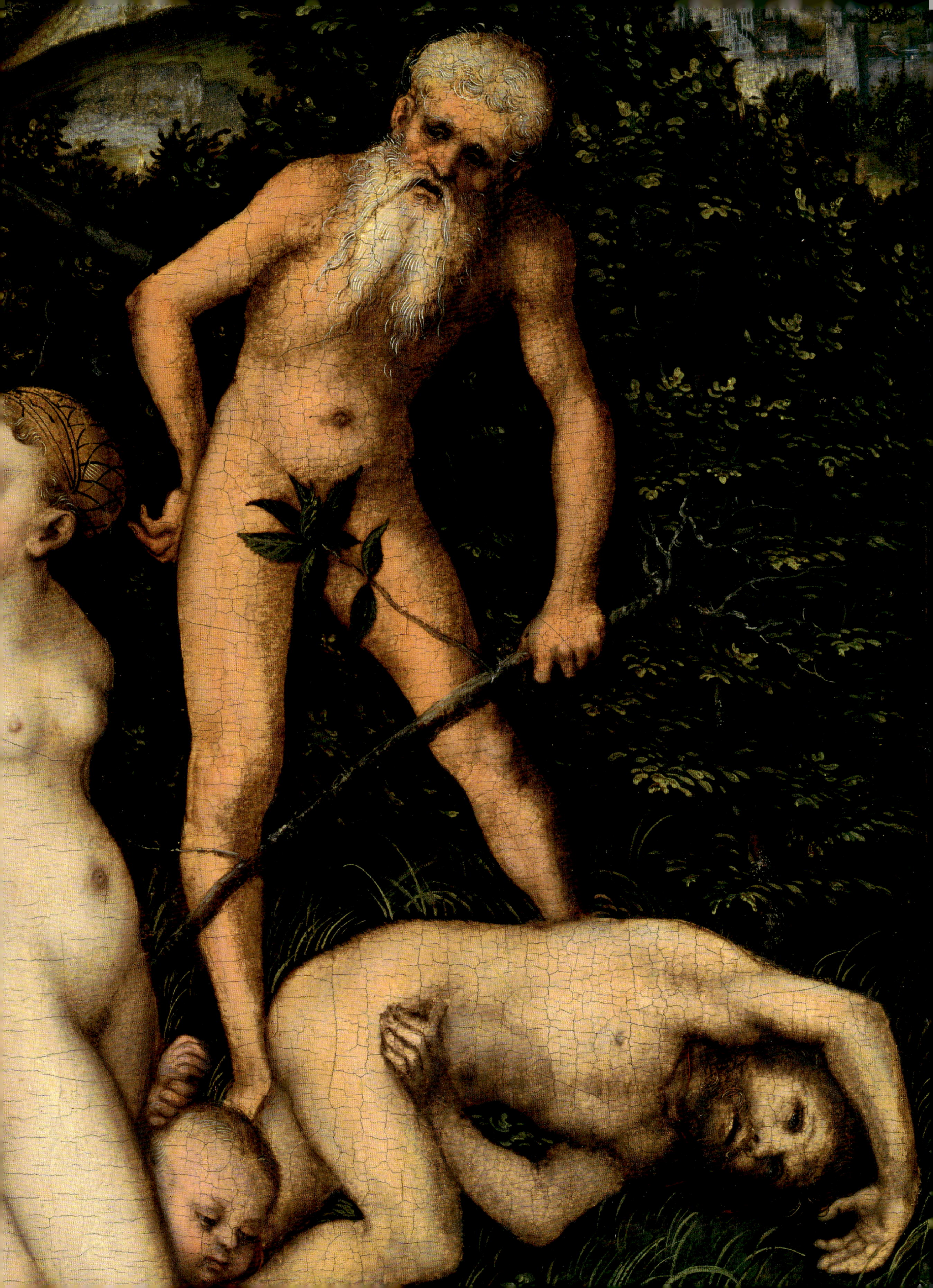

106 A Faun and his Family with a Slain Lion

Wittenberg, *c.* 1526

Signed with the serpent with upright wings facing right on the stone to the left next to the rock

Oil and tempera on wood
82.9 x 56.2 cm

J. Paul Getty Museum, Los Angeles, 2003.100

Provenance:
possibly from the collection of Maximilian I, Elector of Bavaria; since 1948 in various private collections, acquired in 2003 from Hall & Knight in London

(Frankfurt only)

Selected references:
FR 267; Koepplin/Falk 1974/76, vol. 2, pp. 585–93, no. 497. pp. 600 f., no. 500; Koepplin 2003, p. 59; Foister 2003, p. 127; Bierende 2002, pp. 237–49, p. 269; Campbell 2007, pp. 88 f., no. 4; Foister 2007, pp. 59 f.

This tall panel shows one of the mythological depictions of 'wild people', the forest-dwellers and demigods who first appear in Cranach's work in prints and drawings. Shortly before 1530 he began producing these as independent pictorial subjects, using the medium of panel painting, as he has done with this panel, now in the Getty Museum.

A naked man holding a cudgel sits on a block of stone on a strip of ground scattered with pebbles. His pointed ears characterise him as a faun, an antique demigod. At his feet lies a dead lion which clearly he has just killed, as the blood dripping from the animal's nose and mouth confirms. To the right stands a woman with a very delicate figure, also naked; she gives her left hand to a boy, and carries an infant on her right arm. The reciprocal gazes and placid poses clearly denote the figures' intimate trust in one another other, as befits a family. Behind the group lies forest and thick hedge-like undergrowth which in the upper right-hand quarter of the painting falls away to reveal an attractive landscape in the background.

An important feature of this extremely well executed panel is the careful, finely modulated brushwork – visible in the quite different treatments given to foliage, animal fur and hair and the flesh tones of the nude figures – combined with the scrupulous rendering of the smallest details such as the barely noticeable farmhand on the path beneath the rocks in the background, surmounted by a castle, and the wonderfully captured reflection of the town in the water and the lights in the eyes of the faun, the children and the lion. This very carefulness, the artist anticipating that the picture would be viewed in detail from very close range, shows that this work must have been intended as a collector's piece for the well-to-do court circle. Obvious anatomical shortcomings such as the faun's left arm and the woman's hip were clearly tolerated.

It is difficult to decide whether this and other related images stem more from the treatment of an existing pictorial tradition used in other contexts, such as that of the 'wild people', or from illustrations of literary descriptions of mythical demigods, forest-dwellers and primitive people from the works of Lucretius, Ovid, Virgil and others, but both must have played a part and have been influential in one way or another. This, and Cranach's practice of introducing variants, may account for the frequency with which individual motifs bear double meanings which enlarge the range of interpretation: the seated faun with a cudgel and a lion's skin could also be seen as Hercules, and the woman as Charity (cf. cat. 47). Bierende's interpretation, in which he suggests that the figures represent the Germanic-Wendish forest god Zuttibero and another legendary figure, the Virgin of Merseburg (who may have been worshipped in a common shrine), and who for want of pictorial evidence were latinised into Hercules/faun and Venus/Charity, seems far-fetched, however. On the other hand, he also suggests that the seated figure of the satyr, which in terms of motif occurs in earlier woodcuts such as an armed Joshua of 1524, could at least have been inspired by models from Ancient sculpture such as the *Belvedere Torso*, echoes of which can be found in other works, for example the Brussels version of *Apollo and Diana* (cat. 108).

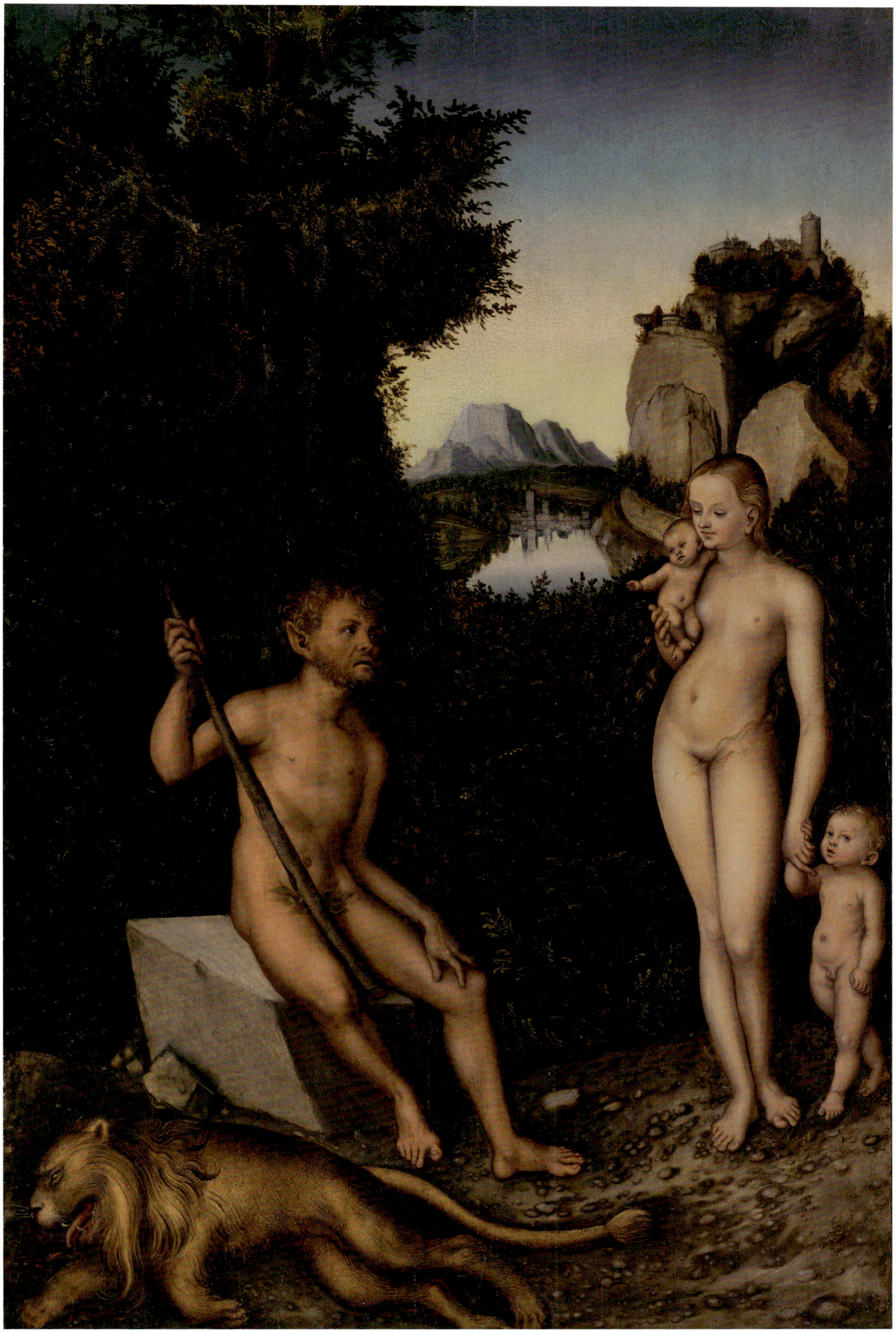

107 Apollo and Diana

Wittenberg, *c.* 1526

Signed at lower left with the serpent with upright wings facing right

Oil and tempera on beechwood
84.6 x 57.2 cm

Her Majesty The Queen, Royal Collection 407294

Provenance:
acquired in 1844–1846 from Friedrich Campe in Nuremberg

Selected references:
FR 271 A; Koepplin/Falk 1974/76, vol. 2, p. 500; Grimm/Erichsen/Brockhoff 1994, p. 350, no. 173 b; Heiser 2002, pp. 65–8; Koepplin 2003, pp. 146 f.; Campbell 2007, pp. 84 f., no. 3; Foister 2007, pp. 59f.

By virtue of its support, format and painting technique, this very fine panel is associated with the *Faun and Family* from the Getty Museum (cf. cat. 106) with which it also has clear compositional similarities. In place of the forest-dwellers of the Getty painting, Cranach here presents the Antique gods Apollo and Diana, who were brother and sister. The composition features many of Cranach's well-tried elements, such as the strip of ground strewn with pebbles in the foreground, the impenetrable 'wall of leaves' behind the main figures, the landscape view in the upper right section and the physical form of the nude figures. However, the actual grouping of the figures is taken from two engravings made in about 1500, or shortly afterwards. Both Jacopo de' Barbari, Cranach's predecessor as court painter in Wittenberg, and Albrecht Dürer tackled the subject in the same medium, Dürer basing his engraving on the other's slightly earlier version. Cranach was already aware of the Dürer engraving during his early period in Vienna, and he probably came across de' Barbari's version soon after he became court painter. Some twenty years later, faced with the ambitious task of creating a panel painting from a subject which previously had been the preserve of graphic works, he recalled the two models and reworked their crucial components. The standing figure of Apollo holding a taut bow comes from the Italian artist's version, which shows the brother and sister as the god and goddess of the Sun and Moon. The poses and the position of the arms in Cranach's painting in the Royal Collection are the same, but he has altered the placing of the arrow, making it point horizontally, as in Dürer's version, and not upwards. From Dürer he also took the motif of the fluttering cloth which holds Apollo's quiver and conceals his private parts. The seated figure of Diana with the deer is also to be found in Jacopo de' Barbari's work, though seen from behind; here Cranach follows Dürer's solution, giving it an original twist in Diana's acrobatically bent leg and by placing her on the deer rather than beside it. In another version of the subject in Brussels (cf. cat. 108), he offers a slightly different variant: here Apollo holds his bow more in the manner of de' Barbari and the deer on which Diana sits is reversed.

Although it is not difficult to describe the motifs which Cranach used as models, taking them quite freely, and then regrouping them in a different form, thereby demonstrating his inexhaustible powers of invention in developing new pictorial subjects, it is not so easy to explain the actual meaning of the picture. While de' Barbari presents Apollo and Diana in a cosmological sense, and Dürer concentrates primarily on the powerful modelling of the nude figures, Cranach's Antique gods seem to be more closely related to 'wild people' and mythological forest-dwellers. Since both Apollo and Diana are connected with hunting, the painting may well belong to this subject area, one which was in high favour in courtly circles; the arms and the deer would also fit this category. There is an interesting parallel to be found in a drawing in a private collection, representing the Fall of Man, in which Eve, like Diana, is shown as a nude seated on a deer. This could well be explained by Cranach's characteristic practice of giving certain figural motifs completely different meanings according to the context in which they appear. As Caroline Campbell has recently suggested, it is possible that Apollo, the embodiment of the male ideal in Ancient times, and Diana, the symbol of chastity, that is, the heathen predecessors of Christ and the Virgin Mary, have here been transformed into their sinful ancestors.

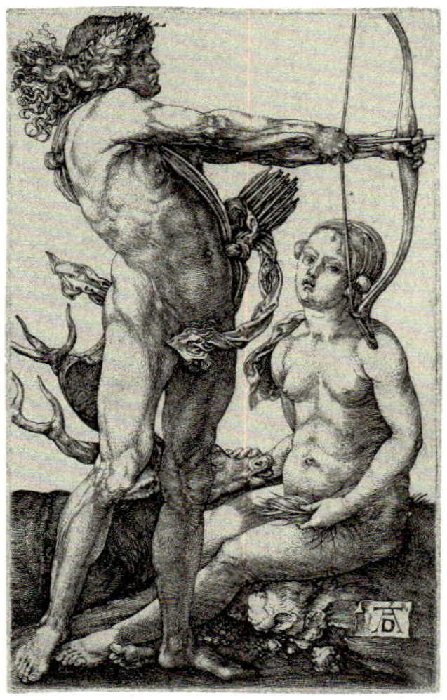

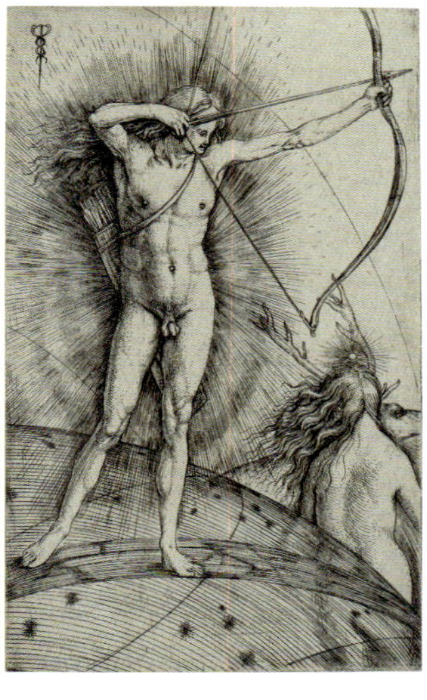

Albrecht Dürer, *Apollo and Diana*, engraving, Städel Museum, Frankfurt, Graphische Sammlung

Jacopo de' Barbari, *Apollo and Diana*, engraving, Staatliche Museen zu Berlin, Kupferstichkabinett

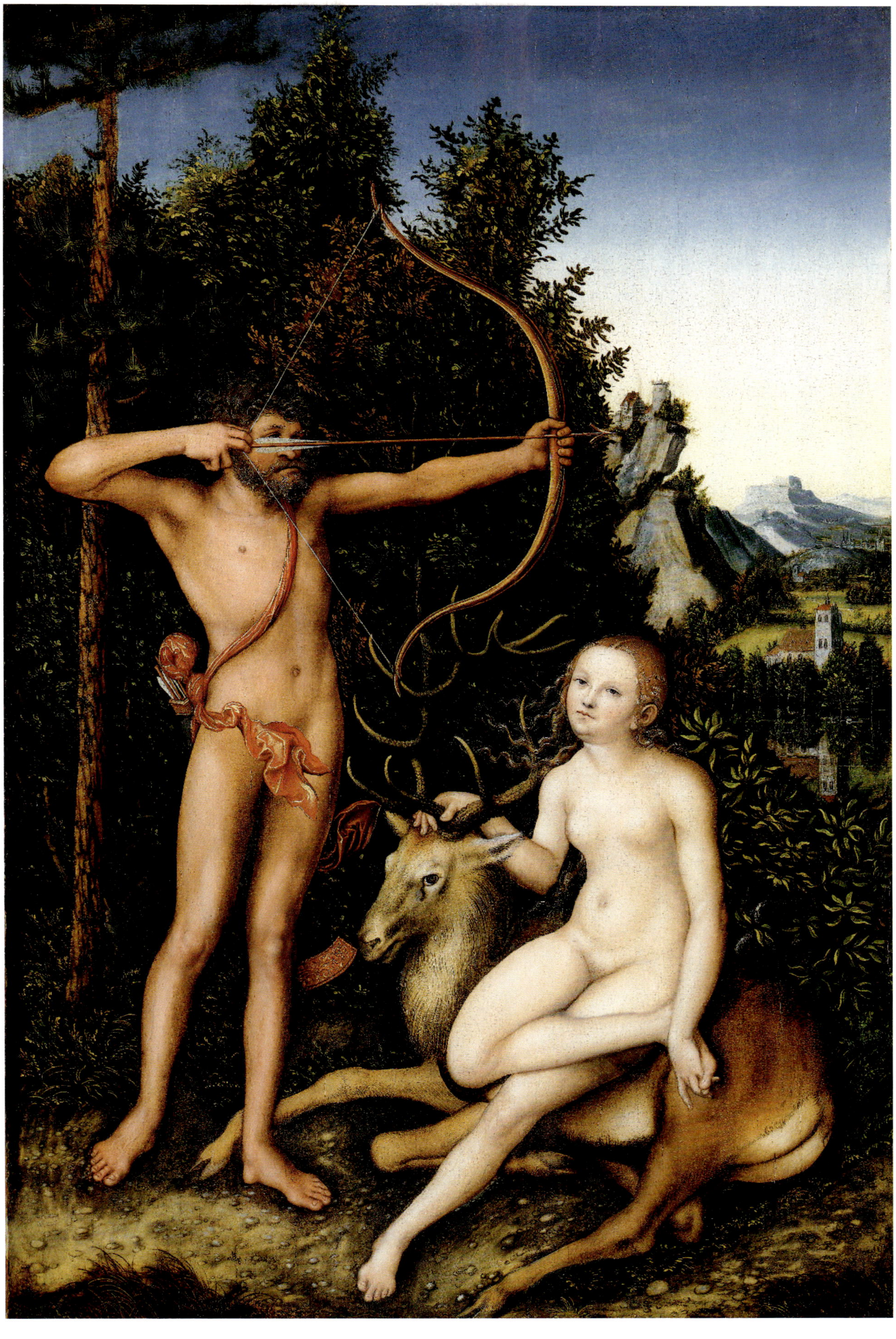

109 Hercules and Antaeus

Wittenberg, *c.* 1530

Signed top right in the black background with the serpent with upright wings facing left

Oil and tempera on wood
26.5 x 17.5 cm

Galerie Neuse Kunsthandel GmbH, Bremen

Provenance:
acquired in 2002 from Nagel in Stuttgart

Selected references:
FR 268; Schade 2003, p. 180, no. 71

The giant Antaeus, son of Poseidon and Gaia, gods of Sea and Earth, challenged all-comers to an unequal fight to the death. As long as he remained in contact with the earth, he could draw new strength from it. When Hercules met him, he understood at the last moment why the giant was invincible, lifted him into the air and crushed him to death.

Cranach painted the subject twice. The picture in Vienna (Akademie der Künste; FR 269) is slightly larger and shows the protagonists entwined in front of a landscape background. Although no time difference between them has been traced, the Bremen version concentrates much more on the figures, placing them in front of a neutral black background.

Although the episode belongs in the sphere of the Twelve Labours of Hercules, it is hard to imagine that this small panel formed part of an organised cycle with a politically charged moralising message. It seems to have been designed much more as a sophisticated chamber piece for a connoisseur, offering scope for deliberations about the artistic theory underpinning it. The two heads can be discussed in terms of their emotional effect, contrasting the confident expression of the winner, already sure of victory, with that of the loser, twisted in pain as he faces an agonising death. The open mouth of the victor, as if he is speaking, and his alert look directed out of the picture give him a cunning, almost mischievous air intended to remind the viewer that Hercules gains his victory not through obvious raw physical power but by using his intellectual abilities to penetrate Antaeus's secret. The latter's straining features and wide-open mouth confirm the outcome. With this motif the artist touches on the question of how to represent things that have no substance. According to medieval beliefs, it was through the open mouth of the dying man that the soul left the body on the moment of death (a detail often seen on the faces of the two Thieves in paintings of the Crucifixion). Showing Antaeus's face upside down with his nostrils on view was a clear breach of decorum which morally discredits the giant. Also dramatic, but at the same time rather comical, is the way the toes of the man being crushed to death are shown splayed and writhing about – a motif whose blunt nature recalls similar details in Matthias Grünewald.

It is also clear that the pointed contrast between the two heads comes about because the trunks of the two figures are almost fused at the hips. Antaeus's torso looks like a folded-out mirror image of his opponent's, demonstrating the theoretical principles of the Gemini (twin figures in mirror image, as depicted countless times by Italian artists since Pollaiuolo's *Martyrdom of St Sebastian* in the National Gallery, London) and the 'stroboscopic layering' seen for example in the famous miniature of the *Lamentation of the Virgin beneath the Cross* in the Book of Hours of the Rohan Master.

The effect of the two figures as 'twins' is particularly evident at waist level, where we see a man's buttocks placed in front of the genitals of the naked Hercules. The sexual connotations of this highly intimate embrace between two completely naked men should not be ignored. However, once the viewer has solved the confusing play of bodies, the core of the composition becomes clear: the hero stands with his legs rooted firmly to the ground, holding the monster in front of him and crushing him so hard that his limbs splay outwards in the shape of a swastika as he flails about in undignified despair. One has the feeling that at any moment Hercules might whirl his opponent round. The composition is thus highly dynamic and works only in two-dimensional projection: if the group were portrayed as a sculpture, the result would be a kind of clumsy windmill. However, small Italian sculptures were indeed a distinct domain for the representation of this subject. Cranach created a composition which, despite its decidedly sculptural structure, could be developed to the full only in the medium of painting. The fact that the painter included the *paragone* in his artistic calculations, in other words the need to compete with the rival art of sculpture, confirms the presumed purpose of the small panel as a collector's piece of high artistic quality.

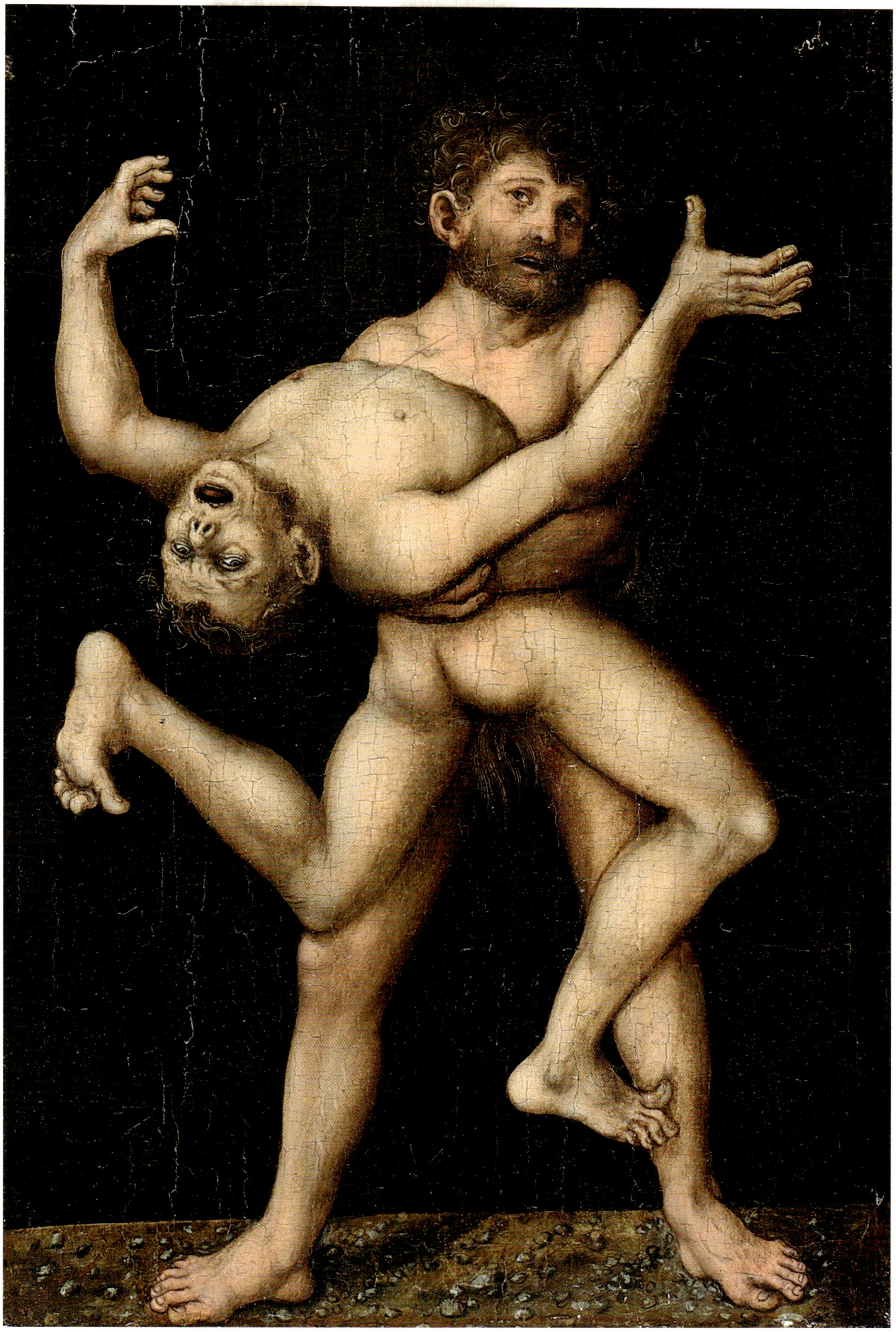

110 Diana and Actaeon

Lucas Cranach the Younger

Wittenberg, *c.* 1550

Oil and tempera on limewood
32 x 73 cm, trimmed at the top

Hessisches Landesmuseum,
Darmstadt, GK 74

Provenance:
acquired in 1829

(Frankfurt only)

Selected references:
FR 409 E; Koepplin/Falk 1974/76, vol 2, pp. 603 f., no. 506; Beeh 1990, pp. 252 f., no. 75

Like a time-lapse photograph, this charming panel summarises the tragic episode that cost the hunter Actaeon his life, as Ovid described it in his *Metamorphoses* (III, 138–252). As he was wandering carefree through the forest, Actaeon surprised Diana, the goddess of hunting, bathing in a spring with her nymphs. The naked goddess blushed deeply under the mortal's gaze. She splashed him with spring water, whereupon he was turned into a stag and was torn to pieces by his own dogs.

Diana stands to the left of her nymphs, distinguished from them by her sumptuous jewellery – necklace, neckband, bracelet and rings. Her cheeks are turning red as with both hands she scoops up water which rises up in thin jets towards the unfortunate spectator on the bank. He has just become a stag but still stands upright and looks at the goddess. Four dogs fall upon him from font and rear. The nymph climbing out of the pool in the foreground seems terrified by Actaeon's fate, and the two beauties in the centre use their bodies to screen themselves against unwanted looks. The fine diaphanous transparent veils with which they have draped themselves conceal nothing. Contemporary viewers were obviously delighted to see these gauze-like creations in pictures (cf. the contribution by Elke Werner (see pp. 99–109). Accordingly, the two nymphs on the far right look directly out at the viewer, involving him. The nymph on the left plays hide-and-seek, using the lone tree as cover; the one on the right turns her body away to conceal her charms from us. Possibly a friendly warning to the beholder is intended, to let the ancient myth be a lesson to him. In an age when hunting fever had gripped the entire nobility, the subject also perhaps offered a chance to hold up a mirror in a light-hearted way to a distinguished client. At any rate Lucas Cranach the Elder issued a bill in Augsburg in 1552 for a painting on canvas 'with Diana splashing the hunter so that he is turned into a stag'. The rounded, doll-like and rather summary body shapes of the nudes suggest, however, that the Darmstadt panel was actually painted by his son.

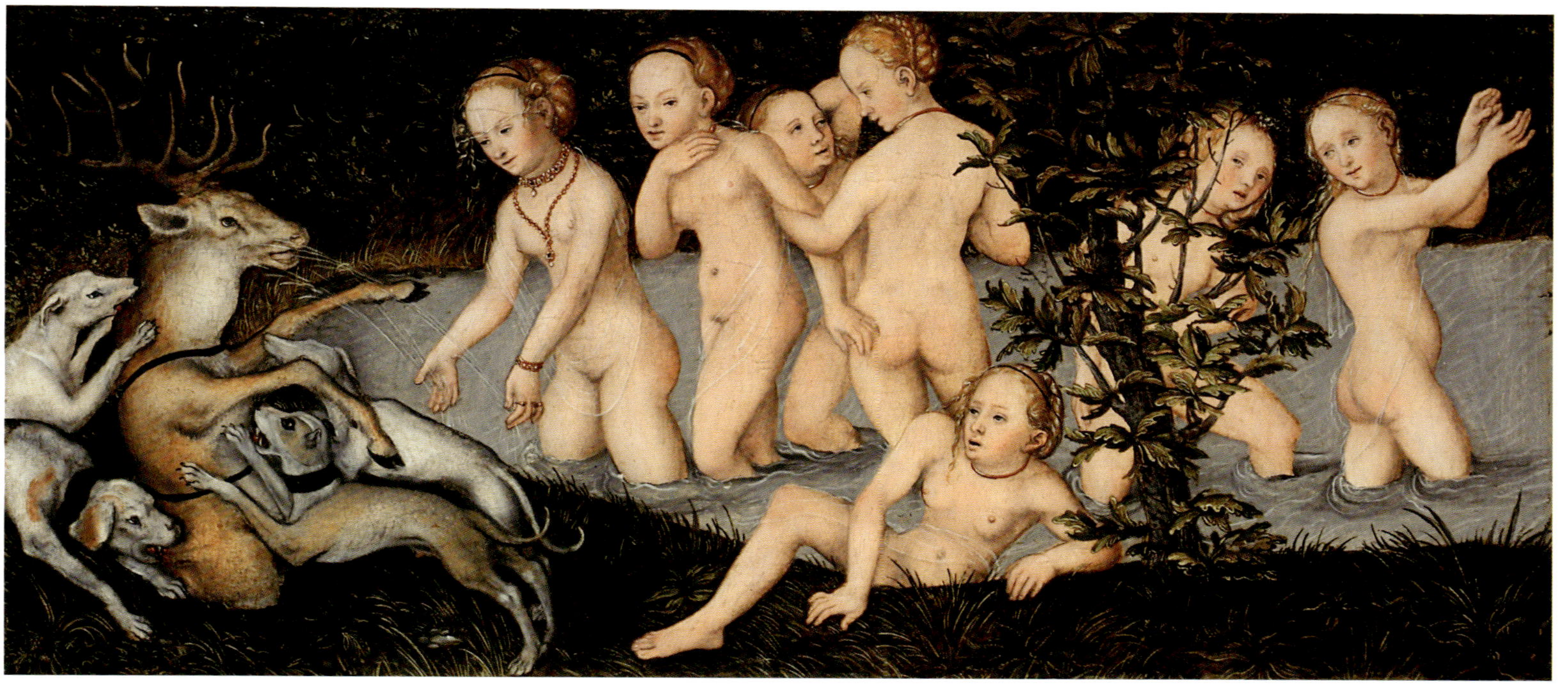

III Venus with Cupid the Honey Thief

Wittenberg, *c.* 1530

Signed and dated below on the tree trunk with the serpent with upright wings facing right; the year probably not genuine. At top right in the black background:
DVM PVER ALVEOLO FVRATVR
MELLA CV[PIDO]
FVRA[N]TI DIGITVM CVSPITE
FIXIT APIS
SIC ETIA[M] NOBIS BREVIS ET
PERITVRA VOLVPTA[S]
QUA[M] PETIMVS TRISTI MIXTA
DOLORE NOCET

Oil and tempera on red beechwood
169 x 67 cm

Galleria Borghese, Rome, 326

Provenance:
acquired from Scipione Borghese; first mentioned in this gallery in 1650

(Frankfurt only)

Selected references:
FR 245; della Pergola 1959, pp. 159 f., no. 229; Hermann-Fiore 1997, p. 17; Koepplin 2003, pp. 34–51; Pérez d'Ors 2007

'As the Infant Cupid was stealing honey from the hollow, the bee stung the thief on the finger. Thus does brief and transitory pleasure harm us too: it is mingled with sharp pain.' So run the lines in Latin in the top corner of the panel. They refer to a description in the nineteenth idyll of Theocritus (*c.* 310–250 BC), *Keriokleptes* (The Honey Thief), though this authorship is now doubted by philologists. Cranach may have learned of the story from Philipp Melanchthon (cf. cat. 124), who discussed the Greek poet in his lectures at Wittenberg University. The author of the verses which paraphrase Theocritus's Greek text seems to have been Georg Sabinus (1508–1560), Melanchthon's pupil and son-in-law.

At all events, Lucas Cranach took up the delightful parable, transforming it into pictures that are as clear as the ancient text. Here the young Cupid, with all the naivety of a child at play, takes the sweet honeycomb from the hollow tree and is stung by the startled bees. Crying, he turns to his mother Venus, who seeks out the gaze of the beholder as if begging for adult support over the boy's foolish behaviour. At the same time she presents the viewer with the moralising inscription couched in the first person plural: just as the spontaneous desire for sweet honey brings with it the risk of being stung by a bee, so the short-lived joys of love can bring us long-lasting pain.

Although Albrecht Dürer was also aware of the subject, as we know from a watercolour dated 1514, in the Kunsthistorisches Museum, Vienna, its circulation in the form of a panel painting became a speciality of the Cranach workshop, which produced at least fifteen versions of it. The first of these, according to Dieter Koepplin, was a painting with a landscape background, dating from about 1526–27, and now in the National Gallery, London (FR 245 L). The *Venus* in the Galleria Borghese is perhaps the earliest of the life-size versions with a black background. Later variants such as the painting in the Kröller-Müller Museum, Otterlo (FR 396) and the Gemäldegalerie, Berlin (FR 395), were painted after 1537, since they bear the device of the serpent with folded wings, and – at least in the case of the latter – were possibly the work of Lucas the Younger. In addition, in these the hollow tree is omitted. These factors indicate a tendency for the pictorial treatments to become more emblematic and independent. As Pablo Perez d'Ors has explained, this trend towards abstraction even allowed a Lutheran version of the subject to be devised in which Christ and Cupid were placed in opposition to each other. Cupid looks for sweet pleasure and is punished by long-lasting pain; in contrast, Christ takes upon himself the agony of the Passion and so acquires the infinite gift of redemption for humanity. Such refined interpretations remained limited to the medium of book illustration, however. Like them, though, Cranach's depictions of *Venus with Cupid the Honey Thief* stem from the spiritual openness and liveliness of the Wittenberg University milieu.

The famous art collector Cardinal Scipione Caffarelli-Borghese (1576–1633) hung the Cranach *Venus* in the same room as his *Venus* by Andrea Brescianino (*c.* 1485–after 1525), which was almost the same size, to show the contrast between Antique and Northern ideals of beauty.

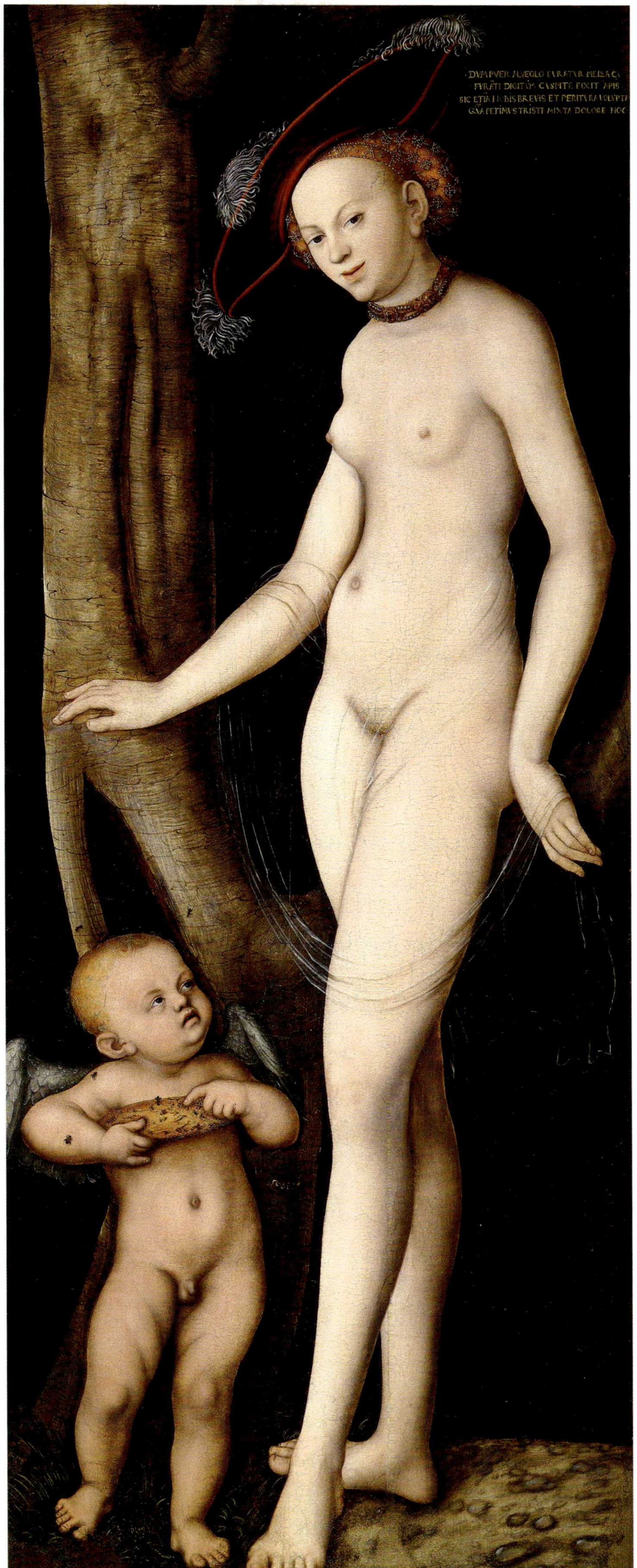

112 Venus with Cupid Stealing Honey

Wittenberg, 1529

Signed at bottom right on a pebble with the serpent with upright wings facing left between the pairs of numbers denoting the year. On the panel fixed to the tree:
DVM PVER ALVEOLO FVRATVR
MELLA CVPIDO
FVRANTI DIGITUM CVSPIDE
FIXIT APIS
SIC ETIAM NOBIS BREVIS ET
PERITVRA VOLV[P]TAS
QVAM PETIMVS TRISTI MIXTA
DOLORE NOCET

Oil and tempera on red beechwood
38.7 x 25.2 cm

Private collection on loan to the Metropolitan Museum of Art, New York

Provenance:
Sir Herbert Cook collection, Richmond, Surrey

Selected references:
FR 246 B; Cook Collection 1915, vol. 3, no. 476

Lucas Cranach completed at least fifteen versions of this attractive scene, depicted in the manner of a Theocritan idyll (cf. cat. 111). The god of Love, the child Amor or Cupid, has stolen a honeycomb and is now being tormented by a swarm of bees. Whimpering and in search of help, he turns to his mother Venus. She, however, prefers to wink at the viewer, who understands as well as she does what is going on; if not, the last lines of the panel on the tree will tell him: The joys of love are as brief and fleeting as tasting honey, their consequences are all too often long-lasting pain, like bee stings. Grown-ups know this, unlike the inexperienced child; with Venus it is literally written on her face, for above her forehead the band of her hood bears the inscription *ES IST ALS* (a contraction of 'Es ist alles eitel', or 'All is vanity'), which those who know their Bible will easily recognise as the famous opening lamentation of the preacher Solomon (Ecclesiastes 1, 2; for this information I am indebted to Joshua Waterman, at Princeton). The behaviour of the goddess is thus thoroughly ambivalent. On the one hand she presents her beauty to the viewer in a provocative pose, draping her long gauze veil, which conceals nothing, most elegantly over her shoulder and raising it wantonly with her left hand. On the other, her 'costume' illustrates the transitory nature of such beauty. It is left to the viewer to draw a moral.

This dialectical expansion of the subject indicates that this is not Cranach's first treatment of the subject. Dieter Koepplin suggests that the earliest surviving version of a Venus with Cupid stealing honey set against a landscape is the painting in the National Gallery, London (FR 245L), painted *c.* 1526–27. In our version Cranach produces variations of certain forms that he had developed in another context. It is notable, for example, that Venus devotes herself enthusiastically to her coquettish play with the veil instead of attending to her child. In this respect she prepares the way for the graceful gesture of the Frankfurt Venus, who appears alone in the picture, which is certainly more consistent (cat. 114). It is possible that the nude featured here was conceived as a single figure or for a Judgement of Paris. The child is another of Cranach's movable figures. His dancing feet have no real place here, but in the life-size version in Rome, where he appears in a mirror image of our picture, his raised foot is actually resting on the root of the tree (cat. 111). This collage-like way of working is not unusual in Cranach's later period.

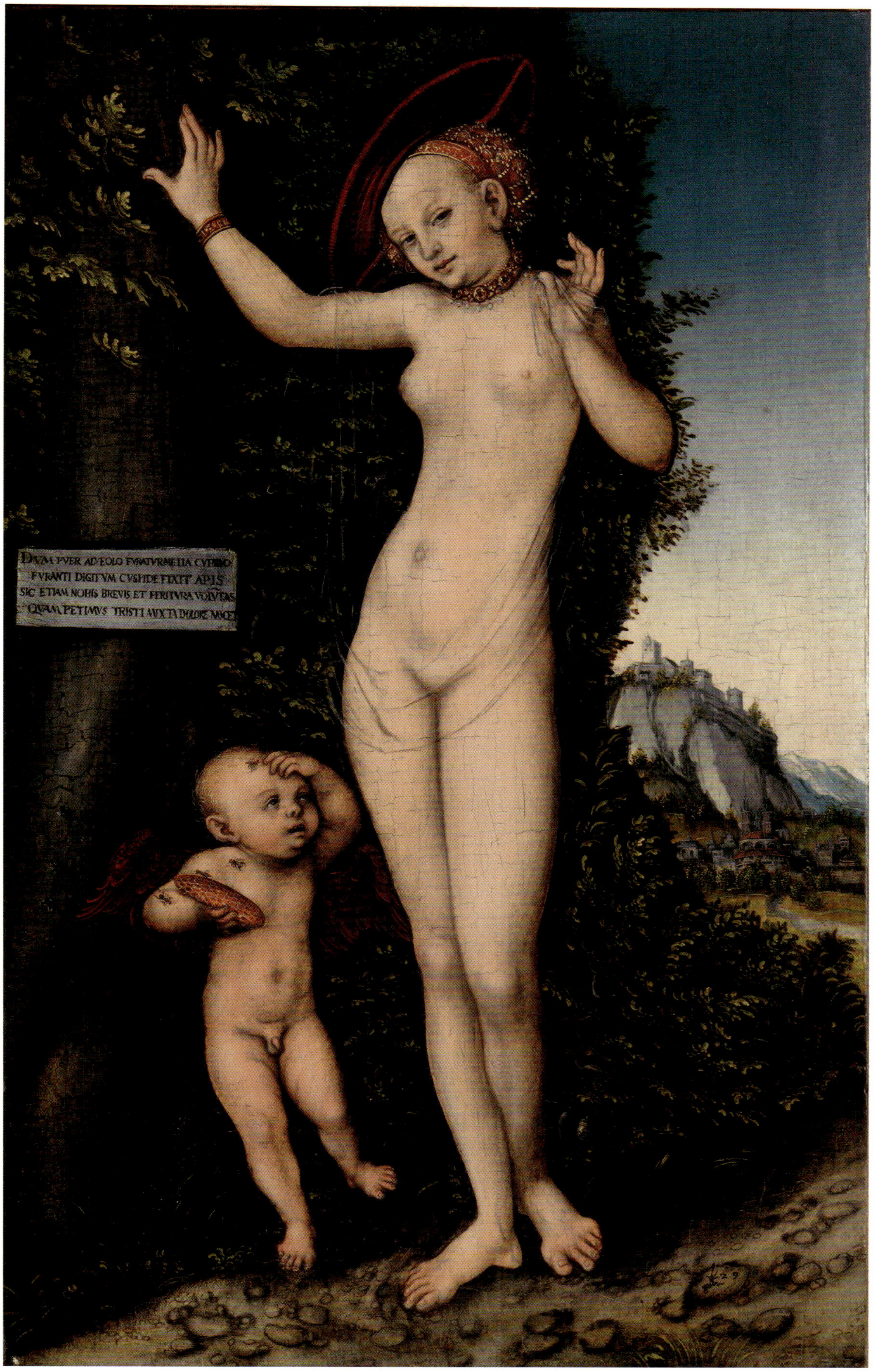
DVM PVER ALVEOLO FVRATVR MELLA CVPIDO
FVRANTI DIGITVM CVSPIDE FIXIT APIS
SIC ETIAM NOBIS BREVIS ET PERITVRA VOLVPTAS
QVAM PETIMVS TRISTI MIXTA DOLORE NOCET

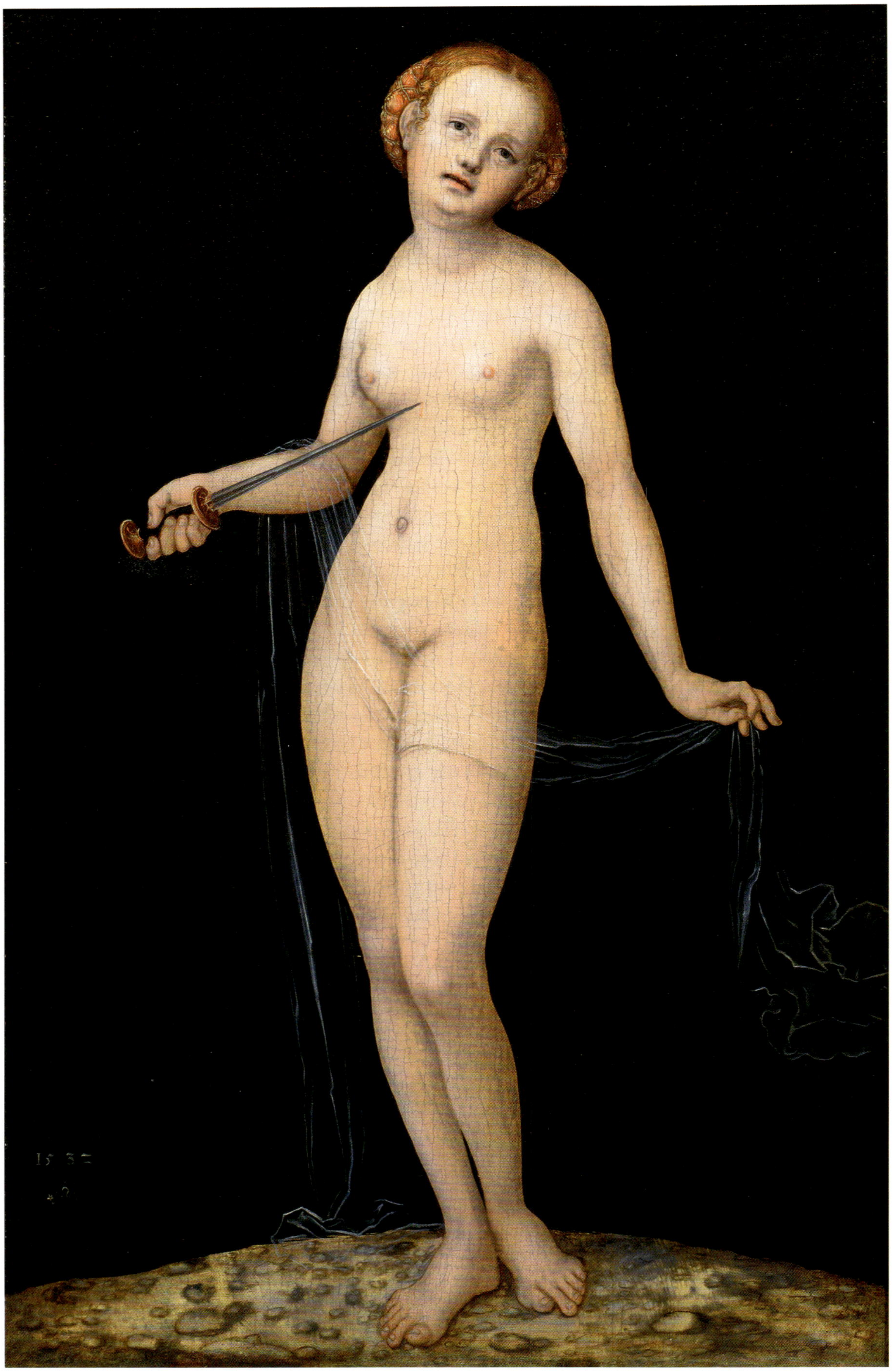

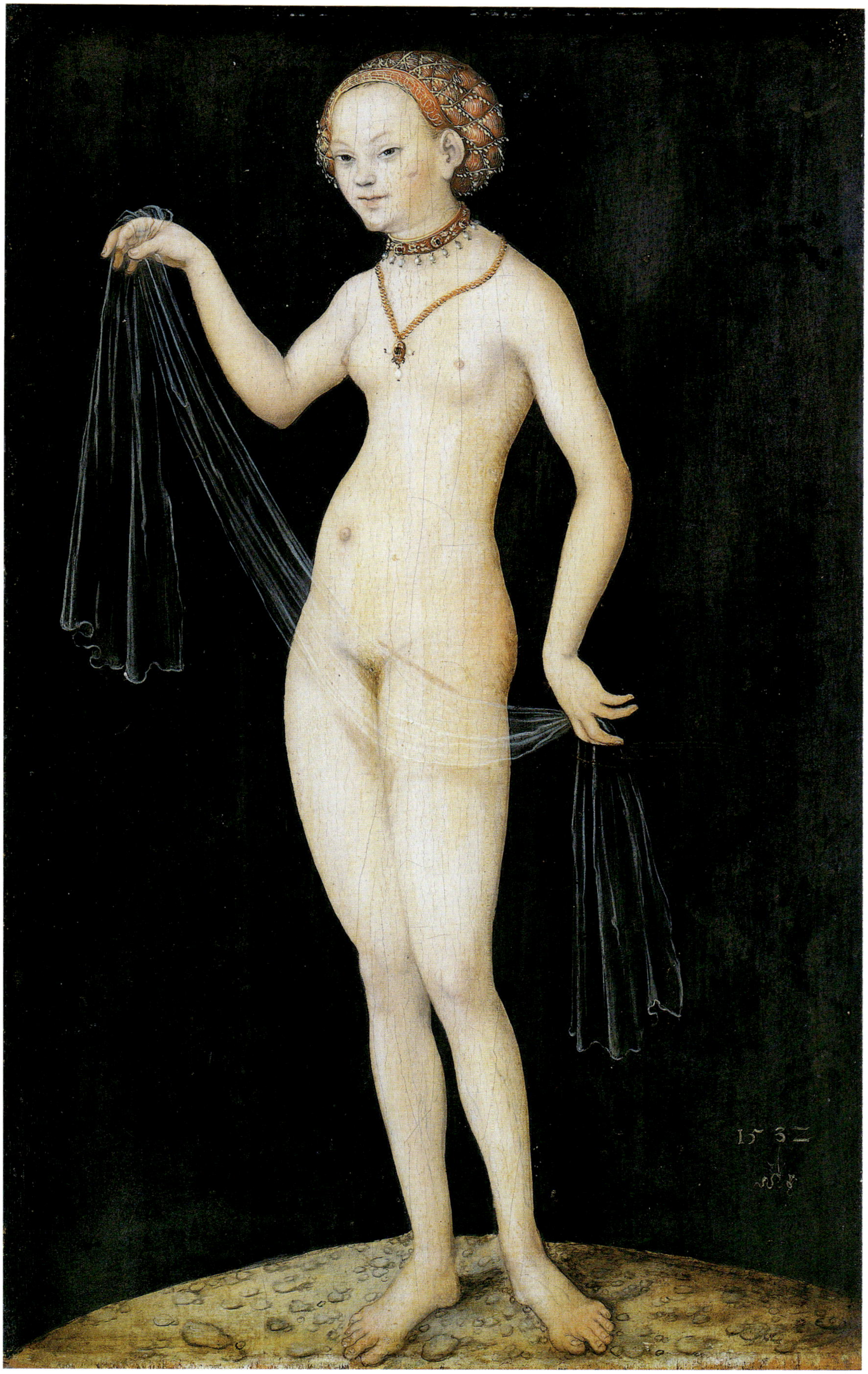
1532

115 The Three Graces

Wittenberg, 1535

Dated bottom left in the black background; beneath this the serpent with upright wings facing right

Oil and tempera on wood
49 x 34 cm

Nelson Atkins Museum of Art, Kansas City, 57-1

Provenance:
before 1915 in the Cook Collection, Richmond, England; acquired in 1957

Selected references:
FR 251; Backlin-Landmann 1969, no. 2; Mertens 1994, p. 78, note 81; for Cuspinian's Exlibris: Koepplin 1973, pp. 142 f.

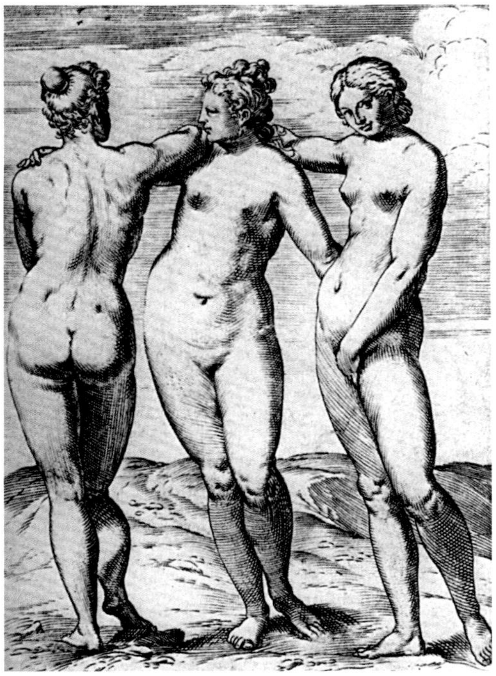

Agostino Carracci, *The Three Graces*, engraving, Städel Museum, Frankfurt, Graphische Sammlung

The Three Graces are figures of Roman mythology who derive from the Greek *Charites*. They are the daughters of Zeus, and are called Euphrosyne, Thalia and Aglaia, meaning Joyfulness, Bloom, and Brightness. In antiquity, towards the end of the Middle Ages and in the Renaissance, they were most often depicted as naked young women, and part of the entourage of Venus. According to Veronika Mertens's research, their allegorical significance changed between the sixteenth and eighteenth centuries. Their association with aesthetic categories such as grace and beauty, as they are understood today, came only in fairly recent times. At first they represented moral qualities such as charity, friendship and generosity. Cranach may have been aware of these associations through his contact with the humanist Johannes Cuspinian (1473–1529), whose portrait he painted around 1502 in Vienna. A decade later, Cuspinian commissioned an unknown artist to depict the three allegorical figures for his *Ex Libris*, accompanied by inscriptions emphasising the virtues of giving and receiving. Two or three panel pictures by Lucas Cranach showing the Three Graces survive – the third version, in the Law Collection in Cambridge (FR 251A), may in fact represent the three goddesses in the *Judgement of Paris*; this attribution remains controversial. In the version formerly in the Seligmann Collection in Paris (FR 250), he gave one of the three naked figures a hat decorated with a feather, and necklaces to all three, but in the picture from Kansas City he shows them naked, in the Antique manner, standing on a narrow balustrade. Their pose is like that of a sculptural group. It is thus astonishing that the composition does not follow the twin-view type which was much more commonly found, with the three women in a row, the outer ones shown frontally and the middle one in back view, their hands laid on each other's shoulders. Raphael's small panel in Chantilly (Musée Condé) is the most famous post-Antique interpretation of this type. Cranach, on the other hand, seems to have had another model in mind, one which Agostino Carracci made popular in the seventeenth century in an engraving (000 Städel, GS, 28757/*Illustrated Bartsch* 39, No. 130 [108]). This type shows the figures from left to right in back, front and side view, possibly in order to display feminine beauty from all three angles. Furthermore, Cranach does not let the Graces touch one another, substituting looks and gestures for physical contact so that the women seem to be holding a debate. Meanwhile their unity is emphasised by the long veil, the ends of which are held by the two outer figures at hip level, and in the middle is draped over the shoulder of the third figure. This central Grace has the most remarkable pose, looking upwards and pointing with the index finger of her right hand. She immediately recalls the personification of Truth in Sandro Botticelli's *The Calumny of Apelles* in the Uffizi, Florence.

Here is perhaps also the place to touch on the more concrete allegorical message. Whatever this may be, it drew Cranach to create three of the most beautiful feminine nudes of his entire oeuvre. The painter adopted Classical ideals of physique more whole-heartedly and, instead of his usual affected depiction of long snaking extremities, produced a consistent pattern of elegantly foreshortened limbs.

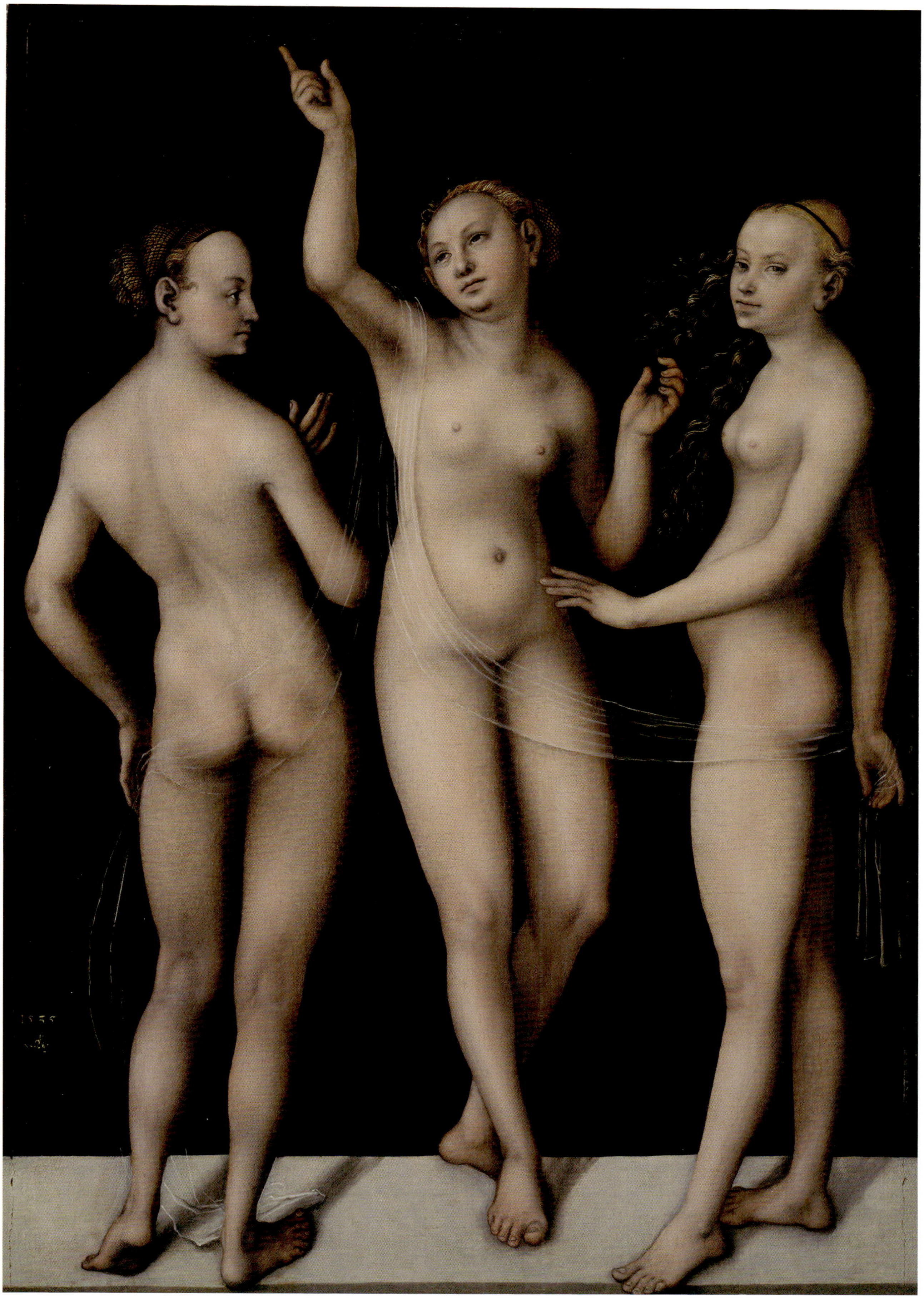

116 Adam and Eve

Lucas Cranach the Elder (?)

Wittenberg, *c.* 1508–10 (?)

Signed at bottom right on the tree trunk with the serpent with upright wings facing left between the pairs of numbers denoting the year

Oil and tempera on red beechwood each panel 139 x 53.9 cm

Musés des Beaux-Arts et d'Archéologie, Besançon, 896.1.54

(Frankfurt only)

Selected references:
not in FR; Koepplin/Falk 1974/76, vol. 2, p. 654, no. 565; Heydenreich 2007, pp. 318 f.; Heydenreich, in Campbell 2007, pp. 18–25

These two large wood panels from Besançon have a surprisingly unusual format. The figures are not quite life-size, though not far from it, and are presented in separate panels against a neutral black background. Their spatial connection is provided by the Tree of Knowledge which is placed in the central axis and divided between the two panels, though only the moss-covered base of the trunk and a dead branch are visible. Adam and Eve are shown as nude figures turning towards each other, Adam looking at Eve while she looks out at the viewer. The serpent next to Eve's head has already done most of its work of seduction, for Eve has already bitten into one of the two apples she is holding and Adam holds the forbidden fruit in his left hand.

In contrast to his woodcut dated 1509, Cranach set his earliest depictions of the Fall of Man against a neutral background rather than a landscape – this applies also to the versions in Warsaw (FR 44, cat. 117), Munich (FR 43) and Würzburg (FR 114) which were probably completed in about 1510 and shortly after. There are many points of comparison between these and the two panels from the Musée des Beaux-Arts et d'Archéologie, though the Warsaw version comes closest, not only in the positioning of Adam's feet, his head type and the mossy trunk but also in Eve's face, clearly derived from models by Dürer, and the long hair falling in parallel wavy tresses. As a result of infra-red reflectography we are now aware of further similarities; it shows that in the preliminary drawing Eve's feet were placed in a manner close to those in the Warsaw picture. On the other hand, certain stylistic differences are apparent, while the format and the use of two separate panels are unusual for Cranach at this time, something which has led observers on several occasions to think that this was not one of his own works but a contemporary copy in his style. However, after detailed investigations, Gunnar Heydenreich has recently established so many similarities with works firmly attributed to Cranach from around 1508–10, in terms of the production of the support, its preparation, the type of underdrawing and the build-up of paint layers, that the panels from Besançon can unquestionably be counted among them.

Some of the elements untypical of Cranach, such as the structure of the figures, which can be seen as striving for anatomical correctness, and Adam's classical contrapposto, certainly bear the influence of Dürer, as Heydenreich has also shown. Dürer's famous life-size panels of Adam and Eve of 1507 (Prado, Madrid), which also provided models for Cranach's other early paintings of the Fall of Man, reveal such striking parallels with Cranach's work that it must be assumed that he was closely acquainted with these panels or with copies of them. We can see these similarities in the choice of perspective, the poses of the two figures – Cranach's adjustment to the positioning of Eve's feet seems to have been an attempt to correct a mistake and return to his model – the direction of the light and, not least, the monumental format of the panels. The motif of Eve's bent arm, with the hand turned inwards to conceal an apple, may on the other hand have come from a pen drawing of *Lucretia* which Dürer completed in 1508. Thus the two spectacular panels from Besançon illustrate in a unique way the relationship between Cranach and Dürer, which in the former's early years as the Wittenberg court painter clearly amounted to much more than the borrowing of individual motifs or certain head types. Cranach not only gleaned ideas from Dürer, he seems to have become competitively involved with him; while he copied the work of the Nuremberg artist extensively, at the same time he did not abandon his own pictorial inclinations, producing a personal style that did not easily match other works from the same period, and for a long time this created problems for Cranach scholars. All these factors strongly suggest that Cranach spent some time in Dürer's studio, or at least paid a visit to it. It is on record that he stayed in Nuremberg in January 1508 when he was awarded his coat of arms, and this would have given him a suitable opportunity.

GD

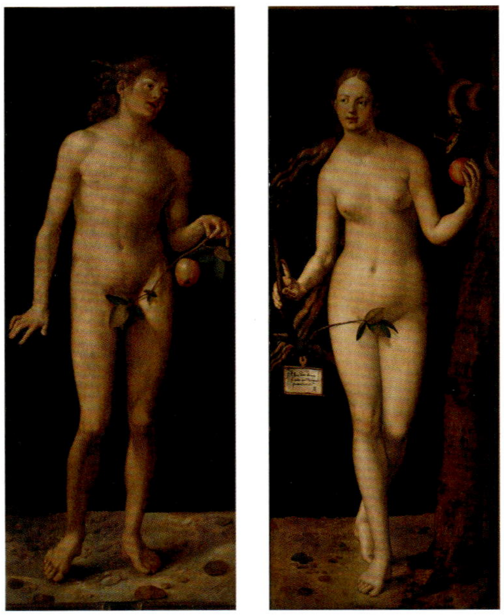

Albrecht Dürer, *Adam and Eve*, 1507, Museo Nacional del Prado, Madrid

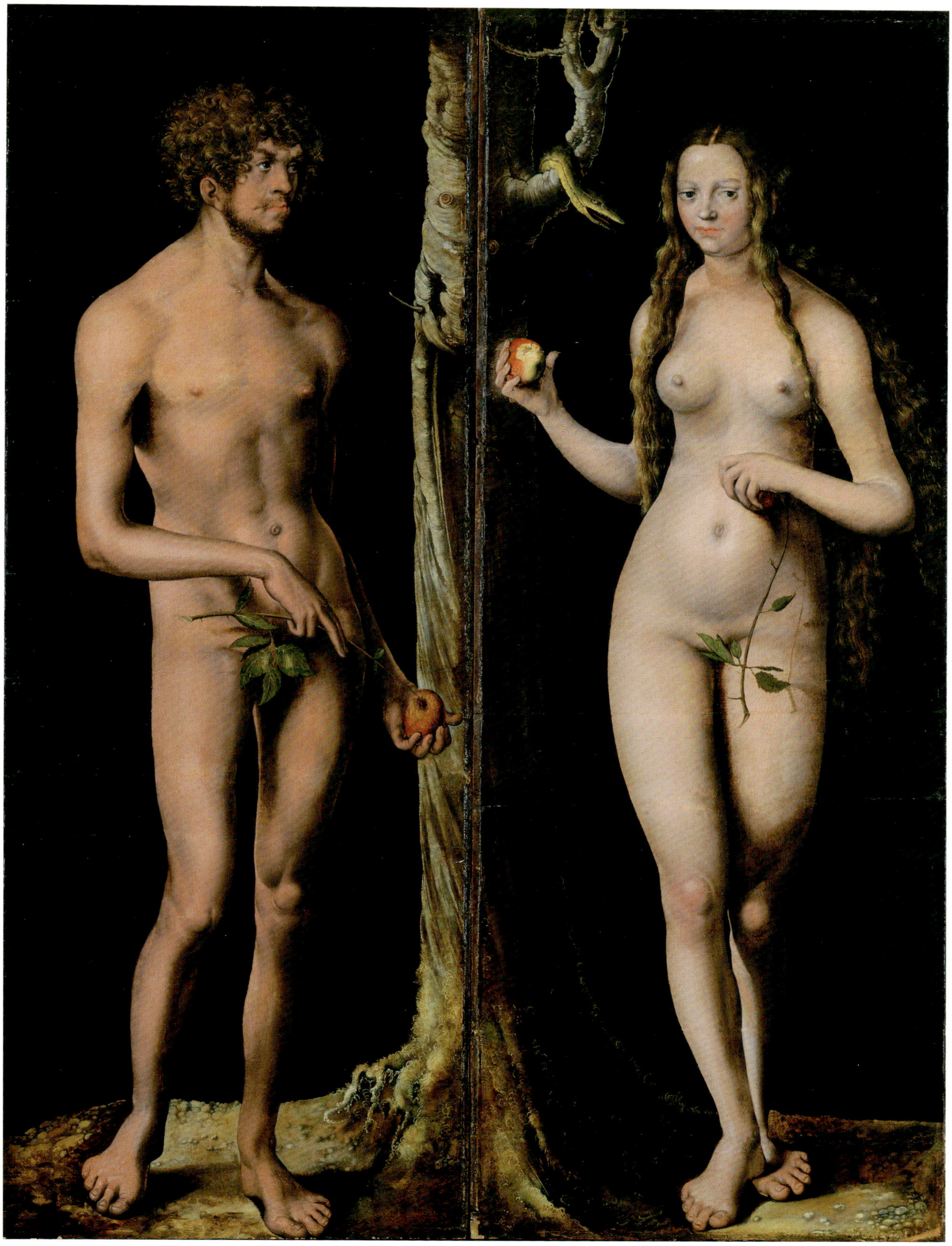

117 Adam and Eve

Wittenberg, *c.* 1510

Oil and tempera on limewood
58 x 44 cm

National Museum, Warsaw,
M. Ob. 588

Provenance:
in the nineteenth century in the collection of the Prince of Hohenzollern-Hechingen; acquired by the Silesian Museum of Fine Arts, Breslau (Wroclaw) in 1925; transferred in 1946

Selected references:
FR 44; Steinborn/Ziemba 2000, pp. 44–7, no. 8; Heydenreich, in Campbell 2007, pp. 21–3, 25

Cranach's first datable attempt to depict the Fall of Man was made in 1509, in a woodcut showing Adam and Eve embracing, with Adam as a seated figure surrounded by numerous animals of various species in the Garden of Eden. However, the earliest surviving panel pictures of the subject, including the version from Warsaw, probably completed around 1510, follow a completely different scheme. Adam and Eve are shown as monumental, standing nude figures against a neutral black background, placed on either side of the Tree of Knowledge. Apart from a narrow strip of ground covered with pebbles, there is no further pictorial space, so the action is limited to the foremost picture plane. The naked figures are lit by a harsh light from the left, giving them a plasticity that, unusually for Cranach, is supported by the powerful and naturalistic modelling of their anatomical details. In contrast, the Tree of Knowledge is notably lifeless: only a few leaves grow on its otherwise barren, apparently dead branches – enough, however, to cover Adam's genitalia. The crested serpent slithers almost vertically down the tree trunk and turns towards Eve, and while she looks out at the viewer and holds an apple between her hand and cheek, Adam watches the serpent's appearance with interest and some misgivings.

This painting and contemporary versions of the subject (those, for example, in Munich, FR 43, Würzburg, FR 113, and Besançon, (cat. 116) reveal unmistakeably the influence of Dürer and the models he provided with his masterly engraving of 1504 and the two life-size panels of Adam and Eve from 1507 (now in the Prado, Madrid). There are clear similarities, particularly with the panels in the Prado, in the motifs employed, including the positioning of Adam's feet, the direction of the light and the perspective, which shows a downward view of the feet and an upward view of the faces. It is also possible to detect the influence of Jan Gossaert in the comparatively well-rounded physiques, the hard lighting and certain similarities in the head types; in 1508 Cranach could have met him on his journey to the Low Countries. However, a comparison with the version in Besançon shows that this painting relied more closely on a thorough study of models drawn from Dürer, whereas they are less strongly apparent in the Warsaw picture. The contrapposto in the shoulders induced by the positioning of Adam's feet is not carried through, and as a result the stance is not convincing, whereas in the Besançon picture the shoulders make the necessary counter-movement. The physique of the nude figures in the Warsaw picture is altogether more stylised and dictated more by a desire for flowing lines than for anatomical correctness. It is also important to consider the format of the Besançon panels, which are almost life-size, and also the use there of individual panels. All this suggests that these were painted shortly before the Warsaw panel and can therefore be regarded as Cranach's earliest surviving panel paintings of the Fall of Man.

On the other hand, contrary to the opinion of Friedländer and Rosenberg, there is a technical reason for thinking that the Warsaw panel was completed before the Munich version; like many of Cranach's early Wittenberg works, the support in Warsaw consists of horizontally arranged boards, whereas in Munich they run vertically, which relates to a later production technique made necessary when the workshop changed its supplier.

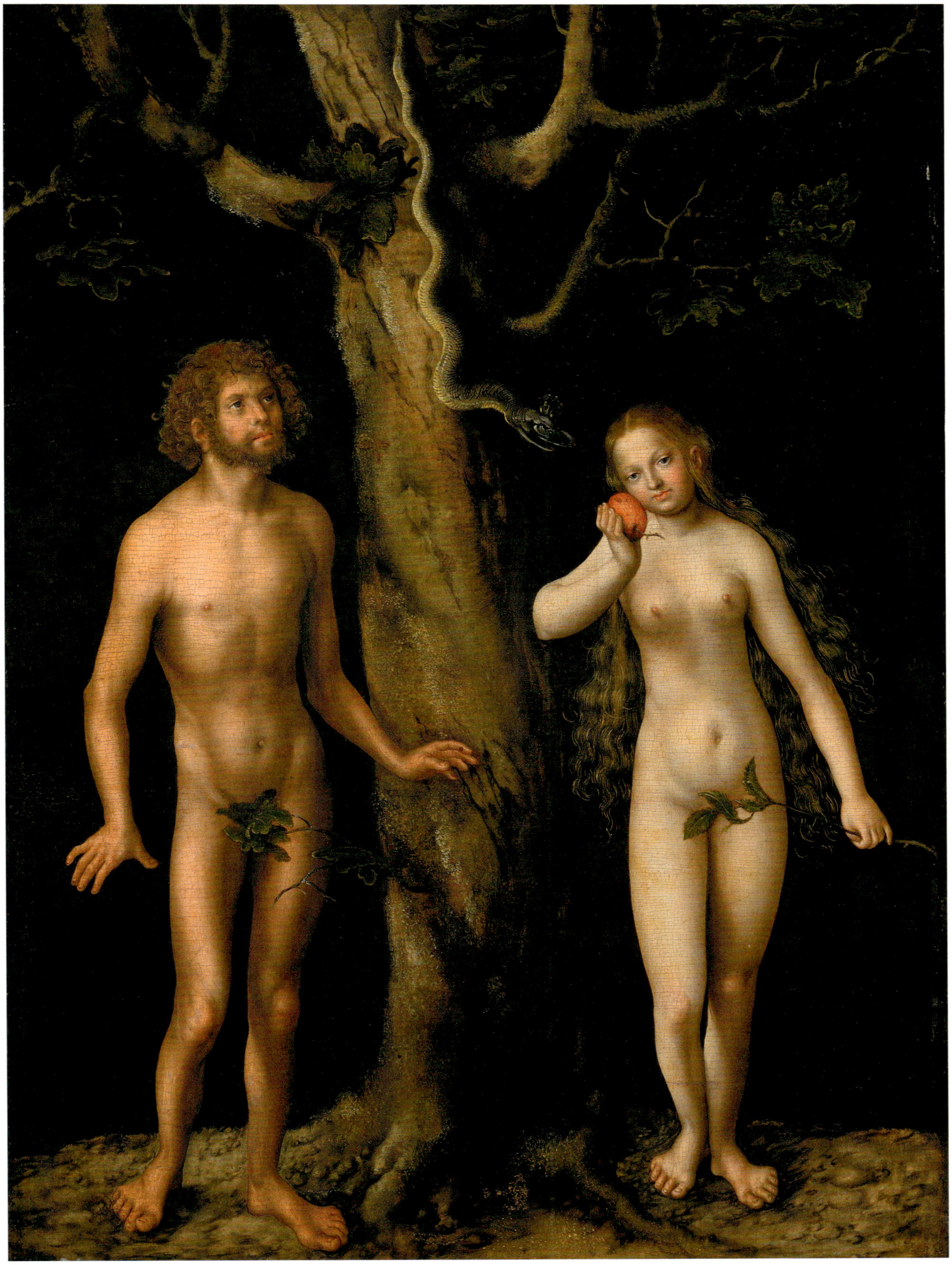

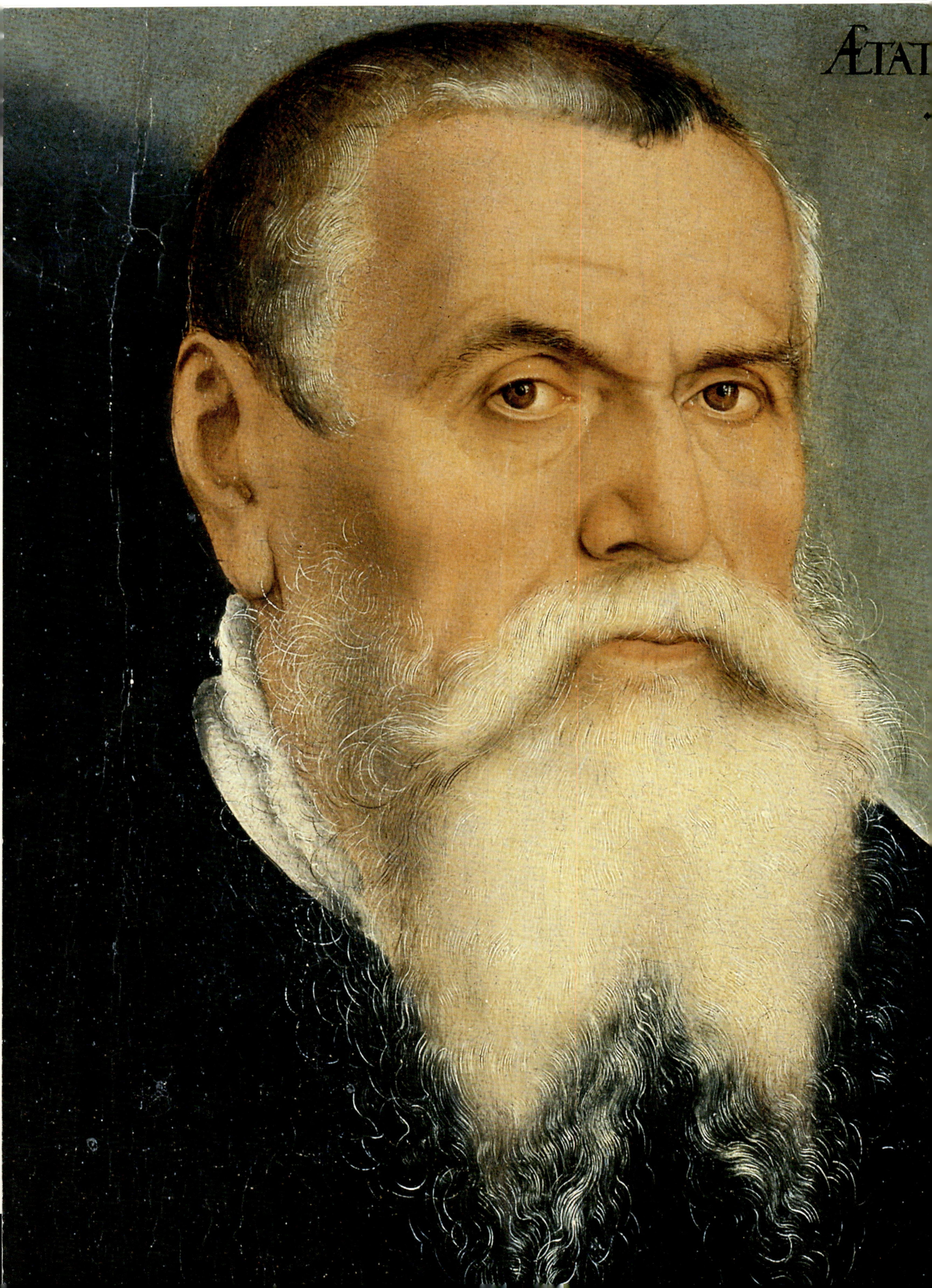
ÆTAT

The Painter's Sons: Hans and Lucas the Younger

The two sons of Lucas Cranach the Elder, Hans and Lucas, seem to have been already active in the studio while they were still children. There are many indications that Hans had a significant talent. Though his style differed only slightly from his father's, two paintings have survived bearing his personal monogram. After he died young in Bologna while on an Italian journey that we can follow through the pages of his personal sketchbook, he was highly praised in a funeral eulogy. His younger brother seems then to have risen to a leading position in the studio, partly to take some of the burden from his father, who was by then aged sixty-five. A few years later, when his father followed the court to Weimar, Lucas the Younger took over as head of the Wittenberg workshop.

120 Portrait of a Bearded Young Man

Hans Cranach

Wittenberg, 1534

Dated half way up the right edge; beneath this the monogram 'HC'

Oil and tempera on beechwood
51.4 x 35.1 cm

Museo Thyssen-Bornemisza, Madrid, 1949.1

Provenance:
sold at auction in Leipzig in 1827; acquired in 1949

(Frankfurt only)

Selected references:
FR 342; Koepplin/Falk 1974/76, vol. 2, p. 701, no. 625; Lübbeke 1991, pp. 178–81, no. 40

The half-length figure of a young man with smooth brown hair wearing a fur *Schaube*, a kind of overcoat, is portrayed against a neutral background in olive green. His facial features are strangely flat and empty, the flabby hands joined in an oddly feeble manner. The mouth is firmly shut, the pale lips pressed together. These features distinguish the portrait in a minor but noticeable manner from other portraits from Lucas Cranach's workshop (see cat. 7). According to the signature it is by Cranach's eldest son Hans, who was probably born around 1513 and died in Bologna during a journey to Italy, at the early age of 24.

There is a portrait in the same format of a woman facing left against a green background in the Musée du Petit Palais, Paris (FR 349 F). Originally this may have been the companion to the male portrait in Madrid, the two forming a diptych of a married couple. The face in the Paris portrait also looks rather empty and masklike, and the hands too are placed together in an oddly limp manner. Although the female portrait is not signed – perhaps superfluous because of the signature on the companion-piece – it may well be by the same painter, particularly since the hands and the small folds in the sleeves are comparable with another signed work by Hans Cranach: a medium-sized version of the episode, often treated in Cranach's workshop, representing Hercules at the court of Queen Omphala, which is also in the Museo Thyssen-Bornemisza (FR 275). This clear and painterly work, dated 1537, marks a further development and bears the serpent emblem and the monogram 'HC'.

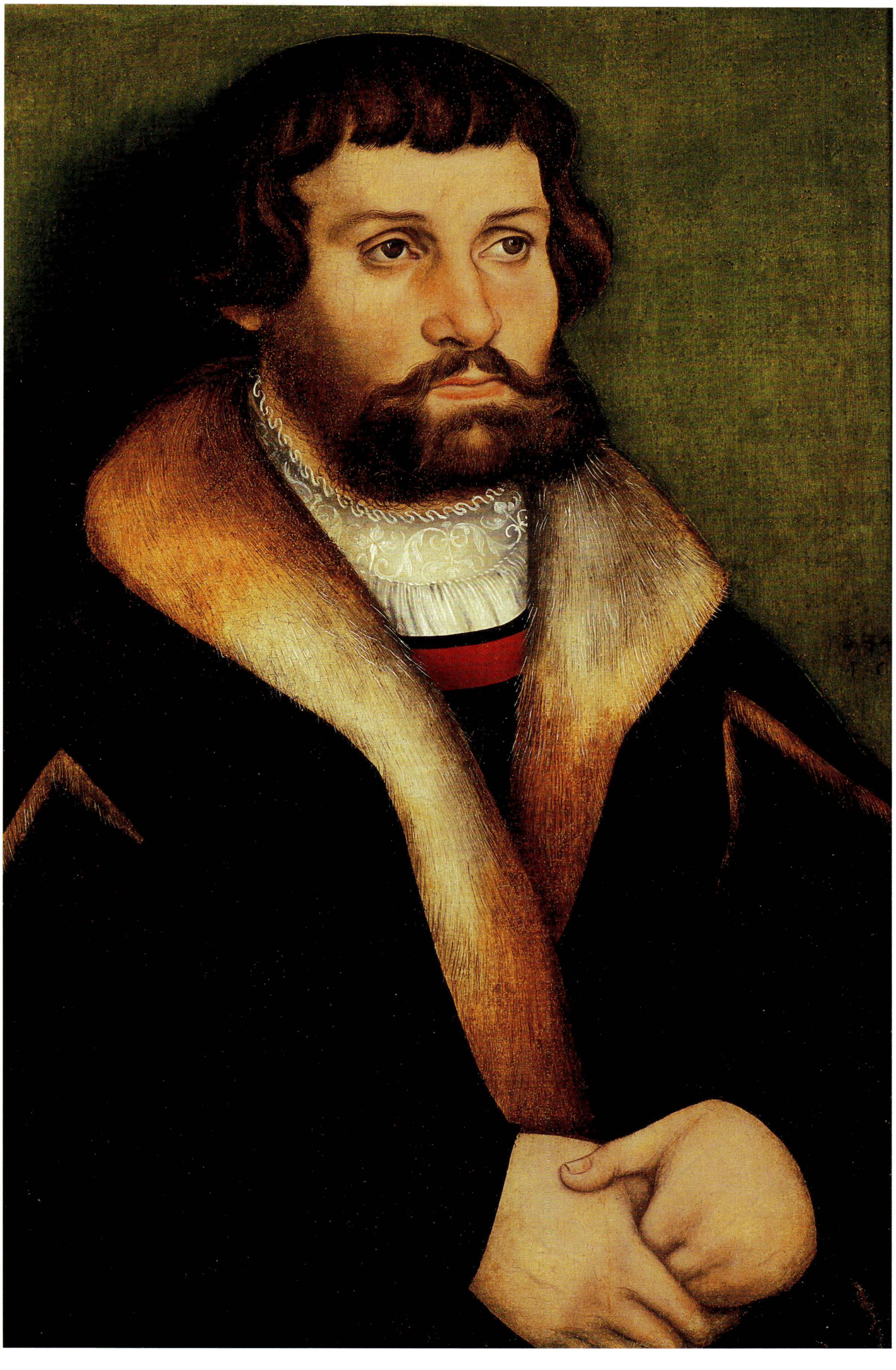

121 Portrait of a Prince

Hans Cranach (?)

Wittenberg, 1529

Dated bottom left in the black background; beneath it the serpent with upright wings facing right

Oil and tempera on wood laid on walnut
36.9 x 28.6 cm

Wallraf-Richartz Museum/Fondation Corboud, Cologne, WRM 874

Provenance:
acquired in 1957 as a gift of the Land Nordrhein-Westfalen

(Frankfurt only)

Selected references:
FR 329; Hiller/Vey 1969, pp. 44 f.; Koepplin/Falk 1974/76, vol. 2, p. 698, no. 620; Krischel 2003, p. 14

The boy is aged about four, and wears a doublet of red silk brocade and a chain with two interwoven ropes – no doubt the work of a goldsmith – and an ostrich feather in his fair hair. Chains like this usually adorned a bride or bridegroom, as can be seen in Cranach's portraits of John Frederick the Magnanimous of Saxony and Sybil of Cleves (Kunstsammlungen zu Weimar, FR 304, 305). The medallion with the Christ monogram on its neck chain indicates that he comes from a family adhering to the old (Catholic) faith. It has been suggested that this is Johann Georg of Brandenburg (1525–1598), though he was not married until 1545. In 1529 Cranach painted his grandfather Joachim I (Berlin, Jagdschloss Grünewald; FR 330), the same year as this child portrait from Cologne. A comparison with the prince and princess portraits from Washington (cats 68, 69) makes it quite clear that this is not the work of Lucas Cranach the Elder. Instead of the painterly glow, the almost Titianesque warmth emerging from darkness and the soulful expressions of the two children, verging on the sentimental, this portrait reveals a definite flatness, both in the face and hands and in the rendering of the brocade pattern. Similar features can be found in the portrait from Madrid (cat. 120), signed by Hans Cranach, as well as the somewhat indecisive folding of the hands and the narrow lips.

If the Cologne portrait is by Lucas Cranach's eldest son, it must have been one of his first paintings. In 1529 Hans Cranach can barely have been more than fifteen or sixteen years old. By that time he had possibly acquired just enough experience in his father's workshop to be able work independently on his first assignments.

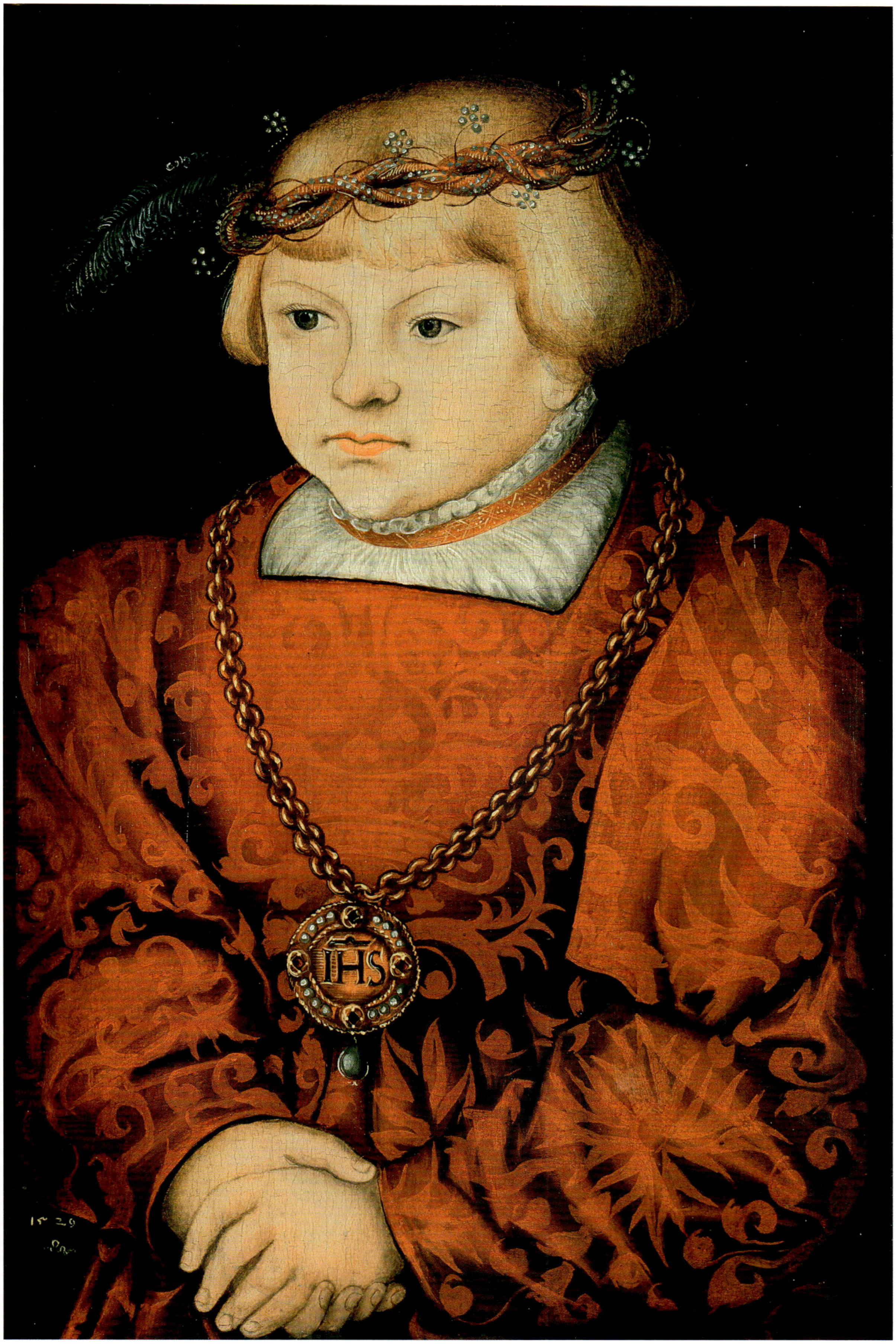
IHS
1529

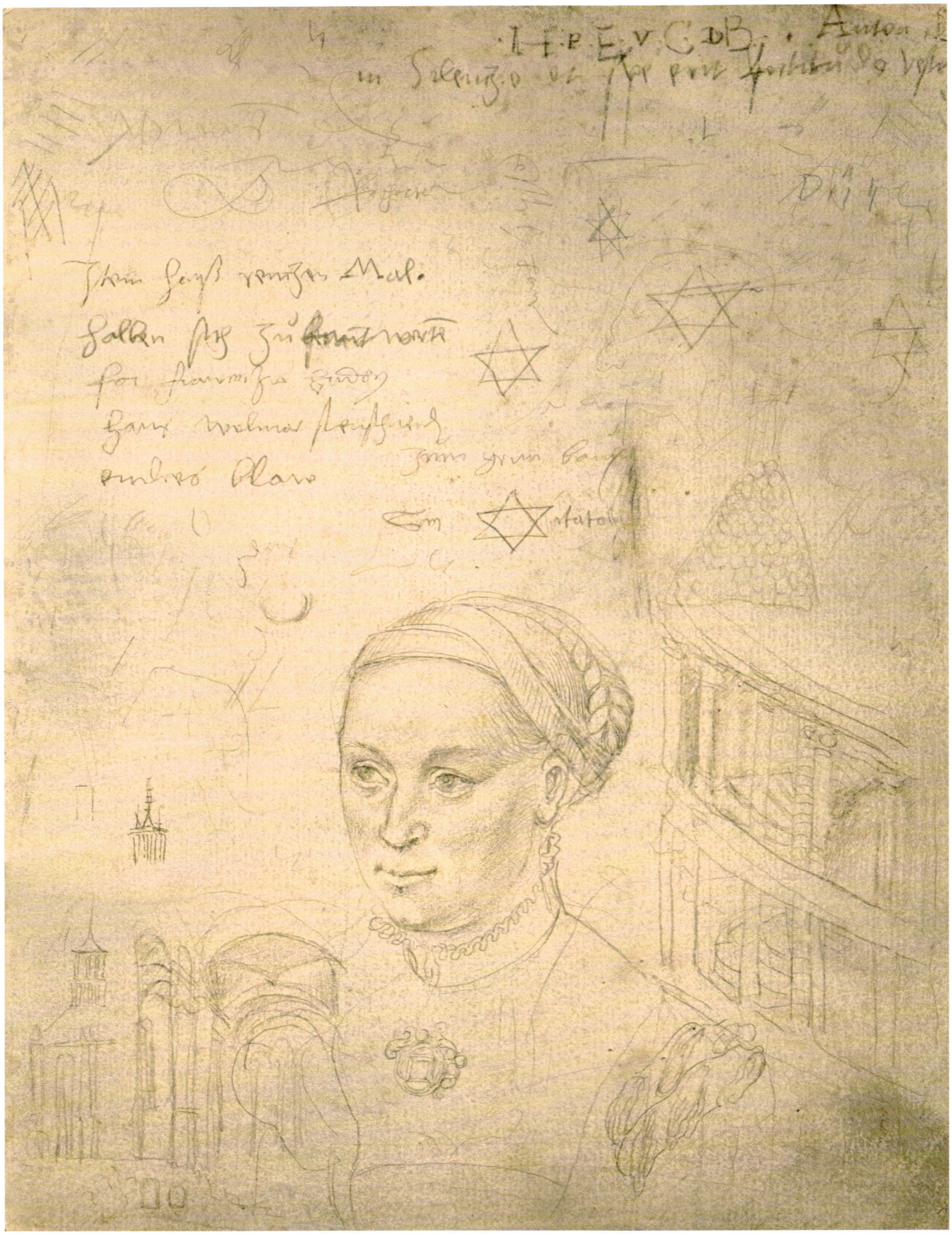

f. 1 r: This attractive portrait study of a young woman is so carefully executed with so much attention given to her costume and the jewel on her breast that the drawing may have been done in preparation for a painting to be completed en route. Hans later added the exterior view and the interior of a Gothic church, and in the process drew over the shoulder area of the portrait. He was equally careless with his sketch of a Renaissance-style spiral staircase on the right. Some of the monograms and pen exercises above were made by another hand.

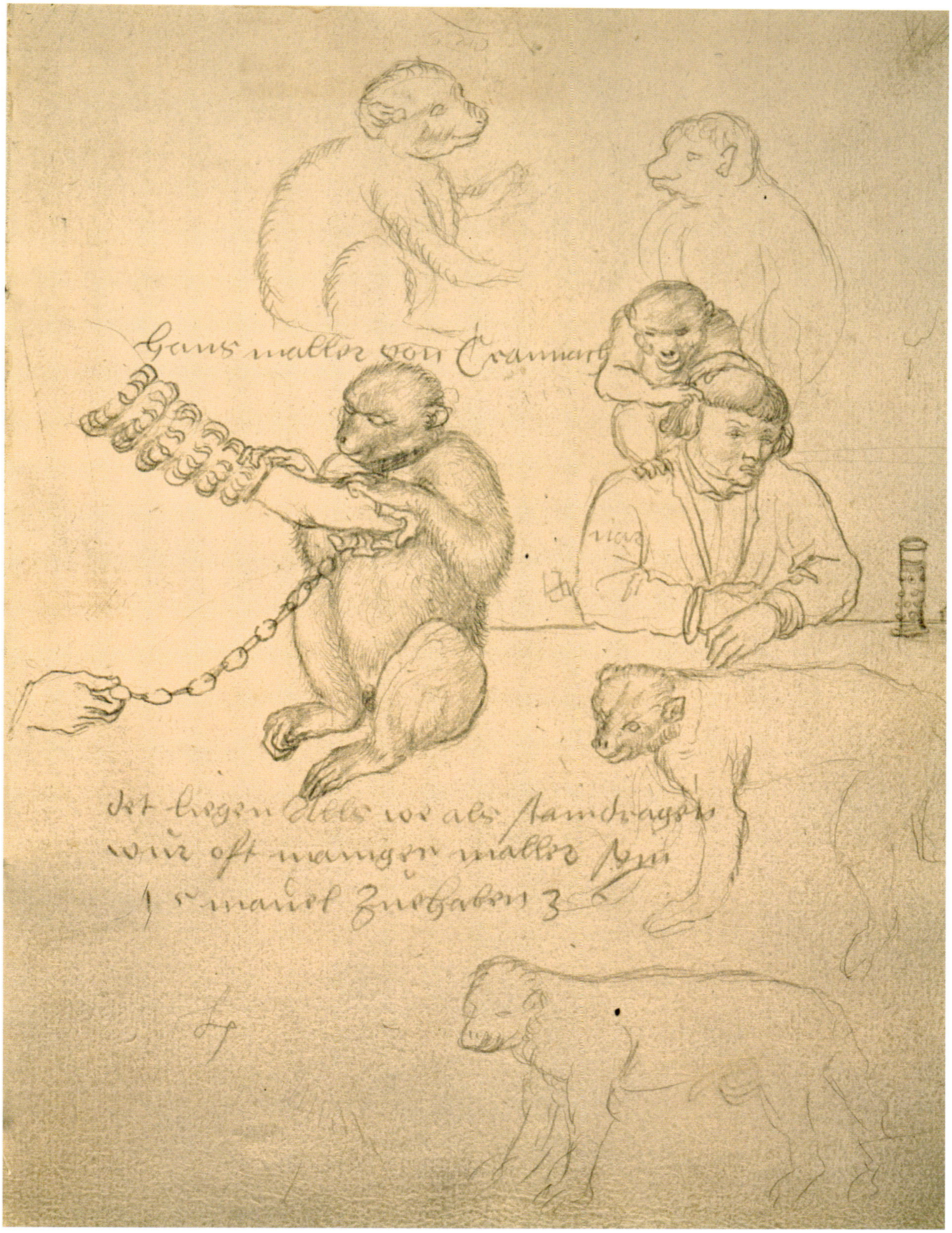

f. 5 r: Sketches of five meerkats surround a self-portrait of the artist, who while being deloused by a monkey looks morosely and wearily at a knobbled glass and a pack of cards on his left. He is identified by the inscription 'Hans maller von Crannach' and some lines which seem to explain his mood: 'Det liegen Alls we als staindragen / wur[d] oft maniger maller sein / maul zue haben' (If lying hurt as much as carrying rocks, then many painters would have a face like his). The year 1536 on either side of the last line shows that this touching little note was written before his Italian journey.

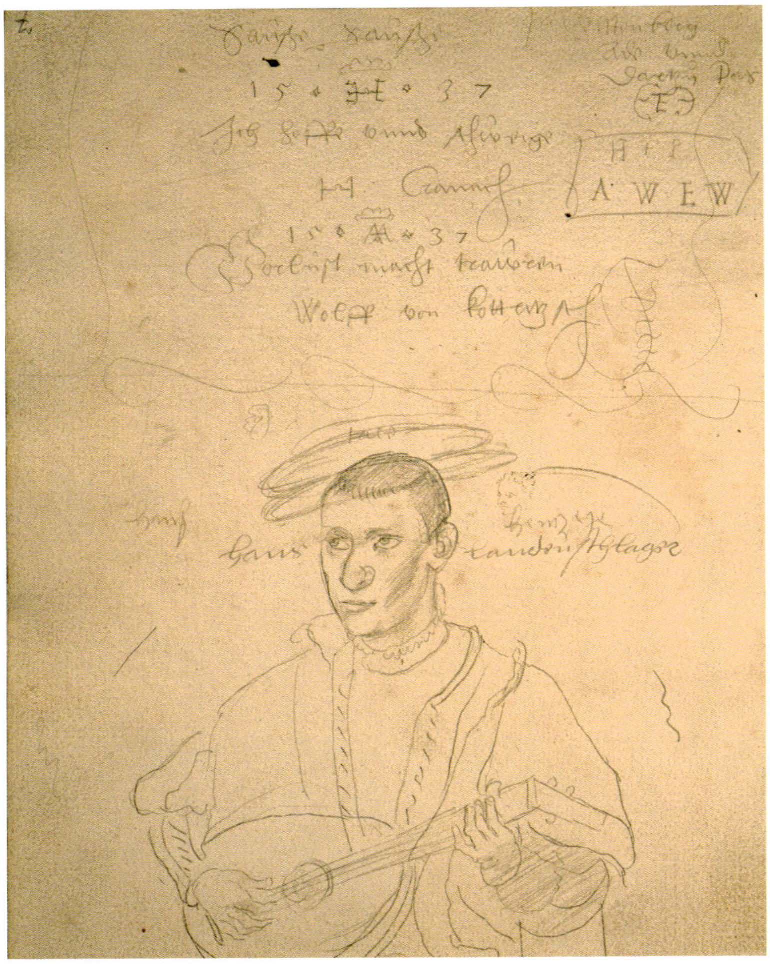

f. 7 r: A sad occasion – possibly Hans Cranach's death – seems to have been the reason for this affirmation of friendship written in another hand in the following year, which reads like an entry in a family register: '1537 / I hope and keep my silence / H Cranach' and '1537 / Loss brings grief / Wolff von Kottenich'. However, the artist himself made the very sketchy drawing below of a young man playing the lute, marked 'hans laudenschlager'. The two strange ellipses may perhaps indicate the place for a flat beret in a portrait to be painted later.

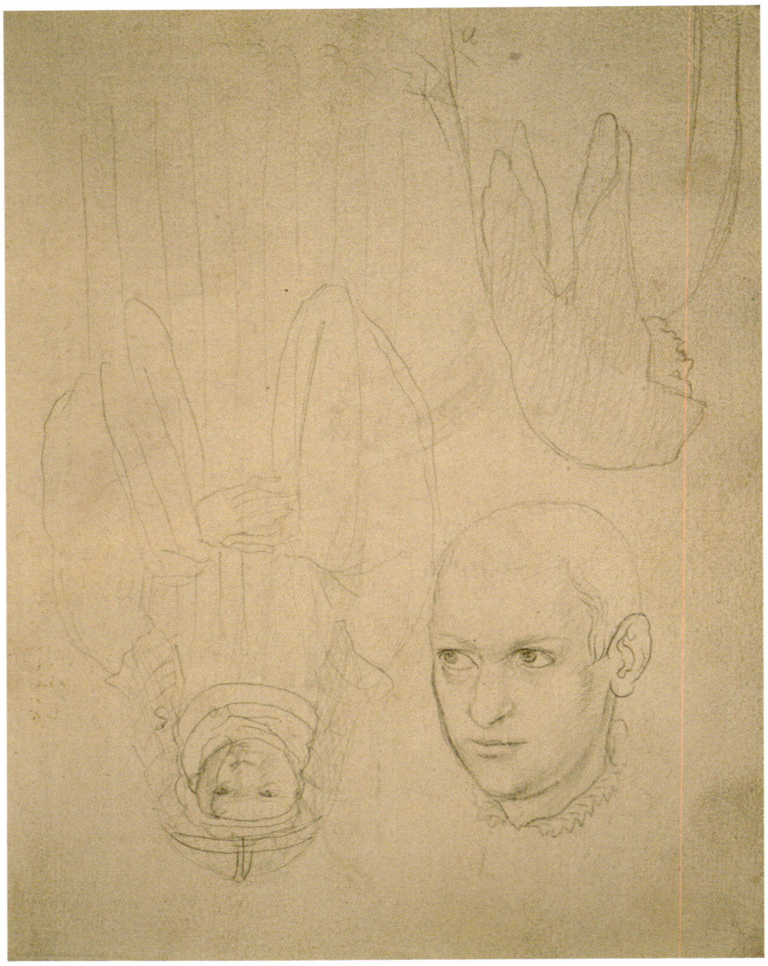

f. 7 v: The finely executed head may be a more detailed drawing of the Hans Lautenschlager on the recto of this sheet. There is controversy over whether Hans Cranach also drew the nun seen in full face and in profile, but the sketch is of good quality.

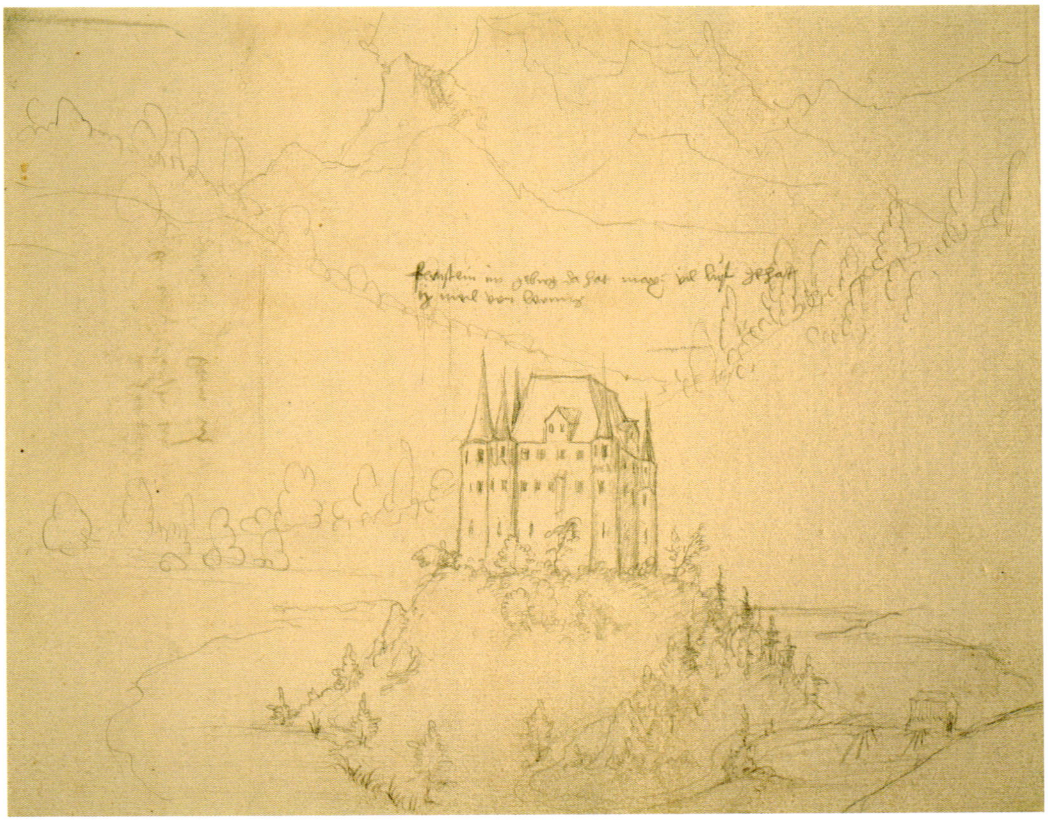

f. 2 v: Here Hans Cranach captured Berg Fernstein in the Tirol in its dramatic Alpine setting. Not only is the inscription proof of this but also the route of his journey listed on the opposite page.

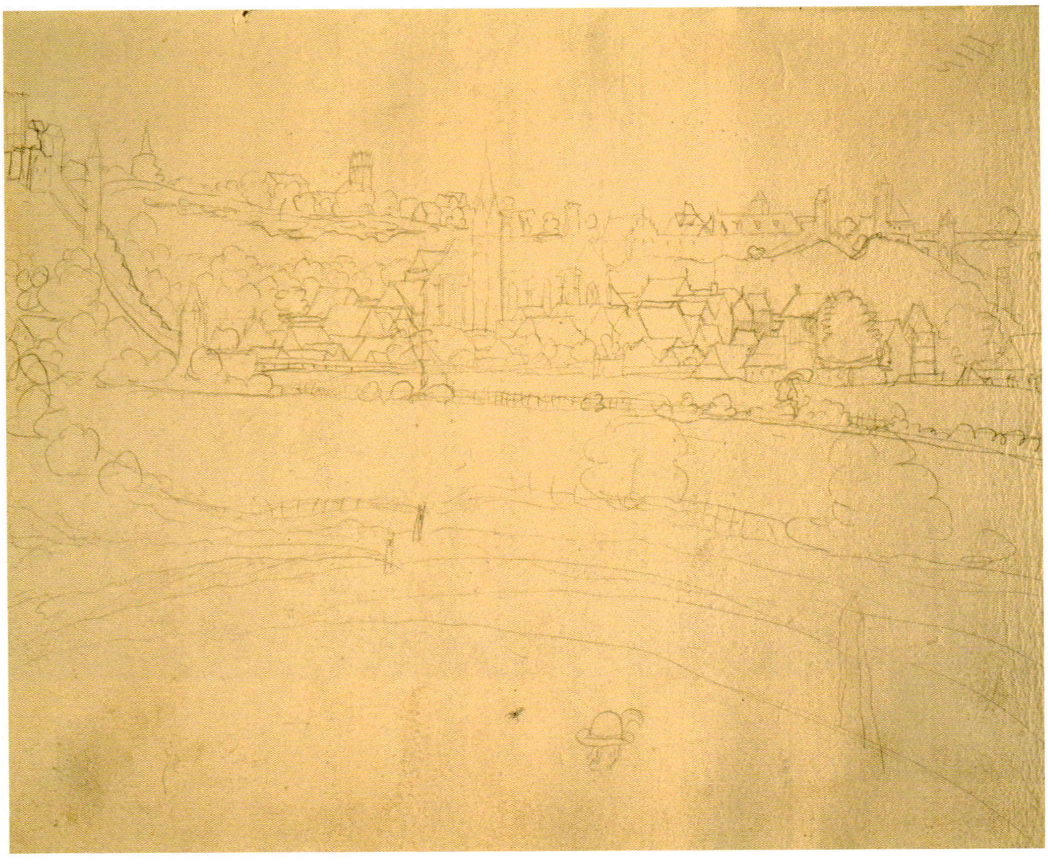

f. 38 v: Hans Cranach, View of a Town in the Northern Alps.

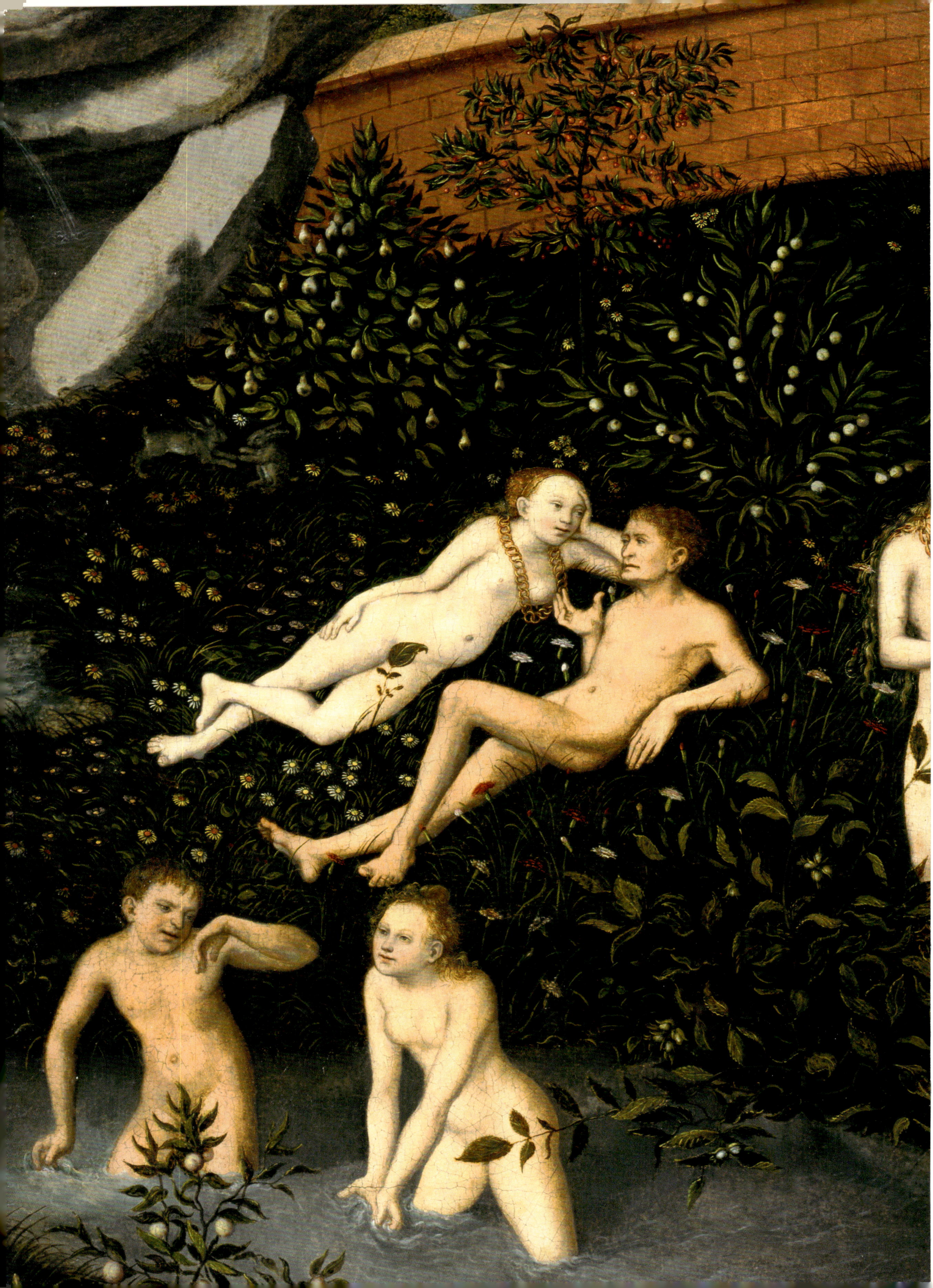

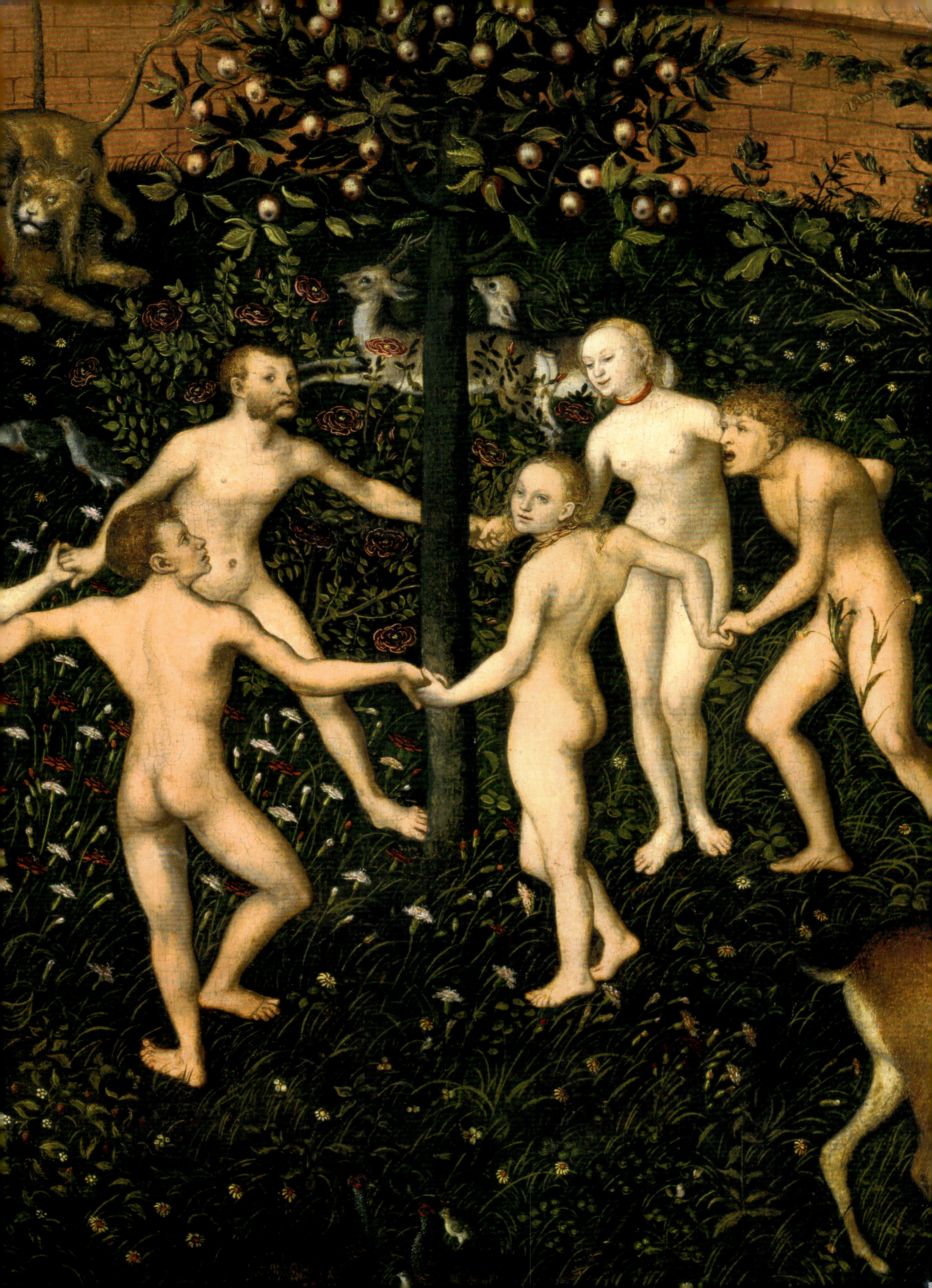

Bibliography

Abbreviations
AKL: *Allgemeines Künstler-Lexikon. Die bildenden Künstler aller Zeiten und Völker*, vol. 1, Munich and Leipzig, 1992
FR: Max J. FRIEDLÄNDER and Jakob ROSENBERG, *The Paintings of Lucas Cranach*, London 1978 (first edition Berlin, 1932)
Hind: Arthur M. HIND , *Early Italian Engravings. A Critical Catalogue with Complete Reproductions of All the Prints Described*, 6 vols, London, 1938–48
Hollstein: Friedrich Wilhelm Heinrich HOLLSTEIN, *German Engravings, Etchings and Woodcuts, c.* 1400–1700, vol. 1, Amsterdam, 1953
IIIB: Walter L. Strauss (ed.), *The Illustrated Bartsch*, vol. 1, New York, 1978
JB: Johannes JAHN (ed.) and Marianne BERNHARD (asst.), *1472–1553 Lucas Cranach d. Ä. Das gesamte graphische Werk. Mit Exempeln aus dem graphischen Werk Lucas Cranach d. J. und der Cranachwerkstatt*, Munich, 1972
LCI: *Lexikon der Christlichen Ikonographie*, edited by Wolfgang Braunfels, vols 1–8, Rome and elsewhere, 1968–1976
R: Jakob ROSENBERG, *Die Zeichnungen Lucas Cranachs d. Ä.*, Berlin, 1960
RDK: *Reallexikon zur deutschen Kunstgeschichte*
SMS: Rainer SCHOCH, Matthias MENDE and Anna SCHERBAUM, *Albrecht Dürer. Das druckgraphische Werk*, 3 vols, Munich, London and New York, 2001–05
ThB: *Allgemeines Lexikon der bildenden Künstler von der Antike bis zur Gegenwart*, ed. Ulrich THIEME and Felix BECKER, vols 1–37, Leipzig, 1908–50
WA: Weimar edition of the *Works of Luther*

ALBRECHT DÜRER 1471–1971, exh. cat., Ausstellung des Germanischen Nationalmuseums Nuremberg, Munich, 1971
ALTDEUTSCHE ZEICHNUNGEN. Museum der bildenden Künste, Leipzig. Graphische Sammlung (*Kataloge der Graphischen Sammlung*, 1), Leipzig o. J. [1972]
ALTE PINAKOTHEK MÜNCHEN [an account of the paintings on display], Bayerische Staatsgemälde Sammlungen, Munich, 1983
Francis AMES-LEWIS and Mary Rogers (eds), *Concepts of Beauty in Renaissance Art*, Aldershot, 1998
Jaynie ANDERSON, *Giorgione. Peintre de la 'Brièveté Poétique'*, Paris, 1996
Christiane ANDERSSON, 'Religiöse Bilder Cranachs im Dienste der Reformation', Lewis W. Spitz (ed.), *Humanismus und Reformation als kulturelle Kräfte in der deutschen Geschichte. Ein Tagungsbericht*, Berlin and New York, 1981, pp. 43–79
Fedja ANZELEWSKY, 'Studien zur Frühzeit Lukas Cranachs d. Ä.', *Städel-Jahrbuch*, NF, 17, 1999, pp. 125–44
Fedja ANZELEWSKY, *Albrecht Dürer. Das malerische Werk*, Berlin, 1971 (enlarged new edition, 2 vols, 1991)
Karl ARNDT and Bernd MOELLER, *Albrecht Dürers 'Vier Apostel'. Eine kirchen- und kunsthistorische Untersuchung* (*Schriften des Vereins für Reformationsgeschichte*, 202), Gütersloh, 2003
Hedy BACKLIN-LANDMANN, *Symbols in Transformation. Iconographic Themes at the Time of the Reformation. An Exhibition of Prints in Memory of Erwin Panofsky*, exh. cat., University Art Museum, Princeton, 1969
Katharine BAETJER, *European Paintings in The Metropolitan Museum of Art by Artists Born in or before 1865: A Summary Catalogue*, New York, 1980
Christopher BAKER and Tom HENRY, *The National Gallery Complete Illustrated Catalogue*, London, 1995
Nicolas BARKER, Hugh BRIGSTOCKE and Timothy CLIFFORD, *'A Poet in Paradise': Lord Lindsay and Christian Art*, exh. cat., Edinburgh, 2000
P. BARKOWSKY, *Die Restaurierung der Barbaratafel vom Altar Georg des Bärtigen aus dem Dom zu Meissen*, unpublished degree thesis, Hochschule für Bildende Künste, Dresden, 1980
Anna BARTL, 'Ein Original von Albrecht Dürer?', *Restauro* 105, 1999, pp. 26–31
Giulia BARTRUM (ed.), *German Renaissance Prints, 1490–1550*, London, 1995
Gustav BAUCH, 'Zur Cranachforschung', *Repertorium für Kunstwissenschaft*, 17, 1894, pp. 425–32
Gabriele BAUMBACH, '"SIC ECIAM INGENTES ANIMOS INSANA VOLVPTAS". Die Herkules und Omphale-Darstellungen der Cranach-Werkstatt und ein Gemälde Lucas Cranachs d. J. für Kardinal Albrecht von Brandenburg', in TACKE, *'... wir wollen der Liebe Raum geben'*, 2006, pp. 369–92
Michaela BAUTZ, *Virtutes. Studien zu Funktion und Ikonographie der Tugenden im Mittelalter und im 16. Jahrhundert*, Berlin, 1999
Michael BAXANDALL, *The Limewood Sculptors of Renaissance Germany*, New Haven and London 1980
Michael BAXANDALL and Ernst Horst GOMBRICH, 'Beroaldus on Francia', *Journal of the Warburg and Courtauld Institutes*, 25, 1962, pp. 113–15
Wolfgang BEEH, *Deutsche Malerei um 1260 bis 1550 im Hessischen Landesmuseum Darmstadt. Abbildungsteil* (plates only; W. Beeh (ed.), *Kataloge des Hessischen Landesmuseums*, 15), Darmstadt, 1990
Sven BEHRISCH, *Die Justitia. Eine Annäherung an die Allegorie der Gerechtigkeit*, Weimar, 2006
Edgar BIERENDE, *Lucas Cranach d. Ä. und der deutsche Humanismus. Tafelmalerei im Kontext von Rhetorik, Chroniken und Fürstenspiegeln*, Munich and Berlin, 2002
Edgar BIERENDE, 'Demut und Bekenntnis – Cranachs Bildnisse von Kurfürst Johann Friedrich I. von Sachsen', Volker Leppin, Georg Schmidt and Sabine Wefers, *Johann Friedrich I. – der lutherische Kurfürst*, Gütersloh, 2006, pp. 327–57
Phyllis Pray BOBER and Ruth RUBINSTEIN, *Renaissance Artists and Antique Sculpture: A Handbook of Sources*, London, 1986
Elfried BOCK and Jakob ROSENBERG, *Staatliche Museen zu Berlin. Die niederländischen Meister. Beschreibendes Verzeichnis sämtlicher Zeichnungen* (Max J. Friedländer [ed.], *Die Zeichnungen alter Meister im Kupferstichkabinett*), 2 vols, Berlin, 1930
Anne-Marie BONNET, 'Der Akt im Werk Lucas Cranachs. Bedeutung und Spezifität der 'nacketen Bilder' innerhalb der deutschen Renaissance-Malerei', in GRIMM/ERICHSEN/BROCKHOFF 1994, pp. 139–49
Anne-Marie BONNET, 'Akt' bei Dürer (*Atlas. Bonner Beiträge zur Renaissanceforschung*, 4), Cologne, 2001
Karel G. BOON, 'Patientia dans les gravures de la Réforme aux Pays-Bas', *Revue de l'Art*, 56, 1982, pp. 7–24
Heiner BORGGREFE, 'Cranachs Cuspinian-Bildnisse neu interpretiert', in TACKE 2007, pp. 15–41
Heinrich BORNKAMM (ed.), *Luthers Vorreden zur Bibel*, Frankfurt am Main, 1983
Karin BORNKAMM, *Luthers Auslegungen des Galaterbriefs von 1519 und 1531. Ein Vergleich*, Berlin, 1963
Helmut BÖRSCH-SUPAN, 'Cranachs Quellnymphen und sein Gestaltunsprinzip de Variation', in KOEPPLIN 1977
Emil BOSSHARD, '"Ein Werk von fünf Tagen". Anmerkungen zu Dürers zweiter Italienreise', *Restauro* 99, 1993, pp. 325–28
Horst BREDEKAMP, *Antikensehnsucht und Maschinenglaube. Die Geschichte der Kunstkammer und die Zukunft der Kunstgeschichte*, Berlin, 2002
Bodo BRINKMANN, 'Jenseits von Vorbild und Faltenform: Bemerkungen zur Modernität Stefan Lochners', in Frank Günter Zehnder (ed.), *Stefan Lochner Meister zu Köln. Herkunft – Werke – Wirkung*, exh. cat., Cologne, 1993, pp. 81–96
Bodo BRINKMANN, *Hexenlust und Sündenfall. Die seltsamen Phantasien des Hans Baldung Grien*, exh. cat., Frankfurt am Main, Petersberg, 2006
Bodo BRINKMANN and Stephan KEMPERDICK, *Deutsche Gemälde im Städel 1500–1550* (*Kataloge des Städelschen Kunstinstituts*, 5), Mainz, 2005
Bodo BRINKMANN and Wolfgang SCHMID (eds), *Hans Holbein und der Wandel in der Kunst des frühen 16. Jahrhunderts*, Turnhout, 2005
David Alan BROWN (ed.), *Virtue and Beauty: Leonardo's Ginevra de' Benci and Renaissance Portraits of Women*, exh. cat., National Gallery of Art, Washington DC, 2001
David Alan BROWN, Peter HUMFREY and Mauro LUCCO, *Lorenzo Lotto: Rediscovered Master of the Renaissance*, exh. cat., National Gallery of Art, Washington DC, New Haven and London, 1997
Robert BRUCK, *Friedrich der Weise als Förderer der Kunst*, Strasbourg, 1903
Stephanie BUCK, *Wendepunkte deutscher Zeichenkunst. Spätgotik und Renaissance im Städel*, exh. cat., Mainz, 2003
Stephanie BUCK, 'Framing the Image. Lucas Cranach's *Adam and Eve* and Book Illustration', in CAMPBELL 2007, pp. 35–45
Malcolm BULL, *The Mirror of the Gods: Classical Mythology in Renaissance Art*, London, 2005
Bernd BÜNSCHE, 'Holztechnologische und maltechnische Untersuchungen an einem Cranachgemälde von 1546', *Beiträge zur Erhaltung von Kunstwerken* 6, 1995, pp. 55–68
Bernd BÜNSCHE, 'Die Verwendung von Lochpausen bei der Anfertigung der Fürstenporträts durch Lucas Cranach den Älteren', *Zeitschrift für Kunsttechnologie und Konservierung*, 12, 1998, pp. 25–32
BÜRGERLICHE SAMMLUNGEN *in Frankfurt 1700–1830*, exh. cat., Historisches Museum Frankfurt, Frankfurt am Main, 1988
Hans BURGKMAIR, *Das graphische Werk*, exh. cat., Städtische Kunstsammlungen Augsburg, Augsburg, 1973
Jens Ludwig BURK, 'Conrat Meit. Bildhauer der Renaissance', in EIKELMANN 2006, pp. 15–65
Johannes BURKHARDT, 'Reformations- und Lutherfeiern. Die Verbürgerlichung der reformatorischen Jubiläumskultur', in Dieter Düding, Peter Friedemann and Paul Münch (eds), *Öffentliche Festkultur im 19. Jahrhundert. Politische Feste in Deutschland von der Aufklärung bis zum Ersten Weltkrieg*, Reinbek nr. Hamburg, 1988, pp. 212–36
Johannes BURKHARDT, 'Kriegsgrund Geschichte? 1870, 1813, 1756. Historische Argumente und Orientierungen bei Ausbruch des Ersten Weltkriegs', in Johannes Burkhardt and others (eds), *Lange und kurze Wege in den Ersten Weltkrieg. Vier Augsburger Beiträge zur Kriegsursachenforschung* (*Schriften der Philosophischen Fakultäten der Universität Augsburg*, vol. 49), Munich, 1996, pp. 9–86
Johannes BURKHARDT, 'Die kriegstreibende Rolle historischer Jubiläen im Dreissigjährigen Krieg und im Ersten Weltkrieg', in Johannes Burkhardt (ed.), *Krieg und Frieden in der historischen Gedächtniskultur* (*Schriften der Philosophischen Fakultäten der Universität Augsburg*, vol. 62), Munich, 2000, pp. 91–102
Andreas BURMESTER and KREKEL, 'Von Dürers Farben', in GOLDBERG/HEIMBERG/SCHAWE 1998, pp. 54–101
Magdalene BUSHART, *Sehen und Erkennen. Albrecht Altdorfers religiöse Bilder*, Berlin and Munich, 2004
Frank BÜTTNER and Gabriele WIMBÖCK (eds), *Das Bild als Autorität. Die normierende Kraft des Bildes*, Münster, 2004
Paolo CADORIN and Monique VEILLON, 'Über die Holzarten der Tafelbilder Cranachs', in KOEPPLIN/FALK 1974/76, vol. 2, p. 443
Caroline CAMPBELL (ed.), *Temptation in Eden: Lucas Cranach's Adam and Eve*, exh. cat., Courtauld Institute of Art, London, 2007
Lorne CAMPBELL, *Renaissance Portraits. European Portrait Painting in the 14th, 15th and 16th Centuries*, New Haven and London, 1990
Lorne CAMPBELL, *National Gallery Catalogues: The Fifteenth-Century Netherlandish Schools*, London, 1998